READING POPULAR CULTURE

PENGUIN ACADEMICS

READING POPULAR CULTURE

Edited by

Michael Petracca
University of California at Santa Barbara

Madeleine Sorapure
University of California at Santa Barbara

Prentice Hall
Boston   Columbus   Indianapolis   New York   San Francisco   Upper Saddle River
Amsterdam   Cape Town   Dubai   London   Madrid Milan Munich   Paris   Montreal   Toronto
Delhi   Mexico City   Sao Paulo   Sydney   Hong Kong   Seoul   Singapore   Taipei   Tokyo

Senior Editor: Brad Potthoff
Editorial Assistant: Nancy C. Lee
Senior Supplements Editor: Donna Campion
Senior Marketing Manager: Sandra McGuire
Senior Media Producer: Stefanie Liebman
Associate Managing Editor: Bayani Mendoza de Leon
Project Coordination, Text Design, and Electronic Page Makeup:
  PreMediaGlobal
Operations Specialist: Mary Ann Gloriande
Art Director, Cover: Nancy Wells
Cover Designer: Ilze Lemesis
Cover Photo: Getty
Printer and Binder: Edwards Brothers
Cover Printer: Lehigh-Phoenix/Hagerstown

For more information about the Penguin Academics series, please contact us by
mail at Pearson Education, attn: Marketing Department, 51 Madison Avenue,
29th Floor, New York, NY 10010, or visit us online at
www.pearsonhighered.com/english.

For permission to use copyrighted material, grateful acknowledgment is
made to the copyright holders on pages 383–384, which are hereby made
part of this copyright page.

Library of Congress Cataloging-in-Publication Data

Reading popular culture / [edited by] Michael Petracca, Madeleine Sorapure.
  p. cm. — (Penguin academics)
  ISBN 978-0-205-71734-7
  1. College readers. 2. Reading comprehension—Problems, exercises, etc.
3. Popular culture—United States 4. United States—Social life and
customs—21st century. I. Petracca, Michael, 1947- II. Sorapure, Madeleine.
  PE1417R393 2011
  808'.0427—dc22   2010045797

1 2 3 4 5 6 7 8 9 10—EDW—13 12 11 10

Prentice Hall
is an imprint of

www.pearsonhighered.com

ISBN-13: 978-0-205-71734-7
ISBN-10:   0-205-71734-9

dedication

Madeleine dedicates this text to the two people who keep her grounded very happily in this world: Bob and Sophia. Michael dedicates this text to his beloved and favorite niece, Selam Desta Black.

contents

Welcome to *Reading Popular Culture*, a lively, frequently opinionated, always thoughtfully selected, logically sequenced, and deeply satisfying broth of readings about popular culture. *Reading Popular Culture* covers a full range of topics in the field of contemporary popular culture from a variety of theoretical perspectives. In so doing, this book takes up the most important general questions that arise from our immersion in the culture of everyday life: Why do the artifacts popular culture, such as certain movies or Web sites, appeal to us, and what effect does our engagement with each of these phenomena have on us?

Readings in each chapter address issues arising within particular domains of popular culture: the world of technology; popular music, including rock and hip-hop; the advertisements that pervade every medium to which we are exposed daily; television shows and movies past and present and future; and popular literature, from Harry Potter to teen vampire books to comic strips. In the introductory notes to each reading and the questions provided after each selection, *Reading Popular Culture* engages readers in the process of thinking critically and carefully about those parts of their lives that are most familiar to them. In this way, activities within the book provide compelling opportunities for students to bring together their academic and the personal lives in a way that enriches both.

Why Reading Popular Culture?

Although students have much to learn from the teachers they encounter in every classroom setting, they also bring a vast store of knowledge with them—especially in the area of popular culture. They are already deeply immersed and often quite expert in the virtual milieu of YouTube, iPhone, and Wii. Many have played hours of online games, video games, and board games, and they have spent their remaining leisure hours surfing the Web and texting, often simultaneously. All have watched countless movies and television shows and have ingested the messages in advertisements throughout their lives.

The advantage of a course (or cluster of courses) focusing on popular culture, then, is that teachers can draw on the students' expertise and interest, showing students how to think clearly and deeply about specific topics and how to communicate their insights effectively. Indeed, the overarching goal of a course that emphasizes popular culture is to help students improve their critical thinking, reading, and writing skills by concentrating on material that they find inherently interesting and about which they already know a great deal.

Whereas, in some cases, today's twentysomethings may actually know *more* than their teachers about certain aspects of popular culture, few have taken the time to devote much critical consideration to its direct effects: for example, to what hip-hop lyrics might reveal to them about the social and cultural climate around them, or to how they might have been influenced by reading Harry Potter books or comics when they were younger. Because video games, Web sites, and automobile advertisements, for example, are consciously contrived popular objects, they constitute particularly rich sources for analysis. Likewise, since many popular issues (such as the influence of said video games on real-life violence, for example) lend themselves naturally to controversial discourse, readers of this textbook will likely relish the chance to present and defend their own points of view regarding the events, institutions, and social constructions that comprise their world.

Reading Popular Culture Selections: Organizational Schema

Each chapter of *Reading Popular Culture* examines a particular aspect of contemporary U.S. culture. The readings within each chapter draw from a wide range of disciplinary conventions and methods: from the rigorously academic, to the journalistic, to the creative non-fictional, and virtually everything in between.

At its outset, *Reading Popular Culture* presents an introductory chapter that poses the provocative question, "What is popular culture?" and then goes on to provide a concise definition of the term from a variety of theoretical perspectives. The chapter proceeds to explain the reasons why one might benefit from some applied study of popular artifacts, concluding that we—both students and teachers—should examine contemporary culture in order to understand and sometimes guard against its influences. Also included in the introductory chapter is a concise explanation of how one might go about using the book in a systematic way, and how one might employ a strategy called "active reading" in order to approach the readings in each of the succeeding chapters. The introduction further explains some practical, step-by-step instructions for writing essays about pop culture-related topics in a variety of styles and rhetorical modes.

Following this introduction, *Reading Popular Culture* breaks the broad range of field of popular culture into its main parts, with a chapter devoted to each. Chapters alternate between specific media, such as television, movies, and popular literature, and broader cultural phenomena, such as technology and advertising. Obviously, there are Boolean overlaps between all of the chapters, since issues within popular culture are almost always interrelated. For instance, novels become movies, and famous music gets reproduced in popular ads. Moreover, technology, broadly defined, is prevalent in all aspects of popular culture, from how it gets created to how it reaches us in our homes and elsewhere. Nevertheless, each chapter of *Reading Popular Culture* forms an independent conceptual unit, and instructors can easily construct a course around several individual chapters.

Within each chapter readers will encounter two major sections. Typically, the initial section will contain readings that address the chapter's subject generally, and the second section will present texts that explore a specific aspect of the chapter subject with more specificity. For example, in the advertising chapter, readings in the first section explore issues and methodologies of advertising, and then readings in the second section focus on the concept of branding in advertisements. Each of the chapters proceeds in this way and includes the following editorial materials as well.

Beyond the Introduction: Editorial Apparatus

The readings themselves form the heart and soul of *Reading Popular Culture*. One could easily and satisfyingly read this book without paying any attention to the ancillary materials that accompany each chapter and reading. However, a great deal of thought has gone into the apparatus that accompanies every chapter and text, and one's reading experience will certainly be enriched by considering the introductory materials and that precede each chapter and reading, and the writing considerations that follow every text.

Chapter Introductions

Each chapter begins with an engaging introduction that sets out the key issues for that particular branch of popular culture. In order to rev up the processes of questioning and analysis, the introductions point to important, overarching themes that run through many or most of the subsequent readings, and they suggest several points of departure for critical consideration. The chapter introductions also provide very brief overviews of each reading that follows, mapping the twists and turns of each chapter's content.

Headnotes

Each reading begins with a headnote that provides additional starting points for examining the author's ideas. These headnotes typically give students a sense of the context of the reading: where and when it was initially published, who the author is, what else he or she has written. With this information, students can get a better sense of the purpose and audience of the reading, and this can help them orient their interpretation. The headnotes also help to guide students through the reading by highlighting a few of the most important ideas that they will encounter.

"Suggestions for Writing" Questions

Following each reading, students will find three questions that will help them articulate their responses to some of the important ideas raised in the reading. The Suggestions for Writing vary in what they ask from students. They encompass a range of rhetorical approaches, such as exposition, analysis, and argumentation, and they require different levels of sophistication and difficulty in terms of content and style. Some questions prompt students to use the reading as a model and to imitate its form and approach in their own composition. Others ask students to do further research or to make connections between readings in the chapter. Although the questions are phrased as suggestions for writing, they can also be modified to serve as starting points for class discussions or small group activities.

MyCompLab

MyCompLab empowers student writers and facilitates writing instruction by integrating a composing space and assessment tools with market-leading instruction, multimedia tutorials, and exercises for writing, grammar and research. Students can use MyCompLab on their own, benefiting from self-paced diagnostics and a personal study plan that recommends the instruction and practice each student needs to improve her writing skills. The composing space and its integrated resources, tools, and services (such as online tutoring) are also available to each student as he writes.

MyCompLab is an eminently flexible application that instructors can use in ways that best complement their course design and teaching style. Instructors can recommend it to students for self-study, set up courses to track student progress, or leverage the power of administrative features to be more effective and efficient. The assignment builder and commenting tools, developed specifically for writing instruction, bring instructors closer to their student writers, make managing assignments and evaluating papers more efficient, and put powerful assessment within reach. Students receive feedback within the context of their own writing, which encourages critical thinking and revision and helps them to develop skills based on their individual needs. Learn more at www.mycomplab.com.

Acknowledgments

We wish to thank deeply the many reviewers whose sage opinions and suggestions we have taken to heart in the preparation of this text. Notable members of this cadre include Jo Ann Bamdas, Palm Beach Community College; Krista E. Callahan-Caudill, University of Kentucky; Hugh Culik, Macomb Community College; Robin Havenick, Linn-Benton Community College; Susan Labadie, Oakland Community College; Karissa McCoy, Georgia Institute of Technology; and Lisa Niles, Spelman College.

about the authors

MICHAEL PETRACCA teaches writing and has served as Acting Co-Director of the Writing Program at the University of California at Santa Barbara. Several of his classes, including Research Writing for the Social Sciences and Writing for Film, focus on interpreting the artifacts of popular culture, including technology, film, and music. Petracca's research and writing interests include cultural criticism and analysis along with popular culture pedagogy—that is, the use of media artifacts as topics of inquiry in the composition classroom. Publications include: *The Graceful Lie: A Method for Making Fiction; Common Culture,* a reader/textbook on popular culture, coauthored with Madeleine Sorapure; two novels, *Doctor Syntax* and *Captain Zzyzx;* a writing across the curriculum textbook, *Academic Communities/Disciplinary Conventions,* co-authored with Bonnie Beedles; along with extensive creative nonfiction, short stories, and poetry.

MADELEINE SORAPURE is Associate Director of the Writing Program at the University of California at Santa Barbara, where she teaches courses in multimedia composing, professional writing, and academic research writing. She is coauthor (with Michael Petracca) of *Common Culture*, currently in its sixth edition. She has also authored articles on new media, autobiography, popular culture, and contemporary fiction. Her current research focuses on the ways that technologies influence us as individuals and as a culture. She is particularly interested in teaching and learning about how we can engage with technologies in ways that are compelling, creative, and critically savvy.

READING POPULAR CULTURE

CHAPTER 1

Introduction

WHAT IS POPULAR CULTURE? ALTHOUGH YOU WILL FIND literally thousands of definitions and discussions of the term if you do a quick Google search, some common threads of meaning emerge from this background white noise. Briefly rendered, pop culture is composed of the shared knowledge and practices of a specific social group at a specific time. Since people in the United States live in a culture that is mediated by technologies such as the Web, television, radio, movies, print literature, and so forth, much of Americans' common knowledge derives from these sources. Because of this commonality, pop culture both reflects and influences people's ways of life. Furthermore, because it is linked to a specific time and place, pop culture is transitory, subject to change, and often an initiator of change. One can envision a text with articles on the popular culture of eighteenth-century France; however, for the purposes of this text, we are focusing on here and now.

The reason we chose to focus on the popular artifacts of here and now is simple and practical: In our classes, we enjoy talking with students about things they are interested in and about which they often have a great deal of knowledge. We have found that popular culture provides a fertile ground for class discussion—and for writing assignments, as you will find in this text—because virtually every one of our students has heard a hip-hop song, has talked on a cell phone, has seen a Facebook page, has seen the movie *Knocked Up*, has seen a football game or played a video game. As Edward Jay Whetmore notes, "Popular culture represents a common denominator, something that cuts across most economic, social, and educational barriers." If the notion of culture reflects a certain degree of social stratification and differentiation, then popular culture represents the elements of everyday life, the artifacts and institutions shared by a society, and a body of common knowledge. In other words, we spend our lives immersed in popular culture. There's no escaping it; like radio waves and houseflies, pop culture is everywhere.

So Why Study Popular Culture?

Pop culture scholars argue for the validity of studying pop culture phenomena like YouTube, *The National Enquirer*, video games, and the Miss America Pageant, because artifacts such as these serve as a kind of mirror in which we can discern much about our society. George Lipsitz, for instance, suggests that "perhaps the most important facts about people have always been encoded within the ordinary and the commonplace." We see reflected in pop culture certain standards and commonly held beliefs about beauty, success, love, or justice. We also see reflected in it important social contradictions and conflicts— tension between races, attitudes toward genders, or preconceptions about generations, for example. To find out about our society, then, we can turn to our own popular products and pastimes.

On an individual level, as well, the media and other pop culture components are part of the fund of ideas and images that inform our daily activities, sometimes exerting a more compelling influence than family or friends, school or work. When we play basketball, we mimic the gestures and movements of Kobe Bryant or another professional athlete we admire; we learn to dance from videos accompanying downloaded iTunes songs (or, heaven forbid, from imitating *Dancing with the Stars*); we even name our children after popular television characters. More importantly, we discover role models; we learn lessons about villainy and heroism, love and relationships, acceptable and unacceptable behavior; we see interactions with people from other cultures. Even if popular culture is merely low-quality amusement or a means of escaping the demands and stresses of the "real" world, it delivers important messages that we may internalize and later act on— for better or for worse. Analyzing pop culture with a critical eye allows you to begin to free yourself from the manipulation of the media; it is an important step toward living an examined life.

We examine and analyze pop culture, then, in order to assess—and sometimes resist—its influences. Both as individuals and as members of local and national communities, a deeper understanding of pop culture better prepares us to make changes that improve our lives.

How to Use This Book

The readings and assignments in this book give you the chance to explore these issues and determine for yourself the role of popular culture in shaping society and in shaping you as an individual. The book includes chapters on key components of popular culture: technology, music, advertising, movies, popular reading, and television. It may be that you already have expertise in one or more of these areas, either from a massive amount of casual exposure (for instance, thousands of hours spent watching TV) or from a personal passion that has led you to intense study (for instance, a fascination with baseball statistics and trivia that might help your fantasy team win its division). Other facets of pop culture may be less interesting to you, although the more dispassionate and objective view you bring to these subjects can help you develop keen analytical insights, as well. Whether you're an engaged participant or a disinterested observer of a particular facet of popular culture, the readings in this book can help you observe carefully, think critically, and perhaps develop a better understanding of yourself and of the world around you.

The readings we have chosen represent a range of approaches to each topic. Most of the articles come from the Web or from mainstream media and were initially written for a general audience; however, one or two articles in each chapter are more scholarly and represent the research-based, academic approach that you might be asked to reproduce in college classes. Moreover, we often present different perspectives on the same topic—particularly in the casebooks that occupy the second part of each chapter—so that you can see the different techniques and assumptions people have brought to bear on a particular phenomenon. Each article begins with a headnote that typically offers background information about the author and briefly summarizes the key points of the reading to follow. These headnotes ease you into the article and give you a quick overview that can guide your interpretation.

In order to get the most of the materials here, we encourage you to practice an energetic, engaged style of reading—one in which you think of yourself as being in the midst of a conversation or dialogue with the author. While you're mostly listening to what he or she has to say, you're also responding: in your mind's reactions and thoughts; in the notes that you write in the text margins; even in the occasional chuckle or "aha!" that you might utter. If you think of reading as more like a dialogue than a monologue, then you're going to be more involved in the process and ultimately gain greater insight into both what the author has to say and your own position on the topic.

There are a number of stages in the process of active reading. First comes *preparation*: You physically prepare yourself for reading by reducing outside distractions and cutting multitasking to a minimum. You can also prepare by getting a general sense of what the article is about—from the title and headnote—and consciously gathering your own thoughts on that topic. Next, you *read*, but do so with a pen or pencil and some paper to write on (writing in the margins of the article is even better, assuming you're not borrowing a copy of this book from a friend or a library). Record your responses along the way, jotting down key points, noting where you agree and disagree, and writing questions next to statements that strike you as complicated, confusing, or incorrect. Next, *reread* the article; you'll be amazed at how much more you'll be able to understand on a second reading. You have a sense of the author's complete argument, and this can inform your second (or third or fourth) reading and help you focus in on crucial details. Finally, *review* your responses to the article; it might be helpful here for you to write a paragraph or two of notes in which you record your impressions, evaluate the author's argument, and sketch out your own response. In the actual practice of active reading, these four stages circle back on one another as well as spiral outward, and you may even be stimulated to do further reading and exploration in order to clarify your thoughts.

Writing About Popular Culture

Following each article in this book are three "Suggestions for Writing." We see these as prompts designed to encourage you to explore a topic fully by engaging in a serious way with the ideas you have just read. In the same way that one can break down the active process of reading into specific activities, so the writing process can be broken down into distinct stages: prewriting, drafting, distancing, and revising. As you approach the sometimes daunting task of writing an essay, visualizing it as a series of discrete steps can make the process seem much more manageable, and therefore more enjoyable.

The first stage of the writing process, *prewriting* is especially gratifying, because at this point you don't have to concern yourself with writing complete sentences, using correct grammar, or organizing your thoughts in any coherent way. At this stage, all you're required to do is write down (or type onto your computer) anything that comes into your head regarding your assigned topic. This will ensure that you generate a wealth of text, which you will later massage into a more structured form. Toward the end of the prewriting phase, you might also consider developing your material into an outline, which will help you as you move on to the organizational stages.

In the *drafting* stage, you will work from your prewritten material and your nascent outline to begin organizing your material into logical sequence. Also during this stage you will want to consider your audience: If you are writing to your instructor only, your essay will undoubtedly have a different tone than if you are writing for your instructor and your classmates, or an imaginary editor, or someone who knows nothing about popular culture, such as a student from another country—or from another planet or galaxy or dimension. Consider, too, the point about your topic that you want to make to that audience. Unlike the prewriting stage, which by its nature often involves writing in a rambling and disjointed sort of way, your success in the drafting stage will depend upon the degree to which you can focus on a series of specific arguments and develop those points using concrete illustrations and examples.

The easiest part of the writing process—even easier than the stress-free prewriting phase—is *distancing*, since it requires no more effort than setting your now-completed first draft aside. Give yourself a full day or two in which you ignore your essay. Pursue your regular activities: Focus on your job, work on assignments for other classes, take a hike, throw a Frisbee, clip your toenails—generally do anything but read over your draft during this distancing phase. When you return to your writing, you will bring a newly discovered objectivity, and this stance will assist you greatly as you move into the revision process.

It is an accepted axiom among professional writers that *revision* is the single most important stage in the entire composition process. The revision stage provides you with an opportunity to clarify your ideas, to cut and move text around in a way that enhances the logical flow of your arguments, to add genial new turns of phrase and to delete clunky or repetitive ones, even to radically alter your entire thesis and move in a completely different intellectual direction. When you finish revising your work, we advise that you print out this second draft and read it *out loud* to yourself, in order to discover any overly wordy passages, phrasings that sound like a mouthful of marbles, grammatical problems, and so on. Reading your prose out loud may seem highly odd—especially to roommates who can't help overhearing or to neighbors, if you read loudly enough—but we promise that engaging in this last activity will give you some crucial additional perspective on your essay and will ultimately make your final draft that much more polished.

Final Thoughts

Our overarching goal in putting this text together was to find readings that might actually be fun for you to read, both engaging and thought provoking. We have been teaching writing courses that focus on the artifacts of popular culture for a long time, and we continue to be gratified by the degree of insight our students bring to the images, narratives, and texts that they may have passively taken for granted previous to these courses. Of course, over the couple of decades that we have taught these courses, we have aged a bit, while our students always stay the same age: 20 or so. For that reason, it has been equally gratifying for us to learn from our students, as each generation comes to the classroom enterprise with a new set of favorite TV shows, movies, toothpaste brands, video games, cell-phone models, skateboard designs, and music superstars. When we started writing texts about popular culture, Madonna and Michael Jackson were young and in vogue. We've happily persevered through Britney Spears, the Beastie Boys, Tupac, and, currently, the Black Eyed Peas and Jay-Z.

Who's next? You tell us.

CHAPTER 2

Technology

Look around you: everything that isn't natural is the product of technology. Roads, buildings, machines, furniture, clothing—these are all artifacts created by humans to suit certain wants and needs. Even some natural objects are technologically mediated: Think of all the technologies involved in farming, transporting, and selling the food that we eat or in collecting, cleaning, and delivering the water we drink. Our lives are thoroughly infused with and shaped by technology; consider all of the technologies associated with birth, education, work, play, illness, and death. And finally, our culture—particularly popular culture—is dependent on technology and reflects the influence of technology. All of the topics that you read about in this book—music, movies, television, advertising—are cultural endeavors made possible by technology.

Clearly, it's impossible to deal with the full range of technology's influence in the short space of one chapter. So we narrow our focus down to what we might call personal technologies—that is, technologies with which you directly interact on a daily basis. You undoubtedly have a lot of experience with technologies that shape your everyday activities and augment your capabilities. For example, communications technologies like the Internet, text messaging, and cell phones enable you to interact in a relatively inexpensive and immediate way with people who are physically distant from you; video games let you experience unusual sorts of situations, challenges, and puzzles; TVs, DVDs, remote controls, iPods, and MP3 players provide you with customized entertainment; and, of course, computers affect almost every aspect of our lives. Technologies such as these are extremely influential because they're so common. Indeed, like the other subjects in this book, technology exerts a profound and mostly unexamined impact on our lives.

We begin the chapter with an article that aims to bring to our conscious attention some of the typically unexamined dimensions of technology's influence. Robert Samuels writes about what he sees on a visit to his local Borders café, commenting on the behavior of people who are gathered together in a common space but are nevertheless separated and even isolated by the technological objects that command their attention and fill their senses. Neil Postman expands on this narrative by arguing that any technology is both a blessing and a burden, changing our behavior and our culture in ways that we can't predict and can't avoid. By offering a number of examples of technologies that have had strong and unexpected ideological consequences, Postman shows how crucial it is to think critically and carefully about the role of technology in our lives.

The second section of the chapter presents four critical perspectives on cell phones and text messaging. We consider the cell phone a prime example of a technology that has, in a remarkably short amount of time, made a huge impact on many aspects of our lives. Cell phones go everywhere with us, hold some of our most important information, enable us to communicate with friends and family, record our photos and videos, provide access to the Internet, and the list goes on. A technology that barely existed twenty years ago has become seemingly indispensable, and, as the readings in this section show, this technology has deeply affected and shaped who we are, individually and collectively.

In the first article, Louis Menand focuses on the ways that texting on cell phones affects language, making English ("the language of popular culture") even more prominent internationally and causing texters to create words and acronyms that merge English with other languages. Next, Randy Cohen considers the ethics of cell phone use and the ways that texting has changed social interactions; Cohen suggests that we need to develop new standards of propriety and new rules of behavior to help us tame the potential threat that cell phones will make us a ruder and more distracted society.

Looking more broadly at cell phones and culture, Howard Rheingold sees great potential in the "smart mobs" that could potentially be created through our pervasive mobile access to the Internet; here, cell phone technology enables new models for collaborative action in the political and social realm. To complement this sociological approach, we conclude the chapter with Sherry Turkle's article that considers the individual and psychological effects of being perpetually connected to others and to the Internet—of being "always on" because of technologies that are "always on you." Turkle advances the concept of a "tethered self" who could perhaps use just a bit more down time—to reflect, to focus, to be alone. If Rheingold's "smart mobs" are made up of Turkle's "tethered selves," what does this tell us about how individuals and society are evolving under technology's influence?

We hope that the readings in this chapter, taken together, will engage you in a fresh look at very familiar objects in your life. Before you read, it might be helpful for you to make a list of the technologies you use on a regular basis, particularly those associated with media, communication, and culture. How do you think the technologies you regularly use have influenced the way you live your life? What would your everyday life be like without these technologies?

ROBERT SAMUELS

Breaking Down Borders: How Technology Transforms the Private and Public Realms

One important premise of this book is that the culture all around us is worthy of investigation. Indeed, we believe that paying attention to the activities we are involved in every day is particularly important because these activities are highly likely to influence who we are, what we do, and what we value. Robert Samuels, a lecturer in the Writing Programs at UCLA, takes precisely this approach in the article that follows. Samuels reports on a mundane, everyday sort of event: a trip to his local Borders café. But in describing and analyzing what he sees there, he is able to draw conclusions about larger changes and challenges in our culture. Specifically, Samuels focuses his attention on the different technologies used by people at the café, and he analyzes how the use of technologies blurs the borders between public and private and between work and play.

It's a Tuesday morning and I'm walking through the Borders Café just south of the UCLA campus in Westwood, CA. My plan is to find a table, drink my coffee, and read some of the novel that I just bought in the bookstore section. As I head for one of the few empty chairs, I pass by a man sitting at a table, the sports section of the Los Angeles *Times* spread out in front of him, a cup of coffee and a blueberry muffin to one side, his cell phone close at hand on the other side. He's wearing a t-shirt and shorts, but he might as well be in pajamas and slippers; it's as if he's in his own kitchen, reading his paper and having his breakfast, just following his morning routine.

I move past breakfast-man and notice a twenty-something woman sitting in one of the five or six comfy upholstered chairs that Borders provides its customers. She's curled up cozily in the chair with one foot stretched out and resting on a matching upholstered footstool. Actually, the foot isn't resting; it's wagging back and forth in time, I assume, to the music that's coming through the headphones attached to her ears and her iPod. Keeping time to the music, she taps her yellow highlighter pen against the textbook that she's ostensibly reading. As I watch, she begins to hum out loud—it sounds like a wildly out-of-tune version of "Dancing Queen"—and then she abruptly looks up and stops humming, a bit startled, remembering that she's in Borders and not in her living room.

I sit at my own table with my coffee and novel, but I don't get past the first page before I'm distracted by a woman at the table to my left who's talking on her cell phone. I see that she's also got her laptop computer open on the table and a magazine on her lap, but it's her phone conversation that's getting all of her attention—and, of course, the attention of everyone around her. We learn that she's terribly sorry but she has to cancel her job interview that Friday because of a doctor's appointment; our dismay is quickly alleviated when, in her next call, she tells a friend that, yes, the trip to Las Vegas that weekend is back on. The café, it seems, is her personal office.

Each of these people seems to have carved a little semi-private, personalized space out of the larger public, commercial space of Borders Café. As people come and go, these spaces change, so that a time-lapse video of Borders Café would have to show it as not just one space but rather as an aggregate of small, shifting living rooms, kitchens, and offices (no bedrooms—yet!). And of course it's not just Borders; this kind of activity goes on at bookstores and coffee shops across the country. These new commercial public squares have become shared spaces that are neither private nor public. In fact, they compel us to redefine what private and public mean. The cell phone woman, for example, seems to have no problem sharing her Las Vegas plans with everyone sitting around her. But then I look around again and notice that I'm one of the few people who can actually hear her. Most of the other people here have headphones on and they're listening to their own iPods or MP3 players, perhaps precisely in order to avoid having to listen to conversations that should be private in the first place.

What I see at Borders convinces me that there are new rules for how to act in public places and for how to socialize with and around one another. It's clear, as well, that none of these changes would have occurred without new technologies helping to break down borders. For instance, the telephone used to be firmly located in the private realm, physically attached to the kitchen wall or set on a desk in an office. Now, however, cell phones allow for a high level of mobility and access, and thus they help us transform any public place into a setting for a private conversation. The laptop, too, has not only transformed the desktop computer but has also reinvented the desktop itself as any table or flat surface. Indeed, your very own lap becomes a desktop of sorts when you put your laptop computer on it.

With wireless technology, laptops and cell phones not only help us cross back and forth between the public and the private, but they also function to undermine the distinction between work and play. For instance, people often jump quickly from doing work on their computers to emailing their friends and playing video games. Likewise, cell phones can combine work functions and play functions, incorporating games as well as digital cameras, video, and, of course, sound clips for ring tones. Some critics of new communication technologies argue that cell phones, laptops, iPods, and the other devices we take with us throughout our day encourage a high level of multitasking and prevent us from concentrating on any single activity. Thus, they argue, people not only become more superficial, but the constant switching between work and leisure activities creates a fragmented sense of self and gives everyone a bad case of attention deficit disorder.

However, another way of looking at these new technologies is to see how they allow people to re-center their sense of self by creating what can be called "personal culture." In other words, instead of seeing culture as a social and public activity, like going to a concert hall, devices like iPods and laptops allow people to take culture with them wherever they go. More importantly, instead of having to let the radio station tell them what to listen to or the newspaper limit their choice of news sources, people are able to personalize their own media and decide on their own what culture they want to consume.

Personal culture derives much of its power from the fact that many of the new media devices are highly immersive: people on cell phones and laptops can become so involved in their own mediated worlds that they forget where they actually are and what they are supposed to be doing. Some states have laws now against driving while talking on a cell phone, but in addition to the physical danger there also may be a social cost. After all, we are social beings who live in public worlds, and therefore we cannot simply forget that other people exist. As I look around me at the people who have temporarily transformed Borders Café into a set of small personal spaces, I realize that although we're all together here there's very little chance that we'll interact with one another. Most of us are plugged in to technologies that, while allowing us to personalize our environment, also effectively isolate us from our neighbors.

But is there really anything wrong with that? We adapt to our new technologies and to the new spaces these technologies create; we adapt, in fact, by using more technologies. To tune out the cell phones, we put on our headphones. There seems to be no way of escaping from a technologically mediated environment, even in a place devoted to selling those old-fashioned, low-tech items called books. But, in Borders, at least, on this sunny Tuesday morning, we seem to be coping well enough even as the borders all around us are shifting and transforming

SUGGESTIONS FOR WRITING

1. After rereading the description of "personal culture" forwarded by Samuels, write a brief definition of this concept in your own words. How do technologies help us create personal culture? Do you think the role of personal culture is increasing in our society, and, if so, what do you think are the consequences of this shift?

2. Samuels discusses two different borders in this article: the border between public and private, and the border between work and play. Choose one of these borders, and make a list of all the technologies that contribute to breaking down this border. You can begin with the technologies that Samuels himself describes; for instance, he discusses how the cell phone helps to break down the border between public and private as well as the border between work and play. Be sure to continue your list with examples of other technologies. Then list any technologies that you think help to maintain or increase the border. Once you've completed your lists, write a brief expository essay

explaining role of technology in the particular border area you're discussing.

3. Samuels acts as an amateur anthropologist in this essay in the sense that he goes to a particular place, observes how people act there, and records and analyzes his observations in an article. Your assignment is to do something similar. Choose a place where people congregate: a coffee shop, a dorm lounge, an outdoor park or playground, a living room. Ideally, the place you choose will be somewhere where you can sit and observe and take notes without being too distracted and without distracting others. Spend an hour or two at the place, watching to see what technologies people use and how the people interact with each other. Then write an essay modeled after Samuels' article. Begin the essay with a couple of detailed descriptions of specific people or activities you observed. In the body of the essay, discuss and analyze the ways that you saw technologies influence people's interactions. You might want to cite Samuels' article in your essay, perhaps in order to argue for or against the conclusions he draws.

NEIL POSTMAN

The Judgment of Thamus

Neil Postman was a highly regarded critic and theorist of popular American culture and a professor of media ecology at New York University. The article that follows comes from one of Postman's later books—Technopoly (1992)—in which he looks at how technology influences our society. Although Postman was accused of being a technophobe, his argument here is balanced: "Every technology is both a burden and a blessing; not either-or but this-and-that." Moreover, Postman believes that technological change is "ecological" in the sense that "[O]ne significant change generates total change." For Postman, the stakes are high when a new technology is introduced into a culture, and it is important that we think critically about technology if we are to live well with it.

You will find in Plato's *Phaedrus* a story about Thamus, the king of a great city of Upper Egypt. For people such as ourselves, who are inclined (in Thoreau's phrase) to be tools of our tools, few legends are more instructive than his. The story, as Socrates tells it to his friend Phaedrus, unfolds in the following way: Thamus once entertained the god Theuth, who was the inventor of many things, including numbers, calculation, geometry, astronomy, and writing. Theuth exhibited his inventions to King Thamus, claiming that they should be made widely known and available to Egyptians. Socrates continues:

> Thamus inquired into the use of each of them, and as Theuth went through them expressed approval or disapproval, according as he judged Theuth's claims to be well or ill founded. It would take too long to go through all that Thamus is reported to have said for and against each of Theuth's inventions. But when it came to writing, Theuth declared, "Here is an accomplishment, my lord the King, which will improve both the wisdom and the memory of the Egyptians. I have discovered a sure receipt for memory and wisdom." To this, Thamus replied, "Theuth, my paragon of inventors, the discoverer of an art is not the best judge of the good or harm which will accrue to those who practice it. So it is in this; you, who are the father of writing, have out of fondness for your off-spring attributed to it quite the opposite of its real function. Those who acquire it will cease to exercise their memory and become forgetful; they will rely on writing to bring things to their remembrance by external signs instead of by their own internal resources. What you have discov-ered is a receipt for recollection, not for memory. And as for wisdom, your pupils will have the reputation for it without the reality: they will receive a quantity of information without proper instruction, and in consequence be thought very knowledgeable when they are for the most part quite ignorant. And because they are filled with the conceit of wis-dom instead of real wisdom they will be a burden to society."[1]

I begin my book with this legend because in Thamus' response there are several sound principles from which we may begin to learn how to think with wise circumspection about a technological society. In fact, there is even one error in the judgment of Thamus, from which we may also learn something of importance. The error is not in his claim that writing will damage memory and create false wisdom. It is demonstrable that writing has had such an effect. Thamus' error is in his believing that writing will be a burden to society and *nothing but a burden*. For all his wisdom, he fails to imagine what writing's benefits might be, which, as we know, have been considerable. We may learn from this that it is a mistake to suppose that any technological innova-tion has a one-sided effect. Every technology is both a burden and a blessing; not either-or, but this-and-that.

Nothing could be more obvious, of course, especially to those who have given more than two minutes of thought to the matter. Nonetheless, we are currently surrounded by throngs of zealous Theuths, one-eyed prophets who see only what new technologies can do and are incapable of imagining what they will *undo*. We might call such people Technophiles. They gaze on technology as a lover does on his beloved, seeing it as without blemish and entertaining no apprehension for the future. They are therefore dangerous and are to be approached cautiously. On the other hand, some one-eyed prophets, such as I (or so I am accused), are inclined to speak only of burdens (in the manner of Thamus) and are silent about the opportunities that new technologies make possible. The Technophiles must speak for themselves, and do so all over the place. My defense is that a dissenting voice is sometimes needed to moderate the din made by the enthusiastic multitudes. If one is to err, it is better to err on the side of Thamusian skepticism. But it is an error nonetheless. And I might note that, with the exception of his judgment on writing, Thamus does not repeat this error. You might notice on rereading the legend that he gives arguments *for* and *against* each of Theuth's inventions. For it is inescapable that every culture must negotiate with technology, whether it does so intelligently or not. A bargain is struck in which technology giveth and technology taketh away. The wise know this well, and are rarely impressed by dramatic technological changes, and never overjoyed. Here, for example, is Freud on the matter, from his doleful *Civilization and Its Discontents*:

> One would like to ask: is there, then, no positive gain in pleasure, no unequivocal increase in my feeling of happiness, if I can, as often as I please, hear the voice of a child of mine who is living hundreds of miles away or if I can learn in the shortest possible time after a friend has reached his destination that he has come through the long and difficult voyage unharmed? Does it mean nothing that medicine has succeeded in enormously reducing infant mortality and the danger of infection for women in childbirth, and, indeed, in considerably lengthening the average life of a civilized man?

Freud knew full well that technical and scientific advances are not to be taken lightly, which is why he begins this passage by acknowledging them. But he ends it by reminding us of what they have undone:

> If there had been no railway to conquer distances, my child would never have left his native town and I should need no telephone to hear his voice; if travelling across the ocean by ship had not been introduced, my friend would not have embarked on his sea-voyage and I should not need a cable to relieve my anxiety about him. What is the use of reducing infantile mortality when it is precisely that reduction which

*imposes the greatest restraint on us in the begetting of children, so
that, taken all round, we nevertheless rear no more children than in the
days before the reign of hygiene, while at the same time we have
created difficult conditions for our sexual life in marriage. . . . And,
finally, what good to us is a long life if it is difficult and barren of
joys, and if it is so full of misery that we can only welcome death as a
deliverer?*[2]

In tabulating the cost of technological progress, Freud takes a
rather depressing line, that of a man who agrees with Thoreau's remark
that our inventions are but improved means to an unimproved end.
The Technophile would surely answer Freud by saying that life has
always been barren of joys and full of misery but that the telephone, ocean liners, and especially the reign of hygiene have not only
lengthened life but made it a more agreeable proposition. That is certainly an argument I would make (thus proving I am no one-eyed
Technophobe), but it is not necessary at this point to pursue it. I have
brought Freud into the conversation only to show that a wise man—
even one of such a woeful countenance—must begin his critique of
technology by acknowledging its successes. Had King Thamus been
as wise as reputed, he would not have forgotten to include in his
judgment a prophecy about the powers that writing would enlarge.
There is a calculus of technological change that requires a measure of
evenhandedness.

So much for Thamus' error of omission. There is another omission
worthy of note, but it is no error. Thamus simply takes for granted—and
therefore does not feel it necessary to say—that writing is not a neutral
technology whose good or harm depends on the uses made of it. He
knows that the uses made of any technology are largely determined by
the structure of the technology itself—that is, that its functions follow
from its form. This is why Thamus is concerned not with *what* people
will write; he is concerned *that* people will write. It is absurd to imagine, Thamus advising, in the manner of today's standard-brand
Technophiles, that, if only writing would be used for the production of
certain kinds of texts and not others (let us say, for dramatic literature
but not for history or philosophy), its disruptions could be minimized.
He would regard such counsel as extreme naiveté. He would allow, I
imagine, that a technology may be barred entry to a culture. But we may
learn from Thamus the following: once a technology is admitted,
it plays out its hand; it does what it is designed to do. Our task is to

understand what that design is—that is to say, when we admit a new technology to the culture, we must do so with our eyes wide open.

All of this we may infer from Thamus' silence. But we may learn even more from what he does say than from what he doesn't. He points out, for example, that writing will change what is meant by the words "memory" and "wisdom." He fears that memory will be confused with what he disdainfully calls "recollection," and he worries that wisdom will become indistinguishable from mere knowledge. This judgment we must take to heart, for it is a certainty that radical technologies invite new definitions of old terms, and that this process takes place without our being fully conscious of it. Thus, it is insidious and dangerous, quite different from the process whereby new technologies introduce new terms to the language. In our own time, we have continuously added to our language thousands of new words and phrases having to do with new technologies: "VCR," "binary digit," "software," "front-wheel drive," "window of opportunity," "Walkman." We are not taken by surprise at this. New things require new words. But new things also modify old words, words that have deep-rooted meanings. The telegraph and the penny press changed what we once meant by "information." Television changes what we once meant by the terms "political debate," "news," and "public opinion." The computer changes "information" once again. Writing changed what we once meant by "truth" and "law"; printing changed them again, and now television and the computer change them once more. Such changes occur quickly, surely, and, in a sense, silently. Lexicographers hold no plebiscites on the matter. No manuals are written to explain what is happening, and the schools are oblivious to it. The old words still look the same, are still used in the same kinds of sentences. But they do not have the same meanings; in some cases, they have opposite meanings. And this is what Thamus wishes to teach us—that technology imperiously commandeers our most important terminology. It redefines "freedom," "truth," "intelligence," "fact," "wisdom," "memory," "history" — all the words we live by. And it does not pause to tell us. And we do not pause to ask.

This fact about technological change requires some elaboration, and I will return to the matter in a later chapter. Here, there are several more principles to be mined from the judgment of Thamus that require mentioning because they presage all I will write about. For instance, Thamus warns that the pupils of Theuth will develop an undeserved reputation for wisdom. He means to say that those who cultivate competence in the use of a new technology become an elite group that are granted undeserved authority and prestige by those who have no such competence. There are different ways of expressing the interesting implications of this fact. Harold Innis, the father of modern communication studies, repeatedly spoke of the "knowledge monopolies" created by important technologies. He meant precisely what Thamus had in mind: those who have control over the workings of a particular technology accumulate power and inevitably form a kind of conspiracy against those who have no access to the specialized knowledge made available by the technology. In his book, *The Bias of Communication*, Innis provides many historical examples of how a new technology "busted up" a traditional knowledge monopoly and created a new one presided over by a different group. Another way of saying this is that the benefits and deficits of a new technology are not distributed equally. There are, as it were, winners and losers. It is both puzzling and poignant that on many occasions the losers, out of ignorance, have actually cheered the winners, and some still do.

Let us take as an example the case of television. In the United States, where television has taken hold more deeply than anywhere else, many people find it a blessing, not least those who have achieved high-paying, gratifying careers in television as executives, technicians, newscasters, and entertainers. It should surprise no one that such people, forming as they do a new knowledge monopoly, should cheer themselves and defend and promote television technology. On the other hand and in the long run, television may bring a gradual end to the careers of schoolteachers since school was an invention of the printing press and must stand or fall on the issue of how much importance the printed word has. For four hundred years, schoolteachers have been part of the knowledge monopoly created by printing, and they are now witnessing the breakup of that monopoly. It appears as if they can do little to prevent that breakup, but surely there is something perverse about schoolteachers being enthusiastic about what is happening. Such enthusiasm always calls to my mind an image of some turn-of-the-century blacksmith who not only sings the praises of the automobile but also believes that his business will be enhanced by it. We know now that his business was not enhanced by it; it was rendered obsolete by it, as perhaps the clearheaded blacksmiths knew. What could they have done? Weep, if nothing else.

We have a similar situation in the development and spread of computer technology, for here too there are winners and losers. There can be no disputing that the computer has increased the power of large-scale organizations like the armed forces or airline companies or banks or tax-collecting agencies. And it is equally clear that the computer is now indispensable to high-level researchers in physics and other natural sciences. But to what extent has computer technology been an advantage to the masses of people? To steelworkers, vegetable store owners, teachers, garage mechanics, musicians, bricklayers, dentists, and most of the rest into whose lives the computer now intrudes? Their private matters have been made more accessible to powerful institutions. They are more easily tracked and controlled; are subjected to more examinations; are increasingly mystified by the decisions made about them; are often reduced to mere numerical objects. They are inundated by junk mail. They are easy targets for advertising agencies and political organizations. The schools teach their children to operate computerized systems instead of teaching things that are more valuable to children. In a word, almost nothing that they need happens to the losers. Which is why they are losers.

It is to be expected that the winners will encourage the losers to be enthusiastic about computer technology. That is the way of winners, and so they sometimes tell the losers that with personal computers the average person can balance a checkbook more neatly, keep better track of recipes, and make more logical shopping lists. They also tell them that their lives will be conducted more efficiently. But discreetly they neglect to say from whose point of view the efficiency is warranted or what might be its costs. Should the losers grow skeptical, the winners dazzle them with the wondrous feats of computers, almost all of which have only marginal relevance to the quality of the losers' lives but which are nonetheless impressive. Eventually, the losers succumb, in part because they believe, as Thamus prophesied, that the specialized knowledge of the masters of a new technology is a form of wisdom. The masters come to believe this as well, as Thamus also prophesied. The result is that certain questions do not arise. For example, to whom will the technology give greater power and freedom? And whose power and freedom will be reduced by it?

I have perhaps made all of this sound like a well-planned conspiracy, as if the winners know all too well what is being won and what lost. But this is not quite how it happens. For one thing, in cultures that have a democratic ethos, relatively weak traditions, and a high receptivity to new technologies, everyone is inclined to be enthusiastic about technological change, believing that its benefits will eventually spread evenly among the entire population. Especially in the United States, where the lust for what is new has no bounds, do we find this childlike conviction most widely held. Indeed, in America, social change of any kind is rarely seen as resulting in winners and losers, a condition that stems in part from Americans' much-documented optimism. As for change brought on by technology, this native optimism is exploited by entrepreneurs, who work hard to infuse the population with a unity of improbable hope, for they know that it is economically unwise to reveal the price to be paid for technological change. One might say, then, that, if there is a conspiracy of any kind, it is that of a culture conspiring against itself.

In addition to this, and more important, it is not always clear, at least in the early stages of a technology's intrusion into a culture, who will gain most by it and who will lose most. This is because the changes wrought by technology are subtle, if not downright mysterious, one might even say wildly unpredictable. Among the most unpredictable are those that might be labeled ideological. This is the sort of change Thamus had in mind when he warned that writers will come to rely on external signs instead of their own internal resources, and that they will receive quantities of information without proper instruction. He meant that new technologies change what we mean by "knowing" and "truth"; they alter those deeply embedded habits of thought which give to a culture its sense of what the world is like—a sense of what is the natural order of things, of what is reasonable, of what is necessary, of what is inevitable, of what is real. Since such changes are expressed in changed meanings of old words, I will hold off until later discussing the massive ideological transformation now occurring in the United States. Here, I should like to give only one example of how technology creates new conceptions of what is real and, in the process, undermines older conceptions. I refer to the seemingly harmless practice of assigning marks or grades to the answers students give on examinations. This procedure seems so natural to most of us that we are hardly aware of its significance. We may even find it difficult to imagine that the number or letter is a tool or, if you will, a technology; still less that, when we use such a technology to judge someone's behavior, we have done something peculiar. In point of fact, the first instance of grading students' papers occurred at Cambridge University in 1792 at the suggestion of a tutor named William Farish.[3] No one knows much about William Farish; not more than a handful have ever heard of him. And yet his idea that a quantitative value should be assigned to human thoughts was a major step toward constructing a mathematical concept of reality. If a number can be given to the quality of a thought, then a number can be given to the qualities of mercy, love, hate, beauty, creativity, intelligence, even sanity itself. When Galileo said that the language of nature is written in mathematics, he did not mean to include human feeling or accomplishment or insight. But most of us are now inclined to make these inclusions. Our psychologists, sociologists, and educators find it quite impossible to do their work without numbers. They believe that without numbers they cannot acquire or express authentic knowledge.

I shall not argue here that this is a stupid or dangerous idea, only that it is peculiar. What is even more peculiar is that so many of us do not find the idea peculiar. To say that someone should be doing better work because he has an IQ of 134, or that someone is a 7.2 on a sensitivity scale, or that this man's essay on the rise of capitalism is an A– and that man's is a C+ would have sounded like gibberish to Galileo or Shakespeare or Thomas Jefferson. If it makes sense to us, that is because our minds have been conditioned by the technology of numbers so that we see the world differently than they did. Our understanding of what is real is different. Which is another way of saying that embedded in every tool is an ideological bias, a predisposition to construct the world as one thing rather than another, to value one thing over another, to amplify one sense or skill or attitude more loudly than another.

This is what Marshall McLuhan meant by his famous aphorism "The medium is the message." This is what Marx meant when he said, "Technology discloses man's mode of dealing with nature" and creates the "conditions of intercourse" by which we relate to each other. It is what Wittgenstein meant when, in referring to our most fundamental technology, he said that language is not merely a vehicle of thought but also the driver. And it is what Thamus wished the inventor Theuth to see. This is, in short, an ancient and persistent piece of wisdom, perhaps most simply expressed in the old adage that, to a man with a hammer everything looks like a nail. Without being too literal, we may extend the truism: To a man with a pencil, everything looks like a list. To a man with a camera, everything looks like an image. To a man with a computer, everything looks like data. And to a man with a grade sheet, everything looks like a number.

But such prejudices are not always apparent at the start of a technology's journey, which is why no one can safely conspire to be a winner in technological change. Who would have imagined, for example, whose interests and what world-view would be ultimately advanced by the invention of the mechanical clock? The clock had its origin in the Benedictine monasteries of the twelfth and thirteenth centuries. The impetus behind the invention was to provide a more or less precise regularity to the routines of the monasteries, which required, among other things, seven periods of devotion during the course of the day. The bells of the monastery were to be rung to signal the canonical hours; the mechanical clock was the technology that could provide precision to these rituals of devotion. And indeed it did. But what the monks did not foresee was that the clock is a means not merely of keeping track of the hours but also of synchronizing and controlling the actions of men. And thus, by the middle of the fourteenth century, the clock had moved outside the walls of the monastery, and brought a new and precise regularity to the life of the workman and the merchant.

"The mechanical clock," as Lewis Mumford wrote, "made possible the idea of regular production, regular working hours and a standardized product." In short, without the clock, capitalism would have been quite impossible.[4] The paradox, the surprise, and the wonder are that the clock was invented by men who wanted to devote themselves more rigorously to God; it ended as the technology of greatest use to men who wished to devote themselves to the accumulation of money. In the eternal struggle between God and Mammon, the clock quite unpredictably favored the latter.

Unforeseen consequences stand in the way of all those who think they see clearly the direction in which a new technology will take us. Not even those who invent a technology can be assumed to be reliable prophets, as Thamus warned. Gutenberg, for example, was by all accounts a devout Catholic who would have been horrified to hear that accursed heretic Luther describe printing as "God's highest act of grace, whereby the business of the Gospel is driven forward." Luther understood, as Gutenberg did not, that the mass-produced book, by placing the Word of God on every kitchen table, makes each Christian his own theologian—one might even say his own priest, or, better, from Luther's point of view, his own pope. In the struggle between unity and diversity of religious belief, the press favored the latter, and we can assume that this possibility never occurred to Gutenberg.

Thamus understood well the limitations of inventors in grasping the social and psychological—that is, ideological—bias of their own inventions. We can imagine him addressing Gutenberg in the following way: "Gutenberg, my paragon of inventors, the discoverer of an art is not the best judge of the good or harm which will accrue to those who practice it. So it is in this; you, who are the father of printing, have out of fondness for your off-spring come to believe it will advance the cause of the Holy Roman See, whereas in fact it will sow discord among believers; it will damage the authenticity of your beloved Church and destroy its monopoly."

We can imagine that Thamus would also have pointed out to Gutenberg, as he did to Theuth, that the new invention would create a vast population of readers who "will receive a quantity of information without proper instruction... [who will be] filled with the conceit of wisdom instead of real wisdom"; that reading, in other words, will compete with older forms of learning. This is yet another principle of technological change we may infer from the judgment of Thamus: new technologies compete with old ones—for time, for attention, for money, for prestige, but mostly for dominance of their world-view. This competition is implicit once we acknowledge that a medium contains an ideological bias. And it is a fierce competition, as only ideological competitions can be. It is not merely a matter of tool against tool—the alphabet attacking ideographic writing, the printing press attacking the illuminated manuscript, the photograph attacking the art of painting, television attacking the printed word. When media make war against each other, it is a case of world-views in collision.

In the United States, we can see such collisions everywhere—in politics, in religion, in commerce—but we see them made most clearly in the schools, where two great technologies confront each other in uncompromising aspect for the control of students' minds. On the one hand, there is the world of the printed word with its emphasis on logic, sequence, history, exposition, objectivity, detachment, and discipline. On the other, there is the world of television with its emphasis on imagery, narrative, presentness, simultaneity, intimacy, immediate gratification, and quick emotional response. Children come to school having been deeply conditioned by the biases of television. There, they encounter the world of the printed word. A sort of psychic battle takes place, and there are many casualties—children who can't learn to read or won't, children who cannot organize their thought into logical structure even in a simple paragraph, children who cannot attend to lectures or oral explanations for more than a few minutes at a time. They are failures, but not because they are stupid. They are failures because there is a media war going on, and they are on the wrong side—at least for the moment. Who knows what schools will be like twenty-five years from now? Or fifty? In time, the type of student who is currently a failure may be considered a success. The type who is now successful may be regarded as a handicapped learner—slow to respond, far too detached, lacking in emotion, inadequate in creating mental pictures of reality. Consider: what Thamus called the "conceit of wisdom"—the real knowledge acquired through the written word—eventually became the pre-eminent form of knowledge valued by the schools. There is no reason to suppose that such a form of knowledge must always remain so highly valued.

To take another example: In introducing the personal computer to the classroom, we shall be breaking a four-hundred-year-old truce between the gregariousness and openness fostered by orality and the introspection and isolation fostered by the printed word. Orality stresses group learning, cooperation, and a sense of social responsibility, which is the context within which Thamus believed proper instruction and real knowledge must be communicated. Print stresses individualized learning, competition, and personal autonomy. Over four centuries, teachers, while emphasizing print, have allowed orality its place in the classroom, and have therefore achieved a kind of pedagogical peace between these two forms of learning, so that what is valuable in each can be maximized. Now comes the computer, carrying anew the banner of private learning and individual problem-solving. Will the widespread use of computers in the classroom defeat once and for all the claims of communal speech? Will the computer raise egocentrism to the status of a virtue?

These are the kinds of questions that technological change brings to mind when one grasps, as Thamus did, that technological competition ignites total war, which means it is not possible to contain the effects of a new technology to a limited sphere of human activity. If this metaphor puts the matter too brutally, we may try a gentler, kinder one: Technological change is neither additive nor subtractive. It is ecological. I mean "ecological" in the same sense as the word is used by environmental scientists. One significant change generates total change. If you remove the caterpillars from a given habitat, you are not left with the same environment minus caterpillars: you have a new environment, and you have reconstituted the conditions of survival; the same is true if you add caterpillars to an environment that has had none. This is how the ecology of media works as well. A new technology does not add or subtract something. It changes everything. In the year 1500, fifty years after the printing press was invented, we did not have old Europe plus the printing press. We had a different Europe. After television, the United States was not America plus television; television gave a new coloration to every political campaign, to every home, to every school, to every church, to every industry. And that is why the competition among media is so fierce. Surrounding every technology are institutions whose organization—not to mention their reason for being—reflects the world-view promoted by the technology. Therefore, when an old technology is assaulted by a new one, institutions are threatened. When institutions are threatened, a culture finds itself in crisis. This is serious business, which is why we learn nothing when educators ask, Will students learn mathematics better by computers than by textbooks? Or when businessmen ask, Through which medium can we sell more products? Or when preachers ask, Can we reach more people through television than through radio? Or when politicians ask, How effective are messages sent through different media? Such questions have an immediate, practical value to those who ask them, but they are diversionary. They direct our attention away from the serious social, intellectual, and institutional crises that new media foster.

Perhaps an analogy here will help to underline the point. In speaking of the meaning of a poem, T. S. Eliot remarked that the chief use of the overt content of poetry is "to satisfy one habit of the reader, to keep his mind diverted and quiet, while the poem does its work upon him: much as the imaginary burglar is always provided with a bit of nice meat for the house-dog." In other words, in asking their practical questions, educators, entrepreneurs, preachers, and politicians are like the house-dog munching peacefully on the meat while the house is looted. Perhaps some of them know this and do not especially care. After all, a nice piece of meat, offered graciously, does take care of the problem of where the next meal will come from. But for the rest of us, it cannot be acceptable to have the house invaded without protest or at least awareness.

What we need to consider about the computer has nothing to do with its efficiency as a teaching tool. We need to know in what ways it is altering our conception of learning, and how, in conjunction with television, it undermines the old idea of school. Who cares how many boxes of cereal can be sold via television? We need to know if television changes our conception of reality, the relationship of the rich to the poor, the idea of happiness itself. A preacher who confines himself to considering how a medium can increase his audience will miss the significant question: In what sense do new media alter what is meant by religion, by church, even by God? And if the politician cannot think beyond the next election, then *we* must wonder about what new media do to the idea of political organization and to the conception of citizenship.

To help us do this, we have the judgment of Thamus, who, in the way be legends, teaches us what Harold Innis, in his way, tried to. New technologies alter the structure of our interests: the things we think *about*. They alter the character of our symbols: the things we think *with*. And they alter the nature of community: the arena in which thoughts develop. As Thamus spoke to Innis across the centuries, it is essential that we listen to their conversation, join in it, revitalize it. For something has happened in America that is strange and dangerous, and there is only a dull and even stupid awareness of what it is—in part because it has no name. I call it Technopoly.

NOTES

1. Plato, p. 96.
2. Freud pp. 38–39.
3. This fact is documented in Keith Hoskin's "The Examination, Disciplinary Power and Rational Schooling," in *History of Education*, vol. VIII, no. 2 (1979), pp. 135–46. Professor Hoskin provides the following story about Farish: Farish was a professor of engineering at Cambridge and designed and installed a movable partition wall in his Cambridge home. The wall moved on pulleys between downstairs and upstairs. One night, while working late downstairs and feeling cold, Farish pulled down the partition. This is not much of a story, and history fails to disclose what happened next. All of which shows how little is known of William Farish.
4. For a detailed exposition of Mumford's position on the impact of the mechanical clock, see his *Technics and Civilization*.

SUGGESTIONS FOR WRITING

1. Write a summary of Postman's argument about the practice of assigning grades in school. In what ways is this practice a kind of technology? In what ways is grading ideological? What reasons does Postman give for objecting to it, and what do you think of his argument here?
2. One reason we chose this article is that we admire Postman's writing style; we think that he crafted some particularly delightful phrases and sentences in this article. For this assignment, go back through

Postman's article and underline any segments of his writing that you find especially pleasing to your own stylistic sensibilities. Choose your five favorites, and for each phrase or sentence, write a one-paragraph explanation of what makes it stylistically pleasing.

3. Postman argues that "technology imperiously commandeers our most important terminology. It redefines 'freedom,' 'truth,' 'intelligence,' 'fact,' 'wisdom,' 'memory,' 'history'—all the words we live by. And it does not pause to tell us. And we do not pause to ask." For this writing assignment, choose one of these terms, or another similarly important and broad term, and explore the ways in which technology has changed its definition. Here are several prewriting activities that can help you begin this assignment:

- Make a list of all the different types of technology that may impact the definition of the term; consider how technologies related to communication, entertainment, medicine, travel, education, politics, and family life, for example, cause us to differently define the term you have chosen.
- Write about how you imagine the term might have been defined in the nineteenth century (or earlier), before the advent of many of the technologies that strongly impact our lives today.
- Think of the way your own understanding of this term has evolved during your life. Have any of the technologies that you use frequently caused you to think differently about this term?

After completing these prewriting activities, compose an essay with a thesis that states both how the term you have chosen is currently defined and how technologies have influenced this definition. Support your argument with specific examples drawn from your prewriting activities.

On Your Phone

LOUIS MENAND

Thumbspeak

Louis Menand is the Robert M. and Anne T. Bass Professor of English and American Literature and Language at Harvard University and a frequent contributor to The New Yorker *magazine and* The New York Review of Books. *In the following article, taken from the October 20, 2008, issue of* The New Yorker, *Menand takes on the weighty subject of texting. He contextualizes his discussion in the review of a book on texting by British linguist David Crystal.*

Although the book, appropriately entitled Txtng: The Gr8 Db8, *argues that texting has no real impact on language or culture, Menand posits that the trillion-plus text messages sent worldwide each year have at least had an effect on the way we use language; he gives a number of examples of how texting in other languages "Englishes" them by creating blends of words and acronyms that have components of English along with the original language. Menand suggests several other consequences of our massive adoption of texting before concluding his essay with a speculation on the future of this technology.*

Is texting bringing us closer to the end of life as we currently tolerate it? Enough people have suggested that it is to have inspired David Crystal to produce *Txtng: The Gr8 Db8* (Oxford). "I don't think I have ever come across a topic which has attracted more adult antagonism," he says. (On the other hand, Crystal has written more than a hundred books, so he does not require extraordinary encouragement to share his views.) Crystal is a professional linguist, and professional linguists, almost universally, do not believe that any naturally occurring changes in the language can be bad. So his conclusions are predictable: texting is not corrupting the language; people who send text messages that use emoticons, initialisms ("g2g," "lol"), and other shorthands generally know how to spell perfectly well; and the history of language is filled with analogous examples of nonstandard usage. It is good to know that the estimated three billion human beings who own cell phones, and who use them to send more than a trillion text messages every year, are having no effect on anything that we should care about. A trillion text messages, Crystal says, "appear as no more than a few ripples on the surface of the sea of language."

The texting function of the cell phone ought to have been the special province of the kind of people who figure out how to use the television remote to turn on the toaster: it's a huge amount of trouble relative to the results. In some respects, texting is a giant leap backward in the science of communication. It's more efficient than semaphore, maybe, but how much more efficient is it than Morse code? With Morse code, to make an "s" you needed only three key presses. Sending a text message with a numeric keypad feels primitive and improvisational—like the way prisoners speak to each other by tapping on the walls of their cells in "Darkness at Noon," or the way the guy in *The Diving Bell and the Butterfly* writes a book. And, as Crystal points out, although cell phones keep getting smaller, thumbs do not. Usually, if you can text a person you can much more quickly and efficiently call that person. But people sometimes text when they are close enough to talk face to face. People *like* to text. Why is that?

Crystal's answer is that texting is, partly, a game. It's like writing a sonnet (well, sort of): the requirement is to adapt the message to immutable formal constraints. A sonnet can't have more than fourteen lines, and a mobile-phone message can't have more than a hundred and forty bytes, which is usually enough for a hundred and sixty characters. This is a challenge to ingenuity, not an invitation to anarchy.

Most of the shortcuts used in texting are either self-evident (@ for "at" and "b" for "be") or new initialisms on the model of the old "A.S.A.P.," "R.S.V.P.," and "B.Y.O.B.": "imho" for "in my humble opinion," and so on. More imaginatively, there are the elaborated emoticons, such as 7:-) for baseball cap, and pictograms, such as @(——— for a rose and ~(_8^(|) for Homer Simpson. These are for thumb-happy aficionados, though, not the ordinary texter notifying her partner that the flight is late. There is a dialect that is used mainly by kids: "prw" for "parents are watching"; "F?" for "Are we friends again?" But Crystal thinks that texting is not the equivalent of a new language. "People were playing with language in this way long before mobile phones were invented," he points out. "Texting may be using a new technology, but its linguistic processes are centuries old." Acronyms, contractions, abbreviations, and shortened words ("phone" for "telephone," and so forth) are just part of the language. Even back in the days when the dinosaurs roamed the earth and men wrote with typewriters, the language of the office memo was studded with abbreviations: "re:," "cc.," "F.Y.I." "Luv" for "love" dates from 1898; "thanx" was first used in 1936. "Wassup," Crystal notes, originally appeared in a Budweiser commercial. @(——— is something that e. e. Cummings might have come up with.

Still, despite what they say, size matters. A trillion of anything has to make some change in cultural weather patterns. Texting is international. It may have come late to the United States because personal computers became a routine part of life much earlier here than in other countries, and so people could e-mail and Instant Message (which shares a lot of texting lingo). Crystal provides lists of text abbreviations in eleven languages besides English. And it is clear from the lists that different cultures have had to solve the problem of squeezing commonly delivered messages onto the cell-phone screen according to their own particular national needs. In the Czech Republic, for example, "hosipa" is used for "*Hovno si pamatuju*": "I can't remember anything." One can imagine a wide range of contexts in which Czech texters might have recourse to that sentiment. French texters have devised "ght2v1," which means "*J'ai acheté du vin.*" In Germany, "nok" is an efficient solution to the problem of how to explain "*Nicht ohne Kondom*"—"not without condom." If you receive a text reading "aun" from the fine Finnish lady you met in the airport lounge, she is telling you "*Älä unta nää*"—in English, "Dream on."

But the lists also suggest that texting has accelerated a tendency toward the Englishing of world languages. Under the constraints of the numeric-keypad technology, English has some advantages. The average English word has only five letters; the average Inuit word, for example, has fourteen. English has relatively few characters; Ethiopian has three hundred and forty-five symbols, which do not fit on most keypads. English rarely uses diacritical marks, and it is not heavily inflected. Languages with diacritical marks, such as Czech, almost always drop them in text messages. Portuguese texters often substitute "m" for the tilde. Some Chinese texters use Pinyin—that is, the practice of writing Chinese words using the Roman alphabet.

But English is also the language of much of the world's popular culture. Sometimes it is more convenient to use the English term, but often it is the aesthetically preferred term—the cooler expression. Texters in all eleven languages that Crystal lists use "lol," "u," "brb," and "gr8," all English-based shorthands. The Dutch use "2m" to mean "tomorrow"; the French have been known to use "now," which is a lot easier to type than "*maintenant.*" And there is what is known as "code-mixing," in which two languages—one of them invariably English—are conflated in a single expression. Germans write "mbsseg" to mean "mail back so *schnell es geht*" ("as fast as you can"). So texting has probably done some damage to the planet's cultural ecology, to lingo-diversity. People are better able to communicate across national borders, but at some cost to variation.

The obvious appeal of texting is its speed. There is, as it happens, a Ten Commandments of texting, as laid down by one Norman Silver, the author of "Laugh Out Loud :-D". The Fourth of these commandments reads, "u shall b prepard @ all times 2 tXt & 2 recv." This is the new decorum in communication: you can be sloppy and you can be blunt, but you have to be fast. To delay is to disrespect. In fact, delay is the only disrespect. Any other misunderstanding can be cleared up by a few more exchanges.

Back when most computing was done on a desktop, people used to complain about how much pressure they felt to respond quickly to e-mail. At least, in those days, it was understood that you might have walked away from your desk. There is no socially accepted excuse for being without your cell phone. "I didn't have my phone": that just does not sound believable. Either you are lying or you are depressed or you have something to hide. If you receive a text, therefore, you are obliged instantaneously to reply to it, if only to confirm that you are not one of those people who can be without a phone. The most common text message must be "k." It means "I have nothing to say, but God forbid that you should think that I am ignoring your message." The imperative to reply is almost addictive, which is probably one reason that texting can be not just rude (people continually sneaking a look at their cell phones, while you're talking with them, in case some message awaits) but deadly. It was reported that the engineer in the fatal Los Angeles commuter-train crash this fall was texting seconds before the accident occurred. The *Times* noted recently that four of ten teen-agers claim that they can text blindfolded. As long as they don't think that they can drive blindfolded.

A less obvious attraction of texting is that it uses a telephone to avoid what many people dread about face-to-face exchanges, and even about telephones—having to have a real, unscripted conversation. People don't like to have to perform the amount of self-presentation that is required in a personal encounter. They don't want to deal with the facial expressions, the body language, the obligation to be witty or interesting. They just want to say "flt is lte." Texting is so formulaic that it is nearly anonymous. There is no penalty for using catchphrases, because that is the accepted glossary of texting. C. K. Ogden's "Basic English" had a vocabulary of eight hundred and fifty words. Most texters probably make do with far fewer than that. And there is no penalty for abruptness in a text message. Shortest said, best said. The faster the other person can reply, the less you need to say. Once, a phone call was quicker than a letter, and face-to-face was quicker than a phone call. Now e-mail is quicker than face-to-face, and texting, because the respondent is almost always armed with his or her device and ready to reply, is quicker than e-mail.

"For the moment, texting seems here to stay," Crystal concludes. Aun, as the Finns say. It's true that all technology is, ultimately, interim technology, but texting, in the form that Crystal studies, is a technology that is nearing its obsolescence. Once the numeric keypad is replaced by the QWERTY keyboard on most mobile messaging devices, and once the capacity of those devices increases, we are likely to see far fewer initialisms and pictograms. Discourse will migrate back up toward the level of e-mail. But it will still be important to reach out and touch someone. Nok, though. Danke.

SUGGESTIONS FOR WRITING

1. While Menand spends much of the article discussing the linguistic qualities of text messages and the way they seem to be infusing English into other languages, he does, toward the end, point to several social and cultural implications of our obsession with texting. Reread the final few paragraphs of the article, and write a brief summary of Menand's points about the social impact of texting. What do you see as the strengths and weaknesses of Menand's argument here?

2. This assignment asks you to analyze the text messages that you or a friend have sent and received over a period of time. Select 20 or 30 of the most recent texts, and copy or type them out so that you have a written record of them. Keep the original spelling, punctuation, and other features of the text (you may have to turn off the auto-correct function of your word processing program). Next, after rereading these messages (and perhaps reading them aloud to discover their oral qualities), write an analytical paper in which you comment on the three or four most striking features of your use of language. If any of Menand's observations are relevant, draw them into your essay to support and extend your analysis.

3. Choose a specific person with whom you frequently communicate—a friend or parent, for example—and consider the circumstances that would cause you either to text, phone, e-mail, or talk in person with him or her. For each of these modes of communication, write a paragraph in which you describe the kinds of conversation topics and goals that would be most appropriate for each different mode. What can you conclude from this comparison about the relative strengths and weaknesses of each mode of communication?

RANDY COHEN

When Texting Is Wrong

What are the ethics of texting? This question has surely occurred to you if you've ever tried to have a conversation with a friend who was more interested in typing on her cell phone than in listening to you. At what point does obsessive texting leave the realm of mildly compulsive behavior and become just plain rude? In the article that follows, Randy Cohen tries to answer that question by considering a couple of scenarios and drawing on current research about texting and cell phone use. Cohen has become something of an expert in contemporary ethical dilemmas: He writes a weekly column on ethics for The New York Times Magazine, *and many of his columns are collected in a book entitled* The Good, the Bad and the Difference: How to Tell Right From Wrong in Everyday Situations. *Cohen brings a light touch to the sometimes heavy philosophical discussions of ethics, given his background as an Emmy Award–winning writer for* Late Night with David Letterman.

The Issue

You're having dinner with your teenage kids, and they text throughout: you hate it; they're fine with it. At the office, managers are uncertain about texting during business meetings: many younger workers accept it; some older workers resist. Those who defend texting regard such encounters as the clash of two legitimate cultures, a conflict of manners not morals. If a community—teenagers, young workers—consents to conduct that does no harm, does that make it O.K., ethically speaking?

The Argument

Seek consent and do no harm is a useful moral precept, one by which some couples, that amorous community of two, wisely govern their erotic lives, but it does not validate ubiquitous text messaging. When it comes to texting, there is no authentic consent, and there is genuine harm.

Neither teenagers nor young workers authorized a culture of ongoing interruption. No debate was held, no vote was taken around the junior high cafeteria or the employee lounge on the proposition: Shall we stay in constant contact, texting unceasingly? Instead, like most people, both groups merely adapt to the culture they find themselves in, often without questioning or even being consciously aware of its norms. That's acquiescence, not agreement.

Few residents of Williamsburg, Va., in, say, 1740 rallied against the law that restricted voting to property-owning white men. For decades, there was little active local opposition to the sexual segregation in various Persian Gulf states. A more benign example: few of us are French by choice, but most French people act much like other French people, for good and ill. Conformity does not imply consent. It simply attests to the influence of one's neighbors.

So it is with incessant texting, a noxious practice that does not merely alter our in-person interactions but damages them. Even a routine conversation demands continuity and the focus of attention: it cannot, without detriment, be disrupted every few moments while someone deals with a text message. More intimate encounters suffer greater harm. In romantic comedy, when someone breaks a tender embrace to take a phone call, that's a sure sign of love gone bad. After any interruption, it takes a while to regain concentration, one reason few of us want our surgeon to text while she's performing a delicate neurological procedure upon us. Here's a sentence you do not want to hear in the operating room or the bedroom: "Now, where was I?"

Various experiments have shown the deleterious effects of interruption, including [a study] that, unsurprisingly, demonstrates that an interrupted task takes longer to complete and seems more difficult, and that the person doing it feels increased annoyance and anxiety.

Mine is not a Luddite's argument, not broadly anti-technology or even anti-texting. (I'm typing this by electric light on one of those computing machines. New fangled is my favorite kind of fangled.) There are no doubt benefits and pleasures to texting, and your quietly texting while sitting on a park bench or home alone harms nobody. But what is benign in one setting can be toxic in another. (Chainsaws: useful in the forest, dubious at the dinner table. Or as Dr. Johnson put it in a pre-chainsaw age, "A cow is a very good animal in the field; but we turn her out of a garden.")

Nor am I fretful that relentless texting hurts the texter herself. Critics have voiced a broad range of such concerns: too much texting damages a young person's intelligence, emotional development and thumbs. That may be so, but it is not germane here. When you injure yourself, that is unfortunate; when you injure someone else, you are unethical. (I can thus enjoy reading about a texting teen who fell into a manhole. When a man is tired of cartoon mishaps, he is tired of life. And yes, that teen is fine now.)

Last week, a Massachusetts grand jury indicted a Boston motorman who crashed his trolley into another, injuring 62 people: he was texting on duty. Last month, Patti LuPone berated an audience member who pulled out an electronic device during her show in Las Vegas. (Theaters forbid the audience to text during a performance, a rule routinely flouted. Perhaps stage managers could be issued tranquilizer darts and encouraged to shoot audience members who open any device during a show. At intermission, ushers can drag out the unconscious and con-fiscate their phones. Or we might institute something I call Patti's Law: Any two-time Tony winner would be empowered to carry a gun on-stage and shoot similar offenders.)

These are the easy cases, of course: clearly it is unethical to text when doing so risks harming other people. And formal regulation can easily address them; a dozen states and the District of Columbia pro-hibit texting while driving, for example. But the problem of perpetual texting in more casual settings cannot be solved by legislation. No par-ent will call the cops if a son or daughter texts at table. Instead, we need new manners to be explicitly introduced at home and at work, one way social customs can evolve to restrain this emerging technology.

Lest casual texting seem a trivial concern, remember that some political observers trace the recent stalemate in the New York Senate to the wrath of power-broker Tom Golisano, who was offended that majority leader Malcolm Smith fiddled with his BlackBerry throughout a meeting between them. When the dust settled, the State Senate had been transformed from merely disheartening to genuinely grotesque. I wouldn't want that on my conscience.

SUGGESTIONS FOR WRITING

1. Cohen begins the article by discussing some of the ways in which texting contradicts the precepts "seek consent" and "do no harm." Briefly summarize the points Cohen makes about how texting in fact operates without consent (but rather just with compliance) and does harm. After your summary, explain what you think of Cohen's argument.

2. The solution that Cohen suggests toward the end of his article is that "we need new manners to be explicitly introduced at home and at work, one way social customs can evolve to restrain this emerging technology." For this assignment, draft a code of manners for texting, either at home or at work. For inspiration, do a Web search for the codes of conduct of various organizations (for example, the U.S. Military Code of Conduct, the Hippocratic Oath, the Journalist's Creed). Then compose a set of rules that would govern the texting behavior of individuals in the home or workplace. After finishing the rules, you might add a paragraph that speculates on the likelihood of their success in solving the ethical problems associated with texting.

3. Try your hand at creative nonfiction in this assignment by writing about an episode that you experienced or heard about in which someone was either texting or using the cell phone in an impolite or ethically questionable way—disturbing others or causing interruptions, for

instance. For your story, create characters, a setting, and a plot with a beginning, middle, and end. Try your best to make the episode come to life through your writing and to convey the particular frustrations caused by the errant texter/phoner. You might end by appending a moral to the story.

HOWARD RHEINGOLD

How to Recognize the Future When It Lands on You

The article that follows is the first chapter of Howard Rheingold's influential book, Smart Mobs, *which was published in 2002. In it, Rheingold considers the ways in which pervasive wireless technology will "makes certain kinds of human actions possible that were never possible before." In the hordes of people talking and texting on their cell phones and in the increasing saturation of our environment with wireless connections to the Internet, Rheingold sees a key convergence of technologies that will enable people to act together and cooperate in new ways. While he acknowledges "dark scenarios" that might eventuate if technology-equipped smart mobs have nefarious intentions, Rheingold is mostly upbeat and excited about the possibilities of mobile computing, and here he makes interesting predictions about how humans might adapt to the technology and change some of their behavior as a result. Given that Rheingold was writing before texting really took off in the United States and before Facebook, MySpace, or Twitter, it's interesting to read this article and see how his predictions have played out.*

The first signs of the next shift began to reveal themselves to me on a spring afternoon in the year 2000. That was when I began to notice people on the streets of Tokyo staring at their mobile phones instead of talking to them. The sight of this behavior, now commonplace in much of the world, triggered a sensation I had experienced a few times before—the instant recognition that a technology is going to change my life in ways I can scarcely imagine. Since then the practice of exchanging short text messages via mobile telephones has led to the eruption of subcultures in Europe and Asia. At least one government has fallen, in part because of the way people used text messaging. Adolescent mating rituals, political activism, and corporate management styles have mutated in unexpected ways.

I've learned that "texting," as it has come to be called, is only a small harbinger of more profound changes to come over the next ten years. My media moment at Shibuya Crossing was only my first encounter with a phenomenon I've come to call "smart mobs." When I learned to recognize the signs, I began to see them everywhere—from barcodes to electronic bridge tolls.

The other pieces of the puzzle are all around us now but haven't joined together yet. The radio chips designed to replace barcodes on manufactured objects are part of it. Wireless Internet nodes in cafés, hotels, and neighborhoods are part of it. Millions of people who lend their computers to the search for extraterrestrial intelligence are part of it. The way buyers and sellers rate each other on the Internet auction site eBay is part of it. At least one key global business question is part of it: Why is the Japanese company DoCoMo profiting from enhanced wireless Internet services while U.S. and European mobile telephony operators struggle to avoid failure?

When you piece together these different technological, economic, and social components, the result is an infrastructure that makes certain kinds of human actions possible that were never possible before. The "killer apps" of tomorrow's mobile infocom industry won't be hardware devices or software programs but social practices. The most far-reaching changes will come, as they often do, from the kinds of relationships, enterprises, communities, and markets that the infrastructure makes possible.

Smart mobs consist of people who are able to act in concert even if they don't know each other. The people who make up smart mobs cooperate in ways never before possible because they carry devices that possess both communication and computing capabilities. Their mobile devices connect them with other information devices in the environment as well as with other people's telephones. Dirt-cheap microprocessors are beginning to permeate furniture, buildings, and neighborhoods; products, including everything from box tops to shoes, are embedded with invisible intercommunicating smartifacts. When they connect the tangible objects and places of our daily lives with the Internet, handheld communication media mutate into wearable remote-control devices for the physical world.

Within a decade, the major population centers of the planet will be saturated with trillions of microchips, some of them tiny computers, many of them capable of communicating with each other. Some of these devices will be telephones, and they will also be supercomputers with the processing power that only the Department of Defense could muster a couple of decades ago. Some devices will read barcodes and send and receive messages to radio-frequency identity tags. Some will furnish wireless, always-on Internet connections and will contain global positioning devices. As a result, large numbers of people in industrial nations will have a device with them most of the time that will enable them to link objects, places, and people to online content and processes. Point your device at a street sign, announce where you want to go, and follow the animated map beamed to the box in your palm, or point at a book in a store and see what the *Times* and your neighborhood reading group have to say about it. Click on a restaurant and warn your friends that the service has deteriorated.

These devices will help people coordinate actions with others around the world—and, perhaps more importantly, with people nearby. Groups of people using these tools will gain new forms of social power, new ways to organize their interactions and exchanges just in time and just in place. Tomorrow's fortunes will be made by the businesses that find a way to profit from these changes, and yesterday's fortunes are already being lost by businesses that don't understand them. As with the personal computer and the Internet, key breakthroughs won't come from established industry leaders but from the fringes, from skunkworks and startups and even associations of amateurs. *Especially* associations of amateurs.

Although it will take a decade to ramp up, mobile communications and pervasive computing technologies, together with social contracts that were never possible before, are already beginning to change the way people meet, mate, work, fight, buy, sell, govern, and create. Some of these changes are beneficial and empowering, and some amplify the capabilities of people whose intentions are malignant. Large numbers of small groups, using the new media to their individual benefit, will create emergent effects that will nourish some existing institutions and ways of life and dissolve others. Contradictory and simultaneous effects are likely: People might gain new powers at the same time we lose old freedoms. New public goods could become possible, and older public goods might disappear.

When I started looking into mobile telephone use in Tokyo, I discovered that Shibuya Crossing was the most mobile-phone-dense neighborhood in the world: 80 percent of the 1,500 people who traverse that madcap plaza at each light change carry a mobile phone.[1] I took that coincidence as evidence that I was on the right track, although I had only an inkling of how to define what I was tracking. It had not yet become clear to me that I was no longer looking for intriguing evidence about changing techno-social practices, but galloping off on a worldwide hunt for the shape of the future.

I learned that those teenagers and others in Japan who were staring at their mobile phones and twiddling the keyboards with their thumbs were sending words and simple graphics to each other—messages like short emails that were delivered instantly but could be read at any time. When I looked into the technical underpinnings of telephone texting, I found that those early texters were walking around with an always-on connection to the Internet in their hands. The tingling in my forebrain turned into a buzz. When you have a persistent connection to the Internet, you have access to a great deal more than a communication channel.

A puzzling problem troubles those who understand the possibilities inherent in a mobile Internet: The potential power of connecting mobile devices to the Internet has been foreseen and hyped recently, but with the exception of DoCoMo, no company has yet created significant profits from wireless Internet services. The dotcom market collapse of 2001, accompanied by the even larger decline in value of global telecommunication companies, raised the question of whether any existing enterprises will have both the capital and the savvy to plug the Internet world into mobile telephony and make a successful business out of it.

Forecasting the technical potential of wireless Internet is the easy part. I knew that I should expect the unexpected when previously separate technologies meet. In the 1980s, television-like display screens plus miniaturized computers added up to a new technology with properties of its own: personal computers. PCs evolved dramatically over twenty years; today's handheld computer is thousands of times more powerful than the first Apple PC. Then PCs mated with telecommunications networks and multiplied in the 1990s to create the Internet, again spawning possibilities that neither of the parent technologies exhibited in isolation. Again, the new hybrid medium started evolving rapidly; my Internet connection today is thousands of times faster than my modem of the early 1980s. Then the Web in the late 1990s put a visual control panel on the Net and opened it to hundreds of millions of mainstream users. What's next in this self-accelerating spiral of technological, economic, and social change?

Next comes the mobile Net. Between 2000 and 2010, the social networking of mobile communications will join with the information-processing power of networked PCs. Critical mass will emerge some time after 2003, when more mobile devices than PCs will be connected to the Internet.[2] If the transition period we are entering in the first decade of the twenty-first century resembles the advent of PCs and the Internet, the new technology regime will turn out to be an entirely new medium, not simply a means of receiving stock quotes or email on the train or surfing the Web while walking down the street. Mobile Internet, when it really arrives, will not be just a way to do old things while moving. It will be a way to do things that couldn't be done before.

Anybody who remembers what mobile telephones looked like five years ago has a sense of the pace at which handheld technology is evolving. Today's mobile devices are not only smaller and lighter than the earliest cell phones, they have become tiny multimedia Internet terminals. I returned to Tokyo a year and a half after I first noticed people using telephones to send text between tiny black and white screens. On my most recent visit in the fall of 2001, I conducted my own color videoconference conversations via the current version of high-speed, multimedia, "third-generation" mobile phones. Perhaps even more important than the evolution of color and video screens in telephone displays is the presence of "location awareness" in mobile telephones. Increasingly, handheld devices can detect, within a few yards, where they are located on a continent, within a neighborhood, or inside a room.

These separate upgrades in capabilities don't just add to each other; mobile, multimedia, location-sensitive characteristics multiply each other's usefulness. At the same time, their costs drop dramatically. The driving factors of the mobile, context-sensitive, Internet-connected devices are Moore's Law (computer chips gets cheaper as they grow more powerful), Metcalfe's Law (the useful power of a network multiplies rapidly as the number of nodes in the network increases), and Reed's Law (the power of a network, especially one that enhances social networks, multiplies even more rapidly as the number of different human groups that can use the network increases). Moore's Law drove the PC industry and the cultural changes that resulted, Metcalfe's Law drove the deployment of the Internet, and Reed's Law will drive the growth of the mobile and pervasive Net.

The personal handheld device market is poised to take the kind of jump that the desktop PC made between 1980 and 1990, from a useful toy adopted by a subculture to a disruptive technology that changes every aspect of society. The hardware upgrades that make such a jump possible are already in the product pipeline. The underlying connective infrastructure is moving toward completion.

After a pause to recover from the collapse of the telecommunications economic bubble of the 1990s, the infrastructure for global, wireless, Internet-based communication is entering the final stages of development. The pocket videophone I borrowed in Tokyo was proof that a high-speed wireless network could link wireless devices and deliver multimedia to the palm of my hand. The most important next step for the companies that would deploy this technology and profit from it has nothing to do with chips or network protocols but everything to do with business models, early adopters, communities of developers, and value chains. It's not just about building the tools anymore. Now it's about what people use the tools to do.

How will human behavior shift when the appliances we hold in our hands, carry in our pockets, or wear in our clothing become supercomputers that talk to each other through a wireless mega-Internet? What can we reasonably expect people to do when they get their hands on the new gadgets? Can anyone foresee which companies will drive change and detect which businesses will be transformed or rendered obsolete by it?

We're only seeing the first-order ripple effects of mobile-phone behavior now—the legions of the oblivious, blabbing into their hands or the air as they walk, drive, or sit in a concert and the electronic tethers that turn everywhere into the workplace and all the time into working time. What if these are just foreshocks of a future upheaval? I've learned enough from past technology shifts to expect the second-order effects of mobile telecommunications to bring a social tsunami. Consider a few of the early warning signs:

- The "People Power II" smart mobs in Manila who overthrew the presidency of President Estrada in 2001 organized demonstrations by forwarding text messages via cell phones.[4]
- A Web site, http://www.upoc.com, enables fans to stalk their favorite celebrities in real time through Internet-organized mobile networks and provides similar channels for journalists to organize citizen-reporters on the fly. The site makes it easy for roving phone tribes to organize communities of interest.
- In Helsinki and Tokyo you can operate vending machines with your telephone and receive directions on your wireless organizer that show you how to get from where you are standing to where you want to go.[5]

- "Lovegety" users in Japan find potential dates when their devices recognize another Lovegety in the vicinity broadcasting the appropriate pattern of attributes. Location-based matchmaking is now available on some mobile phone services.[6]
- When I'm not using my computer, its processor searches for extraterrestrial intelligence. I'm one of millions of people around the world who lend their computers to a cooperative effort—distributing parts of problems through the Internet, running the programs on our PCs while the machines are idle, and assembling the results via the Net. These computation collectives produce enough supercomputing power to crack codes, design medicines, or render digital films.[7]

Location-sensing wireless organizers, wireless networks, and community supercomputing collectives all have one thing in common: *They enable people to act together in new ways and in situations where collective action was not possible before.* An unanticipated convergence of technologies is suggesting new responses to civilization's founding question, How can competing individuals learn to work cooperatively?

As indicated by their name, smart mobs are not always beneficial. Lynch mobs and mobocracies continue to engender atrocities. The same convergence of technologies that opens new vistas of cooperation also makes possible a universal surveillance economy and empowers the bloodthirsty as well as the altruistic. Like every previous leap in technological power, the new convergence of wireless computation and social communication will enable people to improve life and liberty in some ways and to degrade it in others. The same technology has the potential to be used as both a weapon of social control and a means of resistance. Even the beneficial effects will have side effects.

We are moving rapidly into a world in which the spying machinery is built into every object we encounter. Although we leave digital traces of our personal lives with our credit cards and Web browsers today, tomorrow's mobile devices will broadcast clouds of personal data to invisible monitors all around us as we move from place to place. We are living through the last years of the long era before sensors are built into the furniture. The scientific and economic underpinnings of pervasive computing have been building for decades, and the social side-effects are only beginning to erupt. The virtual, social, and physical worlds are colliding, merging, and coordinating.

Don't mistake my estimates of the power of the coming technology with unalloyed enthusiasm for its effects. I am not calling for an uncritical embrace of the new regime, but for an informed consideration of what we're getting ourselves into. We have an opportunity now to consider the social implications of this new technological regime as it first emerges, before every aspect of life is reordered.

Online social networks are human activities that ride on technical communications infrastructures of wires and chips. When social communication via the Internet became widespread, people formed support groups and political coalitions online. The new social forms of the last decade of the twentieth century grew from the Internet's capability for many-to-many social communication. The new social forms of the early twenty-first century will greatly enhance the power of social networks.

Since my visits to Tokyo and Helsinki, I've investigated the convergence of portable, pervasive, location-sensitive, intercommunicating devices with social practices that make the technologies useful to groups as well as individuals. Foremost among these social practices are the "reputation systems" that are beginning to spring up online—computer-mediated trust brokers. The power of smart mobs comes in part from the way age-old social practices surrounding trust and cooperation are being mediated by new communication and computation technologies.

In this coming world, the acts of association and assembly, core rights of free societies, might change radically when each of us will be able to know who in our vicinity is likely to buy what we have to sell, sell what we want to buy, know what we need to know, want the kind of sexual or political encounter we also want. As online events are woven into the fabric of our physical world, governments and corporations will gain even more power over our behavior and beliefs than large institutions wield today. At the same time, citizens will discover new ways to band together to resist powerful institutions. A new kind of digital divide ten years from now will separate those who know how to use new media to band together from those who don't.

Knowing who to trust is going to become even more important. Banding together, from lynch mobs to democracies, taps the power of collective action. At the core of collective action is reputation—the histories each of us pull behind us that others routinely inspect to decide our value for everything from conversation partners to mortgage risks. Reputation systems have been fundamental to social life for a long time. In intimate societies, everyone knows everyone, and everyone's biography is an open, if not undisputed, book. Gossip keeps us up to date on who to trust, who other people trust, who is important, and who decides who is important.

Today's online reputation systems are computer-based technologies that make it possible to manipulate in new and powerful ways an old and essential human trait. Note the rise of Web sites like eBay (auctions), Epinions (consumer advice), Amazon (books, CDs, electronics), Slashdot (publishing and conversation) built around the contributions of millions of customers, enhanced by reputation systems that police the quality of the content and transactions exchanged through the sites.[8] In each of these businesses, the consumers are also the producers of what they consume, the value of the market increases as more people use it, and the aggregate opinions of the users provide the measure of trust necessary for transactions and markets to flourish in cyberspace.

Reputation reports on eBay give prospective auction bidders a sense of the track record of the otherwise anonymous people to whom they may trustingly mail a check. Ratings of experts on Epinions make visible the experience of others in trusting each expert's advice. Moderators on Slashdot award "karma points" that make highly knowledgeable, amusing, or useful posts in an online conversation more visible than those considered less insightful.

Wireless devices will take reputation systems into every cranny of the social world, far from the desktops to which these systems are currently anchored. As the costs of communication, coordination, and social accounting services drop, these devices make possible new ways for people to self-organize mutual aid. It is now technologically possible, for example, to create a service that would enable you to say to your handheld device: "I'm on my way to the office. Who is on my route and is looking for a ride in my direction right now—and who among them is recommended by my most trusted friends?"

Wireless communication technologies and the political regimes that regulate their use are a key component of smart mob infrastructure. One can sit in a restaurant in Stockholm or in the atrium of a business building in San Francisco and connect to unprotected or publicly available wireless networks with a laptop computer. Will ad hoc coalitions of wireless Internet enthusiasts create a grassroots network that can challenge the power of established infrastructure providers?

When I examine the potential of new technologies, I have tried to avoid the dangers of "the rhetoric of the technological sublime," in which the miraculous properties of new tools are extolled to the exclusion of critical examination of their shadow sides.[9] I seek to shine light and also to look into the shadows.

Loss of privacy is perhaps the most obvious shadow side of technological cooperation systems. In order to cooperate with more people, I need to know more about them, and that means that they will know more about me. The tools that enable cooperation also transmit to a large number of others a constellation of intimate data about each of us. In the recent past, it was said that digital information technology, such as the magnetic strips on credit cards, leaves a "trail of electronic breadcrumbs" that can be used to track individuals. In the future, the trail will become a moving cloud as individuals broadcast information about themselves to devices within ten yards, a city block, or the entire world. Although there is room for speculation about how quickly the new tools will be adopted, certainly over the next several decades inexpensive wireless devices will penetrate into every part of the social world, bringing efficiencies to the production of snooping power. The surveillance state that Orwell feared was puny in its power in comparison to the panoptic web we have woven around us. Detailed information about the minute-by-minute behaviors of entire populations will become cost-effective and increasingly accurate. Both powerfully beneficial and powerfully dangerous potentials of this new tracking capability will be literally embedded in the environment.

Cooperative effort sounds nice, and at its best, it is the foundation of the finest creations of human civilizations, but it can also be nasty if the people who cooperate share pernicious goals. Terrorists and organized criminals have been malevolently successful in their use of smart mob tactics. A technological infrastructure that increases surveillance on citizens and empowers terrorists is hardly Utopian. Intrusions on individual privacy and liberty by the state and its political enemies are not the only possible negative effects of enhanced technology-assisted cooperation. In addition, profound questions about the quality and meaning of life are raised by the prospect of millions of people possessing communication devices that are "always on" at home and work. How will mobile communications affect family and societal life?

There are opportunities as well as dangers, however, and a major reason I've written this book is my growing belief that what we understand about the future of smart mobs, and how we talk about that future, holds the power to influence that future—at least within a short window of opportunity. The possibilities for the use of smart mob infrastructure do not consist exclusively of dark scenarios. Indeed, cooperation is integral to the highest expressions of human civilization. In counterpoint to the dystopian possibilities I've noted, I introduce sociologists and economists who argue that wireless technologies could make it easier to create public goods, thus affording an unprecedented opportunity for enhancing social capital that can enrich everyone's life.

Just as existing notions of community were challenged by the emergence of social networks in cyberspace, traditional ideas about the nature of place are being challenged as computing and communication devices begin to saturate the environment. As more people on city streets and on public transportation spend more time speaking to other people who are not physically co-present, the nature of public spaces and other aspects of social geography are changing before our eyes and ears; some of these changes will benefit the public good and others will erode it.

Before people who hold stakes in tomorrow's technological civilization can hope to address the social challenges posed by smart mob technologies, we have to know what the issues are, what they imply, and useful ways to think about them. I conclude this book with a strategic briefing for the future, highlighting the strengths, weaknesses, opportunities, and dangers of mobile and pervasive technologies. I believe that our destiny is not (yet) determined by technology, that our freedom and quality of life do not (yet) have to be sacrificed to make us into more efficient components of a global wealth-generating machine.

I also know that beneficial uses of technologies will not automatically emerge just because people hope they will. Those who wish to have some influence on the outcome must first know what the dangers and opportunities are and how to act on them. Such knowledge does not guarantee that the new tools will be used to create a humane, sustainable world. Without such knowledge, however, we will be ill equipped to influence the world our grandchildren will inhabit.

NOTES

1. The Shibuya Crossing in Tokyo, Japan, has the highest mobile phone density in the world. On weekdays an average of 190,000 people and on weekends an average of 250,000 people pass this crossing per day (Source: CCC, Tsutaya), around 1,500 people traverse at each light change, and 80 percent of them carry a mobile phone. <http://nooper.co.jp/showcase/gallery.php?s=4&l=en> (24 January 2002).

2. Karlin Lillington, "Mobile but Without Direction," *Wired News,* 21 September 2000, <http://www.wired.com/news/business/0,1367,38921,00.html> (28 January 2002).

3. Howard Rheingold, *Tools for Thought: The History and Future of Mind-Expanding Technology* (New York: Simon & Schuster, 1985.)

4. Arturo Bariuad, "Text Messaging Becomes a Menace in the Philippines," *Straits Times,* 3 March 2001.

5. Lisa Takeuchi Cullen, "Dialing for Dollars," *Time Magazine* 157 (22), 4 June 2001, <http://www.timeinc.net/time/interactive/business/money_np.html> (4 February 2002). See also: Kevin Werbach, "Location-Based Computing: Wherever You Go, There You Are," *Release* 1.0 18 (6), June 2000, <http://release1.edventure.com/abstracts.cfm?Counter=8096700> (4 February 2002).

6. "Japan's Lonely Hearts Find Each Other with 'Lovegety,'" *CNN.com,* 7 June 1998, <http://www.cnn.com/WORLD/asiapcf/9806/07/fringe/japan.lovegety/> (26 January 2002).

7. Howard Rheingold, "You Got the Power," *Wired* 8.08, August 2000, <http://www.wired.com/wired/archive/8.08/comcomp.html> (29 March 2002).

8. See: eBay, <http://www.ebay.com>; Epinions, <http://www.epinions.com>; Slashdot, <http://www.slashdot.org>; and Plastic, <http://www.plastic.com>.

9. J. Carey, "Space, Time and Communications: A Tribute to Harold Innis," in *Communication as Culture* (New York: Routledge, 1989), 12.

SUGGESTIONS FOR WRITING

1. Rheingold claims that mobile technologies and pervasive computing are changing the way that people "meet, mate, work, fight, buy, sell, govern, and create." Choose one of these verbs (or use one of your own), and make a list of the various technologies (in addition to cell phones and mobile Internet) that shape human behavior in this realm. Then write an explanatory essay in which you discuss the impact of technology on the particular activity you chose. Perhaps you could conclude your essay by identifying the one technology that currently exerts the strongest influence in this area.

2. Rheingold offers a number of concepts to help us understand the new technological developments he discusses: for example, smart mob, convergence, and reputation system. Choose one of these terms — or another key term that you find in the article — and read through the article again to see how Rheingold defines the terms and what examples he provides to illustrate this definition. Then, in an essay of

your own and using your own words and examples, offer your own definition.

3. This reading begins with a scene Rheingold observed in 2000; his book *Smart Mobs* was published in 2002. To what extent have the predictions Rheingold makes here already been realized, and in what ways were his predictions off the mark? Write an essay in which you essentially update Rheingold by identifying some of the claims he made for the future development of mobile Internet and by showing whether these claims have or haven't been fulfilled. Based on your experience now, how accurate were Rheingold's predictions back in 2002?

SHERRY TURKLE

Always-On, Always-On-You

Sherry Turkle is a professor at the Massachusetts Institute of Technology, where she directs the MIT Initiative on Technology and Self. She is also a licensed clinical psychologist, and she brings together her expertise in technology and human psychology in several highly regarded books that explore how computers are shaping our sense of identity and the relationships we have with others. In the article that follows, which was published in a 2008 collection of essays on mobile technology, Turkle proposes the concept of the "tethered self"—a self perpetually connected to technology and communication devices. While Howard Rheingold sees mostly the positive aspects and opportunities of being constantly connected, Turkle focuses on the problems associated with a loss of time and focus that these technologies engender. Most broadly, however, Turkle offers interesting insights into the ways that cell phone technology enables us to define ourselves and our relationships.

In the mid-1990s, a group of young researchers at the MIT Media Lab carried computers and radio transmitters in their backpacks, keyboards in their pockets, and digital displays embedded in their eyeglass frames. Always on the Internet, they called themselves "cyborgs." The cyborgs seemed at a remove from their bodies. When their burdensome technology cut into their skin, causing lesions and then scar tissue, they were indifferent. When their encumbrances led them to be taken for the physically disabled, they patiently provided explanations. They were learning to walk and talk as new creatures, learning to inhabit their own bodies all over again, and yet in a way they were fading away, bleeding out onto the Net. Their experiment was both a re-embodiment—a prosthetic consummation—and a disembodiment: a disappearance of their bodies into still-nascent computational spaces.

Within a few years, the cyborgs had a new identity as the Media Lab's "Wearable Computing Group," harbingers of embedded technologies while the rest of us clumsily juggled cell phones, laptops, and PDAs. But the legacy of the MIT cyborgs goes beyond the idea that communications technologies might be wearable (or totable). Core elements of their experience have become generalized in global culture: the experience of living on the Net, newly free in some ways, newly yoked in others.

Today, the near-ubiquity of handheld and palm-size computing and cellular technologies that enable voice communication, text messaging, e-mail, and Web access have made connectivity commonplace. When digital technologies first came onto the consumer market in the form of personal computers they were objects for psychological projection. Computers—programmable and customizable—came to be experienced as a "second self" (Turkle 2005a). In the early twenty-first century, such language does not go far enough; our new intimacy with communications devices compels us to speak of a new state of the self, itself.

A New State of the Self, Itself

For the most part, our everyday language for talking about technology's effects assumes a life both on and off the screen, it assumes the existence of separate worlds, plugged and unplugged. But some of today's locutions suggest a new placement of the subject, such as when we say "I'll be on my cell," by which we mean "You can reach me; my cell phone will be on, and I am wired into (social) existence through it." *On my cell, online, on the Web, on instant messaging*—these phrases suggest a *tethered* self.

We are tethered to our "always-on/always-on-you" communications devices and the people and things we reach through them: people, Web pages, voice mail, games, artificial intelligences (nonplayer game characters, interactive online "bots"). These very different objects achieve a certain sameness because of the way we reach them. Animate and inanimate, they live for us through our tethering devices, always ready-to-mind and hand. The self, attached to its devices, occupies a liminal space between the physical real and its digital lives on multiple screens (Turner 1969). I once described the rapid movements from physical to a multiplicity of digital selves through the metaphor of "cycling-through." With cell technology, rapid cycling stabilizes into a sense of continual co-presence (Turkle 1995).

For example, in the past, I did not usually perform my role as mother in the presence of my professional colleagues. Now a call from my sixteen-year-old daughter brings me forth in this role. The presence of the cell phone, which has a special ring if my daughter calls, keeps me on the alert all day. Wherever I am, whatever I am doing, I am psychologically tuned to the connections that matter.

The Connections That Matter

We are witnessing a new form of sociality in which the connectedness that "matters" is determined by our distance from working communications technology. Increasingly, what people want out of public spaces is that they offer a place to be private with tethering technologies. A neighborhood walk reveals a world of madmen and women, talking to themselves, sometimes shouting to themselves, little concerned with what is around them, happy to have intimate conversations in public spaces. In fact, neighborhood spaces themselves become liminal, not entirely public, not entirely private (Katz 2006, chapters 1 and 2).

A train station is no longer a communal space, but a place of social collection: tethered selves come together, but do not speak to each other. Each person at the station is more likely to be having an encounter with someone miles away than with the person in the next chair. Each inhabits a private media bubble. Indeed, the presence of our tethering media signal that we do not want to be disturbed by conventional sociality with physically proximate individuals.

When people have personal cell phone conversations in public spaces, what sustains their sense of intimacy is the presumption that those around them treat them not only as anonymous, but as close to disembodied. When individuals hold cell phones (or "speak into the air," indicating the presence of cells with earphone microphones), they are marked with a certain absence. They are transported to the space of a new ether, virtualized. This "transport" can be signaled in other ways: when people look down at their laps during meals or meetings, the change of gaze has come to signify attention to their BlackBerries or other small communications devices. They are focused on elsewhere.

The director of a program that places American students in Greek universities complains that students are not "experiencing Greece" because they spend too much time online, talking with their friends from home. I am sympathetic as she speaks, thinking of the hours I spent walking with my daughter on a visit to Paris as she "texted" her friends at home on her cell phone. I worry that she is missing something I cherished in my youth, the experience of an undiluted Paris that came with the thrill of disconnection from where I was from. But she is happy and tells me that keeping in touch is "comforting" and that beyond this, her text mails to home constitute a diary. She can look back at her texts and remember her state of mind at different points of her trip. Her notes back to friends, translated from instant message shorthand include "Saw Pont D'Avignon," "Saw World Cup Soccer in Paris," and "Went to Bordeaux." It is hard to get in too many words on the phone keyboard and there is no cultural incentive to do so. A friend calls my daughter as we prepare for dinner at our Paris hotel and asks her to lunch in Boston. My daughter says, quite simply: "Not possible, but how about Friday." Her friend has no idea that her call was transatlantic. Emotionally and socially, my daughter has not left home.

Of course, balancing one's physical and electronic connections is not limited to those on holiday. Contemporary professional life is rich in examples of people ignoring those they are physically "with" to give priority to online others. Certain settings in which this occurs have become iconic: sessions at international conferences where experts from all over the world come together but do their e-mail; the communications channels that are set up by audience members at conferences to comment on speakers' presentations during the presentations themselves (these conversations are as much about jockeying for professional position among the audience as they are about what is beings and at the podium). Here, the public presentation becomes a portal to discussions that take people away from it, discussions that tend to take place in hierarchical tiers—only certain people are invited to participate in certain discussions. As a member of the audience, one develops a certain anxiety: have I been invited to chat in the inner circle?

Observing e-mail and electronic messaging during conferences at exotic locations compels our attention because it is easy to measure the time and money it takes to get everyone physically together at such meetings. Other scenes have become so mundane that we scarcely notice them: students do e-mail during classes; business people do e-mail during meetings; parents do e-mail while playing with their children;

couples do e-mail at dinner; people talk on the phone and do their e-mail at the same time. Once done surreptitiously, the habit of electronic co-presence is no longer something people feel they need to hide. Indeed, being "elsewhere" than where you might be has become something of a marker of one's sense of self-importance.

New Forms of Validation

I think of the *inner history* of technology as the relationships people form with their artifacts, relationships that can forge new sensibilities. Tethering technologies have their own inner histories. For example, a mobile phone gives us the potential to communicate whenever we have a feeling, enabling a new coupling of "I have a feeling/Get me a friend." This formulation has the emotional corollary, "I want to have a feeling/Get me a friend." In either case, what is *not* being cultivated is the ability to be alone, to reflect on and contain one's emotions. The anxiety that teens report when they are without their cell phones or their link to the Internet may not speak so much to missing the easy sociability with others but of missing the self that is constituted in these relationships.

When David Riesman remarked on the American turn from an inner- to an other-directed sense of self by 1950 (Riesman 1950), he could not foresee how technology could raise other-directedness to a new level. It does this by making it possible for each of us to develop new patterns of reliance on others. And we develop transference relationships that make others available to us at literally a moment's notice. Some people experienced this kind of transference to the traditional (landline) telephone. The telephone was a medium through which to receive validation, and sometimes the feelings associated with that validation were transferred to the telephone itself. The cell phone takes this effect to a higher power because the device is always available and there is a high probability that one will be able to reach a source of validation through it. It is understood that the validating cell conversation may be brief, just a "check-in," but more is not necessarily desired.

The cell phone check-in enables the new other-directness. At the moment of having a thought or feeling, one can have it validated. Or, one may *need* to have it validated. And further down a continuum of dependency, as a thought or feeling is being formed, *it may need validation to become established*. The technology does not cause a new style of relating, but enables it. As we become accustomed to cell calls, e-mail, and social Web sites, certain styles of relating self to other feel more natural. The validation (of a feeling already felt) and enabling (of a feeling that cannot be felt without outside validation) are becoming commonplace rather than marked as childlike or pathological.

The psychoanalyst Heinz Kohut writes about narcissism and describes how some people, in their fragility, turn other persons into "self-objects" to shore up their fragile sense of self (Ornstein 1978). In the role of self-object, the other is experienced as part of the self, thus in perfect tune with the fragile individual's inner state. They are there for validation, mirroring. Technology increases one's options. One fifteen-year-old girl explains: "I have a lot of people on my contact list. If one friend doesn't get it, I call another." In Kohutian terms, this young woman's contact or buddy list has become a list of spare parts for her fragile adolescent self.

Just as always-on/always-on-you connectivity enables teens to postpone independently managing their emotions, it can also make it difficult to assess children's level of maturity, conventionally defined in terms of autonomy and responsibility. Tethered children know that they have backup. The "check-in" call has evolved into a new kind of contact between parents and children. It is a call that says "I am fine. You are there. We are connected."

In general, the telegraphic text message quickly communicates a state, rather than opens a dialogue about complexity of feeling. Although the culture that grows up around the cell is a talk culture (in shopping malls, supermarkets, city streets, cafes, playgrounds, and parks, cells are out and people are talking into them), it is not necessarily a culture in which talk contributes to self-reflection. Today's adolescents have no less need than previous generations to learn empathic skills, to manage and express feelings, and to handle being alone. But when the interchanges to develop empathy are reduced to the shorthand of emoticon emotions, questions such as "Who am I?" and "Who are you?" are reformatted for the small screen, and are flattened in the process. High technology, with all its potential range and richness, has been put at the service of telegraphic speed and brevity.

Leaving the Time to Take Our Time

Always-on/always-on-you communications devices are seductive for many reasons, among them, they give the sense that one can do more, be in more places, and control more aspects of life. Those who are attached to BlackBerry technology speak about the fascination of watching their lives "scroll by," of watching their lives as though watching a movie. One develops a new view of self when one considers the many thousands of people to whom one may be connected. Yet just as teenagers may suffer from a media environment that invites them to greater dependency, adults, too, may suffer from being overly tethered, too connected. Adults are stressed by new responsibilities to keep up with email, the nagging sense of always being behind, the inability to take a vacation without bringing the office with them, and the feeling that they are being asked to respond immediately to situations at work, even when a wise response requires taking time for reflection, a time that is no longer available.

We are becoming accustomed to a communications style in which we receive a hasty message to which we give a rapid response. Are we leaving enough time to take our time?

Adults use tethering technologies during what most of us think of as down time, the time we might have daydreamed during a cab ride, waiting in line, or walking to work. This may be time that we physiologically and emotionally need to maintain or restore our ability to focus (Herzog et al. 1997; Kaplan 1995). Tethering takes time from other activities (particularly those that demand undivided attention), it adds new tasks that take up time (keeping up with e-mail and messages), and adds a new kind of time to the day, the time of attention sharing, sometimes referred to as *continuous partial attention* (Stone 2006). In all of this, we make our attention into our rarest resource, creating increasingly stiff competition for its deployment, *but we undervalue it as well.* We deny the importance of giving it to one thing and one thing only.

Continuous partial attention affects the quality of thought we give to each of our tasks, now done with less *mind share.* From the perspective of this essay with its focus on identity, continuous partial attention affects how people think about their lives and priorities. The phrases "doing my e-mail" and "doing my messages" imply performance rather than reflection. These are the performances of a self that can be split into constituent parts.

When media does not stand waiting in the background but is always there, waiting to be wanted, the self can lose a sense of conscious choosing to communicate. The sophisticated consumer of tethering devices finds ways to integrate always-on/always-on-you technology into the everyday gestures of the body. One BlackBerry user says: "I glance at my watch to sense the time; I glance at my BlackBerry to get a sense of my life." The term *addiction* has been used to describe this state, but this way of thinking is limited in its usefulness. More useful is thinking about a new state of self, one that is extended in a communications artifact. The BlackBerry movie of one's life takes on a life of its own—with more in it than can be processed. People develop the sense that they cannot keep up with their own lives. They become alienated from their own experience and anxious about watching a version of their lives moving along, scrolling along, faster than they can handle. It is the unedited version of their lives; they are not able to keep up with it, but they are responsible for it (Mazmanian 2005).

Michel Foucault wrote about Jeremy Bentham's panopticon as emblematic of the situation of the individual in modern, "disciplinary" society (Foucault 1979). The Panopticon is a wheel-like structure with an observer (in the case of a prison, a prison guard) at its hub. The architecture of the Panopticon creates a sense of being always watched whether or not the guard is actually present. For Foucault, the task of the modern state is to construct citizens who do not need to be watched, who mind the rules and themselves. Always-on/always-on-you technology takes the job of self-monitoring to a new level. We try to keep up with our lives as they are presented to us by a new disciplining technology. We try, in sum, to have a self that keeps up with our e-mail.

Boundaries

A new complaint in family and business life is that it is hard to know when one has the attention of a BlackBerry user. A parent, partner, or child can be lost for a few seconds or a few minutes to an alternate reality. The shift of attention can be subtle; friends and family are sometimes not aware of the loss until the person has "returned." Indeed, BlackBerry users may not even know where their attention lies. They report that their sense of self has merged with their prosthetic extensions and some see this as a new "high." But this exhilaration may be denying the costs of multitasking. Sociologists who study the boundaries between work and the rest of life suggest that it is helpful when people demarcate role shifts between the two. Their work suggests that being able to use a BlackBerry to blur the line is problematic rather than a skill to be celebrated. (Clark 2000; Desrochers and Sargent 2003; Shumate and Fulk 2004). And celebrating the integration of remote communications into the flow of life may be underestimating the importance of face-to-face connections (Mazmanian 2005).

Attention-sharing creates work environments fraught with new tensions over the lack of primacy given to physical proximity. Face-to-face conversations are routinely interrupted by cell phone calls and e-mail reading. Fifteen years ago, if a colleague read mail in your presence, it was considered rude. These days, turning away from a person in front of you to answer a cell phone has become the norm. Additionally, for generations, business people have grown accustomed to relying on time in taxis, airports, trains, and limousines to get to know each other and to discuss substantive matters. The waiting time in client outer offices was precious time for work and the exchange of news that created social bonds among professional colleagues. Now, things have changed: professionals spend taxi time on their cell phones or doing e-mail on their PDAs. In the precious moments before client presentations, one sees consulting teams moving around the periphery of waiting rooms, looking for the best place for cell reception so that they can make calls. "My colleagues go to the ether when we wait for our clients," says one advertising executive. "I think our presentations have suffered." We live and work with people whose commitment to our presence feels increasingly tenuous because they are tethered to more important virtual others.

Human beings are skilled at creating rituals for demarcating the boundaries between the world of work and the world of family, play, and relaxation. There are special times (the Sabbath), special meals (the family dinner), special attire (the "armor" for a day's labor comes off at home, whether it is the businessperson's suit or the laborer's overalls), and special places (the dining room, the parlor, the bedroom, the beach). Now always-on/always-on-you technology accompanies people to all these places, undermining the traditional rituals of separation.

There is a certain push back. Just as teenagers hide from friends by using their parents' online accounts to do homework, adults, too, find ways to escape from the demands of tethering: BlackBerries are left at the office on weekends or they are left in locked desk drawers to free up time for family or leisure (Gant and Kiesler 2001). "It used to be my home was a haven; but now my home is a media center," says an architect whose clients reach him on his Internet-enabled cell. No longer a safe space or refuge, people need to find places to hide. There are technically none except long plane rides where there is no cell or Internet access, and this, too, may be changing.

A Self Shaped by Rapid Response

Our technology reflects and shapes our values. If we think of a telephone call as a quick-response system enabled by always-on/always-on-you technology, we can forget there is a difference between a scheduled call and the call you make in reaction to a fleeting emotion, because something crossed your mind, or because someone left you a message. The self that is shaped by this world of rapid response measures success by calls made, e-mails answered, and contacts reached. This self is calibrated on the basis of what the technology proposes, by what it makes possible, and by what it makes easy. But in the buzz of activity, there are losses that we are perhaps not ready to sustain.

One is the technology-induced pressure for speed, even when we are considering matters over which we should take our time. We insist that our world is increasingly complex, yet we have created a communications culture that has decreased the time available for us to sit and think uninterrupted. BlackBerry users describe that sense of encroachment of the device on their time. One says, "I don't have enough time alone with my mind." Other phrases come up: "I have to struggle to make time to think." "I artificially make time to think." "I block out time to think." In all of these statements is the implicit formulation of an "I" that is separate from technology, that can put it aside and needs time to think on its own. This formulation contrasts with a growing reality of our lives lived in the continual presence of communications devices. This reality has us, like the early MIT "cyborg" group, learning to see ourselves not as separate but as at one with the machines that tether us to each other and to the information culture. To put it most starkly: to make more "time" in the old-fashioned sense means turning off our devices, disengaging from the always-on culture. But this is not a simple proposition since our devices have become more closely coupled to our sense of our bodies and increasingly feel like extensions of our minds.

In the 1990s, as the Internet became part of everyday life, people began to create multiple online avatars and used them to shift gender, age, race, and class. The effort was to create richly rendered virtual selves through which one could experiment with identity by playing out parallel lives in constructed worlds. The world of avatars and games continues, but now, alongside its pleasures, we use always-on/always-on-you technology to play ourselves. Today's communications technology provides a social and psychological GPS, a navigation system for tethered selves. One television producer, accustomed to being linked to the world via her cell and Palm device, revealed that for her, the Palm's inner spaces were where her self resides: "When my Palm crashed it was like a death. It was more than I could handle. I felt as though I had lost my mind."

Tethered: To Whom and to What?

Acknowledging our tethered state raises the question of to whom or to what we are connected (Katz 2003). Traditional telephones tied us to friends, family, colleagues from school and work, and commercial or philanthropic solicitations. Things are no longer so simple. These days we respond to humans and to objects that represent them: answering machines, Web sites, and personal pages on social-networking sites. Sometimes we engage with avatars that anonymously "stand in" for others, enabling us to express ourselves in intimate ways to strangers, in part because we and they are able to veil who we "really are." And sometimes we listen to disembodied voices, recorded announcements and messages—or interact with synthetic voice recognition protocols that simulate real people as they try to assist us with technical and administrative problems. We no longer demand that as a person we have another person as an interlocutor. On the Internet, we interact with bots, anthropomorphic programs that are able to converse with us, and in online games we are partnered with nonplayer characters, artificial intelligences that are not linked to human players. The games require that we put our trust in these characters. Sometimes it is only these nonplayer characters who can save our "lives" in the game.

This wide range of entities—human and not—is available to us wherever we are. I live in Boston. I write this chapter in Paris. As I travel, my access to my favorite avatars, nonplayer characters, and social networking sites stays constant. There is a degree of emotional security in a good hotel on the other side of the world, but for many, it cannot compare to the constancy of a stable technological environment and the interactive objects within it. Some of these objects are engaged on the Internet. Some are interactive digital companions that can travel with you, now including robots that are built for relationships.

Consider this moment: an older woman, seventy-two, in a nursing home outside of Boston is sad. Her son has broken off his relationship with her. Her nursing home is part of a study I am conducting on robotics for the elderly. I am recording her reactions as she sits with the robot Paro, a seal-like creature, advertised as the first "therapeutic robot" for its ostensibly positive effects on the ill, the elderly, and the emotionally troubled. Paro is able to make eye contact through sensing the direction of a human voice, is sensitive to touch, and has "states of mind" that are affected by how it is treated—for example, it can sense if it is being stroked gently or with some aggression. In this session with Paro, the woman, depressed because of her son's abandonment, comes to believe that the robot is depressed as well. She turns to Paro, strokes him, and says: "Yes, you're sad, aren't you. It's tough out there. Yes, it's hard." And then she pets the robot once again, attempting to provide it with comfort. And in so doing, she tries to comfort herself.

Psychoanalytically trained, I believe that this kind of moment, if it happens between people, has profound therapeutic potential. What are we to make of this transaction as it unfolds between a depressed woman and a robot? The woman's sense of being understood is based on the ability of computational objects like Paro to convince their users that they are in a relationship. I call these creatures (some virtual, some physical robots) "relational artifacts" (Turkle 1999; 2003a; 2003b; 2004a; 2004b; 2004c; 2005b; 2005c; 2006b; Turkle et al. 2006a). Their ability to inspire a relationship is not based on their intelligence or consciousness but on their ability to push certain "Darwinian" buttons in people (making eye contact, for example) that cause people to respond as *though* they were in a relationship.

Do plans to provide relational robots to children and the elderly make us less likely to look for other solutions for their care? If our experience with relational artifacts is based on a fundamentally deceitful interchange (artifacts' ability to persuade us that they know and care about our existence), can it be good for us? Or might it be good for us in the "feel good" sense, but bad for us in our lives as moral beings? The answers to such questions are not dependent on what computers can do today or what they are likely to be able to do in the future. These questions ask what *we* will be like, what kind of people we are becoming, as we develop increasingly intimate relationships with machines.

In *Computer Power and Human Reason*, Joseph Weizenbaum wrote about his experiences with his invention, ELIZA, a computer program that engaged people in a dialogue similar to that of a Rogerian psychotherapist (Weizenbaum 1976). It mirrored one's thoughts; it was always supportive. To the comment "My mother is making me angry," the program might respond "Tell me more about your mother," or "Why do you feel so negatively about your mother?" Weizenbaum was disturbed that his students, knowing they were talking with a computer program, wanted to chat with it, indeed, wanted to be alone with it. Weizenbaum was my colleague at MIT; we taught courses together on computers and society. At the time his book came out, I felt moved to reassure him about his concerns. ELIZA seemed to me like a Rorschach; users did become involved with the program, but in a spirit of "as if." The gap between program and person was vast. People bridged it with attribution and desire. They thought: "I will talk to this program 'as if, it were a person"; "I will vent, I will rage, I will get things off my chest." At the time, ELIZA seemed to me no more threatening than an interactive diary. Now, thirty years later, I ask myself if I under-estimated the quality of the connection. Now, computational creatures have been designed that evoke a sense of mutual relating. The people who meet relational artifacts are drawn in by a desire to nurture them. And with nurturance comes the fantasy of reciprocation. People want the creatures to care about them in return. Very little about these rela-tionships seems to be experienced "as if."

Relational artifacts are the latest chapter in the trajectory of the tethered self. We move from technologies that tether us to people to those that are able to tether us to the Web sites and avatars that repre-sent people. Relational artifacts represent their programmers but are given autonomy and primitive psychologies; they are designed to stand on their own as creatures to be loved. They are potent objects-to-think-with for asking the questions, posed by all of the machines that tether us to new socialities: "What is an authentic relationship with a machine?" "What are machines doing to our relationships with peo-ple?" And ultimately, "What is a relationship?"

Methodology Note

I have studied relational artifacts in the lives of children and the eld-erly since 1997, beginning with the simple Tamagotchis that were avail-able at every toy store to Kismet and Cog, advanced robots at the MIT Artificial Intelligence Laboratory, and Paro, a seal-like creature de-signed specifically for therapeutic purposes. Along the way there have been Furbies, AIBOS, and My Real Babies, the latter a baby doll that like the Paro has changing inner states that respond to the quality of its hu-man care. More than two hundred and fifty subjects have been in-volved in these studies. My investigations of computer-mediated communication date from the mid-1980s and have followed the media from e-mail, primitive virtual communities, and Web-based chat to cell technology, instant messaging, and social networking. More than four hundred subjects have been involved in these studies. My work was done in Boston and Cambridge and their surrounding suburbs. The work on robotics investigated children and seniors from a range of ethnicities and social classes. This was possible because in every case I was providing robots and other relational artifacts to my informants.

In the case of the work on communications technology, I spoke to people, children, adolescents, and adults, who already had computers, Web access, mobile phones, BlackBerries, et cetera. This necessarily makes my claims about their lives in the always-on/always-on-you culture not equally generalizable outside of the social class currently wealthy enough to afford such things.

REFERENCES

Bruckman, A. 1992. Identity workshop: Emergent social and psychological phenomena in text-based virtual reality. Unpublished paper written in partial completion of a doctoral degree at the Media Lab, Massachusetts Institute of Technology, http://www-static.cc.gatech.edu/~asb/papers/ old-papers.html.

Clark, S. Campbell. 2000. Work/family border theory: A new theory of work/family balance. *Human Relations* 53(6): 747–770.

Desrochers, S., and L. D. Sargent. 2003. Work-family boundary ambiguity, gender and stress in dual-earner couples. Paper presented at the Conference "From 9-to-5 to 24/7: How Workplace Changes Impact Families, Work, and Communities," 2003 BPW/Brandeis University Conference, Orlando, Fla.

Foucault, M. 1979. *Discipline and Punish: The Birth of the Prison*. New York: Vintage Books.

Gant, D. B., and S. Kiesler. 2001. Blurring the boundaries: Cell phones, mobility and the line between work and personal life. In *Wireless World: Social and Interactional Aspects of the Mobile Age*, edited by N. G. R. H. Barry Brown. New York: Springer.

Herzog, T. R., A. M. Black, K. A. Fountaine, and D. J. Knotts. 1997. Reflection and attentional recovery as distinctive benefits of restorative environments. *Journal of Environmental Psychology* 17: 165-170.

Jones, C. A. 2006. Tethered. In *Sensorium: Embodied Experience, Technology, and Contemporary Art*, edited by C. A. Jones. Cambridge, Mass.: List Visual Art Center and MIT Press.

Kaplan, S. 1995. The restorative benefits of nature: Toward an integrative framework. *Journal of Environmental Psychology* 15: 169–182.

Katz, J. E. 2006. *Magic in the Air: Mobile Communication and the Transformation of Social Life*. New Brunswick, N.J.: Transaction.

Katz, J. E., ed. 2003. *Machines That Become Us: The Social Context of Personal Communication Technology*. New Brunswick, N.J.: Transaction.

Mazmanian, M. 2005. Some thoughts on blackberries. In Memo.

Ornstein, P. H., ed. 1978. *The Search for the Self: Selected Writings of Heinz Kohut: 1950–1978*: 2. New York: International Universities Press, Inc.

Riesman, D., R. Denney, and N. Glazer. 1950. *The Lonely Crowd: A Study of the Changing American Character*. New Haven: Yale University Press.

Shumate, M., and J. Fulk. 2004. Boundaries and role conflict when work and family are colocated: A communication network and symbolic interaction approach. *Human Relations* 57(1): 55–74.

Stone, L. 2006. Linda Stone's thoughts on attention, and specifically, continual partial attention. http://www.lindastone.net.

Turkle, S. 1995. *Life on the Screen: Identity in the Age of the Internet*. New York: Simon and Schuster.

Turkle, S. 1999. Toys to change our minds. In *Predictions*, edited by S. Griffiths. Oxford: Oxford University Press.

Turkle, S. 2003a. Sociable technologies: Enhancing human performance when the computer is not a tool but a companion. In *Converging Technologies for Improving Human Performance*, edited by M. C. Roco and W. S. Bainbridge. The Netherlands: Kluwer Academic Publishers.

Turkle, S. 2003b. Technology and human vulnerability. *Harvard Business Review*.

Turkle, S. 2004a. *NSF Report: Relational Artifacts*. National Science Foundation. (NSF Grant SES01115668).

Turkle, S. 2004b. Spinning technology. In *Technological Visions*, edited by M. Sturken, D. Thomas, and S. Ball-Rokeach. Philadelphia: Temple University Press.

Turkle, S. 2004c. Whither psychoanalysis in computer culture. *Psychoanalytic Psychology: Journal of the Division of Psychoanalysis* 21(1): 16–30.

Turkle, S. 2005a. *The Second Self: Computers and the Human Spirit* (20th anniversary ed.). Cambridge, Mass.: MIT Press [1984].

Turkle, S. 2005b. Computer games as evocative objects: From projective screens to relational artifacts. In *Handbook of Computer Games Studies*, edited by J. Raessens and J. Goldstein. Cambridge, Mass.: MIT Press.

Turkle, S. 2005c. Relational artifacts/children/elders: The complexities of cybercompanions. IEEE Workshop on Android Science, Stresa, Italy.

Turkle, S., C. Breazeal, O. Dasté, and B. Scassellat. 2006a. First encounters with kismet and cog: Children's relationship with humanoid robots. In *Digital Media: Transfer in Human Communication*, edited by P. Messaris and L. Humphreys. New York: Peter Lang Publishing.

Turkle, S. 2006b. Tamagotchi diary. *The London Review of Books*, April 20.

Turkle, S. 2006c. Tethering. In *Sensorium: Embodied Experience, Technology, and Contemporary Art*, edited by C. A. Jones. Cambridge, Mass.: List Visual Art Center and MIT Press.

Turner, V. 1969. *The Ritual Process: Structure and Anti-structure*. Chicago: Aldine.

Weizenbaum, J. 1976. *Computer Power and Human Reason: From Judgment to Calculation*. San Francisco: W. H. Freeman.

SUGGESTIONS FOR WRITING

1. In describing the contemporary self as "tethered," Turkle calls up certain associations of this word. Look up "tether" in the dictionary, and find out about the etymology, history, and various uses of this word. Use a thesaurus, as well, to look up synonyms of "tether"; what different meanings would each synonym bring to the concept that Turkle is describing? Then write a brief essay in which you explain the implications of describing a self as "tethered."

2. Turkle argues that the communication technologies to which we are tethered create in us a state of continuous partial attention. This assignment asks you to do a one-day, Zen-like experiment in which you try to pay attention in a complete, rather than partial, way to whatever activities you are involved in. If you're reading, turn off your computer and just read; if you're having a conversation, turn off your cell phone and focus on the person you're talking to; if you're surfing the Web, turn off the music playing in the background; if you're washing the dishes, turn off the TV. In short, make a conscious effort to avoid multitasking. After this one-day experiment, write a reflective essay in which you describe how easy or difficult the experiment was for you and what you learned from it.

3. Turkle concludes this article by discussing "relational artifacts"; she provides several examples to illustrate this concept and draws connections to the idea of a tethered self and the redefinition of relationships. After rereading this final section of the article, define "relational artifacts" in your own words and provide one or two of your own examples of these objects and technologies. Conclude your essay by discussing your opinion of Turkle's claim that "relational artifacts are the latest chapter in the trajectory of the tethered self."

CHAPTER

Music

A RECENT ISSUE OF *HUCK*, A MAGAZINE DEVOTED TO ALL things surf/skate/snowboard-related, features an ad for Skull Candy headphones. In this ad, a seriously ganja-lidded Snoop Dogg wears a pair of vibrant blue paisley-print phones, while some steeply canted text reads, "Snoop Dogg Signature Skull Crusher. A pair of mini-subwoofers against your skull makes the bass feel like a swarm attack by the renegades of funk, soldiers of Jah, and hip-hop nation, all at once." Any lover of music—whether reggae, rap, jazz or avant classical—can't help but be lured by the transcendent promise of deeply driven bass, making the ad so appealing to a core group of audiophiles as to be almost irresistible. However, there is a more sinister side to headphones and their baby cousins, the earbuds. A recent *Time* magazine article, along with countless other news stories, warns that prolonged wearing of headphones and/or earbuds at high volume can cause significant hearing loss, even among the young: "The risk of permanent hearing loss ... can increase with just five minutes of exposure a day to music at full volume." These two polar points of view regarding the merits and potential demerits of listening gear—one viewpoint corporate-driven and the other generated by the news media—illustrate that there are at least two sides to many issues related to popular music. The readings that follow examine current trends in musical taste, the recording industry, and the psychology of music appreciation, along with ethnicity- and gender-related concerns as reflected in the music favored by today's twentysomethings.

The first two readings focus on a subgenre of popular music that might be justifiably identified as the sound track for a generation of young people: rap and hip-hop. Some recent commentary within the hip-hop community, and among popular music commentators generally, is that hip-hop is dead—that it is losing its currency and vibrancy as a cutting-edge art form. The first article, "5 Things That Killed Hip-Hop," takes the form of a blog in which the author, a hip-hop artist and producer self-named J-Zone, lists specific points about the current state of hip-hop. In the author's opinion, the music is in fact *not* dead, but it does have some serious problems facing it; J-Zone identifies these and makes some concrete recommendations for their solution. The second reading in the hip-hop "casebook," "The Miseducation of Hip-Hop," looks at the relationship between rap music and college students who listen to it.

The next section of the chapter examines a range of music-related topics from several perspectives: the cultural/economic, the artistic, and the medical. First, David Hadju, a music critic for *The New Republic* and a professor at the Columbia University Graduate School of Journalism, focuses on the cultural and economic implications of musical trends and tastes, with a sobering discussion of ways in which particularly awful contemporary pop songs parallel the catastrophic state of the United States and world economy. Next, the chapter moves into a humanities-based examination of a particular subgenre of popular music, this one widely referred to as independent rock, or, more colloquially, indie rock. This musical form has emerged from bands such as Nirvana and R.E.M. at the beginning of the post-punk era, through well-known indie acts of today, including The White Stripes, Modest Mouse, the Yeah Yeah Yeahs, and The Strokes. While some critics condemn the current state of indie rock, claiming that it has lost some of its soul (one critic in particular is singled out in this piece as a vehicle against whom to argue) Carl Wilson argues for a different set of deficiencies in the current state of independent rock music, asserting that the problem—if there indeed is a problem at all—has more to do with issues of class than with ethnicity. In this chapter's final article, neurologist Oliver Sacks takes an entirely different approach to the study of music, delivering a fascinating, biology-based discussion of those little melodies that keep repeating over and over in our heads, in an essay entitled, "Brainworms, Sticky Music, and Catchy Tunes."

In sum, then, the articles in this chapter explore the ways in which individuals are constructed in part by today's music: that is, how their beliefs, values, attitudes, and morals—and even the sounds inside their head—are manipulated by the tunes they listen to, whether actively or passively. Some observers see this phenomenon as potentially dangerous, since in some cases—as in the case of violent song lyrics, for example—it might encourage young people to transgress the laws and customs of a civilized culture. However, other critics contend that popular music plays a very positive role in modern life, since it allows people to voice feelings and ideas that would otherwise not be widely heard. You will undoubtedly situate yourself between these two poles, and the readings in this chapter will, we hope, assist you in locating your own position within this ongoing debate.

J-ZONE

5 Things That Killed Hip-Hop

This piece by New York rapper/producer J-Zone comes in the form of a blog. As such, it is conversational, at times bordering on the vulgar, often grammatically incorrect (intentionally, one assumes, in the style of street talk), and highly opinionated. All of these qualities are typical of blogs and are certainly less typical of academic discourse, the latter being the currency of most students' college courses and the form suggested throughout most of this book. However, as blogs become increasingly popular vehicles for personal expression, it may be worth the reader's time to consider their value in an academic setting and in the broader context of journalistic writing. Some writing scholars, such as Peter Elbow, believe in the value of setting up contexts—traditionally, in the classroom, but, by extension, in cyberspace, such as on blogging sites—in which writers become experts on topics of their own choosing. Other writing scholars, such as Donald Bartholomae, ask that students assume expert status by very different means, such as by emulating the structures, formal tone, and rhetorical strategies employed by true authorities in the field. The blog, then, more closely resembles the Elbow model in that it strives "to be evocative, to convince by being true to life, to achieve verisimilitude ... [and] often takes the mode of stories."[1] J-Zone's blog/article shows him to be intimately familiar with all things hip-hop; he majored in music at the State University of New York, worked as a head engineer, achieved prominence with several albums of his

---

[1] Mlynarczyk, Rebecca Williams. "Personal and Academic Writing: Revisiting the Debate." Journal of Basic Writing 25:1 (2006): p. 5.

own music, and helped produce numerous releases for other artists. J-Zone
comments on the notion that hip-hop is stagnant and/or dying: a comment
one has frequently heard leveled at the musical form in recent months so
much so that rapper Nas titled one of his recent albums, "Hip Hop Is
Dead." J-Zone makes a number of salient points in the following discus-
sion, noting some concrete reasons why hip-hop has indeed become less
vital and compelling than it may have been in earlier incarnations, but also
making some well-considered recommendations for its revival and contin-
ued popularity.

I realize that arguing about music is pointless cause we all got different opinions. A few people wanted my opinion on the "is hip hop dead?" matter and I just put my opinion on my sites. For some reason, it's gotten a lot of unexpected feedback, but what I'm saying isn't really new, nor is there is there a right or wrong answer to that question. If u agree with me that's cool, if you disagree that's cool too. It's music, not life and death. At the least, to read it is a way to kill some time.

Everybody's saying it. Nas titled his album that. People are debating and a few brothers asked me for my humble opinion. So as I watch the Celtics lose their 17th straight on Sportscenter, I'll do a music related blog for once. After all, it affects me right? 5 things I feel are the biggest culprits of rap's downfall. Well actually before I exercise my freedom of speech and somebody gets upset for nothing, let me clarify.

A. I am NOT saying that there isn't a batch of stellar records released yearly, or a group of dope producers delivering fly shit or a handful of rappers that still make you wanna listen. I also know music is subjective and it's all opinion. The great music of today may be on par with the great of yesterday, but in the grand scheme of things, the negatives far outweigh the positives.

B. There's 3 things you can never argue about ... Religion, Politics and Hip-Hop. Cause no matter your opinion, somebody will tyrannically oppose and get all fuckin emotional. It's just my humble opinion, relax. Who cares anyway?

C. For the record, the politics at major labels, press and radio are not listed here because they've been around since the beginning of time. And we have ourselves to blame for not manning up to take control of those. Yo Flex, drop a bomb on that. OK, where was I?

5. Clans, Posses, Crews & Cliques: Who U Wit?

Safety in numbers. Movements, collaborations, big name guests, teams, crew beef, etc. The days of the solo roller are over. In the prime of rap, you were judged solely on your music. Rakim, Nas & Biggie (early on), LL, Kane ... they all built their legend on music alone. Hell, Rakim had no guests on his first 4 albums. Sure there was Juice Crew, Native Tongues, Lench Mob crew, etc. But it wasn't mandatory. Then for some reason, in the mid-late 90's, it became totally necessary to have a movement. A crew with 1,000 different artists all on the same team. Touring together, crew t-shirts, beef with other crews, collaborations, etc. Not that that's a bad thing, but it's like people cannot identify with one artist, there has to be a movement or somebody else involved to validate them. Look at today's most successful artists. They all have a movement. Roc-A-Fella, Def Jux, Stonesthrow, Rhymesayers, G-Unit, Dipset, Wu-Tang, Hieroglyphics, Okayplayer, etc. Or if you're not part of a movement, you collaborate with other high profile artists. Doom, Danger Mouse, etc. It's all about cross-pollinating fan bases. You don't? You die. And for some reason, I see Da Youngstas album, Da Aftermath, as the beginning of this from a beat standpoint. That and Run DMC's Down With The King (both 1993) were the first albums I can remember to use a lot of different producers with totally different sounds. It worked back then, they were dope albums. But it wound up being a cancer.

Nowadays you need a Timbaland track, a Neptunes track, a Just Blaze track, a Dre track, a Kanye track for people to really care ... and for the most part it sounds like a collection of songs, not an album. Why not let one of them just do the whole fuckin album? Can't please everybody, why make a futile attempt? Good albums are about a vibe. Wu-Tang was a movement, but it was cohesive and made sense because they all vibed together and RZA was the sonic glue. Sans Illmatic, Ready to Die and a few others, every single great rap album had a maximum of 3 producers and 3 guests. In this fascination with movements, name association and special guests, we've lost album cohesiveness and the focus on just music. It's no longer about how dope you are, it's who you rollin with and who's cosigning what you do. And usually 92% of the crew isn't up to par with the few star artists in the crew. Quantity rules, not quality. You can have a 5 mic album, but nobody cares unless there's a bunch of other people involved. 10 producers and 7 guests. And now so and so with a platinum album can put his wack ass brother or cousin on and cheapen the game, cause they're part of the movement and its about who you with. Back in 88, Milk D said he had "a great big bodyguard" on Top Billin. But that was it. In 2007, there would be a Great Big Bodyguard solo album.

4. Too Much Music

Like the crew theory, this is about quantity. People want more, even if it means a dip in quality. Some people can put out music quickly and do it well. Some people just want to bombard the market for the sake of doing it. Rakim did albums every 2 years. EPMD, Scarface and Ice Cube did it every year and that was considered fast. Nowadays, if you don't have 2 albums, 5 mix tapes and 10 guest appearances a year, you're slippin and people forget you. This attempt to keep up with the rush has cheapened the music. Now you have regular mixtapes marketed as albums, just a bunch of thrown together songs for the fuck of it. But to survive these days, you have to do that to stay in the public eye. There's far too many slim line case CD-R mix tapes out, and as important as mix tapes are to rap, the very vehicle that helped it grow is now playing a part in killing it.

Now everybody has forgotten how to make cohesive projects, so we cover it up by labeling it as a mix tape. The value and pride that full length albums used to symbolize are no more. Mixtapes now triple the number official albums in artist's catalog and never has music seemed so cheap and fast food. Not to mention, when the majors went completely awry in the late '90s, the indie rap scene went out of control with too much product.

When I debuted in 1999, there were maybe 25-30 other indie vinyl releases out that mattered. And mine was one of the only full-length albums. So it was only a matter of time before I got a listen, it didn't matter that I had no big names on my record and came outta nowhere. Try that now. To go to a store and see the foot high stack of one sheets for new records, mix CD's and DVD's dropping weekly makes you see you have a snowballs chance to survive in that world. Look at how many releases a week are on Hiphopsite, Sandbox, Fat Beats, UGHH, etc. The high profile artists get some attention, and everybody else gets ordered in ones and twos, if that. So today's new talent making his debut is in for an uphill battle. Great records go unnoticed. Rap is now a disposable art. Mr. Walt of Da Beatminerz once said, "You work 16 months on an album and get a 2 week window of opportunity. After that your record is as good as dead for most people." That sums it up.

3. *Too Cool to Have Fun / No Balance in Rap*

When rap stopped being fun, I knew we were in big trouble. Not too many people are doin music for fun anymore. Ask yourself, "would I still mess with music as a hobby if there wasn't any money in it?" Too many people would say no. We all wanna get paid. Shit, I got bills too, I love money! But too many people just seem like they'd rather be doing other shit. You read in interviews, "I don't care about no rap, I'd rather be hustling. I just do this cause I can." Hey, whatever floats your boat, I can relate, there's been artists like that since the beginning of time, but they were never the majority until now. Having fun is nowhere near as important as your life before you got signed. And there's plenty of battle MC's, political MC's and killer thugs but it seems there's not many funny artists no more. Like on some Biz Mark, Humpty Hump, The Afros shit. Not afraid to go to the extreme and have fun. God forbid you use your imagination or rap about something not involving Hip Hop, the hood, you bein the shit, the end of the world or what color your car interior is.

I live in Queens, less than a mile from 50 Cent's old house. Nobody really knows I make music over here. Some kid from over here saw me in The Source a while back and said "Yo I ain't know you was in it like that, yo why you ain't tryin to pump your shit out here and let people know, you should rep the hood? 50 did it." Why should I? I'm not on the block tryin to push weight, I'm out there walking to Walgreens for my Grandmother, on my way to the park for a game of 21 or to watch a game at the local high school. I'm a grown ass man with a college degree and I like my neighborhood, but I choose to rap about my beat up car, not dancing in clubs, women with bad hygiene and too many kids or ball playin rappers with limited ball skills, cause I ain't a street cat and I'd rather show the lighter side of life. And that was never a problem back in the day.

Okay those ain't completely new topics, but it's like rappin about those things these days gets you marked as novelty rap. Biz rhymed about a lot of this same shit back in the day, but it was still accepted as legit Hip Hop. 2007? He could never do a song like "The Dragon." Little Shawn & Father MC rapped about the ladies with some R&B beats. De La Soul were labeled as hippies. But all those dudes would beat yo fuckin ass if you got out of line! They were soft by no means, they just wanted to do the music they enjoyed, cause rap is supposed to be a way to have fun and get away from the everyday stress, while not limiting yourself. The thing that made rap so dope in the "golden era" was the balance of styles. You had clown princes like Biz, Humpty Hump, Kwame and ODB later on. You had political brothers like X-Clan, PE, Lakim Shabazz, Poor Righteous Teachers, Kam, etc. You had the explicit shit on Rap-A-Lot and the whole 2 Live movement in Miami. Hip-house like Twin Hype, new jack shit like Wrecks-N-Effect, the whole Native Tongues thing, the hard South Central LA shit, the Oakland funk ... and they all co-existed, were all dope and they all had fun regardless of their style. King Sun made On The Club Tip and then did Universal Flag. Lakim Shabazz, Twin Hype and Wrecks-N-Effect had raw battle rap, Geto Boys and Gansksta Nip were hilarious, PE had the yin and yang of Chuck and Flav and ODB was a ferocious battle MC.

Even the more serious political rap ... everybody seemed to be enjoying making music. Gangsta rappers had a fuckin sense of humor back then. Mob Style might have been the hardest group I've ever heard and they lived it. But them dudes also showed other sides and sounded like they enjoyed music, because it was an escape from everyday bull-shit. Tim Dog, was hilarious and hard at the same time. Even if it was a joke to some, the shit was good listening. Suga Free is an ice cold pimp for real, but he has a sense of humor and approaches his music doin what he feels. Who says rappin about a girl with no teeth or going to the store with coupons ain't "real"? Everything is "real", people forget that. Everybody is so concerned with being feared and taken seriously, they can't come off those insecurities and do some guilty pleasure shit. Even the producers. If you can't show your other sides and bug out in your music, where can you do it? Stop being scared and break some fuckin rules. Put some 300 pound girls in your video for once! Laugh at your-self, dog, you ain't no killer 24/7. You ain't battling MC's and being a lyri-cal lyricist mixtape murder 24/7. Havin fun is almost hip-hop faux pas these days. Rap is dead without balance ... period.

2. Law & Order: MPC and Sampling

"Boop Boop, it's the sound of the police!" Yup, the legal police. Hip-hop is based in illegality, but not maliciously. Ironically, many people got into it to stay out of legal troubles, but technically this positive move is also seen as a life of crime by the powers that be. Mix tapes, remixes, sampling, parodies (somewhat) ... the appeal of hip-hop was always re-arranging the old to create the new. It's the lifeline of the music. One man's treasure is apparently another man's trash. In the wake of DJ Drama getting busted by the Feds for selling mix tapes that the labels and artists themselves approve and benefit from, it has never been more evident that the RIAA and their legal vendetta have just pulled the IV. We all knew that the late 80's way of taking 8 bar James Brown loops and not clearing was bound to catch up to us. I can live with that. You have a platinum album and loop somebody's whole shit, break'em off some money and publishing, it's only right. But then the lawyers and courts got tyrannical. Now 1/8 of a second sample can run you the risk of legal action. Ouch. I remember having a beat placed on a TV show and the music supervisor panicked after the fact because he swore the snare I used sounded like it was sampled. Wow. I understand melodies, but somebody can own a snare sound now?

This is pretty lousy, but to this point it only affected some of the major label stuff and big corporate gigs. No more. MySpace is now shutting down pages that post remixes. WHAT!? I find that completely ass backwards. I know a few dudes that were warned, and others shut down without notice for posting remixes of major label songs with COMMERCIALLY AVAILABLE ACAPELLAS! WELL WHAT THE FUCK IS AN ACAPELLA AVAILABLE ON A RECORD FOR?! TO BE REMIXED! DING DING ... MESSAGE! Now to take that remix and release it on a major label and make 50 grand is one thing. But to have fun with remixes and post them on a MySpace page, where ZERO DOLLARS can be made directly off of it, is completely harmless promotion for all parties involved. Not anymore.

Back in the day to be on a Kid Capri, Double R, S&S, Doo Wop, Silver Surfer, etc. mixtape was the best thing to happen to an artist and their label. An unknown producer leaking a dope remix to a popular artists record was a way to get buzz and a way for the industry to find new talent. Taking pieces of old music and creating something new (like the Bomb Squad) wasn't looked upon with the seriousness of a gunpoint mugging. But in a day where album sales are down, no artists or labels are seeing any money, CD's have foolishly been raised in price, interpolating one line of Jingle Bells in your song can get you sued and you can't post a remix for promotional and listening purposes only ... you can see the music and legal industries have officially declared war on rap as a knee jerk reaction to their own failures. And as idiotic and unjust as things have become, they have the loopholes of law on their side.

1. *The Internet*

Talk about a double-edged sword. Never has it been so easy to get your music heard. If I make a dope beat, I can put it on my MySpace page and it's up in an hour (depending on the servers, it may be "processing" for about 3 years). No more spending money and wasting time for records and test presses. Now people in Arkansas that only have MTV and the Internet can hear my music. Limited distribution isn't as big a problem as before. Everybody is almost equal, and we all have MySpace pages. But look at the flipside: everybody is almost equal, and we all have MySpace pages. There is so much shit out and the internet lurks with a million people doing the same thing, it's virtually impossible to stand out. Back in the day, you had to work your way up in the business. Having a record was in most cases a privilege and a reward for your hard work. Catalog meant something. We're in an MP3 world now, and somebody in their bedroom is on an equal plane with somebody that's paid dues and worked hard. That's great for the kid with talent and no vehicle to get heard. That sucks for the no talent hacks on MySpace that post advertisements for their wack music on your comments page.

The Internet also killed rap's number one asset. Anticipation. How many can remember buying a mixtape and hearing 3 dope joints from an upcoming album on a mixtape? You couldn't wait to cop the album. And you didn't hear the album 3 months in advance cause there was no way to spread it that fast. And in rare cases where the album leaked, you had to get a tape dub and even when you did, you still bought it. I remember hearing Lots Of Lovin, Straighten It Out, TROY and Ghettos Of The Mind from Mecca & The Soul Brother 2 months before it came out. But I couldn't find any other songs. That drove the anticipation up and got everybody talking. We were all eager to support. In 2007, the album would leak months in advance, you burn it and that's it. I'm not complaining cause that won't change things, but that was a large part of what appealed to me and many others about music, especially rap. No more. No artwork & physical CD to read the credits and shoutouts (remember those!?), no anticipation, it's old news by street date, the shit don't sell and here we are. Tower's closing, the legendary Beat Street is closed, Music Factory is a wrap ... people don't realize that rap as we know it is done. Labels are fuckin suing common civilians for file sharing! A physical copy no longer matters unless you're a collector.

Back in the day, you would never see Internet beef. It's just stupid junior high shit. People leaving threats and talkin shit via MySpace, people getting hurt over e-beef at shows, kids on message boards flexin muscle and actin hard. Great! Now that we have a bunch of killers on wax, we got a bunch of em posting in forums. Cute. You can sit in a bedroom in Mexico and talk about knockin out somebody in Finland and it will never come back to you. Hip hop bravado and the anonymity of the Web ... it don't get more junior high. The internet was the blessing and the curse of rap music. I may catch heat for this, but I think the best thing is to blow up the industry and start over. There is still great music and I will enjoy making this music til I pass on, even if only as a hobby. I will still be diggin for records, makin beats, playing instruments and watching old movies for inspiration. But sometimes things need to fall apart to give birth to greater things. The fall of rap in its current state may give birth to something bigger and better. It's what I'm banking on, cause realistically, how much longer can it go down this road? I'm not saying go back in time. Classic rap artists may have been influenced by Cold Crush and Melle Mel, but they took that influence and added something different on to it to create something new, and until that principle can be followed again, I say fuck fixing an abandoned building. Hit it with a wrecking ball and rebuild!

SUGGESTIONS FOR WRITING

1. In this blog piece, the author presents a balanced commentary on the role the Internet has played in the current state of hip-hop, in his Reason #1 section. In an essay, summarize J-Zone's points concerning the positive effects of cyber-culture on hip-hop music and production, and then go on to explain the ways in which the Web has negatively affected hip-hop. In the succeeding portion of the essay, expand this discussion beyond the boundaries of rap and hip-hop: how has the Internet affected popular music, the music industry, and your own life personally as a consumer of and listener to music? As you move toward a conclusion and/or central thesis for your essay, you might try to arrive at your own opinion about the effect of the Web on popular music generally: On the whole, has it had a positive or negative effect?

2. Go to one of the many popular blog sites on the Web and create a presence for yourself there. While it's important to remember that the style you use for your blog will differ dramatically from the language, style, and structure you use for your school essays, one of the goals for any writing course is for you to get practice in a variety of styles, and blogging is increasingly becoming an accepted mode of discourse. For example, in the business community, numerous companies, agencies, and other institutions have begun creating a public relations presence through the use of blogs. Professional journalists, likewise, are becoming increasingly reliant on blogging, as are film and music critics,

for example. In this assignment, you will undertake to write a music-related blog for the rest of the current school term. Using this format, communicate your ideas on the current state of the music industry, discuss your favorite kinds of popular music, review recent albums, and/or explore the various possibilities for accessing music, such as satellite and Web-based radio, file-sharing services (the legal ones, of course), brick-and-mortar record emporiums, concerts, and so forth. Your instructor will promise not to grade your grammar, syntax, and organization; this will be a platform where those concerns are temporarily suspended, so that your imagination can range freely over whatever topic you find interesting.

3. In its colloquial tone, lack of concerns for the conventions of the Queen's English, and highly opinionated arguments, "5 Things That Killed Hip-Hop" conforms to certain negative preconceptions about blogging as a form of written communication. However, and perhaps more importantly, this piece disproves those same negative preconceptions in several ways: First, the author is definitely an expert in the field, as a hip-hop artist, producer, and music critic; second, the author develops his arguments through the rigorous example of illustration and example, citing many sources, historical and current, to back up his claims; and finally, the author often presents both sides of an issue, as he does in his section about the effects of the Internet on the current state of hip-hop music. For example, while he acknowledges that commercial artists must be compensated if their songs are sampled extensively and then incorporated into other commercial tracks, he believes that judicious sampling is an acceptable practice, especially when the resulting songs are not placed on the music industry market but instead are shared free of charge on sites such as MySpace. In an argumentative essay, form your own thesis regarding the validity of blogging as a valid subgenre of writing, presenting both sides of the issue and ultimately arriving at your own conclusion/thesis regarding this issue.

JAMILAH EVELYN

The Miseducation of Hip-Hop

It was recently announced that Jamilah Evelyn has been named the editor of Community College Week, *a nationwide independent journalistic voice reporting to community, junior, and technical colleges. She has also worked in the public relations and communications industry as a senior writer for*

Brooklyn College, and as a reporter for the Chronicle of Higher Education, *a weekly news and information source for college and university faculty members, administrators, and students. In these diverse education-related roles, Evelyn has had an opportunity to witness certain cultural trends and their effects on education at both the university and community-college levels. In this article, she points to criticisms currently being leveled at hip-hop music and culture from within a subset of university and college educators— namely, the community of African American faculty. A significant number of these professors and lecturers believe that, although the themes encoded within the lyrics of hip-hop songs may reflect real-life street situations within United States inner cities, the music's influence may be ultimately counter-productive, causing Black students to perform worse in school—which, in turn, will perpetuate the negative economic and social conditions that rappers dramatize in their lyrics. Some observers go so far as to insist that young African American students turn away from this popular art form, while others suggest that some university courses focus their attention on rap, in order to make connections between this popular form and the work of Black historians, sociologists, urban psychologists, and so forth. In synthesizing and reporting on these opinions, Evelyn strives to maintain journalistic objectivity while addressing the central questions regarding this topic: Are today's faculty and administrators simply out of touch with the aesthetic tastes of their students? Has today's popular music corrupted the minds of a whole generation, as some social commentators within the African-American community and elsewhere contend? While reporting that many college and university officials believe that hip-hop culture and lifestyle is eroding the morals, and ultimately the classroom experience, of today's college students, Evelyn balances her reportage by adding that some college students feel pigeonholed by a hip-hop or "gangsta" image that many of them reject, whereas others revere hip-hop as the "sound track to their lives."*

When Jason Hinmon transferred to the University of Delaware two years ago from Morehouse College in Atlanta, the 22-year-old senior says he almost dropped out his first semester.

He says that for financial reasons, he came back here to his hometown. But in many ways, he had never felt so abandoned.

"I came to class and my professors didn't know how to deal with me," he says, between bites of his a-la-carte lunch. "I could barely get them to meet with me during their office hours." Dark-hued, dread-locked and, well, young, he says many of his mostly White professors figured they had him pegged.

"They took one look at me and thought that I was some hip-hop hoodlum who wasn't interested in being a good student," he says.

But if Hinmon represents the "good" students with grounds to resent the stereotype, there are faculty who profess there's no shortage of young people willing to live up—or down—to it. "You see students walking on campus reciting rap lyrics when they should be reciting something they'll need to know on their next test. Some of these same students you won't see back on campus next semester," says Dr. Thomas Earl Midgette, 50, director of the Institute for the Study of Minority Issues at historically Black North Carolina Central University.

"These rap artists influence the way they dress," he continues. "They look like hoochie mamas, not like they're coming to class. Young men with pants fashioned below their navel. Now, I used to wear bell-bottoms, but I learned to dress a certain way if I was negotiating the higher education maze. I had to trim my afro."

The difference between today's students and their parents, faculty and administrators is marked, no doubt. Technology's omnipresence—apparent in kids with little patience for anything less than instant meals, faster Internet information and cellular ubiquity—is certainly at play when it comes to explaining the divide.

But what causes more consternation among many college and university officials is a music form, a culture and a lifestyle they say is eating away at the morals, and ultimately the classroom experience, of today's college students.

Hip-hop—brash, vulgar, in-your-face hip-hop—is indisputably the dominant youth culture today. Its most controversial front men floss mad ice (wear lots of diamonds and other expensive jewelry), book bad bitches (usually scantily clad, less than the take home kind of girl), and in general, party it up. Its most visible females brag about their sexual dexterity, physical attributes, and cunning tactics when it comes to getting their rent paid.

With college completion statistics at an embarrassing low and the Black–White achievement gap getting wider by the semester, perhaps it's time to be concerned whether the culture's malevolent message is at play.

But can atrocious retention rates really be linked to reckless music? Or do university officials underestimate their students? Is it that young folk today have no sense of history, responsibility and plain good manners? Or are college faculty a bunch of old fogies simply more comfortable with Marvin Gaye's "Sexual Healing" than Little Kim's sexual prowess?

Is this no different than the divide we've always seen between young people and their college and university elders? Or do the disparities between this wave of students and those charged with educating them portend something more disparaging?

The Gap

At the heart of the rift between the two groups is a debate that has both sides passionately disturbed.

Young people say they feel pigeonholed by an image many of them don't support. They say the real rub is that their teachers—Black and White—believe the hype as much as the old lady who crosses the street when she sees them coming.

And they'd like their professors to consider this: They can listen to the music, even party to it, but still have a response just as critical, if not more so, than their faculty and administrators.

Others point out that the pervasiveness of hip-hop's immoral philosophies is at least partly rooted in the fact that the civil rights movement—the older generation's defining moment—surely did not live up to all its promises for Black America.

And further, they say it's important to note that not all hip-hop is irresponsible. In fact, some argue that it's ultimately empowering, uplifting and refreshing. After all, when was the last time a biology professor sat down with a Mos Def CD? How many can even pronounce his name?

Older faculty, administrators and parents alike respond that the music is downright filth. And anyone associated with it ought to have their mouths and their morals cleansed.

There's a real problem when a marijuana-smoking ex-con named Snoop Doggy Dog can pack a campus auditorium quicker than Black historian John Hope Franklin; when more students deify the late Tupac Shakur and his abrasive lyrics than those who ever read the great Martin Luther King Jr.'s "I Have a Dream" speech; when kids decked out in sweats more pricey than their tuition complain that they can't afford a semester's books; when the gains they fought so hard for are, in some ways, slowly slipping away.

"I think what causes us the most grief is that hip-hop comes across as heartless, valueless, nihilistic and certainly anachronistic if not atheistic," says Dr. Nat Irvin, president of Future Focus 2020, an urban futures think tank at Wake Forest University in North Carolina. "Anyone who would argue with that needs to take a look for themselves and see what images are prevalent on BET and MTV."

"But I don't think there's any question that the disconnect comes from the fact that old folks don't have a clue. They don't understand technology. The world has changed. And there's an enormous age gap between most faculty on college campuses and the rest of America," he says.

More than 60 percent of college and university faculty are over the age of 45. Meanwhile, nearly 53 percent of African Americans are under 30 and some 40 percent are under 20. That means more than half of all Blacks were born after the civil rights movement and the landmark *Brown vs. Board of Education* case.

"There's no big puzzle why these kids are coming with a different ideology," Irvin, 49, says.

This Is What Blackness Is

It is universally acknowledged that rap began in New York City's Bronx borough nearly 30 years ago, a mix of Jamaican reggae's dancehall, America's funk music, the inner city's pent-up frustrations and Black folks' general propensity to love a good party.

Pioneering artists like the The Last Poets, The Sugar Hill Gang, Kurtis Blow and Run-DMC combined creative genius and street savvy to put hip-hop on the map.

Its initial associations were with graffiti and party music, according to Dr. Robin D. G. Kelley, professor of history and Africana studies at New York University.

"Then in the late '80s, you begin to see more politicized manifestations of that. BDP, Public Enemy ... In essays that students wrote that were not about rap music, but about the urban condition itself, they would adopt the language. They would quote Public Enemy lyrics, they would quote Ghetto Boys," says Kelley, 38.

"This whole generation of Blacks in particular were trying to carve out for themselves an alternative culture," he continues. "I saw a whole generation for the first time say, 'I don't want to go to corporate America. I don't want to be an attorney. I don't want to be a doctor. I don't want to get paid. I want to make a revolution.'"

"The wave that we're in now is all over the place," he explains.

But even hip-hop's fans stop short at endorsing some of the themes prevailing in today's music and mindset.

Kevin Powell, noted cultural critic and former hip-hop journalist, says the biggest difference between the music today and the music at its onset is that "we don't own it."

"Corporate America completely commodified hip-hop," he says. "We create the culture and corporate America takes it and sells it back to us and tells us, 'This is what Blackness is.'"

And while Powell, 34, says he is disappointed in some of the artists, especially the older ones who "should know better," many students are their staunchest defenders.

Caryn Wheeler, 18, a freshman at Bowie State University, explains simply that "every day isn't about love." Her favorite artists? Jay-Z, Out-Kast, Biggie Smalls, Tupac and Little Kim, many of whom are linked to hip-hop's controversial side. "We can relate because we see what they are talking about every day," she says.

Mazi Mutafa, 23, is a senior at the University of Maryland College Park and president of the Black Student Union there. He says he listens to jazz and hip-hop, positive artists and those who capture a party spirit. "There's a time to party and have fun, and Jay-Z speaks to that," he says. "But there needs to be a happy medium."

Interrupting, senior Christine Gonzalez, 22, says a lot of artists like Jay-Z tend to be revered by younger students. "As you get older, you tend to tone down your style and find that happy medium," she says. "It's all a state of mind."

"People have to understand that Jay-Z is kind of like a 100-level class—an intro to hip-hop. He brings a lot of people into its fan base," Mutafa chimes in. "But then you have groups like The Roots, which are more like a 400-level class. They keep you engaged in the music. But one is necessary for the other."

Erick Rivas, 17, a freshman also at the University of Maryland, says he listens to Mos Def, Black Star, Mobb Deep, Wu-Tang Clan and sometimes other, more mainstream acts like Jay-Z. "Hip-hop has been a driving force in our lives. It is the soundtrack to our lives," he explains.

Keepin' It Real

But if hip-hop is the soundtrack to their lives, it may also mark the failure of it.

De Reef Jamison, a doctoral candidate who teaches African American history at Temple University in Philadelphia, surveyed 72 Black male college students last summer for his thesis. Then a graduate student at Florida, A&M State University, Jamison was interested in discovering if there are links between students' music tastes and their cultural identity, their grades and other key indicators.

"While the lines weren't always so clear and distinct, I found that many of the students who had a low African self-consciousness, who overidentified with a European worldview and who were highly materialistic were often the students who listened to the most 'gangster' rap, or what I prefer to call reality rap," he explains.

As for grades, he says the gangster rap devotees' tended to be lower than those students who listened mostly to what he calls more conscious rap. Still, he's reluctant to draw any hard and fast lines between musical preference and student performance.

"I'd recommend that scholars take a much closer look at this," he says.

Floyd Beachum, a graduate student at Bowling Green State University in Ohio, surveyed secondary [school] students to try to ascertain if there was a correlation between their behavior and the music they listened to.

"The more hyper-aggressive students tended to listen to more hardcore, gangster rap," he says. "Those who could identify with the violence, the drive-by shootings, the stereotypes about women—many times that would play out in their lives."

But Beachum, who teamed up with fellow Bowling Green graduate student Carlos McCray to conduct his research, says he isn't ready to draw any sweeping conclusions either.

"Those findings weren't across the board," he says, adding that he believes school systems can play a role in reversing any possible negative trends.

"If hip-hop and rap influence behavior and you bring all that to school, then the schools should create a very different environment and maybe we'll see more individuals go against the grain," he says.

Even undergraduates say they must admit that they see hip-hop's squalid influence on some of their peers.

"It upsets me when some young people complain that they can't get a job but when they go into that interview, they refuse to take off their do-rags, their big gold medallion and their baggy pants," says Kholiswa Laird, 18, a freshman at the University of Delaware. "But for some stupid reason, a lot of them feel like they're selling out if they wear proper clothes."

"That's just keepin it real," explains Davren Noble, 20, a junior at the University of Delaware. "Why should I have to change myself to get a job? If somebody wants to hire me but they don't like my braids, then either of two things will happen: They'll just have to get over it or I just won't get the job."

It's this kind of attitude that many in higher education see as the crux of the problem.

"We're not gonna serve them well in the university if we don't shake their thinking about how dress is going to influence job opportunities," says Central's Midgette.

Noble, from Maplewood, N.J., is a rapper. And he says that while he grew up in a posh suburb, he often raps about violence.

"I rap about positive stuff too, but as a Black person in America, it's hard to escape violence," he explains. "Mad Black people grew up in the ghetto and the music and our actions reflect that."

For sure, art has been known to imitate life. Hip-hop icon Sean "Puffy" Combs—who two years ago gave $750,000 to his alma mater, Howard University—is currently facing charges on his involvement in a Manhattan nightclub shooting last December. Grammy-winning rapper Jay-Z, also was connected with a night club dispute that ended with a record company executive being stabbed last year.

A Bad Rap?

A simple explanation for the boldness of much of rap's lyrics is that "artists have always pushed the limits," Kelley says.

But what's more, there is a politically conscious, stirring, enriching side of hip-hop that many of its fans say is often overlooked.

"Urban radio stations play the same songs every day," says Powell, a former reporter for *Vibe* magazine. "The media is ghettoizing hip-hop. They make it look passé."

Those often included in hip-hop's positive list are Lauryn Hill, Common, Mos Def, Dead Prez, Erykah Badu, Talib Kweli and other underground acts. Indeed, many of them have been active in encouraging young people to vote. Mos Def and other artists recently recorded a song in memory of Amadou Diallo, "Hip-Hop for Respect."

This is the side of hip-hop many young people say they'd like their faculty to recognize. This is also the side that some people say faculty must recognize.

"There are scholars—I've seen them do this before—who will make a disparaging remark about a whole genre of music, not knowing a doggone thing," NYU's Kelley says. "That's the same thing as saying, 'I've read one article on rational choice theory and it was so stupid, I dismissed the whole genre.'...People who are trained in their own fields would never do that with their own scholarship and yet they are willing to make these really sweeping statements."

"And they don't know. They don't have a critical understanding of the way the music industry operates or the way in which people engage music," he says. "But they are willing to draw a one-to-one correlation between the students' failure and music."

Some professors argue that another correlation should be made: "My most serious students are the die-hard hip-hop fans," says Dr. Ingrid Banks, assistant professor of Black Studies at Virginia Tech. "They are able to understand politics because they understand hip-hop."

Banks says that more of her colleagues would be wise to better understand the music and its culture. "You can't talk about Reagan's policies in the '80s without talking about hip-hop," says the 30-something scholar. "If you start where students are, they make these wonderful connections."

Curricular Connections

If the augmentation of hip-hop scholarship is any indication, academe just may be coming around to at least tolerating this formidable medium.

Courses on hip-hop, books, essays and other studied accounts of the genre are being generated by a pioneering cadre of scholars. And while many people see that as notable, there's not yet widespread belief that academe has completely warmed to the idea of hip-hop as scholarship.

Banks, who has taught "Race, Politics and Rap Music in Late Twentieth Century America" at the Blacksburg, Va., school, says she's experiencing less than a speedy response to getting her course included into the department's curriculum.

"I understand that it usually takes a while to get a course approved, but there have been courses in bio-history that were signed off on rather quickly," she says.

But if academe fails to find ways to connect with hip-hop and its culture, then it essentially will have failed an entire generation, many critics say.

"What's happening is that administrators and teachers are faced with a real crisis. And that crisis they can easily attach to the music," Kelley says. "It's the way they dress, the way they talk. The real crisis is their failure to educate; their failure to treat these students like human beings; their failure to come up with a new message to engage students."

"Part of the reason why there is such a generational gap is because so few educators make an effort to understand the times in which they live. You can't apply '60s and '70s methods to teaching in the new millennium. You can't apply a jazz aesthetic to hip-hop heads," says Powell, who lectures at 70 to 80 colleges and universities a year. "You have to meet the students where they are. That's the nature of education. That's pedagogy."

And while Wake Forest's Irvin says he would agree with that sentiment, he also sees a role that students must play.

"What I see as being the major challenge that these kids will deal with is the image of young, urban America," Irvin says. "Young people need to ask themselves, 'Who will control their identity?'"

"If they leave it up to the media to define who they are, they'll be devastated by these images," he says. "That's where hip-hop is killing us."

SUGGESTIONS FOR WRITING

1. Write a rhetorical analysis in which you attempt to determine the author's stance toward her topic. Does Jamilah Evelyn play the role of dispassionate observer, merely recording journalistically the arguments swirling around this hotly debated topic, or can you detect a certain agenda, a persuasive position underlying her reportage or both? In your essay, use direct quotations from the text of this article, as well as paraphrases of it, to support your assertions as you develop the body of your analysis. As you move into the conclusion of your essay, you might also note, and elucidate your own reactions to, points raised during this piece. The commentators presented in this article will probably cause you to have some emotional reaction; try to set your emotions aside momentarily, make note of specific points of agreement or disagreement as they arise, and summarize these succinctly and assertively as a means of lending closure to your essay.

2. Evelyn asks the question concerning hip-hop styles and attitude, "Is this no different than the divide we've always seen between young people and their college and university elders?" In response to this question, write an analytical essay that takes an historical approach, first chronicling the rise of hip-hop and its effect upon young people from its earliest days, keeping in mind that some of the original young listeners of hip-hop are not so young anymore. Next, based upon your own experience as a member of the most recent hip-hop generation (even if you're not a rabid fan of hip-hop), attempt to answer this

question: Are the styles and behaviors of today the same as the bell-bottoms and Afros to which Dr. Midgette refers near the beginning of this article, or has the effect of hip-hop on listeners changed from generation to generation? In formulating your analysis, you might keep in the back of your mind the central questions that underlie the development of Evelyn's article: From the very beginning, was there something insidious and/or negative in hip-hop culture and its effect on students? Has the effect of hip-hop music upon listeners and specifically college students, who are the target population for Evelyn's study changed through time, or has it remained fairly steady in its influence?

3. Write an essay in which you comment on Jamilah's statement, "There's a real problem when a marijuana-smoking ex-con named Snoop Doggy Dogg can pack a campus auditorium quicker than Black historian John Hope Franklin; when more students deify the late Tupac Shakur and his abrasive lyrics than those who ever read the great Martin Luther King Jr.'s 'I have a dream speech.'" As you formulate a thesis, decide first whether or not you agree with this statement by the author: Do you believe that popular music stars exert more real influence on college students of today than do great leaders and/or educators?
(Hint: There's no right answer to this question; just be honest in your response.) Next, spend some time freewriting on the topic, letting your mind range over a broad scope of points of contention or agreement with the provocative statements made here and elsewhere in Evelyn's article. Having accomplished this activity, begin to cut and paste those supporting points into an order that has a coherent logical development, and then fill in that framework with supporting paragraphs that contain concrete evidence and examples from your experience, reading, and music listening.

On Music, Culture, and the Human Brain

DAVID HADJU

Music in the Meltdown

A number of authors and critics have discussed the relationship between popular music and culture, positing causal connections (or the lack of causality) between lyrics and violence in the streets, pointing out the *influence of certain recording artists on the political process and examining ways in which the financially impacted music industry reflects broader economic changes in this country. In this article, David Hadju, music critic for the venerable social commentary magazine, New Republic, extends the latter examination by showing how certain types of contemporary popular music have devolved into barely listenable trash, as a conscious means of mirroring the barely tolerable state of today's economy. To these new musical forms Hadju attaches the quaint and not very flattering term "shitgaze." While four-letter words (and, in this case, their eight-letter extensions) rarely find their way into academic discourse and serious journalism, occasionally a kinder and gentler euphemism simply will not suffice, and that, ultimately, is the point of Hadju's article: The financial meltdown in the new millennium is so excrementally disastrous that it takes a certain kind of music, with its descriptive expletive not deleted or softened in any way, to reflect the current situation adequately and accurately.*

When all this is over, the economic crisis will take lasting form in the American consciousness as a video montage. The images are already familiar: traders gaping in horror at the Stock Exchange ... Paulson testifying before Congress ... A foreclosure notice tacked onto a front-porch door ... Obama selling the bailout ... The Chrysler headquarters posted for sale on Craigslist (well, not really, not yet). It is as easy to envision this string of images as it is to conjure a mental highlight reel of the visual iconography of the Great Depression: the Dust Bowl photography of Dorothea Lange and Walker Evans, newsreel clips of bread lines and Hooverville shacks—and all of it set to the sound of Rudy Vallee singing "Brother, Can You Spare a Dime?" What, then, will play on the soundtrack of the montage of the current crisis? What is the music of our meltdown?

Last time around, popular culture moved a bit more slowly than it does in the Tweet era. The Tin Pan Alley composer Jay Gorney and the lyricist Yip Harburg did not write "Brother, Can You Spare a Dime?" until 1931, two years after Black Thursday. The song was not introduced until 1932, when it was inserted into a gently socio-political Broadway revue called *New Americana*, and it was not a hit until Rudy Vallee and Bing Crosby took it on, in shifts of mode for them both. Vallee's and Crosby's records of the same song ended up among the top-ten hits of 1932.

This time, within a few months of the unraveling of Fannie Mae and Freddie Mac, a dozen credible songs have taken up the collapse of the economy or its consequences, and at least twenty lesser efforts have been posted on MySpace and YouTube. "Brother" has a multiplying brood of great-grandchildren, including songs by old rock-and-roll grousers such as Neil Young ("Fork in the Road," from a new CD with the same title, and "Cough Up the Bucks" from that album), quasi-political hip-hop artists such as Young Jeezy ("The Recession," from a CD with that title), less-reactionary country singers such as John Rich ("Shuttin' Detroit Down"), and inveterately cranky indie-rock bands such as The Members ("International Financial Crisis"). Many more songs must be hatching. After all, Neil Young can dominate this terrain for only so long before we hear from Bruce Springsteen, and Young Jeezy cannot lay claim to this (or any) territory for long without an incursion from Kanye West. And where are Ani DiFranco and Billy Bragg when there is a topical song to be written?

Neil Young arrived early by taking short cuts, to use the kind of driving analogy, tossed-off and corny, that is common to the material on *Fork in the Road*, including the economically themed title song. The record is something of a concept album about car love, biotech, and the recession. Hastily composed and recorded with a ragtag little band in the vein of mid-1970s Crazy Horse, the album reaffirms Young's devotion to the old hippie precepts of indeliberation and zeal, simultaneously applied. Most of the songs—such as "Behind the Wheel," "Off the Road," "Hit the Road"—have interchangeable titles, chords, tunes, and words, and the general idea is to pay tribute (occasionally tempered) to those hoary symbols of American freedom and gluttony, heavy vehicles and highways, while advocating the use of biofuels.

Two of the songs deal explicitly, if simplistically, with the meltdown. In the title song, "Fork in the Road," Young sings, in his wonderfully preserved screechy whine, "There's a bailout coming but it's not for me/It's for all those creeps watching tickers on TV." He goes on:

I'm a big rock star
My sales have tanked
But I still got you—thanks
Download this
Sounds like shit

In "Cough Up the Bucks," he sings, at full croak:

Where did all the money go?
Where did all the cash flow?
Where did all the money go?

He makes a good point. The music does sound like shit, although its unabashed shittiness, its rude willingness to go wrong for good reasons—that is, in service to the whims of its creator and the moment of creation—help to give *Fork in the Road* (and much of Young's better work) its bite and its guileless veracity.

Neil Young's positions on the meltdown amount to puzzlement and bereavement. He does not question the primacy of capital in America or the glory of wealth; he wonders only why he isn't as rich as he used to be. In setting these thoughts to music, he is carrying on a tradition begun with the first songs to capture the country's reaction to the Great Depression. One of the biggest hits of 1929 turned out to be Bessie Smith's record of "Nobody Knows You When You're Down and Out," a song composed six years earlier by Jimmie Cox, a second-card singer and comedian in black vaudeville. As Smith sang,

> Once I lived the life of a millionaire
> Spending my money, I didn't care
> I carried my friends out for a good time
> Buying bootleg liquor, champagne and wine
> Then I began to fall so low
> I didn't have a friend and no place to go

The sentiment of "Nobody Knows You When You're Down and Out" is umbrage at betrayal—not only betrayal by the singer's good-time friends, but also betrayal by wealth itself, with its promise to keep good times and friends in ample supply. The song was one of the first major crossover hits, and it has become a standard of Tin Pan Alley-style blues, recorded over the years by every blues-loving singer from Alberta Hunter and Big Joe Williams to Eric von Schmidt and Eric Clapton. Among the songs of the Great Depression, it is immeasurably significant, probably more consequential than "Brother, Can You Spare a Dime?" in that it played a major role in establishing blues, music of the black experience, in parity with white music in America.

Indeed, the lasting musical legacy of the Depression is not polemical songs overtly fixed on economic matters, but songs that express in vivid, idiosyncratic, personal terms the discontent of people with little hope—and the most potent of those songs were black, sung by African Americans or by whites imitating blacks, composed by African Americans or by whites drawing heavily from black music. In the year of the crash, Charlie Patton, one of the early masters of Delta blues, made his first recordings for Paramount, and they sold fairly well; the following year, he had a national hit with "High Water Everywhere," a story-song about the Louisiana flood that suggested the economic storm of the time as well. By 1933, the number-one record of the year was Ethel Waters's recording of "Stormy Weather" (by the blackest of the white Tin Pan Alley composers, Harold Arlen, with lyrics by Ted Koehler, another white writer who had worked on Cotton Club shows), and versions of the same song by Leo Reisman (a white bandleader) and Duke Ellington were numbers eleven and twelve.

Hip-hop, which deals with lingering issues of racial, social, and economic inequity through caricature and overcompensation, infamously reveling in bravura displays of material conquest and in overweening pride in its own infamy, does not do suffering or despair very well. The Southern rapper Young Jeezy, who recorded *The Recession* last year, before Lehman Brothers and Merrill Lynch fell, is atypically tentative on this, his third CD. The music is simple and blunt, built around lo-fi synth effects. The title track opens with a sound collage of overlapping bits from financial news broadcasts—"No one's whispering about the 'R' word anymore"; "The government has failed.… " Young Jeezy enters the track in his usual persona of every nigga, rapping about gas prices and not having enough money to buy a bigger truck. In the concerns of his lyrics, he sounds unnervingly like Neil Young. Then comes the chorus, a set of declarations as simple and blunt as the music:

It's a recession, everybody broke
So I just came back to give everybody hope
Just looking out for folk, a gift and the whole nine
Nah, you don't owe me shit, and you
keep the whole nine

Keep in mind: when read on the page, Young Jeezy's language, like a lot of rapping, appears considerably more stupid than it feels when it is taken in as it is meant to be, as one element in a soundscape of beat, flow, and attitude. Jeezy's take on the recession is elementally optimistic, even boosterish. That positivity is of a piece with Jeezy's vanity. Jeezy makes clear—here and in several other songs on all three of his albums—that he feels a paternal, somewhat demeaning sense of duty to lift his fans' spirits through the "gift" of his attention, and he acts out of a faith in the self-reliance that helped make him rich and famous. As he sings in "My President," another topical song on *The Recession*,

"History, Black history, no president ever did shit for me." Young Jeezy's self-reliance is such that it has no need for Barack Obama.

Over the past several months, the hard times have prompted hip-hop radio stations to rediscover "Hard Times," a Ludacris track from his 2003 album, *Chicken-n-Beer*. It is a loosely woven patchwork song with ragged-edged sections about common struggles of many sorts—a lover departs, the money is low, friends turn away. A plaintive, melancholy song about timeless hardships, its sentiments unspoiled by self-pity, "Hard Times" is a hip-hop inheritor to Charlie Patton's "High Water Everywhere," a piece of twenty-first-century blues.

Wherever one stands on the music of Young Jeezy and Ludacris, one should not confuse them with the various stunt rappers who have released songs about the economic crisis: Neal Fox, who wrote and performed "F**k the Fed," and Michael Adams, who did "I Want My Bailout Money." Both songs are parodies and employ hip-hop for its amenability to caricature; they are the musical equivalent of political cartoons, and what Ludacris is to Charlie Patton, Neal Fox and Michael Adams are to Ray Stevens and Weird Al Yankovic.

Not that there's anything wrong with a good laugh in bad times, of course. An expression of despair is scarcely the only legitimate artistic response to the experience of despair. In fact, this whole business of considering music in the context of economic upheaval grows unmanageable in scale when one considers the value of sheer entertainment as an escape from hardship. During the height of the Depression, in March 1932, Herbert Hoover called a meeting with Rudy Vallee in the White House, at which Hoover told Vallee that if he could "write a song to drive away the Depression," he would "rate a medal." Vallee demurred, instead recording "Brother, Can You Spare a Dime?" While the song became one of the biggest hits of the year, it was not at the top of the list. The number-one song was Cole Porter's silky "Night and Day," in a recording by Fred Astaire, who had sung it that year in Astaire and Rogers' glimmery, vapid farce, *The Gay Divorcee*. The number-two and number-three songs were "All of Me" and "Dinah." In a real sense, every song that provides release during a depressing time is a song of that depression.

On those terms, we could think of any number of contemporary pop hits as meltdown music. The most popular tunes of our day—the Black Eyed Peas' "Boom Boom Pow," which is number one as I write, and Lady Gaga's "Poker Face," which is number two—are dance tracks, social music of physical and emotional release, just as "Night and Day" and "All of Me" were in their time. (This is just a coincidence, and I don't mean to make too much of it, but the biggest hits of the two eras, "Boom Boom Pow" and "Night and Day" have, as the musical hooks of their title phrases, nearly identical three-note figures.) We certainly could think of songs such as "Boom Boom Pow" and "Poker Face" that way; but let's not.

Instead, let us consider a possibility we cannot yet see. If the events of the Great Depression have bearing on our time as precedent, they demonstrate how the collapse of prevailing economic, political, and social structures—the end of a kind of hegemony—cleared the way for historically disenfranchised people, African Americans and others in the underclasses, to give voice to their discontent in creative forms previously held in disrepute. The Depression brought blues to the pop charts and led to the rise of folk and country music. If new forms (musical or otherwise) emerge from the current meltdown, they might well be ones now held in such low esteem that we cannot begin to take them seriously yet. I do not know what they might be.

For informed counsel, I turned to a colleague whose taste I abhor, and he pointed me to a new genre of intolerable noise constructed either electronically, with computers, or with electrified instruments. Its purpose, he said, is to challenge prevailing standards of normalcy by "sounding as awful as possible." Its early advocates have given it a name, derived from the rock genre "shoegaze." It is called "shitgaze." I tend to doubt that it will blossom to become the dominant music of the coming years, though music critics for publications such as the *New Republic* felt the same way about blues a hundred years ago. For now, I am kind of tickled by the idea of shitgaze, as much as I am maddened by the sound of it. Maybe Neil Young is onto something. Perhaps the music appropriate to this shitty time should properly sound like shit.

SUGGESTIONS FOR WRITING

1. Using the format of this article by David Hadju, compose an analytical piece in which you examine the ways in which popular music has reflected a social phenomenon, both historically and in the present. The first step in constructing your essay would be to select a social issue that you know from experience has been reflected in rock and hip-hop music. For instance, toward the end of the George W. Bush presidency, a number of contemporary recording artists began putting

out songs that were highly critical of him—both his personality and his policies; Green Day's single, "American Idiot," is a prime example of this, and that song eventually morphed into a full-blown rock opera in the mold of The Who's "Tommy." You could next examine other contemporary musical treatments of George W. Bush (Were there any positive ones? Probably not, but if so, be sure to include them), and then go back through the history of popular music to examine ways in which popular songs criticized and/or praised the nation's leaders. This is just one suggestion for a topic, but there are innumerable social issues, such as the environment, abortion, war ("What is it good for? Absolutely nothin'!"), and so forth, that would serve as ripe subjects for your expository examination.

2. Critique the central thesis of this essay: that we are living in dire economic times, and that the popular music that most appropriately reflects these times is terrible to the point of being virtually unlistenable. Since a bit of time has elapsed since David Hadju wrote his article, the government has taken steps to remedy this country's (and the world's) economic meltdown. In your opinion, have these steps had any effect on the economy and the general morale of the U.S. populace? If your answer is yes—that is, that things are better than they were when Hadju wrote the article—then has a new subgenre of music arisen that reflects the current hopefulness? If, on the other hand, you think things haven't changed all that much, then construct an essay in which you synthesize a number of examples in the most recent rock and hip-hop releases that confirm and extend the thesis of David Hadju's article.

3. How do you feel about the use of the "S-word" in this article? Why do you think Hadju resorted to a common street epithet in developing his thesis? Why do writing teachers typically instruct students not to drop F-bombs or use other "inappropriate" language in academic discourse—either in writing or in the classroom? Imagine you are writing a letter to the magazine that published this article by David Hadju and that you are responding to another letter to the editor in which an angry reader has criticized the use of vulgarity in a respectable political publication such as the *New Republic*. In your letter, you can either agree with the angry reader and write in support of his or her imagined points, or you can contradict the reader and defend Hadju's use of curse words on whatever grounds you believe to be true and valid. In either case—and when considering your own tone for the letter—feel free either to employ a rigorously academic voice, or to adopt an over-the-top, ranting style of verbal delivery as you make your points. In other words, you are hereby issued creative license to have fun with this.

CARL WILSON

The Trouble with Indie Rock: It's Not Just Race. It's Class

In the contemporary music press, one often encounters heated controversy regarding tastes and/or interpretations in musical trends or productions. For instance, reviewers argue over whether Lady Gaga is relevant or just the latest faddish flash-in-the-pan, whether today's punk is as edgy as the "original" punk of the seventies, or whether every Jack Johnson song sounds exactly the same. The central topic in the following article is a pop musical sub-genre called alternative rock ... one with which most readers of this text will be familiar, containing bands such as Nirvana and R.E.M. at the beginning of the post-punk era, through well-known indie acts of today, including The White Stripes, Modest Mouse, Yeah Yeah Yeahs, and The Strokes. In this piece Carl Wilson, a Toronto-based music critic for the Globe and Mail, *book author and prolific music blogger, argues pointedly against an article by* New Yorker *reviewer Sasha Frere-Jones, who recently condemned independent rock for having lost any semblance of ethnic diversity. Wilson counters Frere-Jones' position by asserting that the problem with today's alternative rock—if there indeed is a problem at all—has to do with issues of class, not ethnicity.*

New Yorker pop critic Sasha Frere-Jones has often indicated boredom and annoyance with a lot of the critically acclaimed, music-blog, and/or NPR-approved "indie rock" of this decade. This week, in an article, a couple of blog entries, and a podcast, he tries to articulate why. His answer? It's not black enough; it lacks "swing, some empty space and palpable bass frequencies"; it doesn't participate lustily in the grand (and problematic) tradition of musical "miscegenation" that's given American music, especially rock 'n' roll, its kick.

To give bite to the accusation, Frere-Jones names a few names, beginning with the Arcade Fire and adding Wilco, the Fiery Furnaces, the Decemberists, the Shins, Sufjan Stevens, Grizzly Bear, Panda Bear, and Devendra Banhart, plus indie-heroes past, Pavement. He contrasts them with the likes of the Clash, Elvis, the Beatles, the Rolling Stones, Led Zeppelin, Cream, Public Image Ltd., Bob Dylan, the Minutemen, Nirvana, and even Grand Funk Railroad as examples of willful, gleeful, racial-sound-barrier-breaching white rockers of yore.

As indicated in his pre-emptive blog post, the piece is a provocation, as is Frere-Jones's M.O., and that is welcome at a time when musical discussion revolves numbingly around which digital-distribution method can be most effectively "monetized." (Current champ: Radiohead.) But many commentators have pointed out his article's basic problems of consistency and accuracy: Frere-Jones' story is that the rise of Pavement as role models and Dr. Dre and Snoop Dogg as rivals in the 1990s marked a quick indie retreat from bluesiness and danceability. Yet the conscious and iconoclastic excision of blues-rock from "underground" rock goes back to the '70s and '80s origins of American punk and especially hardcore, from which indie complicatedly evolved.

While it's possible to cherry-pick exceptions ever since, Frere-Jones does so selectively, overlooking the likes of Royal Trux or the Afghan Whigs in the 1990s, or more recently, the Yeah Yeah Yeahs, Spoon, Battles and the dance-punks LCD Soundsystem, Hot Chip, and Junior Senior, almost all of whom appear on his own best-of-the-year list in progress. Last March, in direct contradiction to what he says in this week's New Yorker essay, Frere-Jones wrote in an LCD Soundsystem review: "About five years ago, indie rockers began to rediscover the pleasures of rhythm." Where are those indie rockers now? Vanished, because they would mess with his thesis. He isn't really talking about all of indie rock, but a folkier subset that's hardly trying to be rock at all. But to say so would be less dramatic.

The article also tends troublingly to reduce "black music" to rhythm and sexuality, and to elide the differences between, say, funk, soul, disco, folk-blues, Caribbean, and African influences in white rock. While he justifiably frames the issue as an American one, at least half of Frere-Jones' lauded precedents are British, a context in which appropriating black American music has vastly different connotations. His lead example, the Arcade Fire, is likewise un-American, hailing from Montreal (one of its leaders, Régine Chassagne, has family roots in Haiti). The piece also switches at its convenience between mainstream rock history and the "underground" genealogy of indie, while never balancing the scales by addressing current hit-making rockers like Fall Out Boy or the White Stripes, who remain heavier on groove.

One could go on playing "gotcha" at the expense of Frere-Jones' intended thrust, which mainly indicates that this piece needed another draft or two. This is odd, because "indie whiteness" is a subject he's been banging on about in many forums for several years. (Frere-Jones is also a sometime white-indie-rocker himself.) His consistent mistake seems to be to talk about musical issues as if they were nearly autonomous from larger social dynamics. It's the blind spot of a genuine music lover, but it grants music culture too much power and assigns it too much blame.

For instance, the separation of racial influences in American music arguably begins with the 1970s demise of Top 40 radio, which coincided with the Black Power movement and the withering of the integrationist ideals of the civil rights era. Frere-Jones nods in this direction when he talks about "political correctness," but he reduces the issue to an "academic" critique rather than a vast shift in racial relations and, more importantly, expectations. The brands of "authenticity" that both punk and hip-hop came to demand, which tended to discourage the cross-pollination and "miscegenation" of musical forms, are in keeping with the identity politics that became dominant in the 1980s as well as the de facto resegregation of black and white communities that began in the Reagan era. This is the counternarrative to the cultural-level "social progress" that Frere-Jones rightly points out, in which explicit racism has retreated and black entertainers have come to dominate the mainstream.

It's not just because Snoop Dogg and Dr. Dre were such great artists that white people were afraid to imitate them—they're no better than John Coltrane, Jimi Hendrix, James Brown, Muddy Waters, and dozens of others whom white artists have happily mimicked in the past. Rather it's that this kind of "theft" became a capital cultural crime, and not just in the academy (how many '90s indie rockers knew by heart the verses in "Fight the Power," where Public Enemy calls Elvis a "straight-up racist, simple and plain"?). If gangsta rap marked a break, it was because hip-hop became coded to reflect the retrenchment of the "Two Americas" and the resultant combative, near-separatist mood among African-Americans. It was deliberately made less assimilable, a development reinforced by the marketplace when white suburban kids turned out to love its more extremist voice.

You could argue that it's always incumbent on the artists to come back swinging by presenting an alternative vision. Some have tried—unfortunately, often in the form of jam bands and rock-rap groups—but the diminished street-level faith in an integrationist future means there's not as much optimism about integrationist music. What's more, racial lines in the United States no longer divide primarily into black and white. When "miscegenation" does happen in music now, it's likely to be more multicultural than in Frere-Jones' formula, as in rainbow-coalition bands such as Antibalas and Ozomatli.

Ultimately, though, the "trouble with indie rock" may have far more to do with another post-Reagan social shift, one with even less upside than the black-white story, and that's the widening gap between rich and poor. There is no question on which side most indie rock falls. It's a cliche to picture indie musicians and fans as well-off "hipsters" busily gentrifying neighborhoods, but compared to previous post-punk generations, the particular kind of indie rock Frere-Jones complains about is more blatantly upper-middle class and liberal-arts-college-based, and less self-aware or politicized about it.

With its true spiritual center in Richard Florida-lauded "creative" college towns such as Portland, Ore., this is the music of young "knowledge workers" in training, and that has sonic consequences: Rather than body-centered, it is bookish and nerdy; rather than being instrumentally or vocally virtuosic, it shows off its chops via its range of allusions and high concepts with the kind of fluency both postmodern pop culture and higher education teach its listeners to admire. (Many rap MCs juggle symbologies just as deftly, but it's seldom their main point.) This doesn't make coffeehouse-indie shallow, but it can result in something more akin to the 1960s folk revival, with fretful collegiate intellectuals in a Cuban Missile Crisis mood, seeking purity and depth in antiquarian music and escapist spirituality. Not exactly a recipe for a booty-shaking party. While this scene can embrace some fascinating hermetic weirdos such as Joanna Newsom or Panda Bear, it's also prone to producing fine-arts-grad poseurs such as the Decemberists and poor-little-rich-boy-or-girl singer songwriters who might as well be James Taylor. This year even saw several indie bands playing in "Pops" concerts at summer symphony programs; that's no sin (and good for the symphonies), but it's about as class-demarcated as it gets.

Among at least a subset of (the younger) musicians and fans, this class separation has made indie more openly snobbish and narrow-minded. In the darkest interpretation, one could look at the split between a harmony-and-lyrics-oriented indie field and a rhythm-and-dance-specialized rap/R&B scene as mirroring the developing global split between an internationalist, educated comprador class (in which musically, one week Berlin is hot, the next Sweden, the next Canada, the next Brazil) and a far less mobile, menial-labor market (consider the more confining, though often musically exciting, regionalism that Frere-Jones outlines in hip-hop). The elite status and media sway that indie rock enjoys, disproportionate to its popularity, is one reason the cultural politics of indie musicians and fans require discussion in the first place, a point I wish Frere-Jones had clarified in *The New Yorker*; perhaps in that context it goes without saying.

The profile of this university demographic often includes a sojourn in extended adolescence, comprising graduate degrees, internships, foreign jaunts, and so on, which easily can last until their early 30s. Unlike in the early 1990s, when this was perceived as a form of generational exclusion and protested in "slacker"/grunge music, it's now been normalized as a passage to later-life career success. Its musical consequences might include an open but less urgent expression of sexuality, or else a leaning to the twee, sexless, childhood nostalgia that many older critics (including both Frere-Jones and me) find puzzling and irritating. Female and queer artists still have pressing sexual issues and identities to explore and celebrate, but the straight boys often seem to fall back on performing their haplessness and hyper-sensitivity. (Pity the indie-rock girlfriend.)

Yet this is a problem having to do with the muddled state of white masculinity today, and it's not soluble by imitating some image of black male sexuality (which, as hip-hop and R&B amply demonstrate, is dealing with its own crises). Are we supposed to long for the days when Zeppelin and the Stones fetishized fantasies of black manhood, in part as a cover for misogyny? If forced to choose between tolerating some boringly undersexed rock music and reviving the, er, "vigorous" sexual politics of cock rock, I'll take the boring rock, thanks—for now.

If class, at least as much as race, is the elephant in this room, one of the more encouraging signals lately might be the recent mania for Bruce Springsteen—as if a dim memory suddenly has surfaced that white working-class culture once had a kind of significant berth in rock 'n' roll, too. (It's now moved to Nashville.) I was unexpectedly moved by the video of Win and Régine from the Arcade Fire playing "Keep the Car Running" (Frere-Jones' No. 15 song of the year so far) live with the Boss onstage Sunday in Ottawa. The performance itself aside, their presence in front of an arena audience that mostly had no idea who the hell they were shows the chutzpah it takes to resist niche-market fragmentation. (And sure, I'd be at least as happy if they'd been doing it with Stevie Wonder, and even more if they were sharing the stage with Dr. Dre.)

My armchair sociology may be as reductive as Frere-Jones' potted rock history, but the point is that the problem of style segregation can't be solved by calling upon Sufjan Stevens to funk up his rhythm section. I'm as much a devotee of genre-mixing as Frere-Jones, when it works (I've even used the loaded term "miscegenation" in articles for years), but I've noticed that when indie musicians do grapple with hip-hop rhythms, using their own voices and perspectives (my friends in Ninja High School in Toronto, for instance), they're usually lambasted by critics who fancy themselves arbiters of realness for being an insulting joke. The culture-crossing inhibitions exist for reasons beyond mere timidity, and snorting "get over it" is not enough.

The impetus may have to come from the currently dominant side of the pop market—and increasingly that is what we're seeing. Kanye West doesn't much care about the race of the people he samples, while Justin Timberlake cares very much what race his producer is (African-American, please), and OutKast and Gnarls Barkley play teasing, Prince-like crossover games. If it's going to be re-established that such moves are legit, it will happen on the charts for a while before the more cautious and self-conscious rock-in-decline types feel free to do it too. Which, as a turnabout, seems rather like fair play.

SUGGESTIONS FOR WRITING

1. Write an argumentative essay in which you summarize Carl Wilson's thematic points in this article. Having listed and explicated the author's main thematic threads, attempt to articulate your own opinions about the current state of the independent rock genre. How do you feel about the current state of rock music, assuming that you are familiar with the bands being discussed here? Do you agree that deficiencies exist in rock music today that did not exist a decade or three ago? Do you find it natural and/or worthwhile to put popular music into sub-classifications and then to compare the merits and/or drawbacks of each? Whatever your answer to such questions, formulate a thesis that asserts your own position in this discussion, and then argue that point, using evidence from your extensive knowledge of popular music.

2. Using Wilson's article as a model, assume the role of a music-criticism blogger and write a response to a journalistic music review on a piece of music with which you are very familiar—perhaps a new album by one of your favorite (or most despised) artists. To find such a review, you might do a Google search on the Web using the keywords "popular music review" or some combination of like descriptors, or you might go to the local bookstore or your library's unbound periodicals section, and find a print review in such magazines as *Rolling Stone* or *The Source*,

the latter focusing primarily on hip-hop music and containing many excellent reviews. Ideally, you will find a review that contains some points to which you take exception, just as Carl Wilson did in his response to the Frere-Jones piece. As you construct your bloglike essay, be sure to comment on the assertions in the article that you find valid and well supported before you move into your points of difference and criticism. However, it is the latter group of arguments that will ultimately form the thesis—and probably the title—of your essay, just as Wilson did in the above blog.

3. Write a research essay in which you examine the current state of a subgenre of music *other* than independent rock. You might focus on punk, or electronica, or trance, or thrash metal, or even jazz or classical music. Whatever genre you choose, it would probably be a good idea to pick something with which you are quite familiar or something you would like to learn more about. In any case, your essay should synthesize some source material regarding the historical origins of the subgenre under examination, along with a description of some of the foremost proponents and practitioners of the music today. Your concluding section will move from this objective description of the current state of this kind of music to a more subjective analysis and/or criticism of it. Is this subgenre alive and well today, or has it become anemic and less vital for some reason that you can identify? If you find the latter to be the case, then conclude your essay with some prescriptions for improving this music as we move deeper into the new millennium.

OLIVER SACKS

Brainworms, Sticky Music, and Catchy Tunes

When we think of popular music, our thoughts typically turn to the latest dance floor megahit by Shakira or any of the literally thousands of lyrical productions by Lil Wayne. However, there is another type of music that is every bit as popular as your average song on the Billboard Top 100 chart—and in fact may surpass any of those songs in terms of sheer numbers and their effect on listeners: namely, the advertising jingle. The "Mad Men" who produce the songs that accompany sales pitches on TV, radio, and the Web, are really not "mad" at all; in many cases they are creative geniuses and skillful psychologists, creating lyrics and melodies that lodge themselves tenaciously in listeners' brains, so that when we are walking down supermarket aisles, we will remember the Oscar Meyer Wiener song[2] and choose that brand-name product over the less expensive generic weenie. In the following essay, Oliver Sacks, a practicing physician and author of ten best-selling books on a variety of fascinating medical-related topics—including the book on which the movie Awakenings *was based—examines the effect of catchy jingles on the human brain. To these melodies from advertisements, along with the repetitive hooks from popular songs and scraps of melody from long-forgotten songs from childhood or adolescence, he attaches the label "brainworms" because they burrow their way like organic parasites into our consciousness and take up residence there for a while, sometimes playing over and over for an hour and sometimes—maddeningly for certain individuals with brain-related medical conditions—for days or much longer. Sacks concludes the article by noting that, as we become increasingly attached to our iPods and other omnipresent listening devices, our susceptibility to a mass infestation by brainworms will undoubtedly increase, with all of us moving through the world playing private concerts in our highly impressionable noggins.*

Music is playing inside my head
Over and over and over again
. . . There's no end . . .

CAROLE KING

Sometimes normal musical imagery crosses a line and becomes, so to speak, pathological, as when a certain fragment of music repeats itself incessantly, sometimes maddeningly, for days on end. These repetitions—often a short, well-defined phrase or theme of three or four bars—are apt to go on for hours or days, circling in the mind, before fading away. This endless repetition and the fact that the music in question may be irrelevant or trivial, not to one's taste, or even hateful, suggest a coercive process, that the music has entered and subverted a part of the brain, forcing it to fire repetitively and autonomously (as may happen with a tic or a seizure).

---

[2] http://www.youtube.com/watch?v=aNddW2xmZp8

Many people are set off by the theme music of a film or television show or an advertisement. This is not coincidental, for such music is designed, in the terms of the music industry, to "hook" the listener, to be "catchy" or "sticky," to bore its way, like an earwig, into the ear or mind; hence the term "earworms"—though one might be inclined to call them "brainworms" instead. (One newsmagazine, in 1987, defined them, half facetiously, as "cognitively infectious musical agents.")

A friend of mine, Nick Younes, described to me how he had been fixated on the song "Love and Marriage," a tune written by James Van Heusen.[1] A single hearing of this song—a Frank Sinatra rendition used as the theme song of the television show *Married . . . with Children*— was enough to hook Nick. He "got trapped inside the tempo of the song," and it ran in his mind almost constantly for ten days. With incessant repetition, it soon lost its charm, its lilt, its musicality, and its meaning. It interfered with his schoolwork, his thinking, his peace of mind, his sleep. He tried to stop it in a number of ways, all to no avail: "I jumped up and down. I counted to a hundred. I splashed water on my face. I tried talking loudly to myself, plugging my ears." Finally it faded away—but as he told me this story, it returned and went on to haunt him again for several hours.[2]

---

[1] An earlier generation will remember the tune of "Love and Marriage" as the Campbell's soup advertisement "Soup and Sandwich." Van Heusen was a master of the catchy tune and wrote dozens of [literally] unforgettable songs—including "High Hopes," "Only the Lonely," and "Come Fly with Me"—for Bing Crosby, Frank Sinatra, and others. Many of these have been adapted for television or advertising theme songs.

[2] Since the original publication of *Musicophilia*, many people have written to me about ways of dealing with a brainworm—such as consciously singing or playing it to the end of the song, so that it is no longer a fragment circling round and round, incapable of resolution; or displacing it by singing or listening to another tune (though this may only become another brainworm in turn).

Musical imagery, especially if it is repetitive and intrusive, may have a motor component, a subvocal "humming" or singing of which the person may be unaware, but which still may exact a toll. "At the end of a bad music-loop day," wrote one correspondent, "my throat is as uncomfortable as it might have been had I sung all day." David Wise, another correspondent, found that using progressive relaxation techniques to relax the "muscular correlates to the hearing of music involving the tightening and movement of the speech apparatus . . . associated with auditory thinking" was efficacious in stopping annoying brainworms. While some of these methods seem to work for some people, most others have found, like Nick Younes, no cure.

Though the term "earworm" was first used in the 1980s (as a literal translation of the German *Ohrwurm*), the concept is far from new.[3] Nicolas Slonimsky, a composer and musicologist, was deliberately inventing musical forms or phrases that could hook the mind and force it to mimicry and repetition, as early as the 1920s. And in 1876, Mark Twain wrote a short story ("A Literary Nightmare," subsequently retitled "Punch, Brothers, Punch!") in which the narrator is rendered helpless after encountering some "jingling rhymes":

> *They took instant and entire possession of me. All through breakfast they went waltzing through my brain. . . . I fought hard for an hour, but it was useless. My head kept humming. . . . I drifted downtown, and presently discovered that my feet were keeping time to that relentless jingle. . . . [I] jingled all through the evening, went to bed, rolled, tossed, and jingled all night long.*

Two days later, the narrator meets an old friend, a pastor, and inadvertently "infects" him with the jingle; the pastor, in turn, inadvertently infects his entire congregation.

What is happening, psychologically and neurologically, when a tune or a jingle takes possession of one like this? What are the characteristics that make a tune or a song "dangerous" or "infectious" in this way? Is it some oddity of sound, of timbre or rhythm or melody? Is it repetition? Or is it arousal of special emotional resonances or associations?

My own earliest brainworms can be reactivated by the act of thinking about them, even though they go back more than sixty years. Many of them seemed to have a very distinctive musical shape, a tonal or melodic oddness that may have played a part in imprinting them on my mind. And they had meaning and emotion, too, for they were usually Jewish songs and litanies associated with a sense of heritage and

---

[3] Jeremy Scratcherd, a scholarly musician who has studied the folk genres of Northumberland and Scotland, informs me that

> Examination of early folk music manuscripts reveals many examples of various tunes to which have been attributed the title "The piper's maggot." These were perceived to be tunes which got into the musician's head to irritate and gnaw at the sufferer—like a maggot in a decaying apple. There is one such tune in the [1888] *Northumbrian Minstrelsy*. . . . The earliest collection of pipe music was penned in 1733 by another Northumbrian, William Dixon, and this along with other Scottish collections suggests that the "maggot" most probably appeared in the early 18th century. Interesting that despite the disparity of time the metaphor has remained much the same!

history, a feeling of family warmth and togetherness. One favorite song, sung after the meal on Seder nights, was "Had Gadya" (Aramaic for "one little goat"). This was an accumulating and repetitive song, and one that must have been sung (in its Hebrew version) many times in our Orthodox household. The additions, which became longer and longer with each verse, were sung with a mournful emphasis ending with a plaintive fourth. This little phrase of six notes in a minor key would be sung (I counted!) forty-six times in the course of the song, and this repetition hammered it into my head. It would haunt me and pop into my mind dozens of times a day throughout the eight days of Passover, then slowly diminish until the next year. Did the qualities of repetition and simplicity or that odd, incongruous fourth perhaps act as neural facilitators, setting up a circuit (for it felt like this) that reexcited itself automatically? Or did the grim humor of the song or its solemn, liturgical context play a significant part, too?

Yet it seems to make little difference whether catchy songs have lyrics or not—the wordless themes of *Mission: Impossible* or Beethoven's Fifth can be just as irresistible as an advertising jingle in which the words are almost inseparable from the music (as in Alka-Seltzer's "Plop, plop, fizz, fizz" or Kit Kat's "Gimme a break, gimme a break . . .").

For those with certain neurological conditions, brainworms or allied phenomena—the echoic or automatic or compulsive repetition of tones or words—may take on additional force. Rose R., one of the postencephalitic parkinsonian patients I described in *Awakenings*, told me how during her frozen states she had often been "confined," as she put it, in "a musical paddock"—seven pairs of notes (the fourteen notes of "Povero Rigoletto") which would repeat themselves irresistibly in her mind. She also spoke of these forming "a musical quadrangle" whose four sides she would have to perambulate, mentally, endlessly. This might go on for hours on end, and did so at intervals throughout the entire forty-three years of her illness, prior to her being "awakened" by L-dopa.

Milder forms of this may occur in ordinary Parkinson's disease. One correspondent described how, as she became parkinsonian, she became subject to "repetitive, irritating little melodies or rhythms" in her head, to which she "compulsively" moved her fingers and toes. (Fortunately, this woman, a gifted musician with relatively mild parkinsonism, could usually "turn these melodies into Bach and Mozart" and play them mentally to completion, transforming them from brainworms to the sort of healthy musical imagery she had enjoyed prior to the parkinsonism.)

The phenomenon of brainworms seems similar, too, to the way in which people with autism or Tourette's syndrome or obsessive-compulsive disorder may become hooked by a sound or a word or a noise and repeat it, or echo it, aloud or to themselves, for weeks at a time. This was very striking with Carl Bennett, the surgeon with Tourette's syndrome whom I described in *An Anthropologist on Mars*. "One cannot always find sense in these words," he said. "Often it is just the sound that attracts me. Any odd sound, any odd name, may start repeating itself, get me going. I get hung up with a word for two or three months. Then, one morning, it's gone, and there's another one in its place." But while the involuntary repetition of movements, sounds, or words tends to occur in people with Tourette's or OCD or damage to the frontal lobes of the brain, the automatic or compulsive internal repetition of musical phrases is almost universal—the clearest sign of the overwhelming, and at times helpless, sensitivity of our brains to music.

There may be a continuum here between the pathological and the normal, for while brainworms may appear suddenly, fullblown, taking instant and entire possession of one, they may also develop by a sort of contraction, from previously normal musical imagery. I have lately been enjoying mental replays of Beethoven's Third and Fourth Piano Concertos, as recorded by Leon Fleisher in the 1960s. These "replays" tend to last ten or fifteen minutes and to consist of entire movements. They come, unbidden but always welcome, two or three times a day. But on one very tense and insomniac night, they changed character, so that I heard only a single rapid run on the piano (near the beginning of the Third Piano Concerto), lasting ten or fifteen seconds and repeated hundreds of times. It was as if the music was now trapped in a sort of loop, a tight neural circuit from which it could not escape. Towards morning, mercifully, the looping ceased, and I was able to enjoy entire movements once again.[4]

Brainworms are usually stereotyped and invariant in character. They tend to have a certain life expectancy, going full blast for hours or days and then dying away, apart from occasional afterspurts. But even

---

[4] The duration of such loops is generally about fifteen to twenty seconds, and this is similar to the duration of the visual loops or cycles which occur in a rare condition called palinopsia, where a short scene—a person walking across a room, for example, seen a few seconds before—may be repeated before the inner eye again and again. That a similar periodicity of cycling occurs in both visual and auditory realms suggests that some physiological constant, perhaps related to working memory, may underlie both.

when they have apparently faded, they tend to lie in wait; a heightened sensitivity remains, so that a noise, an association, a reference to them is apt to set them off again, sometimes years later. And they are nearly always fragmentary. These are all qualities that epileptologists might find familiar, for they are strongly reminiscent of the behavior of a small, sudden-onset seizure focus, erupting and convulsing, then subsiding, but always ready to reignite.

Certain drugs seem to exacerbate earworms. One composer and music teacher wrote to me that when she was put on lamotrigine for a mild bipolar disorder, she developed a severe, at times intolerable increase in earworms. After she discovered an article (by David Kemp et al.) about the increase of intrusive, repetitive musical phrases (as well as verbal phrases or numerical repetitions) associated with lamotrigine, she stopped the medication (under her physician's supervision). Her earworms subsided somewhat but have remained at a much higher level than before. She does not know whether they will ever return to their original, moderate level: "I worry," she wrote, "that somehow these pathways in my brain have become so potentiated that I will be having these earworms for the rest of my life."

Some of my correspondents compare brainworms to visual afterimages, and as someone who is prone to both, I feel their similarity, too. (We are using "afterimage" in a special sense here, to denote a much more prolonged effect than the fleeting afterimages we all have for a few seconds following, for instance, exposure to a bright light.) After reading EEGs intently for several hours, I may have to stop because I start to see EEG squiggles all over the walls and ceilings. After driving all day, I may see fields and hedgerows and trees moving past me in a steady stream, keeping me awake at night. After a day on a boat, I feel the rocking for hours after I am back on dry land. And astronauts, returning from a week spent in the near-zero-gravity conditions of space, need several days to regain their "earth legs" once again. All of these are simple sensory effects, persistent activations in low-level sensory systems, due to sensory overstimulation. Brainworms, by contrast, are perceptual constructions, created at a much higher level in the brain. And yet both reflect the fact that certain stimuli, from EEG lines to music to obsessive thoughts, can set off persistent activities in the brain.

There are attributes of musical imagery and musical memory that have no equivalents in the visual sphere, and this may cast light on the fundamentally different way in which the brain treats music and vision.⁵ This peculiarity of music may arise in part because we have to *construct* a visual world for ourselves, and a selective and personal character therefore infuses our visual memories from the start—whereas we are given pieces of music already constructed. A visual or social scene can be constructed or reconstructed in a hundred different ways, but the recall of a musical piece has to be close to the original. We do, of course, listen selectively, with differing interpretations and emotions, but the basic musical characteristics of a piece—its tempo, its rhythm, its melodic contours, even its timbre and pitch—tend to be preserved with remarkable accuracy.

It is this fidelity—this almost defenseless engraving of music on the brain—which plays a crucial part in predisposing us to certain excesses, or pathologies, of musical imagery and memory, excesses that may even occur in relatively unmusical people.

There are, of course, inherent tendencies to repetition in music itself. Our poetry, our ballads, our songs are full of repetition. Every piece of classical music has its repeat marks or variations on a theme, and our greatest composers are masters of repetition; nursery rhymes and the little chants and songs we use to teach young children have choruses and refrains. We are attracted to repetition, even as adults; we want the stimulus and the reward again and again, and in music we get it. Perhaps, therefore, we should not be surprised, should not complain if the balance sometimes shifts too far and our musical sensitivity becomes a vulnerability.

Is it possible that earworms are, to some extent, a modern phenomenon, at least a phenomenon not only more clearly recognized, but vastly more common now than ever before? Although earworms have no doubt existed since our forebears first blew tunes on bone flutes or

---

⁵ And yet an earworm may also, more rarely, include a visual aspect, especially for those musicians who automatically visualize a score as they are hearing or imagining music. One of my correspondents, a French horn player, finds that when her brain is occupied by a brainworm,

> reading, writing, and doing spatial tasks like arithmetic are all disturbed by it. My brain seems to be pretty well taken up with processing the [brainworm] in various ways, mainly spatial and kinesthetic: I ponder the relative sizes of the intervals between the notes, I see them laid out in space, I consider the layout of the harmonic structure that they are a part of, I feel the fingerings in my hand, and the muscular movements required to play them, although I don't actually act these out. It's not a particularly intellectual activity; it's rather careless and I don't put any intentional effort into it; it just happens. . . .
>
> I should mention that these unbidden [brainworms] never interfere with physical activity or with activities that don't require visual thought, like engaging in normal conversation.

beat tattoos on fallen logs, it is significant that the term has come into common use only in the past few decades.[6] When Mark Twain was writing in the 1870s, there was plenty of music to be had, but it was not ubiquitous. One had to seek out other people to hear (and participate in) singing—at church, family gatherings, parties. To hear instrumental music, unless one had a piano or other instrument at home, one would have to go to church or to a concert. With recording and broadcasting and films, all this changed radically. Suddenly music was everywhere for the asking, and this has increased by orders of magnitude in the last couple of decades, so that we are now enveloped by a ceaseless musical bombardment whether we want it or not.

Half of us are plugged into iPods, immersed in daylong concerts of our own choosing, virtually oblivious to the environment—and for those who are not plugged in, there is nonstop music, unavoidable and often of deafening intensity, in restaurants, bars, shops, and gyms. This barrage of music puts a certain strain on our exquisitely sensitive auditory systems, which cannot be overloaded without dire consequences. One such consequence is the ever-increasing prevalence of serious hearing loss, even among young people, and particularly among musicians. Another is the omnipresence of annoyingly catchy tunes, the brainworms that arrive unbidden and leave only in their own time—catchy tunes that may, in fact, be nothing more than advertisements for toothpaste but are, neurologically, completely irresistible.

SUGGESTIONS FOR WRITING

1. Creative nonfiction is a prose subgenre in which the writer uses the first-person "I" perspective to reflect on an event in his or her recent or long-term memory and tells an interesting story about that event, perhaps expanding philosophically a bit to draw general conclusions from personal experience. In this kind of writing, the story always

---

[6] It may be that brainworms, even if maladaptive in our own music-saturated modern culture, stem from an adaptation that was crucial in earlier hunter-gatherer days: replaying the sounds of animals moving or other significant sounds again and again, until their recognition was assured—as one correspondent, Alan Geist, has suggested to me:

> I discovered, by accident, that after five or six continuous days in the woods without hearing any music of any kind, I spontaneously start replaying the sounds that I hear around me, mainly birds. The local wildlife becomes "the song stuck in my head." . . . [Perhaps in more primitive times] a traveling human could more readily recognize familiar areas by adding his memory of sounds to the visual clues that told him where he was. . . . And by rehearsing those sounds, he was more likely to commit them to long-term memory.

comes first, and in that way such pieces resemble fictional short stories you may have read—except that, in the case of creative nonfiction, the stories are true. For the purposes of this assignment, write a creative nonfiction personal essay in which you examine a musical brainworm of your own recollection. It might be the refrain from a song you heard this morning, it might be an advertising jingle from a cartoon show in your childhood, or it might be a television show's theme song, for several example. Whatever the musical origin of the brainworm, describe it in as much vivid detail as you can manage, describing the melody itself (and any accompanying lyrics), recounting when, where, and how it wormed its way into your memory, its emotional effect on you (infuriating? calming? amusing?), and its ultimate disappearance into the background white noise of your mind.

2. Expanding on the assignment in Question 1 above, do some prewriting in which you bring to mind as many specific instances as you can of sticky melodies worming their way into your consciousness throughout the entire arc of your personal experience. Make a list of five or six such brainworms, and arrange your list chronologically. In an extended personal analytical essay, describe each of these instances of the insidious brainworm phenomenon in detail as you did in Question 1, and then—and most importantly—extrapolate from each instance to comment on the ways in which these looping scraps of music might serve as metaphorical signposts for broader changes in your life, your social circle, and U.S. popular culture generally.

3. Using Sacks' technically but nevertheless popularly accessible discussion of brainworms as a model, write a research-based essay in which you examine the medical and/or physical ramifications of a different physical phenomenon. For example, a recent issue within the audiophile community is the effect of listening to iPods and other personal music devices on long-term hearing health, as mentioned at the beginning of this chapter on music in reference to Snoop Dogg's new headphone model. Using the Web as a source, summarize the evidence (or lack thereof) regarding the dangers (or lack thereof, again) of listening to music through earbuds or headphones for long periods and/or at high volumes, and then arrive at a thesis in which you assert that such listening does (or does not) endanger individual listeners' hearing in the long term. Of course, the earbud/hearing loss connection is only one example of a topic for this essay assignment; feel free to come up with a topic that interests you even more, and perform the same kind of analysis on it.

CHAPTER 4

Advertising

ADVERTISEMENTS PROVIDE AN EXCELLENT STARTING POINT for an analysis of popular U.S. culture. First of all, they are ubiquitous—not quite in the air we breathe and the water we drink, but pretty much everywhere else: on billboards, Web sites, newspapers and magazines, radio, and television. If you consider logos to be mini-advertisements (think Nike swoosh), then many of the clothes you wear and the products you buy turn you into something of a walking display case for a range of companies.

In addition to being easily (perhaps too easily) accessible, ads are ripe for analysis in the sense that they're relatively finite, self-contained objects in which companies have nevertheless invested a great deal of time and money. Nothing in an ad is there by mistake; every detail is carefully chosen, every word carefully selected, every image carefully arranged. Advertisers know that readers usually spend only a few seconds glancing at ads as they page through a magazine; we drive quickly past billboards and use TV commercial minutes to grab food from the fridge. In those seconds that the advertisers have our attention, they need to make as strong a pitch as possible. Analyzing an ad is essentially speculating about each of the choices made by the ad designers when creating their pitch. In readings in this chapter, you will see more detailed and complete analyses of ads that can serve as models for your own interpretations.

A final reason why advertisements constitute such a rich and revealing facet of popular culture is that they encode many of our most crucial values and beliefs—both individual and cultural. Advertising agencies spend a great deal of time and money trying to understand the complex psychodynamics of their target audiences and then tailoring ads to appeal to those audiences. Even the simplest and most seemingly direct advertisements still carry subtly powerful messages—about appropriate modes of behavior, standards of beauty and success, gender roles, and a variety of other markers for normalcy and status. In tailoring ads to appeal both to basic human impulses and to more culturally conditioned attitudes, they also ultimately reinforce and even engender such impulses and attitudes. So, although many advertisements seem to be thoroughly innocuous and unimportant, the argument of many pop culture critics is that advertisements have quite an influence— perhaps all the more so because we think they're so bland and harmless.

Several readings in this chapter explain in further detail the ways in which we can be manipulated by advertising. Jib Fowles, for example, points out a variety of strategies advertisements use to appeal to our emotions, even though we may think we are making product choices using our intellects. Other readings focus on the complex relationship between advertising and information. John Calfee argues that, even as advertisements try to persuade consumers to buy certain products, they convey valuable information on a range of subjects; he looks in particular at how ads for food and cigarettes have helped to educate consumers about the health-related consequences of the products they use. Mark Penn deals with a different aspect of the relationship between advertising and information by focusing on how people have begun to educate themselves prior to making purchases; the vast amount of information available on the Web diminishes the power of advertisements, as consumer reviews and other informative sites enable us to learn about products from sources that aren't ultimately trying to persuade us to buy. Another interesting way to think about advertising and information is forwarded by Stephen Baker, who describes current efforts by retailers and marketing firms to collect information about consumers so as to target ads and sell products more effectively. With data about purchases we have already made, retailers can make increasingly accurate educated guesses about what we might buy in the future—and can then find ways to make it much more convenient for us to buy that product in *their* store rather than elsewhere. Taken together, then, these four articles reveal a range of ways to study advertising and analyze its cultural relevance.

The chapter concludes with a pair of readings that explore the phenomenon of brands and branding. Brands continue the work of advertising by keeping products as close as they can to the forefront of our consciousness. College football teams compete in the FedEx Orange Bowl and the AT&T Cotton Bowl; men and women have Nike swooshes tattooed on their bodies; we ask for a Kleenex rather than a tissue when we sneeze. This is all evidence of what Naomi Klein describes in the first reading as "an era in which people are brands and brands are culture." Branding is about promoting a product by associating it with positive messages and social connections that carry through in multiple aspects of our lives. However, James Surowiecki suggests in the final article in this chapter that brands—and advertising as a whole—may be in a period of decline, that consumers don't have the same degree of brand loyalty as they used to. Recalling Penn's profile of the "new info shopper," Surowiecki argues that the plethora of information available to consumers, along with healthy competition and innovation, minimize the amount of influence that advertisements and brands have on us.

But even if we accept Surowiecki's argument that advertising is in decline, it's still a crucial element of contemporary society: surrounding us in our daily lives, influencing our behavior and attitudes, and holding up a sometimes uncannily accurate, sometimes intriguingly distorted mirror of our culture.

JIB FOWLES

Advertising's Fifteen Basic Appeals

In the following article, Jib Fowles looks at how advertisements work by examining the emotional, subrational appeals that they employ. We are confronted daily by hundreds of ads, only a few of which actually attract our attention. Those few do so, according to Fowles, through "something primary and primitive, an emotional appeal, that in effect is the thin edge of the wedge, trying to find its way into a mind." Drawing on research done by the psychologist Henry A. Murray, Fowles describes 15 emotional appeals or wedges that advertisements exploit.

Emotional Appeals

The nature of effective advertisements was recognized full well by the late media philosopher Marshall McLuhan. In his *Understanding Media*, the first sentence of the section on advertising reads, "The continuous pressure is to create ads more and more in the image of audience motives and desires."

By giving form to people's deep-lying desires, and picturing states of being that individuals privately yearn for, advertisers have the best chance of arresting attention and affecting communication. And that is the immediate goal of advertising: to tug at our psychological shirt sleeves and slow us down long enough for a word or two about whatever is being sold. We glance at a picture of a solitary rancher at work, and "Marlboro" slips into our minds.

Advertisers (I'm using the term as a shorthand for both the products' manufacturers, who bring the ambition and money to the process, and the advertising agencies, who supply the know-how) are ever more compelled to invoke consumers' drives and longings; this is the "continuous pressure" McLuhan refers to. Over the past century, the American marketplace has grown increasingly congested as more and more products have entered into the frenzied competition after the public's dollars. The economies of other nations are quieter than ours since the volume of goods being hawked does not so greatly exceed demand. In some economies, consumer wares are scarce enough that no advertising at all is necessary. But in the United States, we go to the other extreme. In order to stay in business, an advertiser must strive to cut through the considerable commercial hubbub by any means available—including the emotional appeals that some observers have held to be abhorrent and underhanded.

The use of subconscious appeals is a comment not only on conditions among sellers. As time has gone by, buyers have become stoutly resistant to advertisements. We live in a blizzard of these messages and have learned to turn up our collars and ward off most of them. A study done a few years ago at Harvard University's Graduate School of Business Administration ventured that the average American is exposed to some 500 ads daily from television, newspapers, magazines, radio, billboards, direct mail, and so on. If for no other reason than to preserve one's sanity, a filter must be developed in every mind to lower the number of ads a person is actually aware of—a number this particular study estimated at about seventy-five ads per day. (Of these, only twelve typically produced a reaction—nine positive and three negative, on the average.) To be among the few messages that do manage to gain access to minds, advertisers must be strategic, perhaps even a little underhanded at times.

There are assumptions about personality underlying advertisers' efforts to communicate via emotional appeals, and while these assumptions have stood the test of time, they still deserve to be aired. Human beings, it is presumed, walk around with a variety of unfulfilled urges and motives swirling in the bottom half of their minds. Lusts, ambitions, tendernesses, vulnerabilities—they are constantly bubbling up, seeking resolution. These mental forces energize people, but they are too crude and irregular to be given excessive play in the real world. They must be capped with the competent, sensible behavior that permits individuals to get along well in society. However, this upper layer of mental activity, shot through with caution and rationality, is not receptive to advertising's pitches. Advertisers want to circumvent this shell of consciousness if they can, and latch on to one of the lurching, subconscious drives.

In effect, advertisers over the years have blindly felt their way around the underside of the American psyche, and by trial and error have discovered the softest points of entree, the places where their messages have the greatest likelihood of getting by consumers' defenses. As McLuhan says elsewhere, "Gouging away at the surface of public sales resistance, the ad men are constantly breaking through into the *Alice in Wonderland* territory behind the looking glass, which is the world of subrational impulses and appetites."

An advertisement communicates by making use of a specially selected image (of a supine female, say, or a curly-haired child, or a celebrity) which is designed to stimulate "subrational impulses and desires" even when they are at ebb, even if they are unacknowledged by their possessor. Some few ads have their emotional appeal in the text, but for the greater number by far the appeal is contained in the artwork. This makes sense, since visual communication better suits more primal levels of the brain. If the viewer of an advertisement actually has the importuned motive, and if the appeal is sufficiently well fashioned to call it up, then the person can be hooked. The product in the ad may then appear to take on the semblance of gratification for the summoned motive. Many ads seem to be saying, "If you have this need, then this product will help satisfy it." It is a primitive equation, but not an ineffective one for selling.

Thus, most advertisements appearing in national media can be understood as having two orders of content. The first is the appeal to deep-running drives in the minds of consumers. The second is information regarding the good[s] or service being sold: its name, its manufacturer, its picture, its packaging, its objective attributes, its functions. For example, the reader of a brassiere advertisement sees a partially undraped but blandly unperturbed woman standing in an otherwise commonplace public setting, and may experience certain sensations; the reader also sees the name "Maidenform," a particular brassiere style, and, in tiny print, words about the material, colors, price. Or, the viewer of a television commercial sees a demonstration with four small boxes labeled 650, 650, 650, and 800; something in the viewer's mind catches hold of this, as trivial as thoughtful consideration might reveal it to be. The viewer is also exposed to the name "Anacin," its bottle, and its purpose.

Sometimes there is an apparently logical link between an ad's emotional appeal and its product information. It does not violate common sense that Cadillac automobiles be photographed at country clubs, or that Japan Air Lines be associated with Orientalia. But there is no real need for the linkage to have a bit of reason behind it. Is there anything inherent to the connection between Salem cigarettes and mountains, Coke and a smile, Miller Beer and comradeship? The link being forged in minds between product and appeal is a pre-logical one.

People involved in the advertising industry do not necessarily talk in the terms being used here. They are stationed at the sending end of this communications channel, and may think they are up to any number of things—Unique Selling Propositions, explosive copywriting, the optimal use of demographics or psychographics, ideal media buys, high recall ratings, or whatever. But when attention shifts to the receiving end of the channel, and focuses on the instant of reception, then commentary becomes much more elemental: an advertising message contains something primary and primitive, an emotional appeal, that in effect is the thin end of the wedge, trying to find its way into a mind. Should this occur, the product information comes along behind.

When enough advertisements are examined in this light, it becomes clear that the emotional appeals fall into several distinguishable categories, and that every ad is a variation on one of a limited number of basic appeals. While there may be several ways of classifying these appeals, one particular list of fifteen has proven to be especially valuable. Advertisements can appeal to:

1. The need for sex
2. The need for affiliation
3. The need to nurture

4. The need for guidance
5. The need to aggress
6. The need to achieve
7. The need to dominate
8. The need for prominence
9. The need for attention
10. The need for autonomy
11. The need to escape
12. The need to feel safe
13. The need for aesthetic sensations
14. The need to satisfy curiosity
15. Physiological needs: food, drink, sleep, etc.

Murray's List

Where does this list of advertising's fifteen basic appeals come from? Several years ago, I was involved in a research project which was to have as one segment an objective analysis of the changing appeals made in post–World War II American advertising. A sample of magazine ads would have their appeals coded into the categories of psychological needs they seemed aimed at. For this content analysis to happen, a complete roster of human motives would have to be found.

The first thing that came to mind was Abraham Maslow's famous four-part hierarchy of needs. But the briefest look at the range of appeals made in advertising was enough to reveal that they are more varied, and more profane, than Maslow had cared to account for. The search led on to the work of psychologist Henry A. Murray, who together with his colleagues at the Harvard Psychological Clinic has constructed a full taxonomy of needs. As described in *Explorations in Personality*, Murray's team had conducted a lengthy series of in-depth interviews with a number of subjects in order to derive from scratch what they felt to be the essential variables of personality. Forty-four variables were distinguished by the Harvard group, of which twenty were motives. The need for achievement ("to overcome obstacles and obtain a high standard") was one, for instance; the need to defer was another; the need to aggress was a third; and so forth.

Murray's list had served as the groundwork for a number of subsequent projects. Perhaps the best-known of these was David C. McClelland's extensive study of the need for achievement, reported in his *The Achieving Society*. In the process of demonstrating that a people's high need for achievement is predictive of later economic growth, McClelland coded achievement imagery and references out of a nation's folklore, songs, legends, and children's tales.

Following McClelland, I too wanted to cull the motivational appeals from a culture's imaginative product—in this case, advertising. To develop categories expressly for this purpose, I took Murray's twenty motives and added to them others he had mentioned in passing in *Explorations in Personality* but not included on the final list. The extended list was tried out on a sample of advertisements, and motives which never seemed to be invoked were dropped. I ended up with eighteen of Murray's motives, into which 770 print ads were coded. The resulting distribution is included in the 1976 book *Mass Advertising as Social Forecast*.

Since that time, the list of appeals has undergone refinements as a result of using it to analyze television commercials. A few more adjustments stemmed from the efforts of students in my advertising classes to decode appeals; tens of term papers surveying thousands of advertisements have caused some inconsistencies in the list to be hammered out. Fundamentally, though, the list remains the creation of Henry Murray. In developing a comprehensive, parsimonious inventory of human motives, he pinpointed the subsurface mental forces that are the least quiescent and most susceptible to advertising's entreaties.

Fifteen Appeals

1. **Need for sex.** Let's start with sex, because this is the appeal which seems to pop up first whenever the topic of advertising is raised. Whole books have been written about this one alone, to find a large audience of mildly titillated readers. Lately, due to campaigns to sell blue jeans, concern with sex in ads has redoubled.

The fascinating thing is not how much sex there is in advertising, but how little. Contrary to impressions, unambiguous sex is rare in these messages. Some of this surprising observation may be a matter of definition: the Jordache ads with the lithe, blouse-less female astride a similarly clad male is clearly an appeal to the audience's sexual drives, but the same cannot be said about Brooke Shields in the Calvin Klein commercials. Directed at young women and their credit-card carrying mothers, the image of Miss Shields instead invokes the need to be looked at. Buy Calvins and you'll be the center of much attention, just as Brooke is, the ads imply; they do not primarily inveigle their target audience's need for sexual intercourse.

In the content analysis reported in *Mass Advertising as Social Forecast* only two percent of ads were found to pander to this motive. Even *Playboy* ads shy away from sexual appeals: a recent issue contained eighty-three full-page ads, and just four of them (or less than five percent) could be said to have sex on their minds.

The reason this appeal is so little used is that it is too blaring and tends to obliterate the product information. Nudity in advertising has the effect of reducing brand recall. The people who do remember the product may do so because they have been made indignant by the ad; this is not the response most advertisers seek.

To the extent that sexual imagery is used, it conventionally works better on men than women; typically a female figure is offered up to the male reader. A Black Velvet liquor advertisement displays an attractive woman wearing a tight black outfit, recumbent under the legend, "Feel the Velvet." The figure does not have to be horizontal, however, for the appeal to be present as National Airlines revealed in its "Fly me" campaign. Indeed, there does not even have to be a female in the ad; "Flick my Bic" was sufficient to convey the idea to many.

As a rule, though, advertisers have found sex to be a tricky appeal, to be used sparingly. Less controversial and equally fetching are the appeals to our need for affectionate human contact.

2. Need for affiliation. American mythology upholds autonomous individuals, and social statistics suggest that people are ever more going it alone in their lives, yet the high frequency of affiliative appeals in ads belies this. Or maybe it does not: maybe all the images of companionship are compensation for what Americans privately lack. In any case, the need to associate with others is widely invoked in advertising and is probably the most prevalent appeal. All sorts of goods and services are sold by linking them to our unfulfilled desires to be in good company.

According to Henry Murray, the need for affiliation consists of desires "to draw near and enjoyably cooperate or reciprocate with another; to please and win affection of another; to adhere and remain loyal to a friend." The manifestations of this motive can be segmented into several different types of affiliation, beginning with romance.

Courtship may be swifter nowadays, but the desire for pairbonding is far from satiated. Ads reaching for this need commonly depict a youngish male and female engrossed in each other. The head of the male is usually higher than the female's, even at this late date; she may be sitting or leaning while he is standing. They are not touching in the

Smirnoff vodka ads, but obviously there is an intimacy, sometimes frolicsome, between them. The couple does touch for Martell Cognac when "The moment was Martell." For Wind Song perfume they have touched, and "Your Wind Song stays on his mind."

Depending on the audience, the pair does not absolutely have to be young—just together. He gives her a DeBeers diamond, and there is a tear in her laugh lines. She takes Geritol and preserves herself for him. And numbers of consumers, wanting affection too, follow suit.

Warm family feelings are fanned in ads when another generation is added to the pair. Hallmark Cards brings grandparents into the picture, and Johnson and Johnson Baby Powder has Dad, Mom, and baby, all fresh from the bath, encircled in arms and emblazoned with "Share the Feeling." A talc has been fused to familial love.

Friendship is yet another form of affiliation pursued by advertisers. Two women confide and drink Maxwell House coffee together; two men walk through the woods smoking Salem cigarettes. Miller Beer promises that afternoon "Miller Time" will be staffed with three or four good buddies. Drink Dr. Pepper, as Mickey Rooney is coaxed to do, and join in with all the other Peppers. Coca-Cola does not even need to portray the friendliness; it has reduced this appeal to "a Coke and a smile."

The warmth can be toned down and disguised, but it is the same affiliative need that is being fished for. The blonde has a direct gaze and her friends are firm businessmen in appearance, but with a glass of Old Bushmill you can sit down and fit right in. Or, for something more upbeat, sing along with the Pontiac choirboys.

As well as presenting positive images, advertisers can play to the need for affiliation in negative ways, by invoking the fear of rejection. If we don't use Scope, we'll have the "Ugh! Morning Breath" that causes the male and female models to avert their faces. Unless we apply Ultra Brite or Close-Up to our teeth, it's good-bye romance. Our family will be cursed with "House-a-tosis" if we don't take care. Without Dr. Scholl's antiperspirant foot spray, the bowling team will keel over. There go all the guests when the supply of Dorito's nacho cheese chips is exhausted. Still more rejection if our shirts have ring-around-the-collar, if our car needs to be Midasized. But make a few purchases, and we are back in the bosom of human contact.

As self-directed as Americans pretend to be, in the last analysis we remain social animals, hungering for the positive, endorsing feelings that only those around us can supply. Advertisers respond, urging us to "Reach out and touch someone," in the hopes our monthly bills will rise.

3. Need to nurture. Akin to affiliative needs is the need to take care of small, defenseless creatures—children and pets, largely. Reciprocity is of less consequence here, though; it is the giving that counts. Murray uses synonyms like "to feed, help, support, console, protect, comfort, nurse, heal." A strong need it is, woven deep into our genetic fabric, for if it did not exist we could not successfully raise up our replacements. When advertisers put forth the image of something diminutive and furry, something that elicits the word "cute" or "precious," then they are trying to trigger this motive. We listen to the childish voice singing the Oscar Mayer weiner song, and our next hot-dog purchase is prescribed. Aren't those darling kittens something, and how did this Meow Mix get into our shopping cart?

This pitch is often directed at women, as Mother Nature's chief nurturers. "Make me some Kraft macaroni and cheese, please," says the elfin preschooler just in from the snowstorm, and mothers' hearts go out, and Kraft's sales go up. "We're cold, wet, and hungry," whine the husband and kids, and the little woman gets the Manwiches ready. A facsimile of this need can be hit without children or pets: the husband is ill and sleepless in the television commercial, and the wife grudgingly fetches the NyQuil.

But it is not women alone who can be touched by this appeal. The father nurses his son Eddie through adolescence while the John Deere lawn tractor survives the years. Another father counts pennies with his young son as the subject of New York Life Insurance comes up. And all over America are businessmen who don't know why they dial Qantas Airlines when they have to take a trans-Pacific trip; the koala bear knows.

4. Need for guidance. The opposite of the need to nurture is the need to be nurtured: to be protected, shielded, guided. We may be loath to admit it, but the child lingers on inside every adult—and a good thing it does, or we would not be instructable in our advancing years. Who wants a nation of nothing but flinty personalities?

Parent-like figures can successfully call up this need. Robert Young recommends Sanka coffee, and since we have experienced him for twenty-five years as television father and doctor, we take his word for it. Florence Henderson as the expert mom knows a lot about the advantages of Wesson oil.

The parent-ness of the spokesperson need not be so salient; sometimes pure authoritativeness is better. When Orson Welles scowls and intones, "Paul Masson will sell no wine before its time," we may not know exactly what he means, but we still take direction from him.

There is little maternal about Brenda Vaccaro when she speaks up for Tampax, but there is a certainty to her that many accept.

A celebrity is not a necessity in making a pitch to the need for guidance, since a fantasy figure can serve just as well. People accede to the Green Giant, or Betty Crocker, or Mr. Goodwrench. Some advertisers can get by with no figure at all: "When E.F. Hutton talks, people listen."

Often it is tradition or custom that advertisers point to and consumers take guidance from. Bits and pieces of American history are used to sell whiskeys like Old Crow, Southern Comfort, Jack Daniel's. We conform to traditional male/female roles and age-old social norms when we purchase Barclay cigarettes, which informs us *The pleasure is back.*

The product itself, if it has been around for a long time, can constitute a tradition. All those old labels in the ad for Morton salt convince us that we should continue to buy it. Kool-Aid says "You loved it as a kid. You trust it as a mother," hoping to get yet more consumers to go along.

Even when the product has no history at all, our need to conform to tradition and to be guided are strong enough that they can be invoked through bogus nostalgia and older actors. Country-Time lemonade sells because consumers want to believe it has a past they can defer to.

So far the needs and the ways they can be invoked which have been looked at are largely warm and affiliative; they stand in contrast to the next set of needs, which are much more egoistic and assertive.

5. Need to aggress. The pressures of the real world create strong retaliatory feelings in every functioning human being. Since these impulses can come forth as bursts of anger and violence, their display is normally tabooed. Existing as harbored energy, aggressive drives present a large, tempting target for advertisers. It is not a target to be aimed at thoughtlessly, though, for few manufacturers want their products associated with destructive motives. There is always the danger that, as in the case of sex, if the appeal is too blatant, public opinion will turn against what is being sold.

Jack-in-the-Box sought to abruptly alter its marketing by going after older customers and forgetting the younger ones. Their television commercials had a seventy-ish lady command, "Waste him," and the Jack-in-the-Box clown exploded before our eyes. So did public reaction until the commercials were toned down. Print ads for Club cocktails carried the faces of octogenarians under the headline, "Hit me with a Club"; response was contrary enough to bring the campaign to a stop.

Better disguised aggressive appeals are less likely to backfire: Triumph cigarettes has models making a lewd gesture with their uplifted cigarettes, but the individuals are often laughing and usually in close company of others. When Exxon said, "There's a Tiger in your tank," the implausibility of it concealed the invocation of aggressive feelings.

Depicted arguments are a common way for advertisers to tap the audience's needs to aggress. Don Rickles and Lynda Carter trade gibes, and consumers take sides as the name of Seven-Up is stitched on minds. The Parkay tub has a difference of opinion with the user; who can forget it, or who (or what) got the last word in?

6. Need to achieve. This is the drive that energizes people, causing them to strive in their lives and careers. According to Murray, the need for achievement is signaled by the desires "to accomplish something difficult. To overcome obstacles and attain a high standard. To excel one's self. To rival and surpass others." A prominent American trait, it is one that advertisers like to hook on to because it identifies their product with winning and success.

The Cutty Sark ad does not disclose that Ted Turner failed at his latest attempt at yachting's America Cup; here he is represented as a champion on the water as well as off in his television enterprises. If we drink this whiskey, we will be victorious alongside Turner. We can also succeed with O.J. Simpson by renting Hertz cars, or with Reggie Jackson by bringing home some Panasonic equipment. Cathy Rigby and Stayfree Maxipads will put people out front.

Sports heroes are the most convenient means to snare consumers' needs to achieve, but they are not the only one. Role models can be established, ones which invite emulation, as with the profiles put forth by Dewar's scotch. Successful, tweedy individuals relate they have "graduated to the flavor of Myer's rum." Or the advertiser can establish a prize: two neighbors play one-on-one basketball for a Michelob beer in a television commercial, while in a print ad a bottle of Johnnie Walker Black Label has been gilded like a trophy.

Any product that advertises itself in superlatives—the best, the first, the finest—is trying to make contact with our needs to succeed. For many consumers, sales and bargains belong in this category of appeals, too; the person who manages to buy something at fifty percent off is seizing an opportunity and coming out ahead of others.

7. Need to dominate. This fundamental need is the craving to be powerful—perhaps omnipotent, as in the Xerox ad where Brother Dominic exhibits heavenly powers and creates miraculous copies. Most of us will settle for being just a regular potentate, though. We drink Budweiser because it is the King of Beers, and here comes the powerful

Clydesdales to prove it. A taste of Wolfschmidt vodka and "The spirit of the Czar lives on."

The need to dominate and control one's environment is often thought of as being masculine, but as close students of human nature advertisers know, it is not so circumscribed. Women's aspirations for control are suggested in the campaign theme, "I like my men in English Leather, or nothing at all." The females in the Chanel No. 19 ads are "outspoken" and wrestle their men around.

Male and female, what we long for is clout; what we get in its place is Mastercard.

8. Need for prominence.   Here comes the need to be admired and respected, to enjoy prestige and high social status. These times, it appears, are not so egalitarian after all. Many ads picture the trappings of high position; the Oldsmobile stands before a manorial doorway, the Volvo is parked beside a steeplechase. A book-lined study is the setting for Dewar's 12, and Lenox China is displayed in a dining room chock full of antiques.

Beefeater gin represents itself as "The Crown Jewel of England" and uses no illustrations of jewels or things British, for the words are sufficient indicators of distinction. Buy that gin and you will rise up the prestige hierarchy, or achieve the same effect on yourself with Seagram's 7 Crown, which ambiguously describes itself as "classy."

Being respected does not have to entail the usual accoutrements of wealth: "Do you know who I am?" the commercials ask, and we learn that the prominent person is not so prominent without his American Express card.

9. Need for attention.   The previous need involved being *looked up to*, while this is the need to be *looked at*. The desire to exhibit ourselves in such a way as to make others look at us is a primitive, insuppressible instinct. The clothing and cosmetic industries exist just to serve this need, and this is the way they pitch their wares. Some of this effort is aimed at males, as the ads for Hathaway shirts and Jockey underclothes. But the greater bulk of such appeals is targeted single-mindedly at women.

To come back to Brooke Shields: this is where she fits into American marketing. If I buy Calvin Klein jeans, consumers infer, I'll be the object of fascination. The desire for exhibition has been most strikingly played to in a print campaign of many years' duration, that of Maidenform lingerie. The woman exposes herself, and sales surge. "Gentlemen prefer Hanes" the ads dissemble, and women who want eyes upon them know what they should do. Peggy Fleming flutters her legs for L'eggs, encouraging females who want to be the star in their own lives to purchase this product.

The same appeal works for cosmetics and lotions. For years, the little girl with the exposed backside sold gobs of Coppertone, but now the company has picked up the pace a little: as a female, you are supposed to "Flash 'em a Coppertone tan." Food can be sold the same way, especially to the diet-conscious; Angie Dickinson poses for California avocados and says, "Would this body lie to you?" Our eyes are too fixed on her for us to think to ask if she got that way by eating mounds of guacamole.

10. Need for autonomy.   There are several ways to sell credit card services, as has been noted: Mastercard appeals to the need to dominate, and American Express to the need for prominence. When Visa claims, "You can have it the way you want it," yet another primary motive is being beckoned forward—the need to endorse the self. The focus here is upon the independence and integrity of the individual; this need is the antithesis of the need for guidance and is unlike any of the social needs. "If running with the herd isn't your style, try ours," says Rotan-Mosle, and many Americans feel they have finally found the right brokerage firm.

The photo is of a red-coated Mountie on his horse, posed on a snow-covered ledge; the copy reads, "Windsor—One Canadian stands alone." This epitome of the solitary and proud individual may work best with male customers, as may Winston's man in the red cap. But one-figure advertisements also strike the strong need for autonomy among American women. As Shelly Hack strides for Charlie perfume, females respond to her obvious pride and flair; she is her own person. The Virginia Slims tale is of people who have come a long way from subservience to independence. Cachet perfume feels it does not need a solo figure to work this appeal, and uses three different faces in its ads; it insists, though, "It's different on every woman who wears it."

Like many psychological needs, this one can also be appealed to in a negative fashion, by invoking the loss of independence or self-regard. Guilt and regrets can be stimulated: "Gee, I could have had a V-8." Next time, get one and be good to yourself.

11. Need to escape.   An appeal to the need for autonomy often co-occurs with one for the need to escape, since the desire to duck out of our social obligations, to seek rest or adventure, frequently takes the form of one-person flight. The dashing image of a pilot, in fact, is a standard way of quickening this need to get away from it all.

Freedom is the pitch here, the freedom that every individual yearns for whenever life becomes too oppressive. Many advertisers like appealing to the need for escape because the sensation of pleasure often accompanies escape, and what nicer emotional nimbus could there be for a product? "You deserve a break today," says McDonald's, and Stouffer's frozen foods chime in, "Set yourself free."

For decades men have imaginatively bonded themselves to the Marlboro cowboy who dwells untarnished and unencumbered in Marlboro Country some distance from modern life; smokers' aching needs for autonomy and escape are personified by that cowpoke. Many women can identify with the lady ambling through the woods behind the words, "Benson and Hedges and mornings and me."

But escape does not have to be solitary. Other Benson and Hedges ads, part of the same campaign, contain two strolling figures. In Salem cigarette advertisements, it can be several people who escape together into the mountaintops. A commercial for Levi's pictured a cloudbank above a city through which ran a whole chain of young people.

There are varieties of escape, some wistful like the Boeing "Someday" campaign of dream vacations, some kinetic like the play and parties in soft drink ads. But in every instance, the consumer exposed to the advertisement is invited to momentarily depart his everyday life for a more carefree experience, preferably with the product in hand.

12. Need to feel safe.   Nobody in their right mind wants to be intimidated, menaced, battered, poisoned. We naturally want to do whatever it takes to stave off threats to our well-being, and to our families'. It is the instinct of self-preservation that makes us responsive to the ad of the St. Bernard with the keg of Chivas Regal. We pay attention to the stern talk of Karl Malden and the plight of the vacationing couples who have lost all their funds in the American Express travelers cheques commercials. We want the omnipresent stag from Hartford Insurance to watch over us too.

In the interest of keeping failure and calamity from our lives, we like to see the durability of products demonstrated. Can we ever forget that Timex takes a licking and keeps on ticking? When the American Tourister suitcase bounces all over the highway and the egg inside doesn't break, the need to feel safe has been adroitly plucked.

We take precautions to diminish future threats. We buy Volkswagen Rabbits for the extraordinary mileage, and MONY insurance policies to avoid the tragedies depicted in their black-and-white ads of widows and orphans.

We are careful about our health. We consume Mazola margarine because it has "corn goodness" backed by the natural food traditions of the American Indians. In the medicine cabinet is Alka-Seltzer, the "home remedy"; having it, we are snug in our little cottage.

We want to be safe and secure; buy these products, advertisers are saying, and you'll be safer than you are without them.

13. Need for aesthetic sensations. There is an undeniable aesthetic component to virtually every ad run in the national media: the photography or filming or drawing is near-perfect, the type style is well chosen, the layout could scarcely be improved upon. Advertisers know there is little chance of good communication occurring if an ad is not visually pleasing. Consumers may not be aware of the extent of their own sensitivity to artwork, but it is undeniably large.

Sometimes the aesthetic element is expanded and made into an ad's primary appeal. Charles Jordan shoes may or may not appear in the accompanying avant-garde photographs; Kohler plumbing fixtures catch attention through the high style of their desert settings. Beneath the slightly out of focus photograph, languid and sensuous in tone, General Electric feels called upon to explain, "This is an ad for the hair dryer."

This appeal is not limited to female consumers: J&B scotch says "It whispers" and shows a bucolic scene of lake and castle.

14. Need to satisfy curiosity. It may seem odd to list a need for information among basic motives, but this need can be as primal and compelling as any of the others. Human beings are curious by nature, interested in the world around them, and intrigued by tidbits of knowledge and new developments. Trivia, percentages, observations counter to conventional wisdom—these items all help sell products. Any advertisement in a question-and-answer format is strumming this need.

A dog groomer has a question about long distance rates, and Bell Telephone has a chart with all the figures. An ad for Porsche 911 is replete with diagrams and schematics, numbers and arrows. Lo and behold, Anacin pills have 150 more milligrams than its competitors; should we wonder if this is better or worse for us?

15. Physiological needs. To the extent that sex is solely a biological need, we are now coming around full circle, back toward the start of the list. In this final category are clustered appeals to sleeping, eating, drinking. The art of photographing food and drink is so advanced, sometimes these temptations are wondrously caught in the camera's lens: the crab meat in the Red Lobster restaurant ads can start us salivating, the Quarterpounder can almost be smelled, the liquor in the glass glows invitingly. Imbibe, these ads scream.

Styles

Some common ingredients of advertisements were not singled out for separate mention in the list of fifteen because they are not appeals in and of themselves. They are stylistic features, influencing the way a basic appeal is presented. The use of humor is one, and the use of celebrities is another. A third is time imagery, past and future, which goes to several purposes.

For all of its employment in advertising, humor can be treacherous, because it can get out of hand and smother the product information. Supposedly, this is what Alka-Seltzer discovered with its comic commercials of the late sixties; "I can't believe I ate the whole thing," the sad-faced husband lamented, and the audience cackled so much it forgot the antacid. Or, did not take it seriously.

But used carefully, humor can punctuate some of the softer appeals and soften some of the harsher ones. When Emma says to the Fruit-of-the-Loom fruits, "Hi, cuties. Whatcha doing in my laundry basket?" we smile as our curiosity is assuaged along with hers. Bill Cosby gets consumers tickled about the children in his Jell-O commercials, and strokes the need to nurture.

An insurance company wants to invoke the need to feel safe, but does not want to leave readers with an unpleasant aftertaste; cartoonist Rowland Wilson creates an avalanche about to crush a gentleman who is saying to another, "My insurance company? New England Life, of course. Why?" The same tactic of humor undercutting threat is used in the cartoon commercials for Safeco when the Pink Panther wanders from one disaster to another. Often humor masks aggression: comedian Bob Hope in the outfit of a boxer promises to knock out the knock-knocks with Texaco; Rodney Dangerfield, who "can't get no respect," invites aggression as the comic relief in Miller Lite commercials.

Roughly fifteen percent of all advertisements incorporate a celebrity, almost always from the fields of entertainment or sports. The approach can also prove troublesome for advertisers, for celebrities are human beings too, and fully capable of the most remarkable behavior. If anything distasteful about them emerges, it is likely to reflect on the product. The advertisers making use of Anita Bryant and Billy Jean King suffered several anxious moments. An untimely death can also react poorly on a product. But advertisers are willing to take risks because celebrities can be such a good link between producers and consumers, performing the social role of introducer.

There are several psychological needs these middlemen can play upon. Let's take the product class of cameras and see how different celebrities can hit different needs. The need for guidance can be invoked by Michael Landon, who plays such a wonderful dad on "Little House on the Prairie"; when he says to buy Kodak equipment, many people listen. James Garner for Polaroid cameras is put in a similar authoritative role, so defined by a mocking spouse. The need to achieve is summoned up by Tracy Austin and other tennis stars for Canon AE-1; the advertiser first makes sure we see these athletes playing to win. When Cheryl Tiegs speaks up for Olympus cameras, it is the need for attention that is being targeted.

The past and future, being outside our grasp, are exploited by advertisers as locales for the projection of needs. History can offer up heroes (and call up the need to achieve) or traditions (need for guidance) as well as art objects (need for aesthetic sensations). Nostalgia is a kindly version of personal history and is deployed by advertisers to rouse needs for affiliation and for guidance; the need to escape can come in here, too. The same need to escape is sometimes the point of futuristic appeals but picturing the avant-garde can also be a way to get at the need to achieve.

Analyzing Advertisements

When analyzing ads yourself for their emotional appeals, it takes a bit of practice to learn to ignore the product information (as well as one's own experience and feelings about the product). But that skill comes soon enough, as does the ability to quickly sort out from all the non-product aspects of an ad the chief element which is the most striking, the most likely to snag attention first and penetrate brains farthest. The key to the appeal, this element usually presents itself centrally and forwardly to the reader or viewer.

Another clue: the viewing angle which the audience has on the ad's subjects is informative. If the subjects are photographed or filmed from below and thus are looking down at you much as the Green Giant does, then the need to be guided is a good candidate for the ad's emotional appeal. If, on the other hand, the subjects are shot from above and appear deferential, as is often the case with children or female models, then other needs are being appealed to.

To figure out an ad's emotional appeal, it is wise to know (or have a good hunch about) who the targeted consumers are; this can often be inferred from the magazine or television show it appears in. This piece of information is a great help in determining the appeal and in deciding between two different interpretations. For example, if an ad features a partially undressed female, this would typically signal one appeal for readers of *Penthouse* (need for sex) and another for readers of *Cosmopolitan* (need for attention).

It would be convenient if every ad made just one appeal, were aimed at just one need. Unfortunately, things are often not that simple. A cigarette ad with a couple at the edge of a polo field is trying to hit both the need for affiliation and the need for prominence; depending on the attitude of the male, dominance could also be an ingredient in this. An ad for Chimere perfume incorporates two photos: in the top one the lady is being commanding at a business luncheon (need to dominate), but in the lower one she is being bussed (need for affiliation). Better ads, however, seem to avoid being too diffused; in the study of post–World War II advertising described earlier, appeals grew more focused as the decades passed. As a rule of thumb, about sixty percent have two conspicuous appeals; the last twenty percent have three or more. Rather than looking for the greatest number of appeals, decoding ads is most productive when the loudest one or two appeals are discerned, since those are the appeals with the best chance of grabbing people's attention.

Finally, analyzing ads does not have to be a solo activity and probably should not be. The greater number of people there are involved, the better chance there is of transcending individual biases and discerning the essential emotional lure built into an advertisement.

Do They or Don't They?

Do the emotional appeals made in advertisements add up to the sinister manipulation of consumers?

It is clear that these ads work. Attention is caught, communication occurs between producers and consumers, and sales result. It turns out to be difficult to detail the exact relationship between a specific ad and a specific purchase, or even between a campaign and subsequent sales figures, because advertising is only one of a host of influences upon consumption. Yet no one is fooled by this lack of perfect proof; everyone knows that advertising sells. If this were not the case, then tight-fisted

American businesses would not spend a total of fifty billion dollars annually on these messages.

But before anyone despairs that advertisers have our number to the extent that they can marshal us at will and march us like automatons to the check-out counters, we should recall the resiliency and obduracy of the American consumer. Advertisers may have uncovered the softest spots in minds, but that does not mean they have found truly gaping apertures. There is no evidence that advertising can get people to do things contrary to their self-interests. Despite all the finesse of advertisements, and all the subtle emotional tugs, the public resists the vast majority of the petitions. According to the marketing division of the A. C. Nielsen Company, a whopping seventy-five percent of all new products die within a year in the marketplace, the victims of consumer disinterest which no amount of advertising could overcome. The appeals in advertising may be the most captivating there are to be had, but they are not enough to entrap the wiley consumer.

The key to understanding the discrepancy between, on the one hand, the fact that advertising truly works, and, on the other, the fact that it hardly works, is to take into account the enormous numbers of people exposed to an ad. Modern-day communications permit an ad to be displayed to millions upon millions of individuals; if the smallest fraction of that audience can be moved to buy the product, then the ad has been successful. When one percent of the people exposed to a television advertising campaign reach for their wallets, that could be one million sales, which may be enough to keep the product in production and the advertisements coming.

In arriving at an evenhanded judgment about advertisements and their emotional appeals, it is good to keep in mind that many of the purchases which might be credited to these ads are experienced as genuinely gratifying to the consumer. We sincerely like the goods or service we have bought, and we may even like some of the emotional drapery that an ad suggests comes with it. It has sometimes been noted that the most avid students of advertisements are the people who have just bought the product; they want to steep themselves in the associated imagery. This may be the reason that Americans, when polled, are not negative about advertising and do not disclose any sense of being misused. The volume of advertising may be an irritant, but the product information as well as the imaginative material in ads are partial compensation.

A productive understanding is that advertising messages involve costs and benefits at both ends of the communications channel. For those few ads which do make contact, the consumer surrenders a moment of time, has the lower brain curried, and receives notice of a product; the advertiser has given up money and has increased the chance of sales. In this sort of communications activity, neither party can be said to be the loser.

SUGGESTIONS FOR WRITING

1. Fowles claims that advertisers try to tap into basic human needs and emotions, rather than consumers' intellect. How does he go about proving this claim? What examples or other proof strike you as particularly persuasive? Where do you see weaknesses in Fowles's argument? Write an essay in which you respond to these questions by first summarizing and then responding to Fowles's key points.

2. According to Fowles, advertisers make certain assumptions about the basic personality traits of human beings. Make a list of these assumptions and then shape that list into one or two paragraphs that provide a description of what advertisers think consumers are like. Finally, write a one or two paragraph response in which you point to assumptions about human nature that you think are correct or incorrect.

3. Working with Fowles's list of the fifteen appeals of advertising, survey a recent magazine, looking at all the ads and categorizing them based on their predominant appeal. In an essay, describe what your results tell you about the magazine and its readership. Based on your survey, would you amend Fowles's list? What additions or deletions would you make?

JOHN E. CALFEE

How Advertising Informs to Our Benefit

This article, adapted from John E. Calfee's book Fear of Persuasion: A New Perspective on Advertising and Regulation, *offers a different view of the effect of advertising on our society. Calfee, a former Federal Trade Commission economist and a resident scholar at the American Enterprise Institute, argues that advertising actually provides many benefits to consumers. Calfee relates several specific cases in which advertisements spread important health information to people who might not have learned about it otherwise. Because advertisers have huge budgets and can reach into virtually every home through television, newspapers, billboards, and radio campaigns, advertisements have the potential to spread information in a way that government-sponsored public service initiatives cannot.*

A great truth about advertising is that it is a tool for communicating information and shaping markets. It is one of the forces that compel sellers to cater to the desires of consumers. Almost everyone knows this because consumers use advertising every day, and they miss advertising when they cannot get it. This fact does not keep politicians and opinion leaders from routinely dismissing the value of advertising. But the truth is that people find advertising very useful indeed.

Of course, advertising primarily seeks to persuade and everyone knows this, too. The typical ad tries to induce a consumer to do one particular thing—usually, buy a product—instead of a thousand other things. There is nothing obscure about this purpose or what it means for buyers. Decades of data and centuries of intuition reveal that all consumers everywhere are deeply suspicious of what advertisers say and why they say it. This skepticism is in fact the driving force that makes advertising so effective. The persuasive purpose of advertising and the skepticism with which it is met are two sides of a single process. Persuasion and skepticism work in tandem so advertising can do its job in competitive markets. Hence, ads represent the seller's self interest, consumers know this, and sellers know that consumers know it.

By understanding this process more fully, we can sort out much of the popular confusion surrounding advertising and how it benefits consumers.

How Useful Is Advertising?

Just how useful is the connection between advertising and information? At first blush, the process sounds rather limited. Volvo ads tell consumers that Volvos have side-impact air bags, people learn a little about the importance of air bags, and Volvo sells a few more cars. This seems to help hardly anyone except Volvo and its customers.

But advertising does much more. It routinely provides immense amounts of information that benefits primarily parties other than the advertiser. This may sound odd, but it is a logical result of market forces and the nature of information itself.

The ability to use information to sell products is an incentive to create new information through research. Whether the topic is nutrition, safety, or more mundane matters like how to measure amplifier power, the necessity of achieving credibility with consumers and critics requires much of this research to be placed in the public domain, and that it rest upon some academic credentials. That kind of research typically produces results that apply to more than just the brands sold by the firm sponsoring the research. The lack of property rights to such "pure" information ensures that this extra information is available at no charge. Both consumers and competitors may borrow the new information for their own purposes.

Advertising also elicits additional information from other sources. Claims that are striking, original, forceful or even merely obnoxious will generate news stories about the claims, the controversies they cause, the reactions of competitors (A price war? A splurge of comparison ads?), the reactions of consumers and the remarks of governments and independent authorities.

Probably the most concrete, pervasive, and persistent example of competitive advertising that works for the public good is price advertising. Its effect is invariably to heighten competition and reduce prices, even the prices of firms that assiduously avoid mentioning prices in their own advertising.

There is another area where the public benefits of advertising are less obvious but equally important. The unremitting nature of consumer interest in health, and the eagerness of sellers to cater to consumer desires, guarantee that advertising related to health will provide a storehouse of telling observations on the ways in which the benefits of advertising extend beyond the interests of advertisers to include the interests of the public at large.

A Cascade of Information

Here is probably the best documented example of why advertising is necessary for consumer welfare. In the 1970s, public health experts described compelling evidence that people who eat more fiber are less likely to get cancer, especially cancer of the colon, which happens to be the second leading cause of deaths from cancer in the United States. By 1979, the U.S. Surgeon General was recommending that people eat more fiber in order to prevent cancer.

Consumers appeared to take little notice of these recommendations, however. The National Cancer Institute decided that more action was needed. NCI's cancer prevention division undertook to communicate the new information about fiber and cancer to the general public. Their goal was to change consumer diets and reduce the risk of cancer, but they had little hope of success given the tiny advertising budgets of federal agencies like NCI.

Their prospects unexpectedly brightened in 1984. NCI received a call from the Kellogg Corporation, whose All-Bran cereal held a commanding market share of the high-fiber segment. Kellogg proposed to use All-Bran advertising as a vehicle for NCI's public service messages. NCI thought that was an excellent idea. Soon, an agreement was reached in which NCI would review Kellogg's ads and labels for accuracy and value before Kellogg began running their fiber–cancer ads.

The new Kellogg All-Bran campaign opened in October 1984. A typical ad began with the headline, "At last some news about cancer you can live with." The ad continued: "The National Cancer Institute believes a high-fiber, low-fat diet may reduce your risk of some kinds of cancer. . . . That's why one of their strongest recommendations is to eat high-fiber foods. If you compare, you'll find Kellogg's All-Bran has nine grams of fiber per serving. No other cereal has more. So start your day with a bowl of Kellogg's All-Bran or mix it with your regular cereal."

The campaign quickly achieved two things. One was to create a regulatory crisis between two agencies. The Food and Drug Administration thought that if a food was advertised as a way to prevent cancer, it was being marketed as a drug. Then the FDA's regulations for drug labeling would kick in. The food would be reclassified as a drug and would be removed from the market until the seller either stopped making the health claims or put the product through the clinical testing necessary to obtain formal approval as a drug.

But food advertising is regulated by the Federal Trade Commission, not the FDA. The FTC thought Kellogg's ads were nondeceptive and were therefore perfectly legal. In fact, it thought the ads should be encouraged. The Director of the FTC's Bureau of Consumer Protection declared that "the [Kellogg] ad has presented important public health recommendations in an accurate, useful, and substantiated way. It informs the members of the public that there is a body of data suggesting certain relationships between cancer and diet that they may find important." The FTC won this political battle, and the ads continued.

The second instant effect of the All-Bran campaign was to unleash a flood of health claims. Vegetable oil manufacturers advertised that cholesterol was associated with coronary heart disease, and that vegetable oil does not contain cholesterol. Margarine ads did the same, and added that vitamin A is essential for good vision. Ads for calcium products (such as certain antacids) provided vivid demonstrations of the effects of osteoporosis (which weakens bones in old age), and recounted the advice of experts to increase dietary calcium as a way to prevent osteoporosis. Kellogg's competitors joined in citing the National Cancer Institute dietary recommendations.

Nor did things stop there. In the face of consumer demand for better and fuller information, health claims quickly evolved from a blunt tool to a surprisingly refined mechanism. Cereals were advertised as high in fiber and low in sugar or fat or sodium. Ads for an upscale brand of bread noted: "Well, most high-fiber bran cereals may be high in fiber, but often only one kind: insoluble. It's this kind of fiber that helps promote regularity. But there's also a kind of fiber known as soluble, which most high-fiber bran cereals have in very small amounts, if at all. Yet diets high in this kind of fiber may actually lower your serum cholesterol, a risk factor for some heart diseases." Cereal boxes became convenient sources for a summary of what made for a good diet.

Increased Independent Information

The ads also brought powerful secondary effects. These may have been even more useful than the information that actually appeared in the ads themselves.

One effect was an increase in media coverage of diet and health. *Consumer Reports*, a venerable and hugely influential magazine that carries no advertising, revamped its reports on cereals to emphasize fiber and other ingredients (rather than testing the foods to see how well they did at providing a complete diet for laboratory rats). The health-claims phenomenon generated its own press coverage, with articles like "What Has All-Bran Wrought?" and "The Fiber Furor." These stories recounted the ads and the scientific information that prompted the ads; and articles on food and health proliferated. Anyone who lived through these years in the United States can probably remember the unending media attention to health claims and to diet and health generally.

Much of the information on diet and health was new. This was no coincidence. Firms were sponsoring research on their products in the hope of finding results that could provide a basis for persuasive advertising claims. Oat bran manufacturers, for example, funded research on the impact of soluble fiber on blood cholesterol. When the results came out "wrong," as they did in a 1990 study published with great fanfare in *The New England Journal of Medicine*, the headline in *Advertising Age* was "Oat Bran Popularity Hitting the Skids," and it did indeed tumble. The manufacturers kept at the research, however, and eventually the best research supported the efficacy of oat bran in reducing cholesterol (even to the satisfaction of the FDA). Thus did pure advertising claims spill over to benefit the information environment at large.

The shift to higher fiber cereals encompassed brands that had never undertaken the effort necessary to construct believable ads about fiber and disease. Two consumer researchers at the FDA reviewed these data and concluded they were "consistent with the successful educational impact of the Kellogg diet and health campaign: consumers seemed to be making an apparently thoughtful discrimination between high- and low-fiber cereals," and that the increased market shares for high-fiber non-advertised products represented "the clearest evidence of a successful consumer education campaign."

Perhaps most dramatic were the changes in consumer awareness of diet and health. An FTC analysis of government surveys showed that when consumers were asked about how they could prevent cancer through their diet, the percentage who mentioned fiber increased from 4% before the 1979 Surgeon General's report to 8.5% in 1984 (after the report but before the All-Bran campaign) to 32% in 1986 after a year and a half or so of health claims (the figure in 1988 was 28%). By far the greatest increases in awareness were among women (who do most of the grocery shopping) and the less educated: up from 0% for women without a high school education in 1984 to 31% for the same group in 1986. For women with incomes of less than $15,000, the increase was from 6% to 28%.

The health-claims advertising phenomenon achieved what years of effort by government agencies had failed to achieve. With its mastery of the art of brevity, its ability to command attention, and its use of television, brand advertising touched precisely the people the public health community was most desperate to reach. The health claims expanded consumer information along a broad front. The benefits clearly extended far beyond the interests of the relatively few manufacturers who made vigorous use of health claims in advertising.

A Pervasive Phenomenon

Health claims for foods are only one example, however, of a pervasive phenomenon—the use of advertising to provide essential health information with benefits extending beyond the interests of the advertisers themselves.

Advertising for soap and detergents, for example, once improved private hygiene and therefore, public health (hygiene being one of the underappreciated triumphs in twentieth century public health). Toothpaste advertising helped to do the same for teeth. When mass advertising for toothpaste and tooth powder began early in this century, tooth brushing was rare. It was common by the 1930s, after which toothpaste sales leveled off even though the advertising, of course, continued. When fluoride toothpastes became available, advertising generated interest in better teeth and professional dental care. Later, a "plaque reduction war" (which first involved mouthwashes, and later toothpastes) brought a new awareness of gum disease and how to prevent it. The financial gains to the toothpaste industry were surely dwarfed by the benefits to consumers in the form of fewer cavities and fewer lost teeth.

Health claims induced changes in foods, in nonfoods such as toothpaste, in publications ranging from university health letters to mainstream newspapers and magazines, and of course, consumer knowledge of diet and health.

These rippling effects from health claims in ads demonstrated the most basic propositions in the economics of information. Useful information initially failed to reach people who needed it because information producers could not charge a price to cover the costs of creating and disseminating pure information. And this problem was alleviated by advertising, sometimes in a most vivid manner.

Other examples of spillover benefits from advertising are far more common than most people realize. Even the much-maligned promotion of expensive new drugs can bring profound health benefits to patients and families, far exceeding what is actually charged for the products themselves.

The market processes that produce these benefits bear all the classic features of competitive advertising. We are not analyzing public service announcements here, but old-fashioned profit-seeking brand advertising. Sellers focused on the information that favored their own products. They advertised it in ways that provided a close link with their own brand. It was a purely competitive enterprise, and the benefits to consumers arose from the imperatives of the competitive process.

One might see all this as simply an extended example of the economics of information and greed. And indeed it is, if by greed one means the effort to earn a profit by providing what people are willing to pay for, even if what they want most is information rather than a tangible product. The point is that there is overwhelming evidence that unregulated economic forces dictate that much useful information will be provided by brand advertising, and only by brand advertising.

Of course, there is much more to the story. There is the question of how competition does the good I have described without doing even more harm elsewhere. After all, firms want to tell people only what is good about their brands, and people often want to know what is wrong with the brands. It turns out that competition takes care of this problem, too.

Advertising and Context

It is often said that most advertising does not contain very much information. In a way, this is true. Research on the contents of advertising typically finds just a few pieces of concrete information per ad. That's an average, of course. Some ads obviously contain a great deal of information. Still, a lot of ads are mainly images and pleasant talk, with little in the way of what most people would consider hard information. On the whole, information in advertising comes in tiny bits and pieces.

Cost is only one reason. To be sure, cramming more information into ads is expensive. But more to the point is the fact that advertising plays off the information available from outside sources. Hardly anything about advertising is more important than the interplay between what the ad contains and what surrounds it. Sometimes this interplay is a burden for the advertiser because it is beyond his control. But the interchange between advertising and environment is also an invaluable tool for sellers. Ads that work in collaboration with outside information can communicate far more than they ever could on their own.

The upshot is advertising's astonishing ability to communicate a great deal of information in a few words. Economy and vividness of expression almost always rely upon what is in the information environment. The famously concise "Think Small" and "Lemon" ads for the VW "Beetle" in the 1960s and 1970s were highly effective with buyers concerned about fuel economy, repair costs, and extravagant styling in American cars. This was a case where the less said, the better. The ads were more powerful when consumers were free to bring their own ideas about the issues to bear.

The same process is repeated over again for all sorts of products. Ads for computer modems once explained what they could be used for. Now a simple reference to the Internet is sufficient to conjure an elaborate mix of equipment and applications. These matters are better left vague so each potential customer can bring to the ad his own idea of what the Internet is really for.

Leaning on information from other sources is also a way to enhance credibility, without which advertising must fail. Much of the most important information in advertising—think of cholesterol and heart disease, antilock brakes and automobile safety—acquires its force from highly credible sources other than the advertiser. To build up this kind of credibility through material actually contained in ads would be cumbersome and inefficient. Far more effective, and far more economical, is the technique of making challenges, raising questions and otherwise making it perfectly clear to the audience that the seller invites comparisons and welcomes the tough questions. Hence the classic slogan, "If you can find a better whiskey, buy it."

Finally, there is the most important point of all. Informational sparseness facilitates competition. It is easier to challenge a competitor through pungent slogans—"Where's the beef?", "Where's the big saving?"—than through a step-by-step recapitulation of what has gone on before. The bits-and-pieces approach makes for quick, unerring attacks and equally quick responses, all under the watchful eye of the consumer over whom the battle is being fought. This is an ideal recipe for competition.

It also brings the competitive market's fabled self-correcting forces into play. Sellers are less likely to stretch the truth, whether it involves prices or subtleties about safety and performance, when they know they may arouse a merciless response from injured competitors. That is one reason the FTC once worked to get comparative ads on television, and has sought for decades to dismantle government or voluntary bans on comparative ads.

"Less-Bad" Advertising

There is a troubling possibility, however. Is it not possible that in their selective and carefully calculated use of outside information, advertisers have the power to focus consumer attention exclusively on the positive, i.e., on what is good about the brand or even the entire product class? Won't automobile ads talk up style, comfort, and extra safety, while food ads do taste and convenience, cigarette ads do flavor and lifestyle, and airlines do comfort and frequency of departure, all the while leaving consumers to search through other sources to find all the things that are wrong with products?

In fact, this is not at all what happens. Here is why: Everything for sale has something wrong with it, if only the fact that you have to pay for it. Some products, of course, are notable for their faults. The most obvious examples involve tobacco and health, but there are also food and heart disease, drugs and side effects, vacations and bad weather, automobiles and accidents, airlines and delay, among others.

Products and their problems bring into play one of the most important ways in which the competitive market induces sellers to serve the interests of buyers. No matter what the product, there are usually a few brands that are "less bad" than the others. The natural impulse is to advertise that advantage—"less cholesterol," "less fat," "less dangerous," and so on. Such provocative claims tend to have an immediate impact. The targets often retaliate; maybe their brands are less bad in a different respect (less salt?). The ensuing struggle brings better information, more informed choices, and improved products.

Perhaps the most riveting episode of "less-bad" advertising ever seen occurred, amazingly enough, in the industry that most people assume is the master of avoiding saying anything bad about its product.

Less-Bad Cigarette Ads

Cigarette advertising was once very different from what it is today. Cigarettes first became popular around the time of World War I, and they came to dominate the tobacco market in the 1920s. Steady and often dramatic sales increases continued into the 1950s, always with vigorous support from advertising. Tobacco advertising was duly celebrated as an outstanding example of the power and creativity of advertising. Yet amazingly, much of the advertising focused on what was wrong with smoking, rather than what people liked about smoking.

The very first ad for the very first mass-marketed American cigarette brand (Camel, the same brand recently under attack for its use of a cartoon character) said, "Camel Cigarettes will not sting the tongue and will not parch the throat." When Old Gold broke into the market in the mid-1920s, it did so with an ad campaign about coughs and throats and harsh cigarette smoke. It settled on the slogan, "Not a cough in a carload."

Competitors responded in kind. Soon, advertising left no doubt about what was wrong with smoking. Lucky Strike ads said, "No Throat Irritation—No Cough . . . we . . . removed . . . harmful corrosive acids," and later on, "Do you inhale? What's there to be afraid of? . . . famous purifying process removes certain impurities." Camel's famous tag line, "more doctors smoke Camels than any other brand," carried a punch precisely because many authorities thought smoking was unhealthy (cigarettes were called "coffin nails" back then), and smokers were eager for reassurance in the form of smoking by doctors themselves. This particular ad, which was based on surveys of physicians, ran in one form or another from 1933 to 1955. It achieved prominence partly because physicians practically never endorsed non-therapeutic products.[1]

Things really got interesting in the early 1950s, when the first persuasive medical reports on smoking and lung cancer reached the public. These reports created a phenomenal stir among smokers and the public generally. People who do not understand how advertising works would probably assume that cigarette manufacturers used advertising to divert attention away from the cancer reports. In fact, they did the opposite.

Small brands could not resist the temptation to use advertising to scare smokers into switching brands. They inaugurated several spectacular years of "fear advertising" that sought to gain competitive advantage by exploiting smokers' new fear of cancer. Lorillard, the beleaguered seller of Old Gold, introduced Kent, a new filter brand supported by ad claims like these: "Sensitive smokers get real health protection with new Kent," "Do you love a good smoke but not what the smoke does to you?" and "Takes out more nicotine and tars than any other leading cigarette—the difference in protection is priceless," illustrated by television ads showing the black tar trapped by Kent's filters.

Other manufacturers came out with their own filter brands, and raised the stakes with claims like, "Nose, throat, and accessory organs not adversely affected by smoking Chesterfields. First such report ever published about any cigarette," "Takes the fear out of smoking," and "Stop worrying . . . Philip Morris and only Philip Morris is entirely free of irritation used [sic] in all other leading cigarettes."

These ads threatened to demolish the industry. Cigarette sales plummeted by 3% in 1953 and a remarkable 6% in 1954. Never again, not even in the face of the most impassioned anti-smoking publicity by the Surgeon General or the FDA, would cigarette consumption decline as rapidly as it did during these years of entirely market-driven antismoking ad claims by the cigarette industry itself.

Thus advertising traveled full circle. Devised to bolster brands, it denigrated the product so much that overall market demand actually declined. Everyone understood what was happening, but the fear ads

---

[1] The ad ran in many outlets, including *The Journal of the American Medical Association*, which regularly carried cigarette advertisements until the early 1950s. Incidentally, Camel was by no means the only brand that cited medical authorities in an effort to reassure smokers.

continued because they helped the brands that used them. The new filter brands (all from smaller manufacturers) gained a foothold even as their ads amplified the medical reports on the dangers of smoking. It was only after the FTC stopped the fear ads in 1955 (on the grounds that the implied health claims had no proof) that sales resumed their customary annual increases.

Fear advertising has never quite left the tobacco market despite the regulatory straight jacket that governs cigarette advertising. In 1957, when leading cancer experts advised smokers to ingest less tar, the industry responded by cutting tar and citing tar content figures compiled by independent sources. A stunning "tar derby" reduced the tar and nicotine content of cigarettes by 40% in four years, a far more rapid decline than would be achieved by years of government urging in later decades. This episode, too, was halted by the FTC. In February 1960 the FTC engineered a "voluntary" ban on tar and nicotine claims.

Further episodes continue to this day. In 1993, for example, Liggett planned an advertising campaign to emphasize that its Chesterfield brand did not use the stems and other less desirable parts of the tobacco plant. This continuing saga, extending through eight decades, is perhaps the best documented case of how "less-bad" advertising completely offsets any desires by sellers to accentuate the positive while ignoring the negative. *Consumer Reports* magazine's 1955 assessment of the new fear of smoking still rings true:

> . . . companies themselves are largely to blame. Long before the current medical attacks, the companies were building up suspicion in the consumer by the discredited "health claims" in their ads . . . Such medicine-show claims may have given the smoker temporary confidence in one brand, but they also implied that cigarettes in general were distasteful, probably harmful, and certainly a "problem." When the scientists came along with their charges against cigarettes, the smoker was ready to accept them.

And that is how information works in competitive advertising.

Less-bad can be found wherever competitive advertising is allowed. I already described the health-claims-for-foods saga, which featured fat and cholesterol and the dangers of cancer and heart disease. Price advertising is another example. Prices are the most stubbornly negative product feature of all, because they represent the simple fact that the buyer must give up something else. There is no riper target for comparative advertising. When sellers advertise lower prices, competitors reduce their prices and advertise that, and soon a price war is in the works. This process so strongly favors consumers over the industry that one of the first things competitors do when they form a trade group is to propose an agreement to restrict or ban price advertising (if not ban all advertising). When that fails, they try to get advertising regulators to stop price ads, an attempt that unfortunately often succeeds.

Someone is always trying to scare customers into switching brands out of fear of the product itself. The usual effect is to impress upon consumers what they do not like about the product. In 1991, when Americans were worried about insurance companies going broke, a few insurance firms advertised that they were more solvent than their competitors. In May 1997, United Airlines began a new ad campaign that started out by reminding fliers of all the inconveniences that seem to crop up during air travel.

Health information is a fixture in "less-bad" advertising. Ads for sleeping aids sometimes focus on the issue of whether they are habit-forming. In March 1996, a medical journal reported that the pain reliever acetaminophen, the active ingredient in Tylenol, can cause liver damage in heavy drinkers. This fact immediately became the focus of ads for Advil, a competing product. A public debate ensued, conducted through advertising, talk shows, news reports and pronouncements from medical authorities. The result: consumers learned a lot more than they had known before about the fact that all drugs have side effects. The press noted that this dispute may have helped consumers, but it hurt the pain reliever industry. Similar examples abound.

We have, then, a general rule: sellers will use comparative advertising when permitted to do so, even if it means spreading bad information about a product instead of favorable information. The mechanism usually takes the form of less-bad claims. One can hardly imagine a strategy more likely to give consumers the upper hand in the give and take of the marketplace. Less-bad claims are a primary means by which advertising serves markets and consumers rather than sellers. They completely refute the naive idea that competitive advertising will emphasize only the sellers' virtues while obscuring their problems.

SUGGESTIONS FOR WRITING

1. According to Calfee, what are some of the ways that free-market competition in advertising benefits consumers? Does Calfee see any reason for government or industry regulation of advertising? What do

you think of Calfee's argument about regulation? Write a position paper in which you either support or argue against Calfee's perspective.

2. Look through some recent magazines, newspapers, or brochures and find approximately twenty ads that you can examine in order to test Calfee's proposition that ads provide consumers with useful information. Make a list of the useful information that each ad presents. That is, what helpful facts do you learn from the ad? Then list the other kinds of information or content presented in each ad. (You might reread Jib Fowles's "Advertising's Fifteen Basic Appeals" to get some ideas.) What conclusions can you draw from this comparison? Do your conclusions coincide with Calfee's claims? Are certain kinds of ads—or ads for certain products—more likely to contain helpful information?

3. Calfee discusses the history of cigarette advertising, noting the predominance of "less-bad" claims and "fear advertising" in mid-twentieth-century cigarette ad campaigns. Find five or six recent cigarette advertisements in magazines or newspapers and analyze the information these ads present and the strategies they use to sell their product. Then write an analytical essay in which you first summarize Calfee's discussion of the history of cigarette advertising, using quotations and paraphrases from the article to develop your summary. In the remainder of your essay, discuss what you see as the current state of cigarette advertising based on your analysis of recent ads.

MARK PENN

New Info Shoppers

This short article comes from Microtrends, *a book in which Mark Penn identifies small patterns of behavior in contemporary U.S. society. Based on these "microtrends"—which he describes as "the small forces behind tomorrow's big changes"—Penn draws conclusions about the state of our religious beliefs, politics, leisure pursuits, family life, educational system, style and fashion, and other cultural elements. Here Penn looks at shopping patterns and discovers a new type of consumer—the "New Info Shopper"—who vigilantly researches products rather than relying on the information (and emotional appeals) provided in advertising.*

With so much attention on psychological marketing these days—finding new ways to tap into people's heads—perhaps the single most neglected trend out there is the move towards more hard-nosed, information-based shopping and purchasing.

While elites were busy shoveling money into Madoff's black box these past few years, strapped consumers have been poring over product spec sheets, third-party reviews, and expert blog sites. In 2008's past holiday season, they watched every dollar. A special kind of consumer has taken a major role in the marketplace—the New Info Shopper. These people just can't buy anything unless they first look it up online and get the lowdown.

These shoppers have the Internet at work, typically hold information-based or office-park jobs, have been to some college or grad school, and are often making ends meet with two jobs, kids, and pets on a middle- or upper-middle-class income.

They have become highly suspicious of many TV ads: In a shoppers survey conducted by our firm, 78 percent of them said that ads no longer have enough of the information they need. As a result, many of them search online for virtually everything. Window shoppers have become "Windows shoppers." They want, in the phrase often attributed to *Dragnet's* Joe Friday, "just the facts, ma'am."

Of course, there is still a healthy role for big, emotional brand appeals and mega-advertising campaigns. For every trend, there is a countertrend. But that's not the real new thing in consumer behavior.

A whopping 92 percent of respondents in our survey said they have more confidence in information they find online than anything coming from a salesclerk or other source. They believe the information they find, not in the information that is spoon-fed to them; and the vast number of clicks today proves that they really are devoting time and energy to ferreting out detailed info before they buy.

A good example of how information can transform a marketplace is the series of ads a few years ago for the Dyson vacuum cleaner. Founder and inventor James Dyson took a commonplace item and explained how he had transformed it with new scientific principles. Consumers weren't bored with the technical approach. On the contrary, sales took off—and changed the marketplace for vacuum cleaners.

When we asked shoppers in our survey whether they would do online research before buying a vacuum cleaner, a remarkable 58 percent said yes. Dyson's ads helped turn vacuum-cleaner buying into a largely information-based market.

We have seen many of the big-market areas convert to an information-driven model—cars, homes, personal computers, and medical care are areas where nearly 4 in 5 shoppers say they gather information on their own from the Web before buying. "Do-It-Yourself Doctors" (that is, New Info Patients) show up at the doctor with their Web-derived diagnosis in hand, and a list of the medicines they need prescribed. Customers appear at the car dealership with the wholesale price and the model already picked out.

Information-seeking is not just an activity, it's a way of looking at the world. New Info Shoppers are proud of the progress they have made in putting facts over pablum. More companies should treat their customers as Dyson did and let them in on the secrets of their unique success. And they should invest more than ever in helping form their consumers into citizen corps, arming them with PCs, cameras, and even asking them to use the phone's new video cameras to document their product usage and put them online.

But how many marketers today work back from what this new consumer is thinking and doing? Not many. Based on the advertising budgets in the U.S., where a typical company will spend 60 times as much on advertising than they spend on generating publicity, most lag way behind in creating a new model of consumers and acknowledging the steps they take before they buy.

Some industries got it right away. Movies and restaurants have huge word-of-mouth and impulse components, but they are also very information-driven. Zagat's pioneered the concept of survey ratings and reviews, and smart restaurants use them. We're seeing the same in entertainment, where Metacritic and others provide professional and customer ratings of every movie.

Now this trend is spreading down the product chain. In our survey, 24 percent said they do online research before they'll even buy shampoo. The Breck Girl is being replaced by a shopping bot.

And they have questions. How does this shampoo work on different hair types, thicknesses, and colors? Are the bottles recyclable? Has the product been tested on animals?

It used to be that the only time people expected 30-page, prepurchase inspection reports was when they were buying a house. Now New Info Shoppers want them just to buy a tube of toothpaste.

The point is that advertising isn't just moving to the Web. No, it's got to grapple with an entirely new kind of shopper and way of shopping. Marketers now have to balance traditional media, online media, and content that is generated by experts, bloggers, and consumers themselves. An astonishing 70 percent of Americans now say they consult product reviews or consumer ratings before they make their buying decisions. Sixty-two percent say they spend at least 30 minutes online every week to help them decide what and whether to buy. Among Americans under 45, that number shoots up to 73 percent. Seventy-three percent—that's more than 4 times the percentage in that age group who go to church every week. For some, smart shopping is more than a hobby. It's a religion.

Information aggregation sites—the ones that don't generate content themselves but link to others' content, weaving a story about the industry and its products—will become even more important. Much as the Drudge Report tells its readers where to find stories they will like, so consumer aggregation sites could grow and do the same for car buyers, PC buyers, and other consumer groups. So far, however, most of these sites have been too cheesy to really catch on.

Information shopping also means manufacturers have to get back to generating more information on their products, even offbeat factoids that are highly memorable (if not always practical). Timex sold a lot of watches by showing that they were still ticking even after being thrown into a washing machine. To catch the eye of the New Info Shopper, manufacturers should start hauling their wares up Mt. Everest, dropping them out of windows, and putting them in boiling water, and then letting people know how they do. In an info-seeking world, facts can again become the great differentiator.

New Info Shoppers are bigger than a microtrend. They represent a broad shift in the marketplace brought about by the Internet, higher education, and changing economic times. But the question is: When will the marketplace catch up to them?

SUGGESTIONS FOR WRITING

1. Write a brief essay in which you explain in your own words the implications of Penn's claim that "Information seeking is not just an activity, it's a way of looking at the world." In your opinion, what would it mean to see the world as a venue for information seeking? How would this approach be different from the way you currently view and interact with the world around you?
2. Penn sketches out a profile of a new kind of consumer; to what extent do you fit this profile? In an autobiographical examination, explore some of your past experiences as an info shopper. What products were you shopping for? What information did you want to find about these products? How did you search for this information, and how did what

you learned ultimately influence your decisions? Based on this self-examination, what revisions would you suggest for Penn's profile of the new info shopper?

3. This assignment asks you to choose a specific product (for instance, a car, a hairbrush, or a book) and do some info shopping about it. Find and evaluate informational sites about that product, keeping note of your search strategies and results as you go about this task. Once you've found a good amount of information about the product, create a single-page brochure or handout that other people could use to find valid information and to inform their own shopping decisions. In addition to this brochure or handout, write a brief explanation of the strengths and weaknesses of the search strategies that you used to find information about the product. How effective were you as an info shopper?

STEPHEN BAKER

Shopper

We conclude this section of general readings on advertising by turning the tables just a bit. Instead of consumers finding information about products, whether through ads (Calfee) or through their own info shopping activities (Penn), Stephen Baker tells us that advertisers are becoming increasingly skilled at finding information about consumers. Following the lead of Internet merchants like Amazon, who record our clicks and keep track of our past purchases in order to personalize our future shopping experiences, retailers are using strategies such as customer loyalty cards to accumulate data about what we buy. Of course, their goal is to use this information about our personal preferences and buying habits to sell even more products to us even more effectively. As Baker puts it, "To date, retailers have stockpiled untold mountains of our personal data, but they're only now waking up to what they can do with it." With the specific example of the smart shopping cart, Baker describes what may be next in the evolving relationship of advertisers and consumers.

THE CALL COMES from my wife at the supermarket. "Do we need onions?"

I check. "We have one big one," I say, turning it over gingerly. "But it's been sprouting for a while . . ."

"Okay, I'll get some. How about milk?"

You know the routine. A few minutes later, whichever one of us is shopping arrives at the checkout counter. There, if we remember, we dig into a pocket or purse for the frayed customer loyalty card on the key chain. The cashier scans it. We get a discount on the orange juice or razor blades, and the supermarket learns about everything we buy. It's a deal we shoppers have been making for years. Stores give us what amounts to a couple bucks a week in exchange for our shopping lists.

Here's the strange part. To date, retailers have stockpiled untold mountains of our personal data, but they're only now waking up to what they can do with it. Sure, managers have used the scans to keep an eye on inventory. They can see when to order more mangoes or Snickers bars. They've learned plenty about our behavior en masse but next to nothing about us as individuals. When we walk into a store, even if it's the hundredth time this year, the system doesn't recognize us. It's clueless.

This era is coming to an end. Retailers simply cannot afford to keep herding us blindly through stores and malls, flashing discounts on Pampers to widowers in wheelchairs and ham hocks to Jews who keep kosher. It's wasteful, and competitors are getting smarter. Look online. Whether it's Amazon.com or a travel service like Orbitz, Internet merchants are working every day to figure us out.

They're tracking every click on their sites. They know where we come from, what we buy, how much we spend, which advertisements we see. They even know which ones we linger over for a moment or two with our mouse. In the online world, businesses no longer look at us as herds but as vast collections of individuals—each of us represented by scores of equations. They prove every day that merchants who know their customers have a big edge. They can study our patterns of consumption, anticipate our appetites, and entice us to spend money.

Personal service is nothing new for retailers. For centuries, it's been a privilege for the rich. Shopkeepers and tailors know their names and measurements and their taste in premier cru burgundies. They also know where to send the bill. A few generations ago, the rest of us got personal service (on a far more modest scale) in our own neighborhoods. "The retail model was a shopkeeper, a millinery, a rug merchant," says Jeff Smith, a managing partner of the retail practice at Accenture, the tech consulting giant. "You didn't serve yourself," he says. "They stood behind counters and found what you were looking for." Chummy relations with customers gave these merchants an edge.

Following World War II, however, retail took a half-century detour into mass industrialization. Shoppers were handed carts and instructed to find their own stuff. Whether they were pushing those carts through Ikea or Wal-Mart, they had entire warehouses to explore. And the merchandise was cheap, in part because the stores had eliminated the middleman—the shopkeeper at the local store who knew the customers by name. They mastered a startling new efficiency, which came from manufacturing and distributing with martial precision. That's what the brainiacs and their computers were focused on: operations. The customers? As we made our way from the massive lots through the equally massive stores, we were processed like card-carrying herd animals.

Now retailers are changing. Accenture's Smith calls it "back to the future." Instead of deploying millions of shopkeepers to twenty-first-century counters, they're relying on automatic machinery, from video cameras to newfangled customer loyalty cards. The operation runs on data, our data. The goal is to follow our footsteps in much same the way that e-tailers track our clicks. In the marketplace of the Numerati, we'll define ourselves as shoppers in ever-greater detail simply by going about our business in a store. When the stores get to know us, they'll recognize us the moment we walk in the door—just the way the corner grocer used to. And just like that grocer, they'll know our week-to-week routines and our not-so-secret cravings. They may calculate that we're probably running short on cat kibbles, and they won't forget that we spike a gallon or two of eggnog every holiday season. (And wouldn't it taste better with premium Jamaican rum this year?) The automatic systems will calculate not only what we're likely to buy but also how much money we make for the store. Many of them will learn how to lavish big spenders with special attention and nudge cheapskates toward the door.

An old shopping cart is parked next to the wall at Accenture's lab, high above downtown Chicago. The offices are chock full of tech gadgetry. Blinking video cameras hang from the ceilings, staring down on the researchers. (They're guinea pigs in a new surveillance system designed to track shoppers and workers.) In one nook of the lab is a large, always-on video connection with another Accenture lab in Silicon Valley. Around lunchtime in Chicago, you can see the California contingent coming to work, steaming coffee cups in hand. You hear their phones ringing and their footsteps echoing across the lobby 2,000 miles to the west. All of this gadgetry is backed by a wraparound view of Chicago's skyscrapers, with Lake Michigan shimmering in the distance. In this technology showcase, the shopping cart looks out of place and a little forlorn. But it reminds Rayid Ghani and his small team of researchers of their key mission: to predict the behavior of people like my wife, and you, and me as we make our way through stores.

Ghani made a splash in 2002 with a study of how a clothing retailer like The Gap or Eddie Bauer could automatically build profiles of us from the things we buy. This sounds simple, but it adds a thick layer of complexity to data mining. If you unearth an old receipt gathering dust in your bedroom, you'll see that one afternoon a few months ago you bought, say, one pair of gray pants, two cotton shirts, and some socks. What can the retailer possibly learn about you from this data? That you're a human being with a body and, presumably, two feet? They take that much for granted. That you spend an average of $863 per year in the store? That's a tad more interesting. But if each one of the items you bought carried a bit more contextual information, what computer scientists call a layer of "semantic" detail, much more of you would pop into focus.

Let's say the pants are tagged as "urban youth." With this bit of knowledge, the system can move beyond your spending habits and start to delve into your personal tastes—much the way Amazon.com calculates the kind of reader you are from the books you buy. A clothing system with semantic smarts can send you coupons for garments that appeal to urban youth. It can track the proclivities of this "tribe" (that's a word marketers adore). And depending on the store's privacy policy, it might decide to sell that data to other companies eager to market songs or cars to the same group. Some, as we'll see later, might even use tribal data to push members toward one political candidate or another. Complications? No doubt. Maybe you're a 55-year-old woman who bought that pair of pants for your 16-year-old son. Maybe he hated them. That's not really you in the receipt, and it's not him either. Faced with such complexity and contradictions, machines need smart and patient teachers to guide them in making sense of us.

That's how Rayid Ghani views himself—as a personal tutor for the idiot savants we know as computers. Ghani is short, a bit round, and quick to smile. He's one of the friendliest tutors his students could hope for (not that they'd notice). A Pakistani who studied at the computer science powerhouse Carnegie Mellon, Ghani would seem to fit right in with the Numerati. But in their rarefied ranks, he's missing a standard ingredient: a doctorate. Having "only a master's" in his circle is viewed as a handicap. But the 29-year-old outsider has grown accustomed to clawing his way upward. The son of two college professors in

Karachi, Pakistan, he applied to American colleges fully aware that he could afford only those offering a full scholarship. He landed at the University of the South, in Sewanee, Tennessee. Ghani calls it "a liberal arts college in the middle of nowhere." Hardly the ideal spot for a budding computer scientist, it is better known for its theology school. But one summer, Ghani won an internship at Carnegie Mellon, in Pittsburgh. He plunged into a world where classmates were teaching cars to drive by themselves and training computers to speak and read. He developed a passion for machine learning. Upon graduation from Sewanee, he proceeded to a master's program at CMU. Ghani was in a hurry. He started publishing papers nearly as soon as he arrived. And when he got his master's, he decided to look for a job "at places where they hire Ph.D.'s." He landed at Accenture, and now, at an age at which many of his classmates are just finishing their doctorate, he runs the analytics division from his perch in Chicago.

Ghani leads me out of his office and toward the shopping cart. For statistical modeling, he explains, grocery shopping is one of the first retail industries to conquer. This is because we buy food constantly. For many of us, the supermarket functions as a chilly, Muzak-blaring annex to our pantries. (I would bet that millions of suburban Americans spend more time in supermarkets than in their formal living room.) Our grocery shopping is so prodigious that just by studying one year of our receipts, researchers can detect all sorts of patterns—far more than they can learn from a year of records detailing our other, more sporadic purchases. (Most of us, for example, buy zero cars and zero TV sets in any given year.)

Three years ago, Ghani's team at Accenture began to work with a grocery chain. (They're not allowed to name it.) This project came with a windfall: two years of detailed customer records. The stores left out names, ages, and other demographic details, but none of that mattered. The 20,000 shoppers Ghani and his colleagues studied were simply numbers. But by their behavior in the stores, each number produced a detailed portrait of a shopper.

Let's assume you're one of those nameless shoppers. What can researchers learn about you? As it turns out, plenty. By the patterns of your purchases, and the amount you spend week after week, they can see if you're on a budget. They can calculate your spending limit. If they add some semantic tags to the data, they can draw other conclusions. When they see you starting to buy skim milk, or perhaps those miracle milk shakes, they can infer that you're on a diet. And they have no trouble seeing when you lapse. That carton of Ben & Jerry's in your cart, or the big wheel of Roquefort, is a giveaway. But wait! Maybe it's the holiday season, or your birthday. A few more weeks of receipts will spell out whether you're just cheating a little or in free fall. All of this they can do with the kind of statistical analysis an eighth grader could understand.

It gets a bit more complicated when they calculate your brand loyalty. Let's say you like Cherry Coke. You lug home a 12-pack every week. How much would Pepsi have to slash the price of its Wild Cherry Cola to entice you to switch? Ghani and two colleagues, Katharina Probst and Chad Cumby, watch how the shoppers respond to sales and promotional giveaways. They score each shopper on brand loyalty, and even loyalty to certain products within a brand. Some people, they've found, are loyal to certain foods, such as Kraft's macaroni and cheese. But does that loyalty extend to other Kraft products? For a certain group of shoppers, it does. The Accenture team takes note.

What they have on their hands is an enormous catalog of the eating habits of a small group of urban Americans in the first years of this century. Anthropologists of a certain bent would feast on it. But what good does it do a supermarket to know that you, for example, have a $95 weekly budget, are fiercely loyal to Cheetos, and flirted with the Atkins diet last barbecue season? What can they do with all that intelligence when they don't do business with you until you show up, loyalty card in hand, at the checkout counter? At that point, you've done your shopping. The chance to offer you promotions based on your profile has passed. Sure, they can throw a few coupons in your bag. Maybe you'll remember them on your next visit, but probably not. This is why, until now, supermarkets have virtually ignored the records of individual shoppers. They had little opportunity to put them to use.

The real breakthrough will come when retailers can spot you grabbing an empty cart and pushing it into the store. This has been a grocers' dream for decades. In a previous life in the 1990s, that sad little shopping cart at Accenture was a proud prototype of a "smart cart," one that allowed shoppers to swipe their loyalty cards through a computer attached to the cart, which would then lead them to bargains. "Everyone tried to do it," Ghani says. The attempts fell flat. The computers were too pricey, the analytics primitive. But computers are far cheaper now. Companies like Accenture are betting they can make systems so smart that shoppers will view the new smart cart as a personal assistant.

The first of such smart carts are just starting to roll. Stop & Shop is testing them in grocery stores in Massachusetts. Carts powered by a Microsoft program are taking their first turns in ShopRite supermarkets along the East Coast. The German chain Metro is launching them in Düsseldorf. And Samsung-Tesco, a Korean-British venture, has them operating in Seoul. A few things we know even at this early stage. For one, a computer on a shopping cart can ill afford to make dumb mistakes. This sounds axiomatic, but the fact is, we've long given grocery stores the benefit of the doubt when they offer us fliers and coupons that don't match our needs or wants, since they don't pretend to know them. But if a shopper has been buying skim milk for a year and the personalized cart insists on promoting half-and-half, the shopper may well view the smart cart as idiotic (and revert to the traditional dumb cart that specializes in rolling).

The other extreme? If these carts get too smart, we'll likely view them as creepy. I can just imagine rolling through my neighborhood Kings, when the cart starts flashing a message: STEVE: Hurry to aisle three for bargains on two of your favorite FUNGAL MEDICATIONS, plus this bonus SELECTION for the fungus you're most likely to contract NEXT! At that point, I'd be inclined to push it out to the street and under the wheels of an oncoming truck.

Setting aside such troubling scenarios, here's what shopping with one of these carts might feel like. You grab a cart on the way in and swipe your loyalty card. The welcome screen pops up with a shopping list. It's based on the patterns of your past purchases. Milk, eggs, zucchini, whatever. Smart systems might provide you with the quickest route to each item. Or perhaps they'll allow you to edit the list, to tell it, for example, never to promote cauliflower or salted peanuts again. This is simple stuff. But according to Accenture's studies, shoppers forget an average of 11 percent of the items they intend to buy. If stores can effectively remind us of what we want, it means fewer midnight runs to the convenience store for us and more sales for them.

Things get more interesting when store managers begin to manipulate our behavior. Rayid Ghani opens his laptop and shows me the supermarket control panel that he and his team have built. "Let's say you want four hundred shoppers to switch to a certain brand of frozen fish," he says. With a couple of clicks, the manager can see how many shoppers at the store buy this item. They sit in groupings known in marketing lingo as "buckets"—in this case, the frozen-fish bucket. Let's say it includes 5,000 shoppers. Among that group are those who buy rival brands of frozen fish. They're the target audience, and they sit in three smaller buckets, say, 1,000 shoppers per rival brand. Of those shoppers, one-third appear to be brand loyalists. It would likely take big discounts to pry them from the fish they usually buy. But the others, some 2,000, are more flexible when it comes to brands. They switch easily and often.

These buckets, as you can see, are getting increasingly refined. Now we're down to the brand-fickle buyers of certain types of frozen fish. Ghani plays at the controls. If he cuts the price by just 50 cents a pound—and sends word of the discount to their smart carts—he can entice a projected 150 of them to jump to the target brand. Ghani lowers the price by another 75 cents. At that level, an additional 300 bargainhunters would line up to buy the fish. The manager can play with endless variables. He can adjust the formula to raise profits, to goose sales, to promote brands, to slash inventory. It's a virtual puppet show, all of it based on probability. The puppets, needless to say, are mathematical representations of us.

Let's say you're notoriously fickle when it comes to brands. Even the smallest fluctuations will push you from Cheerios to Wheaties and back again. If the manager is interested in slashing inventory, you're likely to be in the first bucket he picks up. You're an easy sell. But if the goal is to switch your allegiance from one brand to another, you're a lousy bet. No offense, but you're disloyal, at least in this context. You'll pocket the discount and abandon the brand the very next time you can save a dime. The manager might fare better promoting the discount to those who stick to brands a bit longer than you do. Naturally, they're in another bucket.

You may also lose out on discounts if you hew to a weekly budget. Let's say you spend about $120 a week on groceries. The system calculates that you're on a budget because, say, 87 percent of the time you spend between $113 and $125 a week. If you're not restricted to a formal limit, you might as well be. Assume that the manager is eager to get rid of a mountain of detergent moldering in the warehouse. He's offering jumbo boxes at two for the price of one. Should he send the word to your screen? Maybe not, Ghani says. The reason is simple. For every dollar you spend on discounted products, that's one less dollar you have in your budget to spend at full price. That hurts profits. To get rid of that detergent, it's smarter to target people in freer-spending buckets.

Among the most unpleasant buckets a manager must confront are those loaded with "barnacle" shoppers. That term comes from

V. Kumar, a consultant and marketing professor at the University of Connecticut. Barnacles, from a retailer's perspective, are detestable creatures. We all know a few of them. They're the folks who drive from store to store, clipped coupons in hand, buying discounted goods—and practically nothing else. Kumar calls them barnacles because, like the mollusks clinging to a ship, they hitch free rides and contribute nothing of value. In fact, they cost the retailer money. With all the consumer data pouring in, Kumar says, it's becoming a snap to calculate a projected profit (or loss) for each customer. Kumar, who sells his advice to Ralph Lauren and Procter & Gamble, says that retailers should "fire" customers who look likely to drag down profits.

This doesn't mean hiring musclebound bouncers to block these shoppers at the door. But retailers can take steps in that direction. They can start by removing barnacles from their mailing lists. Increasingly, they'll also have the means to make adjustments inside the store. If bona fide barnacles are pushing smart carts through a supermarket, for example, it might make sense to fill their screens with off-putting promotions for full-priced caviar and truffles. (Discouraging unwanted shoppers is far easier on the Internet. Already, online merchants are assailing their barnacles with advertisements. And if these bargain hunters click to browse the pages of a book or gawk at the free photos on a paid-porn site, they get shunted to the slowest servers, so that they wait and wait.)

If you think about it, barnacles thrive in markets where we're all treated alike. They feast on opportunities that the rest of us, for one reason or another, miss. But now retailers are gaining tools not only to spot barnacles but also to discriminate against them. Barnacles, of course, are the first to notice when this happens. It's their nature to keep their eyes wide open. And you can bet that they'll challenge this type of discrimination in court. In a class-action suit in 2005, lawyers representing some 6 million subscribers to Netflix, the film-by-mail rental service, charged that the service was taking longer to send movies to its most active customers. Those were the film buffs who paid a flat monthly fee of $17.99 for limitless rentals and tried to see as many movies as they could for their money. This involved watching a movie or two the very day they arrived in the mail and rushing to mail them back the next morning. (I know the routine; for my first few months on Netflix, I was an eager barnacle.) Netflix officials admitted that they favored less active (and more profitable) customers with prompt mailings. And in a settlement, they gave millions of subscribers a free month of service. But, significantly, they did not vow to change their barnacle-punishing ways. They simply adjusted the wording in their rental contracts.

Barnacles aren't the only creatures in Kumar's menagerie. He also warns retailers about "butterflies," customers who drop in at the store on occasion, spend good money, and then flit away, sometimes for months or years on end. They're unreliable, and retailers are warned to avoid lavishing attention on them. "You shouldn't chase the butterflies," the professor says. However, by studying their patterns of behavior, smart retailers may learn which butterflies they can turn into reliable customers—a bucket that Kumar calls "true friends."

As merchants learn more about us, it's going to be easier for them to figure out which customers to reward and which ones to punish. This won't make much difference to butterfly shoppers. They're oblivious. But in the age of the retailing Numerati, life for barnacles might get grim.

SUGGESTIONS FOR WRITING

1. Here's a simple yes-or-no question: If a smart cart were available to you at the grocery store where you usually shop, would you use it? Following up on your one-word answer, write an essay in which you elaborate on your reasons for either selecting or avoiding the smart cart. In what ways do you think your choice might be influenced by other personal service shopping experiences you've had, such as getting recommendations from Amazon.com or from storekeepers where you are a frequent customer?

2. The information-gathering practices of retailers and marketers raise important questions about the privacy and ownership of our personal data. Although Baker doesn't delve very deeply into this issue, others have objected to what they see as an invasion of privacy that happens when our shopping or Internet or other activities are recorded and accessed by other people without our knowledge. After a prewriting exercise in which you examine what privacy means to you and how you might define its limits, write an essay in which you discuss whether you think your privacy is violated when companies collect personal information about you. Do you think that certain types of data should have stricter privacy regulations (e.g., information about your finances, your health, your political views)?

3. Drawing on the other readings in this chapter, speculate on some of the ways in which you think advertising will change as a result of the information-gathering practices described in Baker's article. For instance, do you think companies are likely to spend less money on

advertising if they can develop more detailed profiles of consumers? Do you think there might be different advertising strategies for different media (television, print, Internet)? Will ads be more targeted to individuals than to groups? Will they appeal more to reason and less to emotion? In short, write a speculative piece on what you think the future holds for advertising.

On Brands and Branding

NAOMI KLEIN

The Brand Expands

The following article is excerpted from Naomi Klein's book No Logo: Taking Aim at the Brand Bullies. *In her book, Klein combines a detailed analysis of pop cultural artifacts with a stinging critique of the exploitive practices of multinational corporations, the "Brand Bullies" in her subtitle. In the excerpt that follows, Klein coins some powerful terms to describe her view of the current state of marketing and advertising: "the reign of logo terror," the "cultural expansionism" of branding, "the age of the brandasaurus," "the absurdities of branded life." Klein begins with a brief history of logos and moves on to a detailed analysis of a "branded star"—Michael Jordan— and what his relationship with Nike tells us about how brands, culture, and identity have fused together in rather disturbing ways.*

> *Since the crocodile is the symbol of Lacoste, we thought they might be interested in sponsoring our crocodiles.*
>
> —Silvino Gomes, commercial director of the Lisbon Zoo,
> on the institution's creative corporate
> sponsorship program, March 1998

I was in Grade 4 when skintight designer jeans were the be-all and end-all, and my friends and I spent a lot of time checking out each other's butt for logos. "Nothing comes between me and my Calvins," Brooke Shields assured us, and as we lay back on our beds Ophelia-style and yanked up the zippers on our Jordache jeans with wire hangers, we knew she was telling no word of a lie. At around the same time, Romi, our school's own pint-sized Farrah Fawcett, used to make her rounds up and down the rows of desks turning back the collars on our sweaters and polo shirts. It wasn't enough for her to see an alligator or a leaping horseman—it could have been a knockoff. She wanted to see the label behind the logo. We were only eight years old but the reign of logo terror had begun.

About nine years later, I had a job folding sweaters at an Esprit clothing store in Montreal. Mothers would come in with their six-year-old daughters and ask to see only the shirts that said "Esprit" in the company's trademark bold block lettering. "She won't wear anything without a name," the moms would confide apologetically as we chatted by the change rooms. It's no secret that branding has become far more ubiquitous and intrusive by now. Labels like Baby Gap and Gap Newborn imprint brand awareness on toddlers and turn babies into mini-billboards. My friend Monica tells me that her seven-year-old son marks his homework not with check marks but with little red Nike swooshes.

Until the early seventies, logos on clothes were generally hidden from view, discreetly placed on the inside of the collar. Small designer emblems did appear on the outside of shirts in the first half of the century, but such sporty attire was pretty much restricted to the golf courses and tennis courts of the rich. In the late seventies, when the fashion world rebelled against Aquarian flamboyance, the country-club wear of the fifties became mass style for newly conservative parents and their preppy kids. Ralph Lauren's Polo horseman and Izod Lacoste's alligator escaped from the golf course and scurried into the streets, dragging the logo decisively onto the outside of the shirt. These logos served the same social function as keeping the clothing's price tag on: everyone knew precisely what premium the wearer was willing to pay for style. By the mid-eighties, Lacoste and Ralph Lauren were joined by Calvin Klein, Esprit and, in Canada, Roots; gradually, the logo was transformed from an ostentatious affectation to an active fashion accessory. Most significantly, the logo itself was growing in size, ballooning from a three-quarter-inch emblem into a chest-sized marquee. This process of logo inflation is still progressing, and none is more bloated than Tommy Hilfiger, who has managed to pioneer a clothing style that transforms its faithful adherents into walking, talking, life-sized Tommy dolls, mummified in fully branded Tommy worlds.

This scaling-up of the logo's role has been so dramatic that it has become a change in substance. Over the past decade and a half, logos have grown so dominant that they have essentially transformed the clothing on which they appear into empty carriers for the brands they represent. The metaphorical alligator, in other words, has risen up and swallowed the literal shirt.

This trajectory mirrors the larger transformation our culture has undergone since Marlboro Friday, sparked by a stampede of manufacturers looking to replace their cumbersome product-production apparatus with transcendent brand names and to infuse their brands with deep, meaningful messages. By the mid-nineties, companies like Nike, Polo and Tommy Hilfiger were ready to take branding to the next level: no longer simply branding their own products, but branding the outside culture as well—by sponsoring cultural events, they could go out into the world and claim bits of it as brand-name outposts. For these companies, branding was not just a matter of adding value to a product. It was about thirstily soaking up cultural ideas and iconography that their brands could reflect by projecting these ideas and images back on the culture as "extensions" of their brands. Culture, in other words, would add value to their brands. For example, Onute Miller, senior brand manager for Tequila Sauza, explains that her company sponsored a risqué photography exhibit by George Holz because "art was a natural synergy with our product."[1]

Branding's current state of cultural expansionism is about much more than traditional corporate sponsorships: the classic arrangement in which a company donates money to an event in exchange for seeing its logo on a banner or in a program. Rather, this is the Tommy Hilfiger approach of full-frontal branding, applied now to cityscapes, music, art, films, community events, magazines, sports and schools. This ambitious project makes the logo the central focus of everything it touches—not an add-on or a happy association, but the main attraction.

Advertising and sponsorship have always been about using imagery to equate products with positive cultural or social experiences What makes nineties-style branding different is that it increasingly seeks to take these associations out of the representational realm and make them a lived reality. So the goal is not merely to have child actors drinking Coke in a TV commercial, but for students to brainstorm concepts for Coke's next ad campaign in English class. It transcends logo-festooned Roots clothing designed to conjure memories of summer camp and reaches out to build an actual Roots country lodge that becomes a 3-D manifestation of the Roots brand concept. Disney transcends its sports network ESPN, a channel for guys who like to sit

---

[1] *Business Week*, 24 May 1999, and *Wall Streeet Journal*, 12 February 1999.

around in sports bars screaming at the TV, and launches a line of ESPN Sports Bars, complete with giant-screen TVs. The branding process reaches beyond heavily marketed Swatch watches and launches "Internet time," a new venture for the Swatch Group, which divides the day into one thousand "Swatch beats." The Swiss company is now attempting to convince the on-line world to abandon the traditional clock and switch to its time-zone-free, branded time.

The effect, if not always the original intent, of advanced branding is to nudge the hosting culture into the background and make the brand the star. It is not to sponsor culture but to *be* the culture. And why shouldn't it be? If brands are not products but ideas, attitudes, values and experiences, why can't they be culture too? As we will see later in the chapter, this project has been so successful that the lines between corporate sponsors and sponsored culture have entirely disappeared. But this conflation has not been a one-way process, with passive artists allowing themselves to be shoved into the background by aggressive multinational corporations. Rather, many artists, media personalities, film directors and sports stars have been racing to meet the corporations halfway in the branding game. Michael Jordan, Puff Daddy, Martha Stewart, Austin Powers, Brandy and *Star Wars* now mirror the corporate structure of corporations like Nike and the Gap, and they are just as captivated by the prospect of developing and leveraging their own branding potential as the product-based manufacturers. So what was once a process of selling culture to a sponsor for a price has been supplanted by the logic of "co-branding"—a fluid partnership between celebrity people and celebrity brands.

Nike and the Branding of Sports

Inevitably, any discussion about branded celebrity leads to the same place: Michael Jordan, the man who occupies the number-one spot on all of those ranking lists, who has incorporated himself into the JORDAN brand, whose agent coined the term "superbrand" to describe him. But no discussion of Michael Jordan's brand potential can begin without the brand that branded him: Nike.

Nike has successfully upstaged sports on a scale that makes the breweries' rock-star aspirations look like amateur night. Now of course pro sports, like big-label music, is in essence a profit-driven enterprise, which is why the Nike story has less to teach us about the loss of unmarketed space—space that, arguably, never even existed in this context—than it does about the mechanics of branding and its powers of eclipse.

A company that swallows cultural space in giant gulps, Nike is the definitive story of the transcendent nineties superbrand, and more than any other single company, its actions demonstrate how branding seeks to erase all boundaries between the sponsor and the sponsored. This is a shoe company that is determined to unseat pro sports, the Olympics and even star athletes, to become the very definition of sports itself.

Nike CEO Phil Knight started selling running shoes in the sixties, but he didn't strike it rich until high-tech sneakers became the must-have accessory of America's jogging craze. But when jogging subsided in the mid-eighties and Reebok cornered the market on trendy aerobics shoes, Nike was left with a product destined for the great dustbin of yuppie fads. Rather than simply switching to a different kind of sneaker, Knight decided that running shoes should become peripheral in a reincarnated Nike. Leave sneakers to Reebok and Adidas—Nike would transform itself into what Knight calls "the world's best sports and fitness company."[2]

The corporate mythology has it that Nike is a sports and fitness company because it was built by a bunch of jocks who loved sports and were fanatically devoted to the worship of superior athletes. In reality, Nike's project was a little more complicated and can be separated into three guiding principles. First, turn a select group of athletes into Hollywood-style superstars who are associated not with their teams or even, at times, with their sport, but instead with certain pure ideas about athleticism as transcendence and perseverance—embodiments of the Graeco-Roman ideal of the perfect male form. Second, pit Nike's "Pure Sports" and its team of athletic superstars against the rule-obsessed established sporting world. Third, and most important, brand like mad.

Step 1: Create Sport Celebrities

It was Michael Jordan's extraordinary basketball skill that catapulted Nike to branded heaven, but it was Nike's commercials that made Jordan a global superstar. It's true that gifted athletes like Babe Ruth and Muhammad Ali were celebrities before Nike's time, but they never reached Jordan's otherworldly level of fame. That stratum was reserved for movie and pop stars, who had been transformed by the special effects, art direction and careful cinematography of films and music videos. Sport stars pre-Nike, no matter how talented or worshiped,

---

[2] Willigan, "High-Performance Marketing," 94.

were still stuck on the ground. Football, hockey and baseball may have been ubiquitous on television, but televised sports were just real-time play-by-plays, which were often tedious, sometimes exciting and high tech only in the slow-mo replay. As endorsing products, their advertisements and commercials couldn't quite be described as cutting-edge star creation—whether it was Wilt Chamberlain goofily grinning from a box of Wheaties or Rocket Richard being sentenced to "two minutes for looking so good" in Grecian Formula commercials.

> *I wake up every morning, jump*
> *in the shower, look down at the*
> *symbol, and that pumps me up*
> *for the day. It's to remind me*
> *every day what I have to do,*
> *which is, "Just Do It."*
> —*Twenty-four-year-old Internet entrepreneur Carmine Collettion on his decision to get a Nike swoosh tattooed on his navel, December 1997*

Nike's 1985 TV spots for Michael Jordan brought sports into the entertainment world: the freeze frame, the close-up and the quick cuts that allowed Jordan to appear to be suspended in mid-jump, providing the stunning illusion that he could actually take flight. The idea of harnessing sport-shoe technology to create a superior being—of Michael Jordan flying through the air in suspended animation—was Nike mythmaking at work. These commercials were the first rock videos about sports and they created something entirely new. As Michael Jordan says, "What Phil [Knight] and Nike have done is turn me into a dream."[3]

Many of Nike's most famous TV commercials have used Nike superstars to convey the *idea* of sports, as opposed to simply representing the best of the athlete's own team sport. Spots often feature famous athletes playing a game other than the one they play professionally, such as tennis pro Andre Agassi showing off his version of "rock-and-roll golf." And then there was the breakthrough "Bo Knows" campaign, which lifted baseball and football player Bo Jackson out of his two professional sports and presented him instead as the perfect all-around cross-trainer. A series of quick-cut interviews with Nike stars—McEnroe, Jordan, Gretzky—ironically suggested that Jackson

---

[3]Katz, *Just Do It*, 8.

knew their sports better than they did. "Bo knows tennis," "Bo knows basketball" and so on.

At the 1998 Winter Olympics in Nagano, Nike took this strategy out of the controlled environment of its TV commercials and applied it to a real sports competition. The experiment started in 1995 when Nike's marketing department dreamed up the idea of turning a couple of Kenyan runners into Africa's first Olympic ski team. As Mark Bossardet, Nike's director of global athletics, explained, "We were sitting around the office one day and we said, 'What if we took Kenyan runners and transferred their skills to cross-country skiing?[4] Kenyan runners, who have dominated cross-country track-and-field competitions at the Olympics since 1968, have always represented the "idea of sports" at Nike headquarters. ("Where's the Kenyans running?" Phil Knight has been heard to demand after viewing a Nike ad deemed insufficiently inspiring and heroic. In Nike shorthand it means, "Where's the Spirit of Sports?").[5] So according to Nike marketing logic, if two Kenyan runners—living specimens of sports incarnate—were plucked out of their own sport and out of their country and their native climate, and dumped on a frozen mountaintop, and if they were then able to transfer their agility, strength and endurance to cross-country skiing, their success would represent a moment of pure sporting transcendence. It would be a spiritual transformation of Man over nature, birthright, nation and petty sports bureaucrats—brought to the world by Nike, of course. "Nike always felt sports shouldn't have boundaries," the swooshed press release announced. Finally there would be proof.

And if nothing else, Nike would get its name in lots of quirky human-interest sidebar stories—just like the wacky Jamaican bobsled team that hogged the headlines at the 1988 Winter Olympics in Calgary. What sports reporter could resist the heart-warmer of Africa's first ski team?

Nike found its test-tube subjects in two mid-level runners, Philip Boit and Henry Bitok. Since Kenya has no snow, no ski federation and no training facilities, Nike financed the entire extravagant affair, dishing out $250,000 for training in Finland and custom-designed uniforms, and paying the runners a salary to live away from their families. When Nagano rolled around, Bitok didn't qualify and Boit finished last—a full twenty minutes after the gold-medal winner, Bjorn Daehlie

---

[4] *New York Times*, 20 December 1997, A1.
[5] Katz, *Just Do It*, 284.

of Norway. It turns out that cross-country running and cross-country skiing—despite the similarity of their names—require entirely different sets of skills and use different muscles.

But that was beside the point. Before the race began, Nike held a press conference at its Olympic headquarters, catered the event with Kenyan food and beer and showed reporters a video of the Kenyans encountering snow for the first time, skiing into bushes and falling on their butts. The journalists also heard accounts of how the climate change was so dramatic that the Kenyans' skin cracked and their fingernails and toenails fell off, but "now," as Boit said, "I love snow. Without snow, I could not do my sport." As the *Tampa Tribune* of February 12, 1998, put it, "They're just two kooky Kenyans trying to make it in the frozen tundra."

It was quintessential Nike branding: by equating the company with athletes and athleticism at such a primal level, Nike ceased merely to clothe the game and started to play it. And once Nike was in the game with its athletes, it could have fanatical sports fans instead of customers.

Step 2: *Destroy the Competition*

Like any competitive sports player, Nike has its work cut out for it: winning. But winning for Nike is about much more than sneaker wars. Of course Nike can't stand Adidas, Fila and Reebok, but more important, Phil Knight has sparred with sports agents, whose individual greed, he claims, puts them "inherently in conflict with the interests of athletes at every turn";[6] the NBA, which he feels has unfairly piggy-backed on Nike's star-creation machinery;[7] and the International Olympic Committee, whose elitism and corruption Knight derided long before the organization's 1999 bribery scandals.[8] In Nike's world, all of the official sports clubs, associations and committees are actually trampling the spirit of sports—a spirit Nike alone truly embodies and appreciates.

So at the same time as Nike's myth machine was fabricating the idea of Team Nike, Nike's corporate team was dreaming up ways to play a more central role in pro sports. First Nike tried to unseat the sports agents by starting an agency of its own, not only to represent athletes in contract negotiation but also to develop integrated marketing

---

[6] Ibid., 34, 231.
[7] Ibid., 30–31.
[8] Ibid., 36, 119.

strategies for its clients that are sure to complement—not dilute—Nike's own branding strategy, often by pushing its own ad concepts on other companies.

Then there was a failed attempt to create—and own—a college football version of the Super Bowl (the Nike Bowl), and in 1992, Nike did buy the Ben Hogan golf tour and rename it the Nike Tour. "We do these things to be in the sport. We're in sports—that's what we do," Knight told reporters at the time.[9] That is certainly what they did when Nike and rival Adidas made up their own sporting event to settle a grudge match over who could claim the title "fastest man alive" in their ads: Nike's Michael Johnson or Adidas's Donovan Bailey. Because the two compete in different categories (Bailey in the 100-meter, Johnson in the 200), the sneaker brands agreed to split the difference and had the men compete in a made-up 150-meter race. Adidas won.

When Phil Knight faces the inevitable criticism from sports purists that he is having an undue influence on the games he sponsors, his stock response is that "the athlete remains our reason for being."[10] But as the company's encounter with star basketball player Shaquille O'Neal shows, Nike is only devoted to a certain kind of athlete. Company biographer Donald Katz describes the tense meeting between O'Neal's manager, Leonard Armato, and Nike's marketing team:

> Shaq had observed the explosion of the sports-marketing scene ("He took sports-marketing courses," Armato says) and the rise of Michael Jordan, and he'd decided that rather than becoming a part of several varied corporate marketing strategies, an array of companies might be assembled as part of a brand presence that was he. Consumer products companies would become part of Team Shaq, rather than the other way around. "We're looking for consistency of image," Armato would say as he began collecting the team on Shaq's behalf. "Like Mickey Mouse."

The only problem was that at Nike headquarters, there is no Team Shaq, only Team Nike. Nike took a pass and handed over the player many thought would be the next Michael Jordan to Reebok—not "Nike material," they said. According to Katz, Knight's mission "from the beginning had been to build a pedestal for sports such as the world had never seen."[11] But at Nike Town in Manhattan, the pedestal is not holding up

---

9 Ibid., 233.
10 Ibid., 24.
11 Ibid., 24.

Michael Jordan, or the sport of basketball, but a rotating Nike sneaker. Like a prima donna, it sits in the spotlight, the first celebrity shoe.

Step 3: Sell Pieces of the Brand As If It Was the Berlin Wall

Nothing embodies the era of the brand like Nike Town, the company's chain of flagship retail outlets. Each one is a shrine, a place set apart for the faithful, a mausoleum. The Manhattan Nike Town on East Fifty-seventh Street is more than a fancy store fitted with the requisite brushed chrome and blond wood, it is a temple, where the swoosh is worshiped as both art and heroic symbol. The swoosh is equated with Sports at every turn: in reverent glass display cases depicting "The definition of an athlete"; in the inspirational quotes about "Courage," "Honor," "Victory" and "Teamwork" inlaid in the floorboards; and in the building's dedication "to all athletes and their dreams."

I asked a salesperson if there was anything amid the thousands of T-shirts, bathing suits, sports bras or socks that did not have a Nike logo on the outside of the garment. He racked his brain. T-shirts, no. Shoes, no. Track suits? No.

"Why?" he finally asked, sounding a bit hurt. "Is somebody allergic to the swoosh?"

Nike, king of the superbrands, is like an inflated Pac-Man, so driven to consume it does so not out of malice but out of jaw-clenching reflex. It is ravenous by nature. It seems fitting that Nike's branding strategy involves an icon that looks like a check mark. Nike is checking off the spaces as it swallows them: superstores? Check. Hockey? Baseball? Soccer? Check. Check. Check. T-shirts? Check. Hats? Check. Underwear? Check. Schools? Bathrooms? Shaved into brush cuts? Check. Check. Check. Since Nike has been the leader in branding clothing, it's not surprising that it has also led the way to the brand's final frontier: the branding of flesh. Not only do dozens of Nike employees have a swoosh tattooed on their calves, but tattoo parlors all over North America report that the swoosh has become their most popular item. Human branding? Check.

The Branded Star

There is another reason behind Nike's stunning success at disseminating its brand. The superstar athletes who form the building blocks of its image—those creatures invented by Nike and cloned by Adidas and Fila—have proved uniquely positioned to soar in the era of synergy: they are made to be cross-promoted. The Spice Girls can make movies, and film stars can walk the runways but neither can quite win an Olympic medal. It's more practical for Dennis Rodman to write two books, star in two movies and have his own television show than it is for Martin Amis or Seinfeld to play defense for the Bulls, just as it is easier for Shaquille O'Neal to put out a rap album than it is for Sporty Spice to make the NBA draft. Only animated characters—another synergy favorite—are more versatile than sports stars in the synergy game.

But for Nike, there is a downside to the power of its own celebrity endorsers. Though Phil Knight will never admit it, Nike is no longer just competing with Reebok, Adidas and the NBA; it has also begun to compete with another brand: its name is Michael Jordan.

In the three years before he retired, Jordan was easing away from his persona as Nike incarnate and turning himself into what his agent, David Falk, calls a "superbrand." He refused to go along when Nike entered the sports-agent business, telling the company that it would have to compensate him for millions of dollars in lost revenue. Instead of letting Nike manage his endorsement portfolio, he tried to build synergy deals between his various sponsors, including a bizarre attempt to persuade Nike to switch phone companies when he became a celebrity spokesperson for WorldCom.[12] Other highlights of what Falk terms "Michael Jordan's Corporate Partnership Program" include a World-Com commercial in which the actors are decked out in Oakley sunglasses and Wilson sports gear, both Jordan-endorsed products. And, of course, the movie *Space Jam*—in which the basketball player starred and which Falk executive-produced—was Jordan's coming-out party as his own brand. The movie incorporated plugs for each of Jordan's sponsors (choice dialogue includes "Michael, it's show time. Get your Hanes on, lace up your Nikes, grab your Wheaties and Gatorade and we'll pick up a Big Mac on the way!"), and McDonald's promoted the event with *Space Jam* toys and Happy Meals.

Nike had been playing up Jordan's business ambitions in its "CEO Jordan" commercials, which show him changing into a suit and racing to his office at halftime. But behind the scenes, the company has always resented Jordan's extra-Nike activities. Donald Katz writes that as early as 1992, "Knight believed that Michael Jordan was no longer, in sports-marketing nomenclature, 'clean.'"[13] Significantly, Nike boycotted the co-branding bonanza that surrounded *Space Jam*. Unlike McDonald's,

---

[12] "Michael Jordan's Full Corporate Press," *Business Week*, 7 April 1997, 44.
[13] Katz, *Just Do It*, 35.

it didn't use the movie in tie-in commercials, despite the fact that *Space Jam* is based on a series of Nike commercials featuring Jordan and Bugs Bunny. When Falk told *Advertising Age* that "Nike had some reservations about the implementation of the movie,"[14] he was exercising considerable restraint. Jim Riswold, the longtime Nike adman who first conceived of pairing Jordan with Bugs Bunny in the shoe commercials, complained to *The Wall Street Journal* that *Space Jam* "is a merchandising bonanza first and a movie second. The idea is to sell lots of product."[15] It was a historic moment in the branding of culture, completely inverting the traditionally fraught relationship between art and commerce: a shoe company and an ad agency huffing and puffing that a Hollywood movie would sully the purity of their commercials.

For the time being at least, a peace has descended between the warring superbrands. Nike has given Jordan more leeway to develop his own apparel brand, still within the Nike empire but with greater independence. In the same week that he retired from basketball, Jordan announced that he would be extending the JORDAN clothing line from basketball gear into lifestyle wear, competing directly with Polo, Hilfiger and Nautica. Settling into his role as CEO—as opposed to celebrity endorser—he signed up other pro athletes to endorse the JORDAN brand: Derek Jeter, a shortstop for the New York Yankees and boxer Roy Jones Jr. And, as of May 1999, the full JORDAN brand is showcased in its own "retail concept shops"—two in New York and one in Chicago, with plans for up to fifty outlets by the end of the year 2000. Jordan finally had his wish: to be his own free-standing brand, complete with celebrity endorsers.

The Age of the Brandasaurus

On the surface, the power plays between millionaire athletes and billion-dollar companies would seem to have little to do with the loss of unmarketed space that is the subject of this section. Jordan and Nike, however, are only the most broad strokes, manifestations of the way in which the branding imperative changes the way we imagine both sponsor and sponsored to the extent that the idea of unbranded space—music that is distinct from khakis, festivals that are not extensions of beer brands, athletic achievement that is

---

[14] "Space Jam Turning Point for Warner Bros., Jordan," *Advertising Age*, 28 October 1996. 16.

[15] "Merchandise Upstages Box Office," *Wall Street Journal*, 24 September 1996.

celebrated in and of itself—becomes almost unthinkable. Jordan and Nike are emblematic of a new paradigm that eliminates all barriers between branding and culture, leaving no room whatsoever for unmarketed space.

An understanding is beginning to emerge that fashion designers, running-shoe companies, media outlets, cartoon characters and celebrities of all kinds are all more or less in the same business: the business of marketing their brands. That's why in the early nineties, Creative Artists Agency, the most powerful celebrity agency in Hollywood, began to represent not just celebrity people, but celebrity brands: Coke, Apple and even an alliance with Nike. That's why Benetton, Microsoft and Starbucks have leapfrogged over the "magalog" trend and have gone full force into the magazine publishing business: Benetton with *Colors*, Microsoft with the on-line zine *Slate* and Starbucks with *Joe*, a joint venture with Time Inc. That's why teen sensation Britney Spears and sitcom character Ally McBeal each have their own line of designer clothing; why Tommy Hilfiger has helped launch a record label; and rapper Master P has his own sports agency business. It's also why Ralph Lauren has a line of designer household paints, Brooks Brothers has a line of wines, Nike is set to launch a swooshed cruise ship, and auto-parts giant Magna is opening up an amusement park. It is also why market consultant Faith Popcorn has launched her own brand of leather Cocooning armchairs, named after the trend she coined of the same name, and Fashion Licensing of America Inc. is marketing a line of Ernest Hemingway furniture, designed to capture the "brand personality" of the late writer.[16]

As manufacturers and entertainers swap roles and move together toward the creation of branded lifestyle bubbles, Nike executives predict that their "competition in the future [will] be Disney, not Reebok."[17] And it seems only fitting that just as Nike enters the entertainment business, the entertainment giants have decided to try their hand at the sneaker industry. In October 1997, Warner Brothers launched a low-end basketball shoe, endorsed by Shaquille O'Neal. "It's an extension of what we do at retail," explained Dan Romanelli of Warner Consumer products.

It seems that wherever individual brands began—in shoes, sports, retail, food, music or cartoons—the most successful among them have

---

[16] "Armchair Adventures," *Globe and Mail*, 11 January 1999, C12.
[17] Katz, *Just Do It*. 82.

all landed in the same place: the stratosphere of the superbrand. That is where Mick Jagger struts in Tommy Hilfiger, Steven Spielberg and Coke have the same agent, Shaq wants to be "like Mickey Mouse," and everyone has his or her own branded restaurant—from Jordan to Disney to Demi Moore to Puffy Combs and the supermodels.

It was Michael Ovitz, of course, who came up with the blueprint for the highest temple of branding so far, one that would do for music, sports and fashion what Walt Disney long ago did for kids' cartoons: turn the slick world of television into a real-world branded environment. After leaving Creative Artists Agency in August 1995 and being driven out as president of Disney shortly after, Ovitz took his unprecedented $87 million golden handshake and launched a new venture: entertainment- and sports-themed megamalls, a synthesis of pro sports, Hollywood celebrity and shopping. His vision is of an unholy mixture of Nike Town, Planet Hollywood and the NBA's marketing wing—all leading straight to the cash register. The first venture; a 1.5-million-square-foot theme mall in Columbus, Ohio, is scheduled to open in the year 2000. If Ovitz gets his way, another mall, planned for the Los Angeles area, will include an NFL football stadium.

As these edifices of the future suggest, corporate sponsors and the culture they brand have fused together to create a third culture: a self-enclosed universe of brand-name people, brand-name products and brand-name media. Interestingly, a 1995 study conducted by University of Missouri professor Roy F. Fox shows that many kids grasp the unique ambiguities of this sphere intuitively. The study found that a majority of Missouri high-school students who watched Channel One's mix of news and ads in their classrooms thought that sports stars paid shoe companies to be in their commercials. "I don't know why athletes do that—pay all that money for all them ignorant commercials for themselves. Guess it makes everyone like 'em more and like their teams more."[18]

So opined Debbie, a ninth-grader and one of the two hundred students who participated in the study. For Fox, the comment demonstrates a disturbing lack of media literacy, proof positive that kids can't critically evaluate the advertising they see on television. But perhaps these findings show that kids understand something most of us still refuse to grasp. Maybe they know that sponsorship is a far more complicated

---

[18] Roy F. Fox, "Manipulated Kids: Teens Tell How Ads Influence Them," *Educational Leadership*, September 1995, 77.

process than the buyer/seller dichotomy that existed in previous decades and that to talk of who sold out or bought in has become impossibly anachronistic. In an era in which people are brands and brands are culture, what Nike and Michael Jordan do is more akin to co-branding than straight-up shilling, and while the Spice Girls may be doing Pepsi today, they could easily launch their own Spice Cola tomorrow.

It makes a good deal of sense that high-school kids would have a more realistic grasp of the absurdities of branded life. They, after all, are the ones who grew up sold.

SUGGESTIONS FOR WRITING

1. Based on Klein's article, as well as on some of the other readings in this chapter, write brief, one-paragraph definitions of the following closely related terms: advertisement, logo, brand, sponsor. Feel free to draw on your own experience in crafting these definitions as well as on outside reading and research.

2. *No Logo* was originally published in 1996; to what extent do you think Klein's observations hold true today? Are logos still evident on clothing in the way that Klein describes at the beginning of the article? Are celebrity athletes still a cornerstone of branding and marketing? Write an essay in which you update Klein's argument by looking at one or more contemporary examples of how logos and brands operate in U.S. culture.

3. Klein focuses her analysis of celebrity athletes on Michael Jordan, the "superbrand." Choose a more recent example of an athlete who has been branded in a similar way (Tiger Woods, Shaquille O'Neal, Lance Armstrong) and write an analysis of how the branding process has worked for this athlete. Is the athlete associated with a single product (as Jordan was with Nike) or is the athlete able to create his own branded identity (as Jordan ultimately did)? How does the "branded star" represent the products he or she endorses, and how do attributes of the product help define the athlete?

JAMES SUROWIECKI

The Decline of Brands

As an interesting supplement to Naomi Klein's vision of a U.S. landscape covered in logos, James Surowieki argues that brands and branding are in decline. Indeed, the fact that there are more brands than ever is a good indication that the concept of brands and the branding system as a whole aren't working very well. As Surowiecki points out, it wouldn't make sense to launch a new brand if the old brand had a secure lock on consumers: "But because consumers are more promiscuous and fickle than ever, established brands are vulnerable, and new ones have a real chance of succeeding." Companies are still spending millions of dollars creating and marketing their brands, but a more savvy and better informed breed of consumer is less likely to make purchases based on the brand of a product. Surowieki argues that the decline of brands is on the whole a very good thing: As new companies emerge and try to unseat the dominant players by developing innovative technologies and less expensive alternatives, consumers reap the rewards.

The world, it seems, is disappearing beneath a deluge of logos. In the past decade, corporations looking to navigate an ever more competitive marketplace have embraced the gospel of branding with newfound fervor. The brand value of companies like Coca-Cola and IBM is routinely calculated at tens of billions of dollars, and brands have come to be seen as the ultimate long-term asset—economic engines capable of withstanding turbulence and generating profits for decades. So companies spend billions on brand campaigns and try to indelibly mark everything in sight, from the ING New York City Marathon to the Diamond Nuts cup holders at SBC Park.

Since 1991, the number of brands on US grocery store shelves has tripled. Last year, the US Patent and Trademark Office issued an incredible 140,000 trademarks - 100,000 more than in 1983. The average American sees 60 percent more ad messages per day than when the first President Bush left office. A handful of years ago, David Foster Wallace fantasized in Infinite Jest about an America in which corporations sponsor entire years—the Year of the Whopper, the Year of the Depend Adult Undergarment. The fantasy seems more reasonable by the day.

And yet there's something strange going on in branding land. Even as companies have spent enormous amounts of time and energy introducing new brands and defending established ones, Americans have become less loyal. Consumer-goods markets used to be very stable. If you had a set of customers today, you could be pretty sure most of them would still be around two years, five years, ten years from now. That's no longer true. A study by retail-industry tracking firm NPD Group found that nearly half of those who described themselves as highly loyal to a brand were no longer loyal a year later. Even seemingly strong names rarely translate into much power at the cash register. Another remarkable study found that just 4 percent of consumers would be willing to stick with a brand if its competitors offered better value for the same price. Consumers are continually looking for a better deal, opening the door for companies to introduce a raft of new products.

Marketers may consider the explosion of new brands to be evidence of branding's importance, but in fact the opposite is true. It would be a waste of money to launch a clever logo into a world of durable brands and loyal customers. But because consumers are more promiscuous and fickle than ever, established brands are vulnerable, and new ones have a real chance of succeeding—for at least a little while. The obsession with brands, paradoxically, demonstrates their weakness.

The single biggest explanation for fragile brands is the swelling strength of the consumer. We've seen a pronounced jump in the amount of information available about goods and services. It's not just bellwethers like Consumers Union and J. D. Power, established authorities that unquestionably shape people's buying decisions, but also the crush of magazines, Web sites, and message boards scrutinizing products. Consumers have also become more demanding: even as the quality and reliability of products have generally risen, satisfaction ratings have not budged, and in some cases they've actually fallen. Businesses are now dealing with buyers who are armed with both information and harsh expectations. In this environment, companies that slip up—even if it's simply failing to match customer tastes—can no longer count on their good names to carry them through. And consumers have become far more willing to experiment with products, because the amount of information out there makes taking a chance far less risky. By the time you think about buying that digital altimeter barometer, chances are the bleeding edge has already weighed in at Epinions. This gives nascent brands an opportunity to succeed, but it also makes staying power a lot harder to come by. Welcome to the What Have You Done for Me Lately? economy.

Some industries are suffering more than others. In consumer electronics, quality has risen across the board, making product differences harder to discern. Manufacturing has commodified: most of today's computer equipment, television screens, and stereos are made by a small handful of contract manufacturers and then slapped with a logo before hitting store shelves. That doesn't mean that making a better gizmo no longer matters offering genuinely innovative products is, more than ever, the best way to capture market share. But savvy consumers are no longer willing to pay a high premium for an otherwise identical product just because it has a fancy nameplate.

Undoubtedly, there are strong brands that can still command a premium. In one recent survey by Landor Associates, 99.5 percent of people said they'd be willing to pay more for a Sony. But the size of that premium is smaller than ever. Five years ago, Sony charged 44 percent more for its DVD players than the average manufacturer. Today, Sony DVD players cost just 16 percent more than the average. And yet, even though the price of Sony's most expensive DVD player fell 60 percent between 1999 and 2003, CyberHome, maker of absurdly cheap DVD players, has knocked off Sony to become the biggest DVD-machine seller in America. Similarly, in the fashion industry, a stronghold of brand identity and obsession, prices fell an average of 9 percent between 2001 and 2003. At least part of the reason is the uptick in private-label sales, which now account for almost half the market. The rise of retailers like Zara and H&M, which make their own cheap but nice designer knockoffs, and the emergence of a high-low aesthetic (in which top designers no longer dictate taste) have weakened the power of fashion brands and fragmented the industry into myriad small ones. Sure, superbrands like Louis Vuitton and Prada can still command a heft price premium. But they're increasingly the exception.

Marketing types either don't see this trend or choose not to talk about it. In the words of advertising legend Jim Mullen, "Of all the things that your company owns, brands are far and away the most important and the toughest. Founders die. Factories burn down. Machinery wears out. Inventories get depleted. Technology becomes obsolete. Brand loyalty is the only sound foundation on which business leaders can build enduring, profitable growth." Similarly, in the new book *Brands and Branding*, Rita Clifton, chair of Interbrand UK, puts it this way: "Well-managed brands have extraordinary economic value and are the most effective and efficient creators of sustainable wealth." These assertions claim that while factories, source code, and patents are ephemeral, brands are real. But in fact, their long-term value is shrinking. They're becoming nothing more than shadows. You wouldn't expect your shadow to protect you or show you the way. It only goes wherever you do.

Look at Nokia. In 2002, it had the sixth-most-valuable brand in the world, valued by the consultancy Interbrand at $30 billion. But the very next year, Nokia made a simple mistake: It didn't produce the clamshell-design cell phones that customers wanted. Did consumers stick around because of their deep emotional investment in Nokia? Not a chance. They jumped ship, and the company's sales tumbled. As a result, Nokia lost $6 billion in equity. How about Krispy Kreme? In 2003, Fortune called the doughnut maker America's "hottest brand." Then came what might prove to be the hottest name of 2004: Atkins.

Annual rankings of brand value are littered with examples of firms that watched billions of dollars in supposed "brand equity" vanish—not because they messed with their identities, but simply because they didn't make a product or deliver a service that people needed. Even genuinely powerful brand association is no longer a guarantee that a company will make money. TiVo has revolutionized television, and even introduced a word into the consumer vernacular. But it hasn't made a dime in profit. In the past year, the company has cut prices sharply to try to compete with the cheap DVRs coming to market from cable and satellite companies. Similarly, Apple has had to continually introduce better variations on the iPod—and cut prices—to fend off copycats.

Marketers aren't completely deceived (or being deceiving) when they argue that customers make emotional connections with brands, but those connections are increasingly tenuous. If once upon a time customers married brands—people who drove Fords drove Fords their whole lives—today they're more like serial monogamists who move on as soon as something sexier comes along. Gurus talk about building an image to create a halo over a company's products. But these days, the only sure way to keep a brand strong is to keep wheeling out products, which will in turn cast the halo. (The iPod has made a lot more people interested in Apple than Apple made people interested in the iPod.) If a company must constantly deliver new value to its loyal customers just to keep them, those customers aren't loyal at all. Which means, save for a few perennials like Coke, brands have little or no value independent of what a company actually does. "Brands have run out of juice. They're dead," says Kevin Roberts, CEO of advertising giant Saatchi & Saatchi and author of the new book *Lovemarks*. "Now the consumer is boss. There's nowhere for brands to hide."

This is all, of course, a bad thing for marketers. A brand is supposed to provide a haven from competition, offering what Nokia CEO Jorma Ollila calls insurance against missteps. But the disappearance of loyalty means that insurance is vanishing, too—which is great for consumers. When companies can't count on their reputations to carry them through, they're forced to innovate to stay alive. The erosion of brand value, then, means heightened competition—and everything we know about economics tells us that the more competition, the better off consumers will be.

The truth is, we've always overestimated the power of branding while underestimating consumers' ability to recognize quality. When brands first became important in the US a century ago, it was because particular products—Pillsbury flour or Morton salt—offered far more reliability and quality than no-name goods. Similarly, many (and arguably most) of the important brands in American history—Gillette or Disney—became successful not because of clever marketing, but because they offered something you couldn't get anywhere else. (Gillette made the best razors; Disney made the best animated movies.) Even Nike first became popular because it made superior running shoes. Marketers looked at these companies and said they were succeeding because their brands were strong. In reality, the brands were strong because the companies were succeeding.

Over time, certain brands came to connote quality. They did provide a measure of insurance—which in turn made firms less innovative and less rigorous. (Think of the abominable cars General Motors, Ford, and Chrysler made in the late 1960s through the 1970s—remember the Pinto? —in part because they assumed that they had customers for life.) That sense of protection is eroding in industry after industry, and instead of a consumer economy in which success is determined in large part by name, it's now being determined by performance. The aristocracy of brand is dead. Long live the meritocracy of product.

SUGGESTIONS FOR WRITING

1. Surowiecki discusses the decline in brand loyalty, writing, "If once upon a time customers married brands—people who drove Fords drove Fords their whole lives—today they're more like serial monogamists who move on as soon as something sexier comes along." In an autobiographically based essay, examine at least three brands that you've owned and towards which you felt some degree of loyalty. Think about clothing, food, and technology as starting points, and make a list of the names of brands that you own in these categories. After choosing three brands that have some significance for you, describe what it is about these brands that inclines you to purchase them. How loyal are you to these brands? What would make you purchase a different brand? Based on your own experience and analysis, does Surowiecki's perspective on brand loyalty seem accurate to you?

2. Surowiecki presents both sides of the story in this article: That is, he discusses both why brands are important and why their importance is diminishing. Create an outline of the article that lists the points Surowiecki makes for each side, and supplement this outline with any ideas of your own that Surowiecki doesn't mention. You might consider using a table with two columns: In the left column, list the reasons why brands remain important and powerful marketing instruments; in the right column, list the reasons for their decline. Then append a final paragraph to this outline in which you select the perspective that you think more accurately represents the current state of brands and branding.

3. There are several interesting connections between Surowiecki's arguments about the "death of brands" and Penn's profile of the "new info shopper." Write an essay in which you synthesize these two articles and examine their connecting threads. You might structure your essay by articulating the points that each author makes about such key topics as advertising, consumers, information, and the economy. Where do you think Surowiecki and Penn agree and disagree in their assessment of the current state of advertising?

Television

With each passing year, we set new records for *owning televisions and watching them. According to Nielsen Statistics, in 2006 the average American household had more televisions (2.73) than people (2.55). In 2009, Nielsen found that the amount of time the average American spent watching TV had increased again—up to four hours and 35 minutes a day. We now have new ways to watch TV, using what advertisers call the "three screens": mobile devices, the Internet, and the old-fashioned home television (or, if you prefer and can afford it, the deluxe new high-definition flat-screen plasma version). We have a deluge of cable TV stations that cater to narrow individual interests. We have "timeshifted" TV, with technologies like TiVO and DVRs that allow us to personalize our viewing schedules and spend even more time watching our favorite shows. In short, television is a relatively old medium that has proven surprisingly resilient and adaptable to new trends and technologies.*

The first three readings in this chapter take on some of the big questions that naturally follow from television's immense popularity. First, why do we watch TV? Robert Kubey and Mihaly Csikszentmihalyi, in an article originally published in Scientific American, *argue that there are compelling physical and psychological reasons for watching TV; they propose the concept of TV addiction and draw parallels to other addictive substances and activities. Stephen Johnson, by contrast, focuses on the positive effects of TV viewing and forwards the unexpected argument that television may actually make us smarter. In shows like* 24 *and* The West Wing, *viewers see the complicated plot threads of soap opera combined with the realistic characters* and important social issues of nighttime drama. Watching these shows engages viewers in the intellectually stimulating pleasures of solving puzzles and unlocking mysteries. Finally, Clay Shirky argues that despite its appeal and potential benefits, watching television is a passive, solitary activity and a relatively unproductive way for us to spend free time. By contrast, Shirky praises the participatory endeavors facilitated by the Internet. He argues that the time we spend watching TV could be much more usefully spent working on projects like Wikipedia and on similarly collaborative and creative activities.

While the first three readings in this chapter address television viewing in general, the second group of readings focuses on a particular genre of television: reality TV. There are various definitions of reality TV, but we cast a broad net here so as to include classic shows like Survivor, Big Brother, and MTV's The Real World, as well as a range of other relatively unscripted shows in which the cast is comprised of amateurs rather than (or in addition to) professional actors. These include dating shows (The Bachelor, The Bachelorette, Beauty and the Geek); makeover shows (The Biggest Loser, The Swan, Extreme Makeover: Home Edition); talent competitions (American Idol, Nashville Star, America's Next Top Model, Project Runway, Dancing with the Stars, Hell's Kitchen, Top Chef); and celebrity shows (The Simple Life, The Surreal Life, The Osbournes). As you can see from this small sampling (and fuller lists are available online—for instance, at RealityTVWorld.com), the amount and range of reality TV has grown along with the United States's appetite for this type of show. On any given night, you can watch real people enthusiastically engaged in a wide variety of competitions, cohabitations, and other complications.

Popular culture scholars and critics have a lot to say about why viewers enjoy reality television and what effects this genre of TV show might have on U.S. society. In "Reality Check," the first article in this section, Eric Jaffe surveys the ways that psychology scholars have studied reality TV, attempting to answer how it both depicts and influences who we are, how we act, and what we believe. After this overview of reality TV, Richard Huff focuses on American Idol, observing that this wildly popular show is one of many talent competitions that have been reinvigorated by reality TV strategies and technologies. American Idol has been particularly clever at involving the viewers in determining the results of the competition, via telephone and text message voting. Finally, Gareth Palmer offers a close analysis of Extreme Makeover: Home Edition, a popular and seemingly positive, socially responsible example of reality TV in which an extravagant home renovation is provided for a deserving family. Palmer, however, critiques the fairy-tale premise on which this and other makeover shows are based, and he suggests that, although it helps an individual family, the show actually reveals significant problems in the contemporary U.S. family, community, and economy.

The readings in this chapter move, then, from broad approaches to television in general to close readings of specific television shows. They provide a range of starting points for you to think about your own television-viewing habits and the ways that TV has influenced your behaviors, beliefs, and values.

ROBERT KUBEY AND MIHALY
CSIKSZENTMIHALYI

Television Addiction Is No Mere Metaphor

While some social commentators see humor in the idea of couch potatoes spudding out in front of the television, Robert Kubey and Mihaly Csikszentmihalyi bring sociological and biological evidence to bear on their explanation of the addictive power television has over us. Robert Kubey and Mihaly Csikszentmihalyi are both college professors: Kubey is the director of the Center for Media Studies at Rutgers University, and Csikszentmihalyi is the C. S. and D. J. Davidson Professor of Psychology at Claremont Graduate University. In this article, they combine their expertise in media studies and psychology in order to examine the phenomenon of TV addiction.

Perhaps the most ironic aspect of the struggle for survival is how easily organisms can be harmed by that which they desire. The trout is caught by the fisherman's lure, the mouse by cheese. But at least those creatures have the excuse that bait and cheese look like sustenance. Humans seldom have that consolation. The temptations that can disrupt their lives are often pure indulgences. No one has to drink alcohol, for example. Realizing when a diversion has gotten out of control is one of the great challenges of life.

Excessive cravings do not necessarily involve physical substances. Gambling can become compulsive; sex can become obsessive. One activity, however, stands out for its prominence and ubiquity—the world's most popular leisure pastime, television. Most people admit to having a love-hate relationship with it. They complain about the "boob tube" and "couch potatoes," then they settle into their sofas and grab the remote control. Parents commonly fret about their children's viewing (if not their own). Even researchers who study TV for a living marvel at the medium's hold on them personally. Percy Tannenbaum of the University of California at Berkeley has written: "Among life's more embarrassing moments have been countless occasions when I am engaged in conversation in a room while a TV set is on, and I cannot for the life of me stop from periodically glancing over to the screen. This occurs not only during dull conversations but during reasonably interesting ones just as well."

Scientists have been studying the effects of television for decades, generally focusing on whether watching violence on TV correlates with being violent in real life (see "The Effects of Observing Violence," by Leonard Berkowitz; *Scientific American*, February 1964; and "Communication and Social Environment," by George Gerber; September 1972). Less attention has been paid to the basic allure of the small screen—the medium, as opposed to the message.

The term "TV addiction" is imprecise and laden with value judgments, but it captures the essence of a very real phenomenon. Psychologists and psychiatrists formally define substance dependence as a disorder characterized by criteria that include spending a great deal of time using the substance; using it more often than one intends; thinking about reducing use or making repeated unsuccessful efforts to reduce use; giving up important social, family or occupational activities to use it; and reporting withdrawal symptoms when one stops using it.

All these criteria can apply to people who watch a lot of television. That does not mean that watching television, per se, is problematic. Television can teach and amuse; it can reach aesthetic heights; it can provide much needed distraction and escape. The difficulty arises when people strongly sense that they ought not to watch as much as they do and yet find themselves strangely unable to reduce their viewing. Some knowledge of how the medium exerts its pull may help heavy viewers gain better control over their lives.

A Body at Rest Tends to Stay at Rest

The amount of time people spend watching television is astonishing. On average, individuals in the industrialized world devote three hours a day to the pursuit—fully half of their leisure time, and more than on any single activity save work and sleep. At this rate, someone who lives to 75 would spend nine years in front of the tube. To some commentators, this devotion means simply that people enjoy TV and make a conscious decision to watch it. But if that is the whole story, why do so many people experience misgivings about how much they view? In Gallup polls in 1992 and 1999, two out of five adult respondents and seven out of 10 teenagers said they spent too much time watching TV. Other surveys have consistently shown that roughly 10 percent of adults call themselves TV addicts.

To study people's reactions to TV, researchers have undertaken laboratory experiments in which they have monitored the brain waves (using an electroencephalograph, or EEG), skin resistance or heart rate of people watching television. To track behavior and emotion in the normal course of life, as opposed to the artificial conditions of the lab, we have used the Experience Sampling Method (ESM). Participants carried a beeper, and we signaled them six to eight times a day, at random, over the period of a week; whenever they heard the beep, they wrote down what they were doing and how they were feeling using a standardized scorecard.

As one might expect, people who were watching TV when we beeped them reported feeling relaxed and passive. The EEG studies similarly show less mental stimulation, as measured by alpha brain-wave production, during viewing than during reading.

What is more surprising is that the sense of relaxation ends when the set is turned off, but the feelings of passivity and lowered alertness continue. Survey participants commonly reflect that television has somehow absorbed or sucked out their energy, leaving them depleted. They say they have more difficulty concentrating after viewing than before. In contrast, they rarely indicate such difficulty after reading. After playing sports or engaging in hobbies, people report improvements in mood. After watching TV, people's moods are about the same or worse than before.

Within moments of sitting or lying down and pushing the "power" button, viewers report feeling more relaxed. Because the relaxation occurs quickly, people are conditioned to associate viewing with rest and lack of tension. The association is positively reinforced because viewers remain relaxed throughout viewing, and it is negatively reinforced via the stress and dysphoric rumination that occurs once the screen goes blank again.

Habit-forming drugs work in similar ways. A tranquilizer that leaves the body rapidly is much more likely to cause dependence than one that leaves the body slowly, precisely because the user is more aware that the drug's effects are wearing off. Similarly, viewers' vague learned sense that they will feel less relaxed if they stop viewing may be a significant factor in not turning the set off. Viewing begets more viewing.

Thus, the irony of TV: people watch a great deal longer than they plan to, even though prolonged viewing is less rewarding. In our ESM studies the longer people sat in front of the set, the less satisfaction they said they derived from it. When signaled, heavy viewers (those who consistently watch more than four hours a day) tended to report on their ESM sheets that they enjoy TV less than light viewers did (less than two hours a day). For some, a twinge of unease or guilt that they aren't doing something more productive may also accompany and depreciate the enjoyment of prolonged viewing. Researchers in Japan, the U.K. and the U.S. have found that this guilt occurs much more among middle-class viewers than among less affluent ones.

Grabbing Your Attention

What is it about TV that has such a hold on us? In part, the attraction seems to spring from our biological "orienting response." First described by Ivan Pavlov in 1927, the orienting response is our instinctive visual or auditory reaction to any sudden or novel stimulus. It is part of our evolutionary heritage, a built-in sensitivity to movement and potential predatory threats. Typical orienting reactions include dilation of the blood vessels to the brain, slowing of the heart, and constriction of blood vessels to major muscle groups. Alpha waves are blocked for a few seconds before returning to their baseline level, which is determined by the general level of mental arousal. The brain focuses its attention on gathering more information while the rest of the body quiets.

In 1986 Byron Reeves of Stanford University, Esther Thorson of the University of Missouri and their colleagues began to study whether the simple formal features of television—cuts, edits, zooms, pans, sudden noises—activate the orienting response, thereby keeping attention on the screen. By watching how brain waves were affected by formal features, the researchers concluded that these stylistic tricks can indeed trigger involuntary responses and "derive their attentional value through the evolutionary significance of detecting movement. . . . It is the form, not the content, of television that is unique."

The orienting response may partly explain common viewer remarks such as: "If a television is on, I just can't keep my eyes off it,"

"I don't want to watch as much as I do, but I can't help it," and "I feel hypnotized when I watch television." In the years since Reeves and Thorson published their pioneering work, researchers have delved deeper. Annie Lang's research team at Indiana University has shown that heart rate decreases for four to six seconds after an orienting stimulus. In ads, action sequences and music videos, formal features frequently come at a rate of one per second, thus activating the orienting response continuously.

Lang and her colleagues have also investigated whether formal features affect people's memory of what they have seen. In one of their studies, participants watched a program and then filled out a score sheet. Increasing the frequency of edits—defined here as a change from one camera angle to another in the same visual scene—improved memory recognition, presumably because it focused attention on the screen. Increasing the frequency of cuts—changes to a new visual scene—had a similar effect but only up to a point. If the number of cuts exceeded 10 in two minutes, recognition dropped off sharply.

Producers of educational television for children have found that formal features can help learning. But increasing the rate of cuts and edits eventually overloads the brain. Music videos and commercials that use rapid intercutting of unrelated scenes are designed to hold attention more than they are to convey information. People may remember the name of the product or band, but the details of the ad itself float in one ear and out the other. The orienting response is overworked. Viewers still attend to the screen, but they feel tired and worn out, with little compensating psychological reward. Our ESM findings show much the same thing.

Sometimes the memory of the product is very subtle. Many ads today are deliberately oblique: they have an engaging story line, but it is hard to tell what they are trying to sell. Afterward you may not remember the product consciously. Yet advertisers believe that if they have gotten your attention, when you later go to the store you will feel better or more comfortable with a given product because you have a vague recollection of having heard of it.

The natural attraction to television's sound and light starts very early in life. Dafna Lemish of Tel Aviv University has described babies at six to eight weeks attending to television. We have observed slightly older infants who, when lying on their backs on the floor, crane their necks around 180 degrees to catch what light through yonder window breaks. This inclination suggests how deeply rooted the orienting response is.

"TV Is Part of Them"

That said, we need to be careful about overreacting. Little evidence suggests that adults or children should stop watching TV altogether. The problems come from heavy or prolonged viewing.

The Experience Sampling Method permitted us to look closely at most every domain of everyday life: working, eating, reading, talking to friends, playing a sport, and so on. We wondered whether heavy viewers might experience life differently than light viewers do. Do they dislike being with people more? Are they more alienated from work? What we found nearly leaped off the page at us. Heavy viewers report feeling significantly more anxious and less happy than light viewers do in unstructured situations, such as doing nothing, daydreaming or waiting in line. The difference widens when the viewer is alone.

Subsequently, Robert D. McIlwraith of the University of Manitoba extensively studied those who called themselves TV addicts on surveys. On a measure called the Short Imaginal Processes Inventory (SIPI), he found that the self-described addicts are more easily bored and distracted and have poorer attentional control than the nonaddicts. The addicts said they used TV to distract themselves from unpleasant thoughts and to fill time. Other studies over the years have shown that heavy viewers are less likely to participate in community activities and sports and are more likely to be obese than moderate viewers or nonviewers.

The question that naturally arises is: In which direction does the correlation go? Do people turn to TV because of boredom and loneliness, or does TV viewing make people more susceptible to boredom and loneliness? We and most other researchers argue that the former is generally the case, but it is not a simple case of either/or. Jerome L. and Dorothy Singer of Yale University, among others, have suggested that more viewing may contribute to a shorter attention span, diminished self-restraint and less patience with the normal delays of daily life. More than 25 years ago psychologist Tannis M. MacBeth Williams of the University of British Columbia studied a mountain community that had no television until cable finally arrived. Over time, both adults and children in the town became less creative in problem solving, less able to persevere at tasks, and less tolerant of unstructured time.

To some researchers, the most convincing parallel between TV and addictive drugs is that people experience withdrawal symptoms when they cut back on viewing. Nearly 40 years ago Gary A. Steiner of the University of Chicago collected fascinating individual accounts of families whose set had broken—this back in the days when households generally had only one set: "The family walked around like a chicken without a head." "It was terrible. We did nothing—my husband and I talked." "Screamed constantly. Children bothered me, and my nerves were on edge. Tried to interest them in games, but impossible. TV is part of them."

In experiments, families have volunteered or been paid to stop viewing, typically for a week or a month. Many could not complete the period of abstinence. Some fought, verbally and physically. Anecdotal reports from some families that have tried the annual "TV turn-off" week in the U.S. tell a similar story.

If a family has been spending the lion's share of its free time watching television, reconfiguring itself around a new set of activities is no easy task. Of course, that does not mean it cannot be done or that all families implode when deprived of their set. In a review of these cold–turkey studies, Charles Winick of the City University of New York concluded: "The first three or four days for most persons were the worst, even in many homes where viewing was minimal and where there were other ongoing activities. In over half of all the households, during these first few days of loss, the regular routines were disrupted, family members had difficulties in dealing with the newly available time, anxiety and aggressions were expressed. . . . People living alone tended to be bored and irritated. . . . By the second week, a move toward adaptation to the situation was common." Unfortunately, researchers have yet to flesh out these anecdotes; no one has systematically gathered statistics on the prevalence of these withdrawal symptoms.

Even though TV does seem to meet the criteria for substance dependence, not all researchers would go so far as to call TV addictive. McIlwraith said in 1998 that "displacement of other activities by television may be socially significant but still fall short of the clinical requirement of significant impairment." He argued that a new category of "TV addiction" may not be necessary if heavy viewing stems from conditions such as depression and social phobia. Nevertheless, whether or not we formally diagnose someone as TV-dependent, millions of people sense that they cannot readily control the amount of television they watch.

Slave to the Computer Screen

Although much less research has been done on video games and computer use, the same principles often apply. The games offer escape and distraction; players quickly learn that they feel better when playing;

and so a kind of reinforcement loop develops. The obvious difference from television, however, is the interactivity. Many video and computer games minutely increase in difficulty along with the increasing ability of the player. One can search for months to find another tennis or chess player of comparable ability, but programmed games can immediately provide a near-perfect match of challenge to skill. They offer the psychic pleasure—what one of us (Csikszentmihalyi) has called "flow"—that accompanies increased mastery of most any human endeavor. On the other hand, prolonged activation of the orienting response can wear players out. Kids report feeling tired, dizzy and nauseated after long sessions.

In 1997, in the most extreme medium-effects case on record, 700 Japanese children were rushed to the hospital, many suffering from "optically stimulated epileptic seizures" caused by viewing bright flashing lights in a Pokemon video game broadcast on Japanese TV. Seizures and other untoward effects of video games are significant enough that software companies and platform manufacturers now routinely include warnings in their instruction booklets. Parents have reported to us that rapid movement on the screen has caused motion sickness in their young children after just 15 minutes of play. Many youngsters, lacking self-control and experience (and often supervision), continue to play despite these symptoms.

Lang and Shyam Sundar of Pennsylvania State University have been studying how people respond to Web sites. Sundar has shown people multiple versions of the same Web page, identical except for the number of links. Users reported that more links conferred a greater sense of control and engagement. At some point, however, the number of links reached saturation, and adding more of them simply turned people off. As with video games, the ability of Web sites to hold the user's attention seems to depend less on formal features than on interactivity.

For growing numbers of people, the life they lead online may often seem more important, more immediate and more intense than the life they lead face-to-face. Maintaining control over one's media habits is more of a challenge today than it has ever been. TV sets and computers are everywhere. But the small screen and the Internet need not interfere with the quality of the rest of one's life. In its easy provision of relaxation and escape, television can be beneficial in limited doses. Yet when the habit interferes with the ability to grow, to learn new things, to lead an active life, then it does constitute a kind of dependence and should be taken seriously.

SUGGESTIONS FOR WRITING

1. Choose an addiction—for instance, gambling, smoking, or drinking alcohol—and make a list of all that you know about this condition: who suffers from it, what problems it causes, why it occurs, how society has responded, what laws exist that address the addiction, what economic consequences it has, how it might be cured, and so on. Then compare the list you've compiled to the facts about television addiction that Kubey and Csikszentmihalyi discuss in the reading. Based on this comparison, do you think that excessive television viewing can genuinely be considered an addiction? Why or why not?

2. Toward the end of their article, Kubey and Csikszentmihalyi draw comparisons between TV and other more interactive pursuits. Write an essay in which you compare the three leisure activities they discuss: watching TV, playing video games, and surfing the Internet. What kinds of pleasures and problems does each activity pose? Could you argue that one of the three is inherently more healthy than the others?

3. Kubey and Csikszentmihalyi deal with TV addiction in fairly general terms. Test some of the claims they make about TV addiction by writing a focused analysis of a particular type of TV show—for instance, game shows, reality shows, televised sports, soap operas, news, or home improvement shows. What features of this type of show are likely to stimulate an addictive response in viewers? What group of viewers is most likely to be addicted to this type of show? Based on your analysis, would you conclude that all TV shows are equally addictive?

STEVEN JOHNSON

Watching TV Makes You Smarter

If your parents have ever complained that you watch too much TV, just tell them, "But Mom, Dad, watching TV is mentally stimulating and can actually make me smarter!" When they look at you in disbelief, refer them to the following article in which Steven Johnson makes precisely that argument: that watching TV—or at least, watching some of the shows currently on TV—gives you a good cognitive workout. The article, adapted from Johnson's bestseller, Everything Bad Is Good for You: How Today's Popular Culture Is Actually Making Us Smarter, *compares past and present TV shows and concludes that viewers today are required to exercise their mental faculties in order to make sense of complex, multilayered plots and characters.*

The Sleeper Curve

SCIENTIST A: Has he asked for anything special?

SCIENTIST B: Yes, this morning for breakfast . . . he requested something called "wheat germ, organic honey and tiger's milk."

SCIENTIST A: Oh, yes. Those were the charmed substances that some years ago were felt to contain life-preserving properties.

SCIENTIST B: You mean there was no deep fat? No steak or cream pies or . . . hot fudge?

SCIENTIST A: Those were thought to be unhealthy.

From Woody Allen's "Sleeper"

On Jan. 24, the Fox network showed an episode of its hit drama "24," the real-time thriller known for its cliffhanger tension and often-gruesome violence. Over the preceding weeks, a number of public controversies had erupted around "24," mostly focused on its portrait of Muslim terrorists and its penchant for torture scenes. The episode that was shown on the 24th only fanned the flames higher: in one scene, a terrorist enlists a hit man to kill his child for not fully supporting the jihadist cause; in another scene, the secretary of defense authorizes the torture of his son to uncover evidence of a terrorist plot.

But the explicit violence and the post-9/11 terrorist anxiety are not the only elements of "24" that would have been unthinkable on prime-time network television 20 years ago. Alongside the notable change in content lies an equally notable change in form. During its 44 minutes—a real-time hour, minus 16 minutes for commercials—the episode connects the lives of 21 distinct characters, each with a clearly defined "story arc," as the Hollywood jargon has it: a defined personality with motivations and obstacles and specific relationships with other characters. Nine primary narrative threads wind their way through those 44 minutes, each drawing extensively upon events and information revealed in earlier episodes. Draw a map of all those intersecting plots and personalities, and you get structure that—where formal complexity is concerned—more closely resembles "Middlemarch" than a hit TV drama of years past like "Bonanza."

For decades, we've worked under the assumption that mass culture follows a path declining steadily toward lowest-common-denominator standards, presumably because the "masses" want dumb, simple pleasures and big media companies try to give the masses what they want. But as that "24" episode suggests, the exact opposite is happening: the culture is getting more cognitively demanding, not less. To make sense of an episode of "24," you have to integrate far more information than you would have a few decades ago watching a comparable show. Beneath the violence and the ethnic stereotypes, another trend appears: to keep up with entertainment like "24," you have to pay attention, make inferences, track shifting social relationships. This is what I call the Sleeper Curve: the most debased forms of mass diversion—video games and violent television dramas and juvenile sitcoms—turn out to be nutritional after all.

I believe that the Sleeper Curve is the single most important new force altering the mental development of young people today, and I believe it is largely a force for good: enhancing our cognitive faculties, not dumbing them down. And yet you almost never hear this story in popular accounts of today's media. Instead, you hear dire tales of addiction, violence, mindless escapism. It's assumed that shows that promote smoking or gratuitous violence are bad for us, while those that thunder against teen pregnancy or intolerance have a positive role in society. Judged by that morality-play standard, the story of popular culture over the past 50 years—if not 500—is a story of decline: the morals of the stories have grown darker and more ambiguous, and the antiheroes have multiplied.

The usual counterargument here is that what media have lost in moral clarity, they have gained in realism. The real world doesn't come in nicely packaged public-service announcements, and we're better off with entertainment like "The Sopranos" that reflects our fallen state with all its ethical ambiguity. I happen to be sympathetic to that argument, but it's not the one I want to make here. I think there is another way to assess the social virtue of pop culture, one that looks at media as a kind of cognitive workout, not as a series of life lessons. There may indeed be more "negative messages" in the mediasphere today. But that's not the only way to evaluate whether our television shows or video games are having a positive impact. Just as important—if not more important—is the kind of thinking you have to do to make sense of a cultural experience. That is where the Sleeper Curve becomes visible.

Televised Intelligence

Consider the cognitive demands that televised narratives place on their viewers. With many shows that we associate with "quality" entertainment—"The Mary Tyler Moore Show," "Murphy Brown,"

"Frasier"—the intelligence arrives fully formed in the words and actions of the characters on-screen. They say witty things to one another and avoid lapsing into tired sitcom clichés, and we smile along in our living rooms, enjoying the company of these smart people. But assuming we're bright enough to understand the sentences they're saying, there's no intellectual labor involved in enjoying the show as a viewer. You no more challenge your mind by watching these intelligent shows than you challenge your body watching "Monday Night Football." The intellectual work is happening on-screen, not off.

But another kind of televised intelligence is on the rise. Think of the cognitive benefits conventionally ascribed to reading: attention, patience, retention, the parsing of narrative threads. Over the last half-century, programming on TV has increased the demands it places on precisely these mental faculties. This growing complexity involves three primary elements: multiple threading, flashing arrows and social networks.

According to television lore, the age of multiple threads began with the arrival in 1981 of "Hill Street Blues," the Steven Bochco police drama invariably praised for its "gritty realism." Watch an episode of "Hill Street Blues" side by side with any major drama from the preceding decades—"Starsky and Hutch," for instance, or "Dragnet"—and the structural transformation will jump out at you. The earlier shows follow one or two lead characters, adhere to a single dominant plot and reach a decisive conclusion at the end of the episode. Draw an outline of the narrative threads in almost every "Dragnet" episode, and it will be a single line: from the initial crime scene, through the investigation, to the eventual cracking of the case. A typical "Starsky and Hutch" episode offers only the slightest variation on this linear formula: the introduction of a comic subplot that usually appears only at the tail ends of the episode, creating a structure that looks like this graph. The vertical axis represents the number of individual threads, and the horizontal axis is time.

A "Hill Street Blues" episode complicates the picture in a number of profound ways. The narrative weaves together a collection of distinct strands—sometimes as many as 10, though at least half of the threads involve only a few quick scenes scattered through the episode. The number of primary characters—and not just bit parts—swells significantly. And the episode has fuzzy borders: picking up one or two threads from previous episodes at the outset and leaving one or two threads open at the end. Charted graphically, an average episode looks like this:

Critics generally cite "Hill Street Blues" as the beginning of "serious drama" native in the television medium—differentiating the series from the single-episode dramatic programs from the 50's, which were Broadway plays performed in front of a camera. But the "Hill Street" innovations weren't all that original; they'd long played a defining role in popular television, just not during the evening hours. The structure of a "Hill Street" episode—and indeed of all the critically acclaimed dramas that followed, from "thirtysomething" to "Six Feet Under"—is the structure of a soap opera. "Hill Street Blues" might have sparked a new golden age of television drama during its seven-year run, but it did so by using a few crucial tricks that "Guiding Light" and "General Hospital" mastered long before.

Bochco's genius with "Hill Street" was to marry complex narrative structure with complex subject matter. "Dallas" had already shown that the extended, interwoven threads of the soap-opera genre could survive the weeklong interruptions of a prime-time show, but the actual content of "Dallas" was fluff. (The most probing issue it addressed was the question, now folkloric, of who shot J.R.) "All in the Family" and "Rhoda" showed that you could tackle complex social issues, but they did their tackling in the comfort of the sitcom living room. "Hill Street" had richly drawn characters confronting difficult social issues and a narrative structure to match.

Since "Hill Street" appeared, the multi-threaded drama has become the most widespread fictional genre on prime time: "St. Elsewhere," "L.A. Law," "thirtysomething," "Twin Peaks," "N.Y.P.D. Blue," "E.R.," "The West Wing," "Alias," "Lost." (The only prominent holdouts in drama are shows like "Law and Order" that have essentially updated the venerable "Dragnet" format and thus remained anchored to a single narrative line.) Since the early 80's, however, there has been a noticeable increase in narrative complexity in these dramas. The most ambitious show on TV to date, "The Sopranos," routinely follows up to a dozen distinct threads over the course of an episode, with more than 20 recurring characters. An episode from late in the first season looks like this:

The total number of active threads equals the multiple plots of "Hill Street," but here each thread is more substantial. The show doesn't offer a clear distinction between dominant and minor plots; each story line carries its weight in the mix. The episode also displays a chordal mode of storytelling entirely absent from "Hill Street": a single scene in "The Sopranos" will often connect to three different threads at the same time, layering one plot atop another. And every single thread in this "Sopranos" episode builds on events from previous episodes and continues on through the rest of the season and beyond.

Put those charts together, and you have a portrait of the Sleeper Curve rising over the past 30 years of popular television. In a sense, this is as much a map of cognitive changes in the popular mind as it is a map of on-screen developments, as if the media titans decided to condition our brains to follow ever-larger numbers of simultaneous threads. Before "Hill Street," the conventional wisdom among television execs was that audiences wouldn't be comfortable following more than three plots in a single episode, and indeed, the "Hill Street" pilot, which was shown in January 1981, brought complaints from viewers that the show was too complicated. Fast-forward two decades, and shows like "The Sopranos" engage their audiences with narratives that make "Hill Street" look like "Three's Company." Audiences happily embrace that complexity because they've been trained by two decades of multi-threaded dramas.

Multi-threading is the most celebrated structural feature of the modern television drama, and it certainly deserves some of the honor that has been doled out to it. And yet multi-threading is only part of the story.

The Case for Confusion

Shortly after the arrival of the first-generation slasher movies—"Halloween," "Friday the 13th"—Paramount released a mock-slasher flick called "Student Bodies," parodying the genre just as the "Scream" series would do 15 years later. In one scene, the obligatory nubile teenage baby sitter hears a noise outside a suburban house; she opens the door to investigate, finds nothing and then goes back inside. As the door shuts behind her, the camera swoops in on the doorknob, and we see that she has left the door unlocked. The camera pulls back and then swoops down again for emphasis. And then a flashing arrow appears on the screen, with text that helpfully explains: "Unlocked!"

That flashing arrow is parody, of course, but it's merely an exaggerated version of a device popular stories use all the time. When a sci-fi script inserts into some advanced lab a nonscientist who keeps asking the science geeks to explain what they're doing with that particle accelerator, that's a flashing arrow that gives the audience precisely the information it needs in order to make sense of the ensuing plot. ("Whatever you do, don't spill water on it, or you'll set off a massive explosion!") These hints serve as a kind of narrative hand-holding.

Implicitly, they say to the audience, "We realize you have no idea what a particle accelerator is, but here's the deal: all you need to know is that it's a big fancy thing that explodes when wet." They focus the mind on relevant details: "Don't worry about whether the baby sitter is going to break up with her boyfriend. Worry about that guy lurking in the bushes." They reduce the amount of analytic work you need to do to make sense of a story. All you have to do is follow the arrows.

By this standard, popular television has never been harder to follow. If narrative threads have experienced a population explosion over the past 20 years, flashing arrows have grown correspondingly scarce. Watching our pinnacle of early 80's TV drama, "Hill Street Blues," we find there's an informational wholeness to each scene that differs markedly from what you see on shows like "The West Wing" or "The Sopranos" or "Alias" or "E.R."

"Hill Street" has ambiguities about future events: will a convicted killer be executed? Will Furillo marry Joyce Davenport? Will Renko find it in himself to bust a favorite singer for cocaine possession? But the present-tense of each scene explains itself to the viewer with little ambiguity. There's an open question or a mystery driving each of these stories—how will it all turn out?—but there's no mystery about the immediate activity on the screen. A contemporary drama like "The West Wing," on the other hand, constantly embeds mysteries into the present-tense events: you see characters performing actions or discussing events about which crucial information has been deliberately withheld. Anyone who has watched more than a handful of "The West Wing" episodes closely will know the feeling: scene after scene refers to some clearly crucial but unexplained piece of information, and after the sixth reference, you'll find yourself wishing you could rewind the tape to figure out what they're talking about, assuming you've missed something. And then you realize that you're supposed to be confused. The open question posed by these sequences is not "How will this turn out in the end?" The question is "What's happening right now?"

The deliberate lack of hand-holding extends down to the microlevel of dialogue as well. Popular entertainment that addresses technical issues—whether they are the intricacies of passing legislation, or of performing a heart bypass, or of operating a particle accelerator—conventionally switches between two modes of information in dialogue: texture and substance. Texture is all the arcane verbiage provided to convince the viewer that they're watching

Actual Doctors at Work; substance is the material planted amid the background texture that the viewer needs make sense of the plot.

Conventionally, narratives demarcate the line between texture and substance by inserting cues that flag or translate the important data. There's an unintentionally comical moment in the 2004 blockbuster "The Day After Tomorrow" in which the beleaguered climatologist (played by Dennis Quaid) announces his theory about the imminent arrival of a new ice age to a gathering of government officials. In his speech, he warns that "we have hit a critical desalinization point!" At this moment, the writer-director Roland Emmerich—a master of brazen arrow-flashing—has an official follow with the obliging remark: "It would explain what's driving this extreme weather." They might as well have had a flashing "Unlocked!" arrow on the screen.

The dialogue on shows like "The West Wing" and "E.R.," on the other hand, doesn't talk down to its audiences. It rushes by, the words accelerating in sync with the high-speed tracking shots that glide through the corridors and operating rooms. The characters talk faster in these shows, but the truly remarkable thing about the dialogue is not purely a matter of speed; it's the willingness to immerse the audience in information that most viewers won't understand. Here's a typical scene from "E.R.":

[WEAVER AND WRIGHT push a gurney containing a 16-year-old girl. Her parents, JANNA AND FRANK MIKAMI, follow close behind. CARTER AND LUCY fall in.]

WEAVER: 16-year-old, unconscious, history of biliary atresia.
CARTER: Hepatic coma?
WEAVER: Looks like it.
MR. MIKAMI: She was doing fine until six months ago.
CARTER: What medication is she on?
MRS. MIKAMI: Ampicillin, tobramycin, vitamins a, d and k.
LUCY: Skin's jaundiced.
WEAVER: Same with the sclera. Breath smells sweet.
CARTER: Fetor hepaticus?
WEAVER: Yep.
LUCY: What's that?
WEAVER: Her liver's shut down. Let's dip a urine. [To CARTER] Guys, it's getting a little crowded in here, why don't you deal with the parents? Start lactulose, 30 cc's per NG.

> **CARTER:** We're giving medicine to clean her blood.
>
> **WEAVER:** Blood in the urine, two-plus.
>
> **CARTER:** The liver failure is causing her blood not to clot.
>
> **MRS. MIKAMI:** Oh, God. . . .
>
> **CARTER:** Is she on the transplant list?
>
> **MR. MIKAMI:** She's been Status 2a for six months, but they haven't been able to find her a match.
>
> **CARTER:** Why? What's her blood type?
>
> **MR. MIKAMI:** AB. [This hits CARTER like a lightning bolt. LUCY gets it, too. They share a look.]

There are flashing arrows here, of course—"The liver failure is causing her blood not to clot"—but the ratio of medical jargon to layperson translation is remarkably high. From a purely narrative point of view, the decisive line arrives at the very end: "AB." The 16-year-old's blood type connects her to an earlier plot line, involving a cerebral-hemorrhage victim who—after being dramatically revived in one of the opening scenes—ends up brain-dead. Far earlier, before the liver-failure scene above, Carter briefly discusses harvesting the hemorrhage victim's organs for transplants, and another doctor makes a passing reference to his blood type being the rare AB (thus making him an unlikely donor). The twist here revolves around a statistically unlikely event happening at the E.R.—an otherwise perfect liver donor showing up just in time to donate his liver to a recipient with the same rare blood type. But the show reveals this twist with remarkable subtlety. To make sense of that last "AB" line—and the look of disbelief on Carter's and Lucy's faces—you have to recall a passing remark uttered earlier regarding a character who belongs to a completely different thread. Shows like "E.R." may have more blood and guts than popular TV had a generation ago, but when it comes to storytelling, they possess a quality that can only be described as subtlety and discretion.

Even Bad TV Is Better

Skeptics might argue that I have stacked the deck here by focusing on relatively highbrow titles like "The Sopranos" or "The West Wing," when in fact the most significant change in the last five years of narrative entertainment involves reality TV. Does the contemporary pop cultural landscape look quite as promising if the representative show is "Joe Millionaire" instead of "The West Wing"?

I think it does, but to answer that question properly, you have to avoid the tendency to sentimentalize the past. When people talk about the golden age of television in the early 70's—invoking shows like "The Mary Tyler Moore Show" and "All in the Family"—they forget to mention how awful most television programming was during much of that decade. If you're going to look at pop-culture trends, you have to compare apples to apples, or in this case, lemons to lemons. The relevant comparison is not between "Joe Millionaire" and "MASH"; it's between "Joe Millionaire" and "The Newlywed Game," or between "Survivor" and "The Love Boat."

What you see when you make these head-to-head comparisons is that a rising tide of complexity has been lifting programming at the bottom of the quality spectrum and at the top. "The Sopranos" is several times more demanding of its audiences than "Hill Street" was, and "Joe Millionaire" has made comparable advances over "Battle of the Network Stars." This is the ultimate test of the Sleeper Curve theory: even the junk has improved.

If early television took its cues from the stage, today's reality programming is reliably structured like a video game: a series of competitive tests, growing more challenging over time. Many reality shows borrow a subtler device from gaming culture as well: the rules aren't fully established at the outset. You learn as you play.

On a show like "Survivor" or "The Apprentice," the participants—and the audience—know the general objective of the series, but each episode involves new challenges that haven't been ordained in advance. The final round of the first season of "The Apprentice," for instance, threw a monkey wrench into the strategy that governed the play up to that point, when Trump announced that the two remaining apprentices would have to assemble and manage a team of subordinates who had already been fired in earlier episodes of the show. All of a sudden the overarching objective of the game—do anything to avoid being fired—presented a potential conflict to the remaining two contenders: the structure of the final round favored the survivor who had maintained the best relationships with his comrades. Suddenly, it wasn't enough just to have clawed your way to the top; you had to have made friends while clawing. The original "Joe Millionaire" went so far as to undermine the most fundamental convention of all—that the show's creators don't openly lie to the contestants about the prizes—by inducing a construction worker to pose as man of means while 20 women competed for his attention.

Reality programming borrowed another key ingredient from games: the intellectual labor of probing the system's rules for weak spots and opportunities. As each show discloses its conventions, and each participant reveals his or her personality traits and background, the intrigue in watching comes from figuring out how the participants should best navigate the environment that has been created for them. The pleasure in these shows comes not from watching other people being humiliated on national television; it comes from depositing other people in a complex, high-pressure environment where no established strategies exist and watching them find their bearings. That's why the water-cooler conversation about these shows invariably tracks in on the strategy displayed on the previous night's episode: why did Kwame pick Omarosa in that final round? What devious strategy is Richard Hatch concocting now?

When we watch these shows, the part of our brain that monitors the emotional lives of the people around us—the part that tracks subtle shifts in intonation and gesture and facial expression—scrutinizes the action on the screen, looking for clues. We trust certain characters implicitly and vote others off the island in a heartbeat. Traditional narrative shows also trigger emotional connections to the characters, but those connections don't have the same participatory effect, because traditional narratives aren't explicitly about strategy. The phrase "Monday-morning quarterbacking" describes the engaged feeling that spectators have in relation to games as opposed to stories. We absorb stories, but we second-guess games. Reality programming has brought that second-guessing to prime time, only the game in question revolves around social dexterity rather than the physical kind.

The Rewards of Smart Culture

The quickest way to appreciate the Sleeper Curve's cognitive training is to sit down and watch a few hours of hit programming from the late 70's on Nick at Nite or the SOAPnet channel or on DVD. The modern viewer who watches a show like "Dallas" today will be bored by the content—not just because the show is less salacious than today's soap operas (which it is by a small margin) but also because the show contains far less information in each scene, despite the fact that its soap-opera structure made it one of the most complicated narratives on television in its prime. With "Dallas," the modern viewer doesn't have to think to make sense of what's going on, and not having to think is boring. Many recent hit shows—"24," "Survivor," "The Sopranos," "Alias," "Lost," "The Simpsons," "E.R."—take the opposite approach, layering each scene with a thick network of affiliations. You have to focus to follow the plot, and in focusing you're exercising the parts of your brain that map social networks, that fill in missing information, that connect multiple narrative threads.

Of course, the entertainment industry isn't increasing the cognitive complexity of its products for charitable reasons. The Sleeper Curve exists because there's money to be made by making culture smarter. The economics of television syndication and DVD sales mean that there's a tremendous financial pressure to make programs that can be watched multiple times, revealing new nuances and shadings on the third viewing. Meanwhile, the Web has created a forum for annotation and commentary that allows more complicated shows to prosper, thanks to the fan sites where each episode of shows like "Lost" or "Alias" is dissected with an intensity usually reserved for Talmud scholars. Finally, interactive games have trained a new generation of media consumers to probe complex environments and to think on their feet, and that gamer audience has now come to expect the same challenges from their television shows. In the end, the Sleeper Curve tells us something about the human mind. It may be drawn toward the sensational where content is concerned—sex does sell, after all. But the mind also likes to be challenged; there's real pleasure to be found in solving puzzles, detecting patterns or unpacking a complex narrative system.

In pointing out some of the ways that popular culture has improved our minds, I am not arguing that parents should stop paying attention to the way their children amuse themselves. What I am arguing for is a change in the criteria we use to determine what really is cognitive junk food and what is genuinely nourishing. Instead of a show's violent or tawdry content, instead of wardrobe malfunctions or the F-word, the true test should be whether a given show engages or sedates the mind. Is it a single thread strung together with predictable punch lines every 30 seconds? Or does it map a complex social network? Is your on-screen character running around shooting everything in sight, or is she trying to solve problems and manage resources? If your kids want to watch reality TV, encourage them to watch "Survivor" over "Fear Factor." If they want to watch a mystery show, encourage "24" over "Law and Order." If they want to play a violent game, encourage Grand Theft Auto over Quake. Indeed, it might be just as helpful to have a rating system that used mental labor and not obscenity and violence as its classification scheme for the world of mass culture.

Kids and grown-ups each can learn from their increasingly shared obsessions. Too often we imagine the blurring of kid and grown-up cultures as a series of violations: the 9-year-olds who have to have nipple brooches explained to them thanks to Janet Jackson; the middle-aged guy who can't wait to get home to his Xbox. But this demographic blur has a commendable side that we don't acknowledge enough. The kids are forced to think like grown-ups: analyzing complex social networks, managing resources, tracking subtle narrative intertwinings, recognizing long-term patterns. The grown-ups, in turn, get to learn from the kids: decoding each new technological wave, parsing the interfaces and discovering the intellectual rewards of play. Parents should see this as an opportunity, not a crisis. Smart culture is no longer something you force your kids to ingest, like green vegetables. It's something you share.

SUGGESTIONS FOR WRITING

1. Consider the evidence that Johnson uses to support his claim that current TV shows are cognitively stimulating. Select one specific piece of evidence that you find very convincing and one that you find unconvincing. Based on a comparison of these two pieces of evidence, what general conclusions can you draw about the characteristics of good and weak evidence?

2. Reread the last paragraph of the article, in which Johnson discusses how parents and children can benefit from "smart culture" on TV. Make a list of the benefits for kids and the benefits for parents. Then consider whether you think each of the benefits can be realistically achieved by watching smart TV. Draw on your own experiences and your own knowledge of TV programs in order to decide whether Johnson's argument is reasonable or whether he is overstating the positives of watching TV.

3. Johnson provides some visual evidence to support his assertion that TV shows have become increasingly complex. The three graphs included in the article show the number of plot threads in single episodes of *Starsky and Hutch, Hill Street Blues,* and *The Sopranos.* A quick visual comparison of these graphs does indeed suggest that *The Sopranos* has more plot threads and more interweaving of these threads than the two earlier shows. Create a similar chart for a current TV show of your choice. Choose a show to watch, and, as you're watching, keep note of each time a new plot thread occurs or a reference to another thread appears. After the show is over, plot these elements on a simple chart in which the vertical axis represents each plot thread and the horizontal

axis represents time. To make the task easier, label each plot thread on the vertical axis (something Johnson doesn't do). After you've finished the chart, write a brief essay in which you draw conclusions about the relative complexity of the show as compared to the three examples Johnson offers.

CLAY SHIRKY

Gin, Television, and Social Surplus

The following article has an interesting history: It is adapted from a talk that Shirky gave at a 2008 Web 2.0 conference, and it can be found online at a blog that Shirky developed to promote his latest book, Here Comes Everybody: The Power of Organizing Without Organization. *The ideas here have been what we might describe as multiply mediated: oral presentation, online blog, print article. Shirky himself is equally multiple, so to speak. Here's how he describes his career on his home page: "I have been a producer, programmer, professor, designer, author, consultant, sometimes working with people who wanted to create a purely intellectual or aesthetic experience online, sometimes working with people who wanted to use the internet to sell books or batteries or banking." In what follows, Shirky suggests a provocative connection between the Internet and TV in terms of how they offer very different solutions to the "problem" of free time.*

I was recently reminded of some reading I did in college, way back in the last century, by a British historian arguing that the critical technology, for the early phase of the industrial revolution, was gin.

The transformation from rural to urban life was so sudden, and so wrenching, that the only thing society could do to manage was to drink itself into a stupor for a generation. The stories from that era are amazing—there were gin pushcarts working their way through the streets of London.

And it wasn't until society woke up from that collective bender that we actually started to get the institutional structures that we associate with the industrial revolution today. Things like public libraries and museums, increasingly broad education for children, elected leaders—a lot of things we like—didn't happen until having all of those people together stopped seeming like a crisis and started seeming like an asset.

It wasn't until people started thinking of this as a vast civic surplus, one they could design for rather than just dissipate, that we started to get what we think of now as an industrial society.

If I had to pick the critical technology for the 20th century, the bit of social lubricant without which the wheels would've come off the whole enterprise, I'd say it was the sitcom. Starting with the Second World War a whole series of things happened—rising GDP per capita, rising educational attainment, rising life expectancy and, critically, a rising number of people who were working five-day work weeks. For the first time, society forced onto an enormous number of its citizens the requirement to manage something they had never had to manage before—free time.

And what did we do with that free time? Well, mostly we spent it watching TV.

We did that for decades. We watched I Love Lucy. We watched Gilligan's Island. We watch Malcolm in the Middle. We watch Desperate Housewives. [Television] essentially functioned as a kind of cognitive heat sink, dissipating thinking that might otherwise have built up and caused society to overheat.

And it's only now, as we're waking up from that collective bender, that we're starting to see the cognitive surplus as an asset rather than as a crisis. We're seeing things being designed to take advantage of that surplus, to deploy it in ways more engaging than just having a TV in everybody's basement.

This hit me in a conversation I had about two months ago. As Jen said in the introduction [to this presentation], I've finished a book called Here Comes Everybody, which has recently come out, and this recognition came out of a conversation I had about the book. I was being interviewed by a TV producer to see whether I should be on their show, and she asked me, "What are you seeing out there that's interesting?"

I started telling her about the Wikipedia article on Pluto. You may remember that Pluto got kicked out of the planet club a couple of years ago, so all of a sudden there was all of this activity on Wikipedia. The talk pages light up, people are editing the article like mad, and the whole community is in a ruckus—"How should we characterize this change in Pluto's status?" And a little bit at a time they move the article—fighting offstage all the while—from, "Pluto is the ninth planet," to "Pluto is an odd-shaped rock with an odd-shaped orbit at the edge of the solar system."

So I tell her all this stuff, and I think, "Okay, we're going to have a conversation about authority or social construction or whatever." That wasn't her question. She heard this story and she shook her head and said, "Where do people find the time?" That was her question. And I just kind of snapped. And I said, "No one who works in TV gets to ask that question. You know where the time comes from. It comes from the cognitive surplus you've been masking for 50 years."

So how big is that surplus? So if you take Wikipedia as a kind of unit, all of Wikipedia, the whole project—every page, every edit, every talk page, every line of code, in every language that Wikipedia exists in—that represents something like the cumulation of 100 million hours of human thought. I worked this out with Martin Wattenberg at IBM; it's a back-of-the-envelope calculation, but it's the right order of magnitude, about 100 million hours of thought.

And television watching? Two hundred billion hours, in the U.S. alone, every year. Put another way, now that we have a unit, that's 2,000 Wikipedia projects a year spent watching television. Or put still another way, in the U.S., we spend 100 million hours every weekend, just watching the ads. This is a pretty big surplus. People asking, "Where do they find the time?" when they're looking at things like Wikipedia don't understand how tiny that entire project is, as a carve-out of this asset that's finally being dragged into what Tim [O'Reilly] calls an architecture of participation.

Now, the interesting thing about a surplus like that is that society doesn't know what to do with it at first—hence the gin, hence the sitcoms. Because if people knew what to do with a surplus with reference to the existing social institutions, then it wouldn't be a surplus, would it? It's precisely when no one has any idea how to deploy something that people have to start experimenting with it, in order for the surplus to get integrated, and the course of that integration can transform society.

The early phase for taking advantage of this cognitive surplus, the phase I think we're still in, is all special cases. The physics of participation is much more like the physics of weather than it is like the physics of gravity. We know all the forces that combine to make these kinds of things work: there's an interesting community over here, there's an interesting sharing model over there, those people are collaborating on open source software. But despite knowing the inputs, we can't predict the outputs yet because there's so much complexity.

The way you explore complex ecosystems is you just try lots and lots and lots of things, and you hope that everybody who fails fails informatively so that you can at least find a skull on a pikestaff near where you're going. That's the phase we're in now.

Just to pick one example, one I'm in love with, but it's tiny. A couple of weeks ago one of my students at ITP forwarded me a project started by a professor in Brazil, in Fortaleza, named Vasco Furtado. It's a Wiki Map for crime in Brazil. If there's an assault, if there's a burglary, if there's a mugging, a robbery, a rape, a murder, you can go and put a push-pin on a Google Map, and you can characterize the assault, and you start to see a map of where these crimes are occurring.

Now, this already exists as tacit information. Anybody who knows a town has some sense of, "Don't go there. That street corner is dangerous. Don't go in this neighborhood. Be careful there after dark." But it's something society knows without society really knowing it, which is to say there's no public source where you can take advantage of it. And the cops, if they have that information, they're certainly not sharing. In fact, one of the things Furtado says in starting the Wiki crime map was, "This information may or may not exist some place in society, but it's actually easier for me to try to rebuild it from scratch than to try and get it from the authorities who might have it now."

Maybe this will succeed or maybe it will fail. The normal case of social software is still failure; most of these experiments don't pan out. But the ones that do are quite incredible, and I hope that this one succeeds, obviously. But even if it doesn't, it's illustrated the point already, which is that someone working alone, with really cheap tools, has a reasonable hope of carving out enough of the cognitive surplus, enough of the desire to participate, enough of the collective goodwill of the citizens, to create a resource you couldn't have imagined existing even five years ago.

So that's the answer to the question, "Where do they find the time?" Or, rather, that's the numerical answer. But beneath that question was another thought, this one not a question but an observation. In this same conversation with the TV producer I was talking about World of Warcraft guilds, and as I was talking, I could sort of see what she was thinking: "Losers. Grown men sitting in their basement pretending to be elves."

At least they're doing something.

Did you ever see that episode of Gilligan's Island where they almost get off the island and then Gilligan messes up and then they don't? I saw that one. I saw that one a lot when I was growing up. And every half-hour that I watched that was a half an hour I wasn't posting at my blog or editing Wikipedia or contributing to a mailing list. Now I had an ironclad excuse for not doing those things, which is none of those things existed then. I was forced into the channel of media the way it was because it was the only option. Now it's not, and that's the big surprise. However lousy it is to sit in your basement and pretend to be an elf, I can tell you from personal experience it's worse to sit in your basement and try to figure if Ginger or Mary Ann is cuter.

And I'm willing to raise that to a general principle. It's better to do something than to do nothing. Even lolcats, even cute pictures of kittens made even cuter with the addition of cute captions, hold out an invitation to participation. When you see a lolcat, one of the things it says to the viewer is, "If you have some sans-serif fonts on your computer, you can play this game, too." And that's message—I can do that, too—is a big change.

This is something that people in the media world don't understand. Media in the 20th century was run as a single race—consumption. How much can we produce? How much can you consume? Can we produce more and you'll consume more? And the answer to that question has generally been yes. But media is actually a triathlon, it's three different events. People like to consume, but they also like to produce, and they like to share.

And what's astonished people who were committed to the structure of the previous society, prior to trying to take this surplus and do something interesting, is that they're discovering that when you offer people the opportunity to produce and to share, they'll take you up on that offer. It doesn't mean that we'll never sit around mindlessly watching Scrubs on the couch. It just means we'll do it less.

And this is the other thing about the size of the cognitive surplus we're talking about. It's so large that even a small change could have huge ramifications. Let's say that everything stays 99 percent the same, that people watch 99 percent as much television as they used to, but 1 percent of that is carved out for producing and for sharing. The Internet-connected population watches roughly a trillion hours of TV a year. That's about five times the size of the annual U.S. consumption. One per cent of that is 100 Wikipedia projects per year worth of participation.

I think that's going to be a big deal. Don't you?

Well, the TV producer did not think this was going to be a big deal; she was not digging this line of thought. And her final question to me was essentially, "Isn't this all just a fad?" You know, sort of the flagpole-sitting of the early 21st century? It's fun to go out and produce and share a little bit, but then people are going to eventually realize, "This isn't as good as doing what I was doing before," and settle down. And I made a spirited argument that no, this wasn't the case, that this was in fact a big one-time shift, more analogous to the industrial revolution than to flagpole-sitting.

I was arguing that this isn't the sort of thing society grows out of. It's the sort of thing that society grows into. But I'm not sure she believed me, in part because she didn't want to believe me, but also in part because I didn't have the right story yet. And now I do.

I was having dinner with a group of friends about a month ago, and one of them was talking about sitting with his four-year-old daughter watching a DVD. And in the middle of the movie, apropos nothing, she jumps up off the couch and runs around behind the screen. That seems like a cute moment. Maybe she's going back there to see if Dora is really back there or whatever. But that wasn't what she was doing. She started rooting around in the cables. And her dad said, "What you doing?" And she stuck her head out from behind the screen and said, "Looking for the mouse."

Here's something four-year-olds know: A screen that ships without a mouse ships broken. Here's something four-year-olds know: Media that's targeted at you but doesn't include you may not be worth sitting still for. Those are things that make me believe that this is a one-way change. Because four year olds, the people who are soaking most deeply in the current environment, who won't have to go through the trauma that I have to go through of trying to unlearn a childhood spent watching Gilligan's Island, they just assume that media includes consuming, producing and sharing.

It's also become my motto, when people ask me what we're doing—and when I say "we" I mean the larger society trying to figure out how to deploy this cognitive surplus, but I also mean we, especially, the people in this room, the people who are working hammer and tongs at figuring out the next good idea. From now on, that's what I'm going to tell them: We're looking for the mouse. We're going to look at every place that a reader or a listener or a viewer or a user has been locked out, has been served up passive or a fixed or a canned experience, and ask ourselves, "If we carve out a little bit of the cognitive surplus and deploy it here, could we make a good thing happen?" And I'm betting the answer is yes.

SUGGESTIONS FOR WRITING

1. As was noted in the introduction, this article was initially a talk that Shirky presented at a conference. List some of the signs of its beginnings as an oral presentation that you still see in the article.

Then write a brief explanation of whether you think these stylistic features help to advance or detract from Shirky's argument when presented in writing.

2. Toward the end of the article, Shirky returns several times to the idea that the Internet offers opportunities to participate and produce, whereas television offers only opportunities to consume. Make a list of all of the ways in which you have become more of a participant in broader social and cultural activities because of the Internet, whether by creating a MySpace profile, posting videos on YouTube, or playing online games, for example. What benefits do you think you derive from interacting on the Internet, and how are these different from the benefits you get from watching TV? Based on your own experience as a participant and a producer, do Shirky's predictions about the future seem persuasive to you?

3. Shirky's basic premise about television—that it renders us passive consumers of media produced by others—may be undermined by new developments in the television industry that are aimed at engaging viewers and giving them more opportunities to interact with programs. In addition to shows that solicit our votes to affect or determine final outcomes (e.g., *Big Brother, American Idol),* many TV programs have Web sites where fans can contribute to discussions and find additional information about contestants and episodes (e.g., *Biggest Loser, Survivor).* ABC's *Lost* is well-known for the active participation of its fans in alternative forums, including Web sites, novels, podcasts, and other venues. Consider the ways in which television programs use the Internet and other technologies to offer viewers more opportunities to interact and produce. Select what you see as the two or three most significant developments from this list and draft an essay in which you use these developments to argue against Shirky's claims about television. In your essay, discuss specific examples of interactive television programming—perhaps drawing on your own experience with these programs as well.

On Reality TV

ERIC JAFFE

Reality Check

The following article presents an overview of psychological research on the phe-
nomenon of reality TV. Considered objectively, it would make sense that psy-
chologists are keenly interested in knowing more about a form of entertainment

that supposedly depicts real people confronting real challenges and working out the details of real relationships. In fact, some reality shows—Survivor, Big Brother, MTV's The Real World—seem remarkably like laboratories for human behavior: Bring a group of strangers together, introduce some adverse conditions, and see what happens to individuals and relationships. Moreover, psychologists have the expertise to help us understand why reality TV has become so popular: Who watches it, and why? What effect does reality TV have on its viewers? Reflecting the diverse approaches within the field of psychology, Eric Jaffe discusses the range of answers that researchers in psychology have provided to these and other questions about reality TV.

See: the world of reality television. The cast members bear little resemblance to your usual television actors (but they also seem quite unlike you and me). In exotic settings and high-stakes competitions, strangers are stranded and banded together, elevated to star status as long as they are willing to do and say things we could never imagine. Video editors whirl through raw footage, past the mundane, in search of incidental lusts or brawls. Promises are bound and broken in a single breath. Triumph is declared over enemies who, moments before, were friends who, days before, were strangers. True love may or may not be found, depending on whether the check is real.

Such is the world that has advertisers flocking, Juilliard graduates panhandling, and psychologists wondering whether life could ever come to imitate this peculiar art.

Reality television has been vilified as the lowest form of entertainment, a threat to intelligence, and catering to (and rising from) the most prurient of human instincts. As such, the shows would seem to offer a bounty of possible examinations from a behavioral perspective. But until recently, the effects of reality television remained sparsely explored. Bryant Paul, Indiana University, offers two explanations for the dearth of literature. First, reality TV is perpetually changing, making it difficult for researchers to collect and analyze data that remain relevant. The other reason is that some researchers do not think it will last. "It's been around three to five years, which is a blink in the bigger scheme," Paul said. "The novelty is wearing off."

If that is the case, losing popularity has never been so popular. Fifty-one million people tuned in to the first-season finale of "Survivor" in August 2000.[1] In January 2003, reality shows accounted for 85 percent of

---

[1] Nielsen Media Research (2000). Report on television.

the most valuable TV-advertising space in the United States, according to the Cable News Network. Competing plans for entire reality networks—Reality 24-7 and Fox Reality Channel—are in the works. The craze has even reached the classroom. James Hay, University of Illinois at Urbana-Champagne, recently began teaching a course called The Reality TV Syndrome. "I'm often asked, 'Why would you want to teach in higher education the lowest form of television?'" Hay said. "But it's an important matter in everyday life."

And not all researchers believe the fad is fading. "I don't see any signs that it's going away any time soon," said Brad Waite, Central Connecticut State University, who presented reality television research at the American Psychological Society's 16th Annual Convention. "Something so ubiquitous must have an effect on behavior."

Passion for Peeping

Flip back to that first "Survivor" finale. As a frame of reference, 51 million viewers is more than watched the 1983 "M*A*S*H" special—the top Nielson-rated show of all time. (Nielson officially ranks shows by time-share and household percentage, however, so—M*A*S*H—still holds the top spot, and—Survivor—doesn't even crack the top 100.) By watching in such high numbers, viewers told network executives to dump their high-priced writers and lovely actors in favor of identifiable people in familiar conflicts. All we really wanted to see was the same thing we saw in the mirror every morning—ourselves. Only different.

According to Waite, a writers' strike loomed in Hollywood around this time. The airwaves were ripe for inexpensive replacements. After "Survivor," previously impossible profits became, well, a reality.

"It is not difficult to imagine the difference in cost between a whole series where one person wins $1 million and producing a series of 'Friends,' where each cast member earns that much each episode," said James Wiltz, Ohio State University. "One big hit in this genre is worth many attempts."

Network executives thought the same thing. The new strain of television soon spread throughout the viewing community, plagiarizing and mutating into myriad subgenres. But as the number of shows grew, so did the media criticism. A month before the "Survivor" finale, *Time* said we had a passion for peeping and that we enjoyed the suffering, mean-spiritedness, and humiliation endured by others. The *New Statesman* blamed not only reality viewers but also participants for the culture of voyeurism. Nearly a year later, a *Newsweek* headline read: "Another reality show, another IQ point disappears."

It was all the negative publicity that motivated Robin Nabi to conduct some of the earliest research on why people watch. "The press suggested we'd reached an all-time low in taste," said Nabi, a communications professor at University of California, Santa Barbara who takes a social-psychological approach to research. "It's frustrating to see these claims not based on any data. I wanted to know if the claims were reflected in the general public."

Why We Watch

The roots of reality television appear in the 1950s show "Queen for a Day," in which women in dire circumstances competed for the studio audience's sympathy to win fur coats and appliances. Prior to the end of the 20th century, most reality television research centered on the show "Cops," which follows law enforcement officers on their daily beats. But unlike newer reality shows, people on "Cops" were not removed from their natural setting, and the research mostly addressed the show's violence. "The Real World," pioneer of modern reality TV, has aired since 1992, but for years there were too few shows like it to merit a study.

Researching after the turn of the millennium, it did not take Nabi long to debunk some of the criticism. In her *Media Psychology* report, "Reality-Based Television Programming and the Psychology of Its Appeal,"[2] Nabi found the notion of reality watchers as voyeurs questionable at best.

"The idea of voyeurism didn't bear itself out in the data. Viewers wanted to watch other people, but not to see something the characters didn't want them to see," Nabi said, noting that voyeuristic pleasure is undermined when the subject knows he or she is being watched. Besides, said Nabi, viewers are well aware that illicit activity is certain to be censored even if it occurs.

A year later, Ohio State University psychologist Steven Reiss confirmed the absence of voyeurism, though what he found instead was debatably worse. He and collaborator James Wiltz based their research on Reiss's sensitivity theory, which says that most complex human motives can be reduced to 16 basic desires. Each time a desire is realized,

---

[2] Nabi, R. L., Biely, E. N., Morgan, S. J., Stitt, C. R. (2003). "Reality-based television programming and the psychology of its appeal." Media Psychology, 5, 303–330.

a related joy is experienced. Though the motives are universal, they are individually prioritized to reflect our unique comportments, our personal Desire Profiles. Reiss has used these profiles to accurately predict spirituality, underachievement, teamwork—even organ donation.

According to Reiss, media events repeatedly allow people to experience the 16 desires and joys. Drawing on the uses and gratification theory—which suggests that people select media to fulfill certain needs—as well as the sensitivity theory, Reiss predicted that reality viewers would display a collective Desire Profile. Finding any difference from the normal profile would have been intriguing. What he and Wiltz found about the basic needs of reality viewers proved that truth is sometimes scarier than fiction.

Reiss's data showed that the largest significant motive for watching reality television was social status, which leads to the joy of self-importance. Only slightly less strong was the need for vengeance, which leads to vindication. "Some people may watch reality TV partially because they enjoy feeling superior to the people being portrayed," Reiss said. "People with a strong need for vengeance have the potential to enjoy watching people being humiliated."

In a content analysis of the five most popular reality shows and the five top scripted dramas and comedies, Waite and collaborator Sara Booker confirmed that reality shows might reflect a desire for viewing humiliation. Using show raters to code character behaviors, they found that reality shows rated higher in humiliation than scripted dramas. (This even after data from "The Swan"—a reality show on which a homely woman receives a makeover, only to then compete in a beauty pageant—was omitted.)

Humilitainment

Waite and Booker call this phenomenon "humilitainment," the tendency for viewers to be attracted to spectacular mortification. Since their study, similarly indecorous shows have popped up like pockmarks on the genre. "Temptation Island" placed dating couples on opposite ends of an island resort and introduced tempters and temptresses whose main purpose, it seems, was to initiate philandering while wearing as little clothing as possible. Some titles alone are enough to evoke disgust: "I Want a Famous Face," "Trading Spouses: Meet Your New Mommy," "The Virgin," and the ever-popular font of humiliation: "Who's Your Daddy?"

Humilitainment has a more graceful and precise cousin—the German word schadenfreude, which translates to the pleasure one receives at the suffering of others. Colin Wayne Leach and Russell Spears studied schadenfreude as it related to an even more real type of reality contest—World Cup soccer matches. Looking at soccer fans' reactions to their team's losses and rival team's victories, Leach and Spears found that schadenfreude was the result of threatened inferiority. In the wake of losing a competition, schadenfreude is "a covert form of prejudice that is used in the maintenance of self-worth," the authors wrote in the *Journal of Personality and Social Psychology*.

If reality viewers are in fact tuning in to feel better at another person's expense, Waite predicts a maladaptive future for heavy watchers. "They expect it's OK to humiliate and to be humiliated by others, instead of thinking there's something wrong with this behavior," Waite said. "The world they're living in is different from others." In this world according to Waite, the borders separating on-screen from off-screen blend indistinguishably. It is this seamless convergence of fiction and reality that psychologists fear could have a severe behavioral impact.

Real People, Real Problems

Each semester, Bryant Paul demonstrates the power of media to his psychology students. He asks how many of them have been to New York. Half raise their hands. He then asks how many of them perceive New York as a dangerous place. The students draw no connection to the previous response, and nearly all the hands are raised.

The theory Paul sets into action is not a new one. It has been around since the late 1960s, when media psychologist George Gerbner stated that exposure to cultural imagery can shape a viewer's concept of reality. Simply put, the more TV a person watches, the more that person believes in the world of TV. Using his "cultivation theory," Gerbner showed that heavy news viewers believed they resided in a "meaner" world, to the point where they might even approve stricter violence interventions.

"In general, one of the negative things about television is that it gives a distorted image of what the rest of the world is like," said APS Fellow and Charter Member Craig A. Anderson, Iowa State University, who focuses mostly on violent media but sees some overlap with reality shows. "TV changes the perception of what is normative."

Mary Beth Oliver, a communications professor at Pennsylvania State University who researches the psychological effects of media on viewers, also wondered what happens when this mean world is a real world.

"I thought the perceived reality would have a strong impact on viewers' social-reality judgments," said Oliver, who studied "Cops" long before the reality boom. Her analysis of crime shows found that African Americans and Latinos were overwhelmingly cast as criminals and whites as police officers. In addition, police were using aggression frequently, particularly if the criminals were minorities.

"Reality television requires viewers to disengage from the suffering of other people or to derive enjoyment from it," Oliver said.

To test how greatly these shows were actually influencing world-views, Oliver asked regular watchers to estimate the prevalence of crime in the real world. Startlingly, reality crime watchers gave increased crime estimates, particularly for the amount of black crimes. Yet Oliver's most unsettling realization came from a phone call she received from an officer in charge of training at a Roanoke, Virginia police department. The man had read her research and was very nervous, because every trainee who wanted to sign up for the force was addicted to these reality crime shows.

"He told me it wasn't just for the enjoyment," Oliver recalled. "That's what they thought policing would really be like."

The blurry line between fiction and reality should come as less of a surprise considering that the godmother of reality television, Mary-Ellis Bunim, was an executive producer for the soap opera "As the World Turns" before creating "The Real World" with partner Jonathan Murray. Bunim's obituary in the December 26, 2004 *New York Times Magazine* said her idea was to "craft soap-opera storylines with actual people."

Fulfilling this idea requires a luxury unavailable to normal reality—heavy editing. "The Apprentice" and "Survivor" each shoot for almost a month and a half, turning 1,000 hours of life into about 15 hours of programming. "The Real World," reality's longest shoot, tapes for five months before producing two dozen episodes. Many researchers, including Paul, find this manipulation problematic.

"Reality TV is just as real as anything else on TV—it's not," Paul said. "They can create any impression they want. One-eighth of an hour one time a week is all viewers get to construct an opinion about a character."

Douglas Gentile, director of research at the National Institute on Media and the Family and psychology professor at Iowa State University, agreed that reality TV's presentation has a large influence on viewers. "One of the things we know from media violence research is that the more realistic the presentation is, the media violence effect seems to be stronger," Gentile said. "Reality TV is claiming it's real, even though there's a striking lack of resemblance to what's really happening in the world. But the average viewers, who aren't as savvy to know how the shows are being produced, are being told that what they're seeing is true."

In addition to how the shows are marketed, rumors linger that cast members exaggerate their behavior and that producers instigate conflict. According to Booker, the character Toni from "Paradise Hotel" admitted letting her rage get the best of her on camera. The villainy of Omarosa from "The Apprentice" seems nothing more than shrewd self-promotion—she still frequents gossip-columns a year after the show's end. Gentile has a clinical term for the insults and antics that come so naturally to reality characters: relational aggression.

"A lot of reality television is very relationally aggressive," he said, describing the term as *I'm having a party and you're not invited.* "Not only do the characters interact unpleasantly to each other, they also spread rumors. This is a classic example of relational aggression—trying to gang up, enhancing one's own status by bringing others down."

Anderson has seen some evidence that relational aggression does not always stop with words. "Relational aggression frequently escalates into physical aggression," he said. "Many assaults occur between acquaintances, when name-calling escalates beyond saying nasty things."

Waite fears such consistent, ignominious behavior will lead to a modified re-creation of Gerbner's "mean world."

"Is the world of the heavy viewer of modern reality TV a 'mean world' but in a different sense?" he asked. "Is this 'mean world' one in which embarrassment, disrespect, and degradation are common? This to me is one of the most interesting reasons why we study this type of programming."

Improving Reality

If reality television does persist, psychologists may in time grow to understand more about its allure. Waite and Gentile both said that video game users have been recently hooked up to functional Magnetic Resonance Imaging machines; whether for marketing or empirical purposes, reality viewers might not be far behind. Until then, Waite speculates that younger generations are simply accustomed to being on screen. Digital cameras now come standard with most cell phones, and Web cams televise daily adventures, from the quotidian to the erotic, around the clock.

"Expectations of privacy have been eroded," Waite said. "Public disclosure, even of formerly private behaviors and feelings, are the expectation."

This intimacy entitlement might explain why 37 million people tuned in after the "Survivor" finale to watch the reunion. Miles away from the island of Pulau Tiga, plain-clothed cast members discussed their feelings and opinions on the experience. To Reiss, this suggests that these once-regular people now hovered somewhere between the celebrity and pedestrian echelons.

"If you pay attention to ordinary people then you're saying ordinary people are important," he said. "People can watch reality TV shows and see ordinary people like themselves become famous, win cash prizes, and move up in their status."

Paul disagrees that a desire to be famous attracts viewers—after all, he says, these people can be famous for you. Rather, the fact that these people were not groomed for celebrity in the traditional sense, that friends of friends invariably went to camp with someone on one of the shows, "and really good empathy equals really good television."

Nabi stumbled onto this possibility when she found almost as much variety among preference for reality subgenres as she did preference between reality and fiction. In some cases, the very quality that defined one show's enjoyment was anathema to another's—suspense was a draw for reality talent shows, but for a reality crime show it was a major detractor, perhaps because the viewer wondered if the criminal remained at large. To Nabi, this could mean that watching real people, whatever the circumstance, is the real attraction.

"Watching real people on TV is fascinating, just like watching people in the airport is fascinating," she said. "Viewers are interested in people—not pain." This leads her to think that some of the negativity directed toward reality TV may be unjustified, but it does not solve the riddle of why viewing real people is such an attraction. "Something deeper is happening here that we haven't gotten to."

For the time being, Nabi sees a positive side to viewer malleability and the scientific evidence supporting it. "It is possible that the way producers put their programs together may be influenced by the academic research," she said. In fact, she has already seen an improvement in the way some reality shows depict real events. Previously, "Extreme Makeover" was criticized for making plastic surgery seem beneficial, rapid, and risk-free. In its current season, however, Nabi said the show more clearly depicts the multiple, intensive steps involved in surgical procedures.

An altruistic show even lurks on the horizon—"The Scholar," in which 10 exceptional and financially-needy high school seniors from around the country will compete for a full scholarship. "Imagine this concept," wrote Booker at the end of her second study, "using reality television to actually improve reality." Given the genre's impact on behavior, that might not be too unrealistic.

Side bar:
The Reiss Profile

In their 2004 report "Why People Watch Reality TV," published in Media Psychology , lead author Steven Reiss and James Wiltz used the Reiss Profile to explain why certain people watched reality television. Validated by responses from over 10,000 people, the Reiss Profile measures how basic motives result in a particular joy. Reality viewers were found to have significantly higher motives for status and vengeance.

Motive	Joy
Acceptance: Desire for approval	**Self-confidence**
Curiosity: Desire for knowledge	**Wonderment**
Eating: Desire for food	**Satiation**
Family: Desire to raise own children	**Love**
Honor: Desire to obey a traditional moral code.	**Loyalty**
Idealism: Desire to improve society (including altruism, justice)	**Compassion**
Independence: Desire for autonomy	**Freedom**
Order: Desire to organize (including desire for ritual)	**Stability**
Physical Exercise: Desire to exercise muscles	**Vitality**
Romance: Desire for sex (including courting)	**Lust**
Power: Desire to influence (including leadership)	**Efficacy**
Saving: Desire to collect	**Ownership**
Social Contact: Desire for peer companionship (and desire to play)	**Fun**
Status: Desire for prestige (including desire for attention)	**Self-importance**
Tranquility: Desire for inner peace (prudence, safety)	**Safe, relaxed**
Vengeance: Desire to get even (including desire to win)	**Vindication**

REFERENCE

Reiss, S., & Wiltz, J. (2004). Why people watch reality TV. *Media Psychology, 6*, 363–378.

SUGGESTIONS FOR WRITING

1. Jaffe discusses the phenomenon of "humilitainment," which he defines as "the tendency for viewers to be attracted to spectacular mortification." Select a specific reality TV show in which you think humilitainment may be occurring (Jaffe lists some shows in the article), and write an analysis of the particular "mortifications" that are involved. Why do you think viewers find this show appealing? Do you agree with the researchers' prediction of a "maladaptive future" for heavy watchers of this type of show?

2. The sidebar above presents a list of basic motives that drive human behavior, along with their corresponding results or "joys." Use this list to help you think about the appeal of a particular type of reality program (e.g., talent competition, physical competition, dating, home improvement). Which of the motives are most relevant for that type of reality show? In what specific ways does the show satisfy those motives and deliver the desired results? Write an essay in which you explore these questions by applying the list of motives to a type of reality TV show.

3. Jaffe discusses a number of psychological concepts in this article: voyeurism, schadenfreude, cultivation theory, relational aggression, intimacy entitlement. Choose one of these concepts and write a definition-based essay in which you explain the concept in your own words, perhaps after conducting some outside research to learn more about it. Discuss how this concept is relevant for an understanding of reality TV.

RICHARD M. HUFF

Singing for Fame, Fortune, or Just Attention

According to the Nielsen ratings system, American Idol was the most popular TV show in the United States from 2005 to 2009. Everyone knows the formula: Thousands of wanna-be pop stars from all over the nation audition for a spot in the top twelve, where they then deliver weekly performances in front of sometimes-caustic/sometimes-compassionate judges and try to avoid being eliminated. Major musical artists and producers mentor the contestants, whose talents are tested by having to perform a different theme or genre of music each week. The judges offer instant and entertaining feedback on the performances, the viewers vote via text or telephone, and the ultimate winner gets a recording contract and a major head start on fame and fortune. In the article that follows, Richard Huff provides a brief history of this enormously popular show, tracing its roots back to the radio and television talent shows of the 1940s and 1950s. Indeed, American Idol *has fundamentally reinvented the old talent show, reinvigorating it with the techniques of reality TV.*

As a child and a budding singer Wayne Newton won a talent contest in Roanoke, Virginia. He was only nine at the time. After the win, Newton and his family traveled to New York to audition for *The Original Amateur Hour*. Ted Mack hosted the program, which began in 1948 on the Dumont network and in 1949 moved to NBC. The show actually began on radio, with Major Bowes as the host. A year and a half after Bowes died, it was revived on television.

Mack had been an assistant on Bowes radio show and the format for the television version was taken directly from the radio show. Mack played host to a variety of amateurs, real amateurs, ranging from mimes to comics to kazoo players and singers. Viewers voted for their favorite acts by calling the show or sending postcards. The winners were given scholarships. After he auditioned, Newton said he was told, "We'll call you. Don't call us."

Mack's staff never called. And Newton, who in 2005 would go on to be a part of E! Entertainment's reality show *The Entertainer* to find new talent to work in Las Vegas, is quick to note that Elvis Presley also didn't make the cut on *The Original Amateur Hour*.

Little did Newton know when he auditioned for *The Original Amateur Hour* that he would become part of the early influences for a genre of reality programming to find entertainers and people with other talents. One of the most famous finds during the *Amateur Hour*, though on the radio version, was Frank Sinatra. Gladys Knight and Pat Boone were also winners on the television version. For the most part, those appearing on the show never made it big in the entertainment world.

After *The Original Amateur Hour* several similar shows would pop up along the way giving amateurs in a variety of genres a chance at super stardom. Chuck Barris's *Gong Show* was one. By 1983, the syndicated *Star Search* was becoming a platform for future stars and also showcased regular people. Ed McMahon hosted the show, which allowed performers to compete in various categories, such as male or female singers, comics, and a television spokesmodel category. Unlike *The Original Amateur Hour, Star Search* did turn out many future stars, including such performers as Christina Aguilera, Tiffany, and Rosie O'Donnell.

As it was, after the talent show heydays of the 1950s, such shows were marginal hits at best and tended to operate around the fringes of the medium. The reality phase of music and competition began abroad in 1 999, with the launch of *Popstars* in New Zealand. The reality show followed a pop group from its creation to hitting the road to fame. The show was a hit and was quickly made in several countries such as Denmark, Spain, Finland, Australia, and eventually Britain. *Popstars* launched in the United States on the WB and in Britain in 2001. Viewers watched along as potential group members were selected from auditions and then finally put together in a made-for-television band. The American version produced a girl group called Eden's Crush. In the British version, viewers were glued to the set to see who made the band and what happened after. The manufactured group's first single rocketed to the top of the charts.

Before *Popstars* aired in the United States, ABC had launched *Making the Band*, a series that tracked music mogul Lou Pearlman as he created a pop group. The series aired for three seasons on ABC and resulted in the creation of O-Town, a group that had a brief run in the pop world before disbanding. (Ashley Parker Angel, one of the members of O-Town was featured in his own comeback reality show on MTV in early 2006.)

While watching the undeniable success of *Popstars* in Britain, record producers Simon Cowell and Simon Fuller came up with a twist on the idea of *Popstars*. Rather than have a group result from the show, they wanted to have a contest where just one person won in the end of the show's run. Fuller and Cowell then took the show to the production firm Freemantle to see if they would make it. They immediately bought into the concept.

"We had both been auditioning artists in the music business for more than 15 years, and we instinctively knew what was being shown on *Popstars* was not representative of what really goes on in the audition room," Cowell wrote in his book *I Don't Mean to Be Rude, But. . . .* "*Pop Idol* would expose what really happens in an audition. This was going to be the hook of the show and it was not going to be pleasant."

More than 10,000 people applied to audition for the show. Initially, Cowell wrote, the judges were too soft on those auditioning. Realizing it was not going to make for good television, they let loose with their real feelings. The next person who walked in the door was terrible and was told so, Cowell wrote. "We'd put the reality back in reality television," he said. When it launched, the show became a huge hit in Britain. *Pop Idol* yielded first season winner Will Young who went on to sell 2 million records with his first release.

Based on the performance in Britain, Cowell and Fuller decided to take the show to the United States, where reality television was just taking off. They pitched the show to a couple networks, which passed. Eventually, Fox officials said yes. *American Idol* launched on Fox in June 2002 with Cowell, Randy Jackson, and Paula Abdul as the judges. Cowell immediately stood out for providing frank assessments of the contestants' performances, which contrasted often with the softer approach from Abdul.

For instance, early on Cowell addressed Jim Verraros, a 19-year-old singer from Illinois by saying: "I hated your audition. I thought it was terrible. I don't know what that was all about."

His reaction immediately earned him the nickname "Mr. Nasty," and his sparring with fellow judge Paula Abdul over how he treated contestants made for excellent television. Early episodes of *American Idol* were centered on the audition process and included a steady stream of good and terrible singers. Viewers were hooked. Ratings soared for the show. By September, it was a hit. The finale, in which Kelly Clarkson beat out Justin Guarini to become the first *American Idol* champion, was watched by 22.8 million viewers.

"*American Idol* does not belong in the reality category," said Syracuse University Professor Robert Thompson, who runs the school's Center for Popular Television. "You never saw those people [outside of the competition] or if you did it was a short period of time outside the stage. Therefore, it was about all that stuff. What *American Idol* did was reintroduce the viability of the old-fashioned talent show," Thompson said. "Then it invited the marriage of the old-fashioned talent show with the new fashioned reality show." "*American Idol*" executive producer Ken Warwick, refers to the show as "Vareality", a mix of variety and reality.

If anything, *American Idol* had the spirit of a reality show and carried many reality show traits: real people trying out for television and then being voted off in a competition. The winner, like in *Survivor*, had a life-changing experience. *American Idol* worked with audiences for a couple of reasons. Early on, viewers were drawn to the auditioning process for the I-can't-believe-what-I'm-seeing factor when a really bad singer was on stage. Likewise, once the bad ones were cut from the show, then the tide turns toward rooting—and voting—for the ultimate winners. Then it becomes like watching a favorite team. "Without question, if it was done and everyone was fantastic, I don't think anyone would watch *American Idol*," Cowell said, "80 percent of them are terrible."

Cecile Frot-Coutaz, executive producer of *American Idol* said the show works because it's a pure format. "It's a very simple show," she said. "It's about, it's trying to find the next kind of next great singer, and it's about the American dream. It's about taking people who live a normal life in some remote part of the country, but have an amazing talent, discovering that talent and making the dream come true. I think there's something very powerful about that."

Not to be undervalued in the process is the role of the public, which votes on the outcome of *American Idol*. Although judges Cowell, Jackson, and Abdul can say someone is a great singer, it's up to the public to cast a vote for the singer they want to win.

Besides launching the careers of such talented singers as Clarkson, Clay Aiken, Bo Bice, and Carrie Underwood, *American Idol* has also been responsible for the career of William Hung, a very bad singer who turned his awful performance auditioning on *American Idol* into a very small recording career.

Hung wasn't the first bad singer to make it on *American Idol*, though he was the first to turn his appearance into a career of sorts. Otherwise, most really bad singers who go on the show know that going in and are just trying to get some airtime on the hit show. "In truth, with the bad singers, it depends where you come from," said executive producer Nigel Lythgoe. "I love the deluded. I don't love the university [student] and the graduate that comes along, makes himself look stupid because he is on a bet. We record everybody, so we've got it, and we'll normally drop that into a montage of stupidity, but not feature them as a soloist. It's the William Hungs that I love. It's the ones that believe you can be successful—and it's everybody's dream—you can be successful in this country by working hard. And he forgets that you need a modicum of talent as well, which he didn't have. But he believes like so many that come along to the auditions that if we invest our time as professionals in them, we can make them a star."

And that they have. As part of their deals to appear on *American Idol* the winner's first album is produced by and released by record companies associated with the producers. The show producers control what songs and the direction they'll take early on. Anyone making it into the top 10 of *American Idol* is signed to a deal for future work. Some have called the deals restrictive and unfair.

Not so, said Cowell, who. points out the show helps propel a career that might never have happened. "None of them, when they win, are going to turn and give the money to charity," Cowell said. "This is a get rich quick scheme for somebody. If you don't like it, don't play."

Fox attempted to capture the *American Idol* magic in *American Juniors*, an *Idol* spin-off featuring singers between the ages of 6 and 13 in June 2003. The show was similar to the adult *American Idol*, although the judges were different, and as a result spared the juniors the wrath of Simon Cowell. However, many critics said because the show lacked the bite of a Cowell, it just wasn't interesting. Others said the children singers weren't as good as the adults and not worth watching. The first version struggled to get viewers, though Fox officials initially said there would be a second version. That edition was never produced and ultimately scrapped.

The producers of *American Idol* also staged one cycle of *World Idol* on Fox, which put the winners of the various international competitions in one big battle. It, too, lasted one season.

The arrival of *American Idol* also opened the door for even more music-based series, either direct competitions like *American Idol* or shows built around a theme, such as *Making the Band*, which once dropped by ABC in 2003 was picked up, altered, and continued at MTV.

Producers Ben Silverman and H. T. Owens, the team behind *The Restaurant* reality series, capitalized off the *American Idol* momentum in 2003 with their show, *Nashville Star* for the USA Network. Where *American Idol* looked for a pop star, *Nashville Star* searched for a country artist. A dozen contestants competed in the first cycle. They were judged by industry professionals and viewers at home. During the run of the show the finalists lived together in a house on Music Row in Nashville.

In addition to singing, *Nashville Star* also put contestants in what was called the "hot spot," a challenge where they had to act professional in a situation in which most stars routinely find themselves. One in the first season had the five finalists sing the National Anthem at a stock car race.

The first winner was Buddy Jewell, whose first CD hit the No.1 spot on the Billboard country charts. "I had been in Nashville for a decade writing songs," said Jewell. "*Nashville Star* landed me a record deal and gave me the opportunity to perform my own songs on the show in front of millions of Americans each week—with fan reactions via email and through my Web site. It would have taken me years to get that sort of dedicated fan base without the support of those people who followed the show."

The show was a hit for the USA Network, which launched its fourth season of *Nashville Star* in early 2006. *Nashville Star* works because it showcases the best untapped musical talent on television," said Jeff Wachtel, USA Network's executive vice president of original programming in announcing the new season. "One thing we've learned over the past three seasons is that there's an incredible pool of talented performers whose voices have yet to be heard." Even the runners up on *Nashville Star* have done well. Miranda Lambert, who finished third on the show, has since had a successful country singing career. *Nashville Star* has also proven to be a strong draw for celebrities. Singing star LeAnn Rimes was the host early on. Singer Sarah Evans stepped in at one point. And in 2006, Wynonna and Cowboy Troy were the hosts, with a series of big-named stars saving as judges.

American Idol is so good, it also has been spoofed. Mike Fleiss, the man behind *Who Wants to Marry a Multimillionaire?* and *The Bachelor*, took on *American Idol* in 2004 with *The WB's Superstar USA*, a riveting series that took the model of *American Idol* and turned it upside down. Rather than looking for good singers, *Superstar USA* looked for bad singers, truly bad singers, but the contestants were not told they were bad. Like *American Idol* there were three judges, including a former pop star and a cranky judge in the model of Simon Cowell. When a good singer performed they were told they were terrible. A bad singer, however, was showered with praise. It wasn't until the end of the show when the winner was told they were picked because they were really bad.

Because *Superstar USA* was built on a stunt, or more specifically a twist, it wasn't tried twice. In the past, the second cycle of some shows hasn't done as well as the first, especially with twist shows. *Joe Millionaire* didn't work a second time around, nor did *Joe Schmo*, largely because once the stunt is known—and viewers know what to expect—producers tend to shy away from the format.

American Idol served as the model for *So You Think You Can Dance*, a talent search show for dancers produced by *American Idol* backer Nigel

Lythgoe in 2005 and again in 2006. It was also the model for *But Can They Sing?* a VHI reality show with celebrities trying to belt out a tune. Among the performers were Joe Pantoliano, Morgan Fairchild, boxer Larry Holmes, and former model Kim Alexis. "I've embraced the fact that I can't sing," Pantoliano told the *New York Daily News* before the show launched. He couldn't, of course, but that was the idea behind the series in the first place.

The influence of *American Idol* and *Survivor* combined are found in a two reality shows that appeared during 2005 that were designed to find new embers for real-life bands. Mark Burnett, the force behind *Survivor*, also produced *Rock Star* for CBS. The show was created to find a lead singer or the band INXS, which had been without a lead singer since Michael Hutchence killed himself in 1997. Unlike *American Idol*, *Rock Star* did not include any of the audition process as part of the show, and instead began with the field of contestants already picked. Brooke Burke and Dave Navarro served as hosts, and the surviving members of INXS were part of the judging process. Viewers were also shown some of the behind-the-scenes life of the contestants, such as rehearsals and living together in a house. "This was a band, it was going to take a singer, we weren't just going to crank out a pop star," Navarro said. "I thought it was an interesting twist."

"Yes, it's a music show, and somebody does win it," executive producer and former *Idol* producer, David Goffin said before the launch. "But somebody who wins becomes a member of an existing band. It's an incredible prize. I think we've got something that ends in a much bigger and better way [than *American Idol*]."

CBS banked on the show to be a big hit, but it wasn't. Three planned weekly telecasts were cut down, and eventually the show was moved to VH1 to finish out its run. Canadian J. D. Fortune won the show and immediately cut a record with INXS. Tommy Lee, who appeared in an NBC series following him going back to college, agreed to spearhead a new band that would search for a singer on CBS's *Rock Star*, set for summer 2006.

The R&B group TLC also went the reality show route to find a new singer. The group had three members, but one, Lisa Lopes was killed in a car crash. Like *Rock Star*, UPN's *R U the Girl* was about becoming the next member of the group, which members T-Boz and Chilli each said would not be a replacement for Lopes. Yet, it intentionally focused more on T-Boz and Chilli than the competitors. "We've all seen competition shows," executive producer Jay Blumenfield told reporters in

July 2005, before the show launched. "I think there're good things and bad things about them. But we all wanted to try something new and really try to go on a journey with T-Boz and Chilli and see where it took us." Along the way viewers saw the contestants prove their singing and dancing skills, as well as their people skills in dealing with the two remaining members of TLC.

To some extent, NBC's *Last Comic Standing* owes something to *American Idol*. The series was a mix of *Idol's* performance functions and *The Real World's* living together strings. The show lasted a couple of seasons, though it has been hamstrung by controversy when it was clear some of the comics on the show were already professionals, and there were also questions about the judging process. Having worked out the kinks, *Last Comic Standing* was revived and slated to return on NBC in the summer of 2006, with 10 comics, male and female, living together in a house and vying for a talent contract with the network.

The common thread running through most of the performance and musical genre shows is that they tend to appeal to families and encourage family viewing. Families watch together because parents generally do not need to worry about salacious content on a show such as *American Idol* or *Nashville Star* because it's not part of the mix. No one is forced to humiliate themselves to get to the next level. There isn't a lot of behind-the-scenes footage for parents to worry about kids seeing alcohol-fueled parties or dips in a hot tub. And, there is rarely any bad language.

During the 2004-2005 television season, *American Idol* was the most-watched show on television, averaging more than 27 million viewers an episode; that's up from more than 21 million the show earned in 2002-2003, according to Nielsen Media Research. *American Idol's* audience levels stand in contrast to most aging shows, which tend to lose viewers in subsequent seasons, not gain them.

"I think unpredictability is the key to making great reality TV," Cowell told television writers in January 2005. "That is the definition of reality. It's real." Cowell is right. Amazingly, the fifth season of *American Idol* was drawing its largest audiences ever, routinely topping 30 million viewers for each edition. Typically, shows draw their largest audiences in the first season and fall from there. But *American Idol* increased audience with each season.

And it's that aspect of the performance shows that keeps viewers coming back and watching, waiting, and even hoping they'll be setside when a new star is born. Newton, who for decades has been one of Las Vegas's biggest stars, said giving people a shot at fame was one of the reasons he was willing to be part of *The Entertainer*. And if it existed when he was coming up, he would have tried out, too. "The truth of the matter is the thing that propelled me to want to be such an integral part of this show was the realization that what helped me in my embryonic stages of my career, don't exist for these people today, and it really is something that I absolutely would have done," Newton said. "I absolutely would have auditioned. I absolutely would have shown up."

He did in his day, on *The Original Amateur Hour*. Today, young singers are doing the same.

SUGGESTIONS FOR WRITING

1. Drawing on the other articles in this section and on your own experience and research, compose your own definition of reality TV. Based on this definition, is *American Idol* a reality TV show? What criteria does it meet, and in what ways is it different from a typical reality TV show? In order to make your argument more persuasive, draw on some of the quotations provided in Huff's article.

2. Huff offers several explanations as to why talent shows like *American Idol* are inherently interesting to viewers. After reviewing his arguments and recalling your own experience either as a viewer or participant, write an essay in which you attempt to explain the particular appeal of talent shows.

3. In Huff's article, *American Idol* is frequently compared to other, mostly less successful reality TV shows. Choose one of the many talent-focused reality TV shows (e.g., *American's Next Top Model, Dancing with the Stars, Top Chef, Last Comic Standing*) and write an extended comparison and contrast paper in which you describe the similarities and differences between *American Idol* and this show. At the end of your paper, use your comparison to help you support a conclusion about why one of the shows is more successful or popular or interesting than the other.

GARETH PALMER

Extreme Makeover: Home Edition: An American Fairy Tale

Gareth Palmer is a British scholar (hence the article's British spelling of "programme" and "neighbour," for example) whose research focuses on popular media. Here he looks from across the Atlantic at one popular American *reality TV show—*Extreme Makeover: Home Edition—*and draws conclusions about what the popularity of this show suggests about American society, the American economy, and the American Dream. In every episode of* EMHE, *a deserving family, one that has suffered a major setback, gets the gift of an extravagantly renovated house; community members work together on the project with an expert crew assembled by* EMHE *and sponsored by ABC and Sears. On the surface, this charitable expression of friends and neighbors in support of a truly needy family would seem to be unobjectionable and even commendable. Gareth Palmer argues, however, that a closer analysis of the show reveals its distorted depiction of family, community, and capitalism. According to Palmer, deep cracks in the American Dream become apparent in* EMHE *'s attempt to patch up the homes of desperate families.*

It's a fairy tale. It's a guaranteed happy ending (Forman 2005).

ABC's *Extreme Makeover: Home Edition* (hereafter EMHE) was one of the top ten programmes of the 2004/05 season in America and winner of the 2005 EMMY for Outstanding Reality TV Programme. EMHE tells a fascinating story about modern-day America where the return of a strong right-wing ideology privileges the traditional family and the interests of business, yet also affords a glimpse of the crises affecting ordinary Americans. In the model of community proposed by the programme, the state has no role to play: in its place are people coming together out of fellow-feeling for their neighbours. But the repair work is so extreme it throws into relief the mundane quality of most American homes. In promoting such a perspective both in the programme and through its various affiliated enterprises with Sears etc., ABC are championing an America which resonates with its mythical past but which is utterly unrepresentative of family life for most Americans. The programme is, in short, a fairy tale where magic is represented by selfless communities, free goods, labour, and dreams coming true.

I will proceed by considering how the following elements knit together to produce this modern portrait of American life. The centrality of the *family* is the first and primary theme in what follows. Which families have been chosen and why? What do they represent? I then consider the ways in which the programme helps construct the *community* as a natural mechanism founded not on self-interest but on the simple concept of neighbourliness. I then look at how the state has almost completely retreated, and how its work has been replaced by a *magical market* where items such as labour have no price. In the final section I consider the ways in which the programme represents another dimension in the changing role and function of *television*. Rather than being an apparatus that records a world external to it, television is now an increasingly active agent in changing it. The very fact that well over 50,000 people per series have written in to be on the programme is testimony to the fact that, as far as many people are concerned, television can and perhaps even should change their lives. I conclude by considering the programme in the context of the American economy.

The Family

Representations have become a critical battleground in the conflicts over family and family values leading to the spectacularization of the family as the platform on which society's profound debates about sexual and personal morality are performed (Chambers 2001: 176).

EMHE starts every week with a sequence in which the assorted designers who will lead the re-design of the house are situated in a van watching the targeted family's videotape. Team Leader Ty Pennington gives the background to this family and the rest of this sequence involves reaction shots of all involved. What is remarkable about this sequence, at least for this British viewer, is that these video-diary sequences sent in by the family are all extraordinarily revealing about the state of America.

In many cases the desperation of families is a direct result of the fact that agencies of the state have abandoned them. For example, in one case a family had to watch their son die because ambulances and police refused to go into their neighbourhood for fear of their lives. In another video we see a family whose son is dying because he is ineligible for medical aid. In yet another typical episode, an Iraq War veteran has materials provided for him, as the state does not support veterans very generously. Week after week we see first hand video testimony that the state is in retreat and only those lucky enough to have many friends, family and neighbours are able to survive. But it is those who have slipped below ordinary levels of subsistence that form the centrepieces of *EMHE*. As Frances Bonner writes when describing 'ordinary' television: 'When . . . it has to deal with death . . . and given its fascination with medical matters and with hard luck stories (tragedies) it must do this with some regularity—placing it within a 'plucky' family is the principal way to do things' (Bonner 2003: 111).

After watching their tape for a few moments the crew arrive, and the family to be chosen is woken very early in the morning, on the doorstep of their home. This magical moment is only the first of many such otherworldly touches in the narrative. After meeting the team and crying tears of gratitude, the family is then whisked away for a week-long holiday while crew, enlisted community, and contractors go about the business of changing their home.

What follows is a monumental effort to effect the transformation. But why has all this energy been devoted to making the home so central? In the last ten years, makeover shows have become a mainspring of TV schedules in Britain and America. In each case a person with limited resources is assisted into a new look and given the confidence he or she needs to progress. However, at the centre of these 'reveals' is the family. In examples ranging from *This Old House* to *The Swan* it is the family that has inspired the change and the family who are focused on in their reaction to it. In this way the home is remade as a machine for keeping families together, the place to retreat to. It need hardly be said that such an approach brings to mind long and powerful myths about the centrality of the family. Anthony Giddens describes the family as, 'The site for the democratisation of intimate relationships, the family becomes a major platform on which debates about moralities and ethics gets staged' (Giddens 1999: 165).

The makeover show turns individuals into family members, foregrounds the family and makes it a part of the wider community. It is hard to imagine a clearer message about the centrality of the home and the importance of keeping the family together come what may. But, as Young has pointed out, 'The family can of course teach adherence to the values of the community but the presence of a strong family does not magically entail community' (Young 1999: 155).

It might be argued that there are two families at work in *EMHE* – the subject of the makeover and the extended family of the design team. It is after all this family that we get to know every week through their work and their relationships with one another. It is they who represent a modern family with no fixed relationships and no permanent 'home' they can call their own. We might also note that the five men exhibit some of the camp characteristics that are now a trademark of the genre: only in this sense can the hint of homosexuality be tolerated, in a space marked-off from ordinary life. In a sense, the *EMHE* team represent the fluid upwardly mobile petit bourgeoisie against the time-worn virtues of the proletariat. This divide between the classes ensures that the working class are always receptive and thankful for the 'good taste' bestowed upon them by the middle class. But while it is the role of the working class to be properly grateful, the designers are all seen to be humbled by their experience, which extends beyond the show and is maintained through letters and notes pinned to a message board. The coming together of these two family groupings is about 'learning'—a theme that dominates so much American television. While the working class learn taste, the petit bourgeoisie learn about 'real people' (i.e. the sort of people they would not normally ever encounter in their lives as designers for the rich and famous). This learning is a means of bringing groups together, the wider theme that animates the series and which keys it into the classic picture of an America constituted of families connected to communities making one nation (Morley and Robins 1995: 109).

At the end of the show the ramshackle house, held together by the depth of the bonds between the family members, is replaced by a magnificent home. Crucial here is the show's reveal which takes place after a bus is moved aside to show the transformed home. (It has even inspired the catchphrase 'Bus Driver. Move That Bus!') As Charlotte Brunsden has written, 'It is the reaction, not the action, that matters' (Brunsden 2001: 35).

As we are lead through the magically transformed home at the same time as the family, we too can be awestruck by the changes wrought by the designers and of course the wider community. In one sense, we marvel at the high quality of the work achieved but perhaps more significant is the fact that we are reminded that this transformation is also a reward—it is because people have held the family together in very difficult situations that they deserve this home. In clips and segments that remind us of the past, we are moved to see that these people have got what they deserve. The home is an extension of the love that the family hold for one another. By undergoing this transformation as a reward for their dedication to the family, the individuals go from being objects of our pity to ones of our envy.

It seems almost churlish to mention it in the presence of so much joy, but this portrait of a family transformed is so unrealistic it might even be counter-productive. This is a classic example of what Chambers calls 'the massive discrepancy between complex lived experiences of human relationships and those popular discourses that invent and promote an imaginary nuclear familiarism' (Chambers 2004: 175). But such discrepancies are hidden in the magic of transformation.

Community

'A better community—get involved and help—click here' (ABC website).

Makeover programmes are the most overt sign of the ways television perceives itself to be engaged in a project of advising ordinary viewers about their transformation into happier, more satisfied, up-to-date versions of their selves (Bonner 2002: 136).

The community plays a central role in *EMHE*. It is made clear throughout the programme and in all accompanying materials that it is the community that are responsible for making the whole thing come together. While it may be designers who provide the creative impetus, it is the community that are seen doing all the unglamorous heavy work. Unlike the virtual shadow communities inspired to 'call the cops' in response to televised police appeals which dissolve once their contribution is made, *EMHE* features real communities showing us all how to work together.

To begin with, the community has often been the sponsor of the families who are featured. As Forman has said: 'Most of the families we end up doing are nominations. The kind of families we're looking for don't say "Gee, I need help". They are quietly trying to solve their problems themselves and it's a neighbour or co-worker who submits an application on their behalf (Forman 2005).

We see the community, shortly after the programme begins, giving testimony to the deserving family, then later throughout the show at work in various jobs. They play small but significant roles in the drama as the glue in the cracks of the community holding everything together. And yet they are also there in the reveal. They 'star' here because of what they have done to bring about these changes. Whether as contractors, friends, tradesmen or simply labourers, all have a role to play and are defined not so much as individuals but as part of a greater whole. No individual pulls focus: it is always about the larger community. But what actually constitutes this community?

It is important to see the entire series in context as a trigger for activating a wide variety of communities. For example, the local press are often keen to highlight the series if a local family is involved. In Salt Lake City we learn of the '1,500 workers and volunteers working 24 hours a day to build a bigger home for the Johnson family.' In the *Boston Globe* we read about how residents had 'been routing for more than a year for a family to be picked up by the show.'

Once they had been selected, the community were all too keen to get involved.

Two allied supporters of this community effort are local businesses and the Church. John McMurria has pointed out how Sears has benefited from the programme (McMurria 2005). But plenty of other local services are represented in *EMHE*, not as profit-led businesses but as benevolent organizations. The value of PR here can be enormous as big cardboard cheques are presented to tearful local residents. As one business said of a veteran—'He has such a sweet and humble spirit and we wanted to thank him for the way he loves for his country and his family.'

It is important also to note that American Christian groups have been generous in praising the show. As Evangelical journalist Holly Vincente Robaina wrote, 'It's a rare phenomenon. Believers of every age, ethnicity and denomination are embracing the primetime television show ABC's Extreme *Makeover: Home Edition*' (Robaina 2005).

Executive producer Tom Forman was specifically asked whether any plan was made to 'include elements that would connect specifically with Christian values.' Forman responded that the show appealed because 'good things happen to good people. That's possibly why it resonates with the Christian community and all of our viewers' (Forman, ABC interview).

Church leaders are quoted by the local press, such as Mr. A. Wigston in the *Cass County Democrat of Missouri*. 'It was really neat to see God working through the hearts of the designers for people with disabilities.' Some other churches have set out on 'copy-cat' schemes in which members decorate or attempt mini-makeovers of their own in just the way that producer Forman had hoped they would. Not only does this imitative practice privilege the role of the Church in the community, but the reporting and celebration of this role presents a clear ideological message on the centrality of helping heterosexual families. But is this at the expense of other communities?

These timeless myths of the American 'heartland', featuring the happy smiling community working for nothing but love, bring to mind classic American TV fictions such as *Little House on the Prairie* and *The Waltons*. These idealized versions of perfect family life may be instructive about nostalgia in the 1970s and 1980s, and for settled family life in a time of great upheaval. But of course these fictions were located in the past when such a myth may have been feasible. But what are we to make of *EMHE*'s portrait of American life, which suggests such ideals are here with us now?

It is of course possible to take a different view of the community. A few questions might be worth asking here: what other possible communities may be excluded here? To what extent are alternative family groupings given time and attention? Or perhaps a more useful question might concern the location of this community. In almost every edition of the show, the house to be modified is placed centre screen without any sort of context. What are the neighbour's houses like? What else is on the street? The framing of the house in this way also helps us to consider the home as somehow separate from others, but it excludes any arguments we might make concerning the collapse of American communities. What if we were to see other broken-down homes? The danger here might be that we could make wider arguments about poverty and the role played by corporate America as it seeks to maximize profit without any thought for communities. I think here of Flint, Michigan in Michael *Moore's Roger and Me* where the collapse of the community after the departure of Chrysler is denoted in showing hundreds of boarded-up homes. But there are no shortage of communities who have borne the brunt of America's economic boom and bust. For example, on Public Housing, the Bush administration has twice proposed the elimination of the HOPE VI programme, which provided for the revitalization of more than 20,000 severely distressed public units as well as the demolition of another 63,000 severely distressed units (Alliance for Healthy Homes).

To try and deal with change on this scale would perhaps be a makeover too far. Furthermore, according to the embedded logic of the industry, such a programme would not be 'good television'. As the old maxim goes 'The death of millions is just a statistic: the death of one is a tragedy.'

But to return to the programme as it currently stands: is it small-minded to think of the after-show effect? Is it just possible that, after the cameras have gone, the community become jealous of the fact that their neighbour's house now towers above them all? Will the idealized family always be so well thought of by other members of the community? One wonders how the community will fare after one of its members has been both symbolically and financially elevated.

The Magical Market

What I want to do in this section is analyse how the market is disguised as part of the magical narrative of *EMHE*. One of the most unusual factors about the programme for British viewers is the complete absence of cost. In contrast to many UK makeover shows, costs are never mentioned in *EMHE*. Why is this? The instinctual answer has to be that costs have no place in a fairy tale. Do we know where the Prince bought the glass slippers? Of course not—these are crass questions. It is our role simply to be enchanted by the transformations wrought. But, at the risk of breaking the spell, there are various economic elements that I think merit discussion, for they speak to the real and entirely nonmagical base of the programme.

In the first place, we might consider the costs of labour. What would it cost to hire such designers or to employ upwards of 150 people for 24 hours a day, seven days a week? Secondly, we might look at the cost of the furnishings, the materials and the many other artful purchases that go into the ideal home. It is only at the end of the show that we have any sort of opportunity to calculate the cost of this transformation, but by then we are too emotionally involved to make such calculations. The point is that all of these costs are hidden in the service of repairing families. But not mentioning costs makes these repairs appear free or even magical. As most communities know, the economic is determining and not at all magical. The fact is that there are many who profit enormously from the show.

While it is clearly the case that one family will benefit from the makeover, the Public Relations benefits to others involved are extraordinary. The most obvious recipient of good PR is the Sears corporation. The programme's website makes it clear that the company is a major partner in the production of the show. It is worth noting that Sears also sponsor *EMHE* host Ty Pennington. Pennington's 'can-do' attitude represents something that Sears wants—as long as the 'can-do' he recommends is connected to Sears products. As PR, Pennington legitimates Sears as a caring company through his leadership of such obvious good works.

But Sears is only the most high profile of sponsors. Every week we hear of many other local organizations that have devoted their goods and services to the families in need. At this point we are encouraged to think of local businesses not as profit driven but as charitable organizations. The PR benefit of this publicity is enhanced when favourable coverage appears in the local papers about the *EMHE* projects in their town. This would be a good time for local businesses to place adverts reminding consumers of their modest role in the transformation.

Thirdly, and perhaps most obviously, the benefits to ABC will be very considerable. Firstly, there are the benefits in revenue that accrue to shows that are doing well. This factor is particularly important when competition from other stations and other media is more intensive than ever before. During the show the families often thank ABC while the presenters and others also make subtle mention of how the programme has only been possible through the good offices of the station. Again, this will represent an invaluable opportunity for the station to define itself as family-driven in contrast to its more ruthless rivals CBS, Fox and NBC. This benefit sometimes informs the company's well-advertised outreach programmes and also helps to inspire other shows. The praise heaped on the programme by churches and other religious groups helps ABC reposition itself in the family market. The Disney channel owns the station, whose sponsorship of gay-friendly corporate policies and broadcast of gay-themed sitcoms such as *Ellen* has resulted in criticism from Christian groups. *EMHE* redefines ABC as a wholesome family station.

Finally, is it not also the case that the programme is of enormous benefit to the eight designers who appear on the show? The 'good works' they do here will drive business to their companies as well as raise their price in the celebrity market as guest speakers, seminar leaders etc.

But what is crucial to all of this is that the market appears to be driven not by the hunt for profit but by the simple desire to do 'good works'. In this way, capitalism is sold to audiences as a warm and responsive mechanism reacting to community needs rather than a system for maximizing profits. It is not money that pulls people together, but a sort of magic.

But might it be possible to read the lavish life styling of these homes in another way? Might we also look at this extravagance as masking a sort of crisis? Barthes would describe such lavish furnishings as a 'spectacle of excess', behind the exuberance of which we can detect some deeper crisis (Barthes 1988). Can we read the excesses of

EMHE as a frantic attempt to disguise the actual breakdown of families (caused in no small part by the logic of capitalism) with an over-abundance of consumer goods?

Television That Works

'An ethics of care as presented in lifestyle programmes is primarily about care and responsibility . . . good and bad ways to live their lives' (Hill 2005: 184).

EMHE is part of a growing number of television programmes that are not simply recording or reflecting on society but becoming active elements, working practically and ideologically to change the world. As Jack Bratich points out in this volume, [*Makeover Television*], 'Reality TV may be less about representing reality than intervening in it, less mediating and more involving.'

In one sense, television has always done this. Magical solutions to practical problems for everyday people have been the staple of quiz and games shows for decades. But the past twenty years have seen a distinct rise in the number of programmes that focus on intervening in the lives of the public. In a curious historical quirk, commercial television is engaging with the public in a way that PBS can no longer afford to do. But commercial interests inspire all these interventions. *Wife Swap*, *Big Brother* and *Temptation Island* are not there to help the public (despite the rhetoric) but to offer mutual exploitation opportunities. They work, however, and this fact is proved night after night in reality TV shows, makeover shows, talk shows, cosmetic surgery shows, and many other programmes made at the behest of commercial institutions. Like any other product maker, the apparatus of ABC has a vested interest in producing 'good' (i.e. repeatable) results. Furthermore, if it does this in a way which makes it look socially responsible, then it gets a double-whammy. Not only does this help to keep the profile of the medium high but it also foregrounds television as a site for the validation of the person. To be on television is now one of the highest honours that can be accorded someone.

There is another significant point underscoring and helping to guarantee the effects of *EMHE* and others in the lifestyle genre: and it is in the craft of performance. *EMHE* is a very polished production that pulls together emotionally moving performances with the use of music, lighting and photography. Not only does the styling of the show borrow creatively from drama, it also emphasizes a theatrical transformation that will impress children—the next generation whose devotion to the medium all stations need to cherish. It is also interesting to note that many of the designers have experience in drama. Of the eight designers in the 2004/5 season, four have stage or screen credits in theatre or television—i.e. they know how to emote on screen. The rest all have experience on makeover shows of one kind or another that make them perfectly primed for *EMHE*'s excesses. This is not suggesting anything as crude as engineering but, given their histories, it is certainly significant. Those on screen know how to enhance their performances of concern. Television works here because the effects on all the participants are plain to see—crying, hugging, laughing, etc.

It would be comforting to think that our own responses to the transformations, led by the families and designers, heralded some sort of emotional literacy, but even if we try to gain comfort from this we cannot escape the fact that this is all wrought for commercial profit (Littler 2002: 20). It is sad to reflect upon, but the radical changes to one family's life that we see in *EMHE* would simply not happen if it were not for television. Despite the powerful and manipulative devices that bring forth our involvement, at base the programme is a device for selling audiences to advertisers. It is not an engine for social change.

Television works here in four ways—as a mechanism for information and entertainment, as a space for validation and legitimating, as an apparatus that can effect transformations and, last but by no means least, as a way of embedding consumer goods in our lives. More than ever—symbolically, economically and commercially—'television works.'

Conclusion

Commercial culture does not manufacture ideology, it relays and reproduces and processes and packages and focuses ideology that is constantly arising set forth both from social elites and from active social groups and movements throughout the society (Gitlin 1994: 518).

We have seen that *EMHE* produces a vision of America that has powerful emotional resonances. Its view of the world articulates connections with families, the Christian right and the neo-conservative policies of the Bush era. Yet the programme also provides gaps and fissures through which we can see massive cracks appearing in the American Dream. Although *EMHE* might seem like an unadulterated paean of praise to Capitalism, it fails to completely convince because of what it reveals as the inspirations to the makeover: things have got to be so bad because of the retreat of the state, that radical, even magical, consumer surgery is necessary.

Any acquaintance with government sources, such as the Census Bureau, provides plentiful evidence that America is a rich country that is systematically neglecting its poor. For the past five years all indexes indicate that poverty is rising year-on-year. According to the 2004 Census, 35.9 million people live below the poverty line in America. Furthermore, programmes to assist the poor such as 'America's Second Harvest' record that, since 1997, 2 million more people have turned to them, making a total of 23.3 million people requesting emergency food. We might, for example, compare the *EMHE* children whose tear-soaked faces of joy at the makeover contrast with the 33 per cent of children whose parents cannot secure full-time year-round employment (Toppo 2005). It is against these harsh economic facts that we ought to understand the work that ABC does to promote the family.

The fact is that in modern-day America many families and communities have been wrecked by policies that force them to uproot and look for work elsewhere. While the statistics attest to the breakdown of the family unit, ABC is doing the massive ideological labour of shoring it up. In the face of this breakdown *EMHE* deploys its excesses. The revamped houses look like sets because they are there to provide ideal templates for the performance of family roles.

As capitalism continues to deepen divisions between rich and poor, ABC offers the cold comfort of the *EMHE* fairy tale, the belief that if the family holds together despite everything that can be thrown against it, then the reward will eventually come.

Hope may be all they have.

REFERENCES

Barthes, Roland. *Mythologies*. London: Paladin, 1988.
Bonner, Frances. *Ordinary Television: Analyzing Popular TV*. London: Sage, 2003.

Brunsdon, C., C. Johnson, R. Moseley and H. Wheatley. "Factual Entertainment on British Television: The Midlands TV Research Group's '8–9 Project.'" *European Journal of Cultural Studies.* 4:1 (2001): 29–62.

Chambers, D. *Representing the Family.* London: Sage, 2001.

Forman, T. Interview at official ABC website. (2005) www.abc.go.com/primetime/xtremehome/index.html

Giddens, Anthony. *Modernity and Self-identity: Self and Society in the Late Modern Age.* Stanford, California: Stanford University Press, 1991.

____. *Runaway World: How Globalisation is Reshaping our Lives.* London: Profile Books, 1999.

Hill, Annette. *Reality TV: Audiences and Popular Factual Television.* London: Routledge, 2005.

Littler, J. "Making Fame Ordinary: Intimacy, Reflexivity, Keeping it Real." *Mediactive.* 2 (2002): 8–25.

McMurria, John. "Desperate Citizens." *Flow.* 3:3 (2005) http://jot.communication.utexas.edu/flow/?jot=view&id=1047.

Morley, D. and K. Robins. *Spaces of Identity: Global Media, Electronic Landscapes and Cultural Boundaries.* London: Routledge, 1995.

Robaina, Holly Vincente. "A Foundation of Faith." *Christianity Today.* www.christianitytoday.com *Salt Lake City Tribune.* (2006) www.sltrib.com

Young, J. *The Exclusive Society.* London: Sage, 1999.

SUGGESTIONS FOR WRITING

1. Palmer argues that *Extreme Makeover: Home Edition* and other makeover shows use the formula of the fairy tale to provide a magical solution to a real problem. To test this premise, select one fairy tale that you're familiar with—for example, Sleeping Beauty, Jack and the Beanstalk, or Beauty and the Beast—and write a paper in which you compare and contrast elements of that fairy tale to elements in *EMHE*. What themes do they share? In what ways are the characters and plots similar? What key differences do you see? Based on your comparison, does Palmer's argument seem valid to you?

2. Palmer points out a number of ways in which he thinks *EMHE* misrepresents family, community, and the economy. Choose one of these three topics and summarize Palmer's objections. Then, after viewing an episode of *EMHE,* write an argumentative essay in which you support or dispute Palmer's claims on this topic. Be sure to provide evidence from the specific episode that you watch in order to back up your assertions.

3. Palmer describes *EMHE* and makeover reality shows in general as "mutual exploitation opportunities." Choose another makeover reality show—for instance, *The Biggest Loser, Supernanny,* or *The Swan*—and watch a few episodes of it to remind yourself of the general formula. Then develop an analysis, modeled after the one presented by Palmer, in which you look closely at the presuppositions and implications of the show. Could you argue, as Palmer does, that the makeovers produced by the show are ultimately unrealistic and exploitive?

CHAPTER 6

Movies

A RECENT ARTICLE IN *MOVIE MAKER* MAGAZINE NOTED THAT
the digital revolution, along with attendant innovations in entertainment technology, are threatening the viability of the traditional movie theater. The article's author comments, "The big-screen, high definition televisions with surround sound that many people have in their very own living rooms rival many neighborhood movie theaters," and as a result, "today's movie theaters are under attack." A number of theater upgrades have been posited to counter this passive attack by stay-at-homes, including retro movie houses with Egyptian or 1950s themes and upscale dining facilities, plush leather or even vibrating seats, live music before the feature begins, expanded 3-D and IMAX formats, and futuristic "4-D" formats that might include spraying water and varying smells to tickle the senses. Whether any of these imagined innovations (is smell-o-vision really an improvement?) actually comes to pass, there's no doubt that the external trappings of the movie-going experience will change to some degree in the next decade or two. Nevertheless, the reasons people go to movies will remain pretty much the same as they were in the days of the nickel matinee, the double feature, newsreels, Looney Tunes and Merrie Melodies cartoons, and the drive-in theater, where many a teenage couple learned human anatomy in the back seat of a Ford Fairlane. People will go out to movies in great numbers in order to leave the house and escape the routine of their daily lives; to be part of an audience community transported by a narrative experience; to find a romantic setting where conversation is at a

minimum; to indulge, for one night, in a veritable orgy of junk food; and, above all, to be entertained and, perhaps, touched emotionally.

As there are many reasons for going out to see movies, so there are many ways of studying them, as this chapter will illustrate. From a sociopolitical perspective, movies can reflect, define, or redefine norms and values, and politically motivated filmmakers such as Michael Moore use the big screen to illuminate pressing social ills such as injustices in the health care system (see Moore's *Sicko,* for instance). From a psychological perspective, audiences can identify with a film's central characters and project their own feelings into the narrative, providing them with a sense of emotional connection to a protagonist along with the sensation of psychic tension and, ultimately, release: a healthy catharsis in the eyes of some psychologists; potentially dangerous role modeling in the eyes of other commentators and observers. From a literary perspective, movies can be interpreted in terms of genres, such as science fiction films, or *noir* crime dramas, or menaced-female stories—or by examining narrative elements such as plot construction, characterization, imagery, and so forth. From an economic perspective, movies may be seen profitably as a consumable product, defined solely by marketplace forces and subject to the same marketing scrutiny as, say, a case of cornflakes. To the cultural critic, on the other hand, such economic concern might seem to be worthy of criticism, reducing a potentially powerful artistic form to the lowest common denominator: money.

This chapter introduces film study and discussion arising from several of these views. The first readings focus on the social impacts and implications of film. The chapter begins with a summary overview of modern filmmaking by the late Sydney Pollack, a Hollywood director, writer, producer, and actor of great renown and impeccable reputation. Following Pollack's discussion, *Time* magazine movie reviewer Richard Schickel discusses the nature of his profession, drawing a crucial distinction between film reviewing, which he practices regularly, and film criticism, which he sees as a more scholarly (and, at its worst, more pretentious) pursuit. Schickel believes that reviewers are successful insofar as they write in clear and engaging voices, expressing filmic preferences that aid audiences in determining which films to see and which to avoid. By contrast, the next piece in the chapter provides an example of film criticism, which is definitely more scholastic than that which Schickel describes: not pretentious, one hopes, but rather, piquant and thought provoking. In this article, film scholar, director, and producer Jethro Rothe-Kushel examines the film *Fight Club*, bringing to bear a wide range of social-scientific theory and psychological research in order to arrive at certain conclusions regarding the movie's appeal and the messages encoded within it.

Following this general overview of the movie industry, film reviewing, and film criticism, this chapter moves into an examination of specific cinematic subgenres. The next two readings deal with the horror genre, beginning with a discussion by famed novelist of the macabre and film author Stephen King, who believes that scary movies play an important function in society, helping individuals to discharge primal urges, thereby maintaining a certain psychological balance in our society. After King's broad speculation comes another relatively scholastic piece on horror films; in this one, Kyle Bishop, a literature professor and expert in all things horrific, examines a certain kind of film monster—the zombie—as a worthy subject for study, revealing certain concerns, uncertainties, and unease of modern viewers. Then, in striking contrast to the gruesome subjects of the horror section of this chapter, the final section is devoted to a lighter and brighter subgenre, the romantic comedy. The first reading in this section serves two functions: It provides an example of a movie review, as described by Richard Schickel in the earlier reading contrasting film reviewing and film criticism; and it gives readers some crucial background on the history of romantic comedy. The author of this piece, *New Yorker* reviewer David Denby, traces the ancestry of romantic comedies from their beginnings, through the screwball comedies of the thirties and forties and up to the present, focusing on one in particular, *Knocked Up*. This recent film by Judd Apatow, he says, serves as an example of modern romantic comedy that reveals perhaps the zeitgeist of the new millennium, while at the same time bringing us a new and different kind of male romantic lead: the slacker. Finally, the last piece in this chapter also examines romantic comedy, but from a female perspective. Kira Cochrane's "Where Have All the Good Women Gone?" leaves us with a well-argued complaint: that today's heroines unfortunately perpetuate certain negative stereotypes in romantic comedy, which through film history has been a "genuinely positive genre" for its portrayals of women.

SYDNEY POLLACK

The Way We Are

We begin this chapter with a general overview of the state of contemporary movies by Sydney Pollack, one of the world's most prolific filmmakers for several decades. Pollack, who passed away recently, directed more than twenty films—including The Way We Were, Tootsie, Out of Africa, *and* The Firm—*and worked occasionally as an actor as well: For example, he was Dustin Hoffman's agent in* Tootsie. *In the course of fulfilling these roles, Pollack kept a sensitive forefinger on the pulse of mass taste, specifically with regard to cinema, and he both observed and helped shape Hollywood's response to public predilections and preferences. The following article— actually an address Pollack delivered at a conference about the influence of the popular media on American values—makes a central point:, The kinds of movies we see today,including certain levels of violence, sexuality, and so forth, reflect the moral fabric of the United States. As such, Pollack believes, movies do not directly cause changes in moral values. In the course of developing this argument Pollack notes that although screenwriters and directors may very well wish to imply certain moral points in their films, the economics of the film industry demand first and foremost that movies entertain audiences—and that they make money; therefore, Hollywood films must appeal to a ticket- and DVD-purchasing audience whose values may in fact differ markedly from those of the filmmakers.*

Six weeks ago, I thought I was going to be happy to be a part of this conference, which shows you how naive I am. The agenda—for me at least—is a mine field. Normally, I spend my time worrying about specific problems and not reflecting, as many of you on these panels do. So I've really thought about this, and I've talked to anyone who would listen. My colleagues are sick and tired of it, my wife has left for the country and even my agents—and these are people I pay—don't return my phone calls. By turns, I have felt myself stupid, unethical, a philistine, unpatriotic, a panderer, a cultural polluter, and stupid. And I've completely failed to solve your problems, except in one small way. You have delayed by at least six weeks the possibility of my contributing further to the problems you see.

I know your concerns have to do with American values and whether those values are being upheld or assaulted by American entertainment— by what I and others like me do. But which values exactly?

In the thirties, forties, and fifties, six men in the Valley, immigrants really, ran the movie industry. Our society was vastly different. The language of the movies was a language of shared values. If you put forward a virtuousness on the part of your hero, everybody responded to it.

When Sergeant York, played by Gary Cooper, refused to endorse a breakfast cereal, knowing he'd been asked because he'd won the Medal of Honor, he said: "I ain't proud of what I've done. You don't make money off of killing people. That there is wrong." We expected him to behave that way.

But society's values have changed. That kind of scrupulous, ethical concern for the sanctity of human life doesn't exist in the same way, and that fact is reflected in the movies. There's a nostalgia now for some of the old values, but so many people embrace other expressions of values that it's hard to say these other expressions aren't reality.

Their idea of love, for example, is a different idea of love. It's a much less chaste, much less idealized love than was depicted in the earlier films. We are seeing some sort of return to the ideal of marriage. There was a decade or two when marriage really lost its popularity, and while young people are swinging toward it again, I don't believe one could say that values have not changed significantly since the thirties, forties, and fifties.

Morality, the definitions of virtue, justice, and injustice, the sanctity of the individual, have been fairly fluid for American audiences in terms of what they choose to embrace or not embrace.

Take a picture like *Dances With Wolves*. You could not have made it in the thirties or forties. It calls into question every value that existed in traditional Westerns. It may not reflect what everybody thinks now, but it expresses a lot of guilty re-evaluation of what happened in the West, the very things shown in the old Westerns that celebrated the frontier.

If we got the movies to assert or talk about better values, would that fix our society? Well, let me quote Sam Goldwyn. When he was told by his staff how poorly his studio's new—and very expensive—film was doing, Sam thought a minute, shrugged, and said, "Listen, if they don't want to come, you can't stop them."

Now that's as close to a first principle of Hollywood as I can come. It informs everything that we're here to discuss and it controls every solution that we may propose.

Out of Hollywood

Before they can be anything else, American movies are a product. This is not good or bad, this is what we've got. A very few may become art, but all of them, whatever their ambitions, are first financed as commodities. They're the work of craftsmen and artists, but they're soon offered for sale.

Whether we say that we're "creating a film" or merely "making a movie," the enterprise itself is sufficiently expensive and risky that it cannot be, and it will not be, undertaken without the hope of reward. We have no Medicis here. It takes two distinct entities, the financiers and the makers, to produce movies, and there is a tension between them. Their goals are sometimes similar, but they do different things. Financiers are not in the business of philanthropy. They've got to answer to stockholders.

Of course, the controlling influence in filmmaking hasn't changed in 50 years: it still belongs to the consumer. That's the dilemma and, in my view, what we're finally talking about. What do you do about culture in a society that celebrates the common man but doesn't always like his taste?

If you operate in a democracy and you're market-supported and -driven, the spectrum of what you will get is going to be very wide indeed. It will range from trash to gems. There are 53,000 books published in this country every year. How many of them are really good? Tired as I may be of fast-food-recipe, conscienceless, simple-minded books, films, TV, and music, the question remains, who is to be society's moral policeman?

Over the course of their first 30 or 40 years, the movies were a cottage industry, and the morality that was reflected in them was the morality of the early film pioneers. Now, film studios are tiny divisions of multinational corporations, and they feel the pressure for profits that happens in any other repeatable-product business. They look for a formula. Say you get the recipe for a soft drink and perfect it; once customers like it, you just repeat it and it will sell. More fortunes have been lost than made in the movie business pursuing such a formula, but unfortunately today, more junk than anything else is being made pursuing it. And film companies are folding like crazy.

Since we are in the democracy business, we can't tell people what they should or shouldn't hear, or support, or see, so they make their choices. The market tries to cater to those choices, and we have what we have.

Making Films

Are American films bad? A lot of them surely are, and so are a lot of everybody else's, the way a lot of anything produced is bad—breakfast cereals, music, most chairs, architecture, mail-order shirts. There probably hasn't been a really beautiful rake since the Shakers stopped making farm implements. But that is no excuse.

I realize that I am a prime suspect here, but I'm not sure that you really understand how odd and unpredictable a business the making of films actually is. It just doesn't conform to the logic or rules of any other business. It's always been an uneasy merger of two antithetical things: some form of art and sheer commerce.

If the people who make films get the money that is invested in them back to the people who finance them, then they'll get to make more. We know that the business of films is to reach as many people as possible. That works two ways; it's not just a market discipline. You have to remember that most of us who are doing this got into it for the romance, the glory, the applause, the chance to tell stories, even to learn, but rarely for the money. The more people you reach, the greater your sense of success. Given the choice, I'd rather make the whole world cry than 17 intellectuals in a classroom.

But, paradoxically, if you are the actual maker of the film—not the financier—you can't make films and worry about whether they'll reach a large audience or make money, first, because nobody really knows a formula for what will make money. If they did, I promise you we would have heard about it, and studios would not be going broke. Second, and much more practically, if you spent your time while you were making the film consciously thinking about what was commercial, then the real mechanism of choice—the mechanism that is your own unconscious, your own taste and imagination, your fantasy—would be replaced by constant reference to this formula that we know doesn't work.

So the only practical approach a filmmaker can take is to make a film that he or she would want to see. This sounds arrogant, but you try to make a movie for yourself, and you hope that as many people as possible will like it too. If that happens, it's because you've done something in the telling of the story that makes people care. One of the things that makes a film distinct from other American business products is this emotional involvement of the maker. A producer of auto parts can become pretty emotional about a sales slump, but it isn't the same thing. His product hasn't come from his history; it isn't somehow in the image of his life; and it lacks mystery. It is entirely measurable and concrete, which is certainly appropriate in the manufacture of auto parts. I wouldn't want to buy a carburetor from a neurotic, mixed-up auto manufacturer.

Fortunately for those of us in film, no such standards apply. Quite the contrary, in fact. No matter what his conscious intentions are, the best part of what the filmmaker does—the part, when it works, that makes you want to see the film—doesn't come from a rational, consciously controllable process. It comes from somewhere inside the filmmaker's unconscious. It comes from making unlikely connections seem inevitable, from a kind of free association that jumps to odd or surprising places, conclusions that cause delights, something that creates goose pimples or awe.

This conference has suggested a question: While you're actually making the movie, do you think about whether or not it will be doing the world any good? I can't answer it for filmmakers in general. For myself, candidly, no, I don't.

I try to discover and tell the truth and not be dull about it. In that sense, the question has no significance for me. I assume that trying to discover the truth is in itself a good and virtuous aim. By truth I don't mean some grand, pretentious axiom to live by; I just mean the truth of a character from moment to moment. I try to discover and describe things like the motives that are hidden in day-to-day life. And the truth is rarely dull. If I can find it, I will have fulfilled my primary obligation as a filmmaker, which is not to bore the pants off you.

Most of us in this business have enormous sympathy for Scheherazade—we're terrified we're going to be murdered if we're boring. So our first obligation is to not bore people; it isn't to teach.

Most of the time, high-mindedness just leads to pretentious or well-meaning, often very bad, films. Most of the Russian films made under communism were of high quality in terms of craft, but they were soporific because their intent to do good as it was perceived by the state or an all-knowing party committee was too transparent.

I'm sure that you think the person in whose hands the process actually rests, the filmmaker, could exert an enormous amount of control over the film's final worthiness. The question usually goes like this: Should filmmakers pander to the public, or should they try to elevate public taste to something that many at this conference would find more acceptable? Is the job of an American filmmaker to give the public what it wants or what the filmmaker thinks the public should have? This doesn't leave much doubt as to what you think is the right answer.

But framing your question this way not only betrays a misunderstanding of how the filmmaking process works but also is just plain wishful thinking about how to improve society. I share your nostalgia for some of those lost traditional values, but attempting to reinstall them by arbitrarily putting them into movies when they don't exist in everyday life will not get people to go to the movies or put those values back into life. I wish it were that simple.

Engaging an Audience

This conference is concerned with something called popular culture and its effect on society, but I am concerned with one film at a time and its effect. You are debating whether movies corrupt our souls or elevate them, and I'm debating whether a film will touch a soul. As a filmmaker, I never set out to create popular culture, and I don't know a single other filmmaker who does.

Maybe it's tempting to think of Hollywood as some collective behemoth grinding out the same stories and pushing the same values, but it's not that simple. Hollywood, whatever that means, is Oliver Stone castigating war in *Born on the Fourth of July* and John Milius celebrating it in *The Wind and the Lion*. It's Walt Disney and Martin Scorsese. It's Steven Spielberg and Milos Foreman. It's *Amadeus* and *Terminator* and hundreds of choices in between.

I don't want to defend Hollywood, because I don't represent Hollywood—I can't, any more than one particular writer can represent literature or one painter art. For the most part, the impulse toward all art, entertainment, culture, pop culture, comes from the same place within the makers of it. The level of talent and the soul, if you'll forgive the word again, is what finally limits it.

At the risk of telling you more than you need to know about my own work, I make the movies I make because there is in each film some argument that fascinates me, an issue I want to work through. I call this a spine or an armature because it functions for me like an armature in sculpture—something I can cover up and it will support the whole structure. I can test the scenes against it. For me, the film, when properly dramatized, adds up to this idea, this argument.

But there are lots of other ways to go about making a film, and lots of other filmmakers who do it differently. Some filmmakers begin knowing exactly what they want to say and then craft a vehicle that contains that statement. Some are interested in pure escape. Here's the catch. The effectiveness and the success of all our films is determined by exactly the same standards—unfortunately, not by the particular validity of their message but by their ability to engage the concentration and emotions of the audience.

Citizen Kane is an attack on acquisition, but that's not why people go to see it. I don't have any idea if the audience that saw *Tootsie* thought at any conscious level that it could be about a guy who became a better man for having been a woman; or that *The Way We Were*, a film I made 20 years ago, may have been about the tension between passion, often of the moment, and wisdom, often part of a longer view; or that *Out Of Africa* might be about the inability to possess another individual and even the inability of one country to possess another. That's intellectual and stuffy. I just hope the audiences were entertained.

I may choose the movies I make because there's an issue I want to explore, but the how—the framing of that issue, the process of finding the best way to explore it—is a much more mysterious, elusive, and messy process. I can't tell you that I understand it; if I did, I would have a pep talk with myself and go out and make a terrific movie every time.

I would not make a film that ethically, or morally, or politically trashed what I believe is fair. But by the same token, I feel an obligation—and this is more complicated and personal—to do films about arguments. I try hard to give each side a strong argument—not because I'm a fair guy but because I believe it's more interesting. Both things are going on.

I do the same thing on every movie I make. I find an argument, a couple of characters I would like to have dinner with, and try to find the most fascinating way to explore it. I work as hard as I can to tell the story in the way I'd like to have it told to me.

What is really good is also entertaining and interesting because it's closer to a newer way to look at the truth. You can't do that consciously. You can't start out by saying, "I am now going to make a great film."

The virtue in making a film, if there is any, is in making it well. If there's any morality that's going to come out, it will develop as you begin to construct, at every moment you have a choice to make. You can do it the honest way or you can bend it, and the collection of those moments of choice is what makes the work good or not good and is what reveals morality or the lack of it.

I've made many films. I've had some enormous successes and I've had some colossal failures, but I can't tell you what the difference is in terms of what I did.

An American Aesthetic?

In some circles, American films suffer by comparison with European films precisely because a lot of our movies seem to be the product of little deliberation and much instinct. It's been said of European movies that essence precedes existence, which is just a fancy way of saying that

European movies exist in order to say something. Certainly one never doubts with a European film that it's saying something, and often it just comes right out and says it.

American films work by indirection; they work by action and movement, either internal or external, but almost always movement. Our films are more narratively driven than others, which has a lot to do with the American character and the way we look at our lives. We see ourselves and our lives as being part of a story.

Most of our movies have been pro the underdog, concerned with injustice, relatively anti-authority. There's usually a system—or a bureaucracy—to triumph over.

More often than not, American movies have been affirmative and hopeful about destiny. They're usually about individuals who control their own lives and their fate. In Europe, the system was so class-bound and steeped in tradition that there was no democratization of that process.

There's no prior education required to assimilate American movies or American culture. American culture is general, as opposed to the specificity of Japanese or Indian culture. America has the most easily digestible culture.

Our movies seem artless. The best of them keep us interested without seeming to engage our minds. The very thing that makes movies so popular here and abroad is one of the primary things that drives their critics to apoplexy, but seeming artlessness isn't necessarily mindlessness. There's a deliberate kind of artlessness in American movies that has come from a discipline or aesthetic long ago imposed by the marketplace. Our movies began as immigrants' dreams that would appeal to the dreams of other immigrants, and this aesthetic has led American films to transcend languages and cultures and communicate to every country in the world.

The Filmmaker's Responsibility

It has been suggested to some extent in this conference that I ought to study my own and American filmmakers' responsibilities to the public and to the world. I realize I have responsibilities as a filmmaker, but I don't believe that they are as a moralist, a preacher, or a purveyor of values. I know it's tempting to use filmmaking as such, but utility is a poor standard to use in art. It's a standard that has been and is still used by every totalitarian state in the world.

My responsibility is to try to make good films, but "good" is a subjective word. To me at any rate, "good" doesn't necessarily mean "good for us" in the narrow sense that they must elevate our spirits and send us out of the theater singing, or even that they must promote only those values that some think are worth promoting.

Good movies challenge us, they provoke us, they make us angry sometimes. They present points of view we don't agree with. They force us to clarify our positions in opposition to them, and they do this best when they provide us with an experience and not a polemic.

Somebody gave the okay to pay for *One Flew Over the Cuckoo's Nest, Driving Miss Daisy, Stand By Me, Moonstruck, Terms of Endearment,* and *Amadeus,* and despite conventional wisdom that said those films could not be successful, those decisions paid off handsomely because there are no rules. Studio executives and other financiers do exceed themselves. They take chances. They have to, and we have to hope that they'll do it more often.

What we see in movie theaters today is not a simple reflection of today's economics or politics in this country but is a sense of the people who make the movies, and they vary as individuals vary. So what we really want is for this very privileged process to be in the best hands possible, but I know of no force that can regulate this except the moral climate and appetites of our society.

What we're exporting now is largely a youth culture. It's full of adolescent values; it's full of adolescent rage, love, rebelliousness, and a desire to shock. If you're unhappy with their taste—and this is a free market—then an appetite has to be created for something better. How do we do that? Well, we're back to square one: the supplier or the consumer, the chicken or the egg? Let's not even ask the question; the answer is both. Of course filmmakers ought to be encouraged toward excellence, and audiences ought to be encouraged to demand it. How? That's for thinkers and social scientists to figure out. I have no idea. But if I had to play this scene out as an imaginary dialogue, I might say that you must educate the consumer first, and the best places to start are at school and at home. And then you would say that that is my job, that popular entertainment must participate in this education. And I would say, ideally, perhaps, but I do not think that will happen within a system that operates so fundamentally from an economic point of view. On an individual basis, yes, one filmmaker at a time; as an industry, no. An appetite or market will have to exist first.

That's not as bad as it sounds, because in the best of all possible worlds, we do try to satisfy both needs: entertain people and be reasonably intelligent about it. It can be done, and it is done more often than you might think. It's just very difficult.

It's like the two Oxford dons who were sitting at the Boarshead. They were playwrights, grousing because neither one of them could get produced, neither one could get performed. One turned to the other and said, "Oh, the hell with it. Let's just do what Shakespeare did—give them entertainment."

SUGGESTIONS FOR WRITING

1. Pollack describes his interest in making "films about arguments" and giving "each side a strong argument." Write a comparison/contrast essay in which you think back over all the movies you've seen and come up with an example of two different styles of moviemaking: one film in which there is a clear-cut good guy (or girl) or bad guy/girl, and another film that has a more rounded and/or ambiguous attitude toward its characters and, ultimately, its message. As you develop your comparison/contrast supporting points, consider the merits of each approach, both intellectually and rhetorically (i.e., which movie makes its thematic points more effectively?) and emotionally (i.e., which film do you like better, and why?).

2. Pollack, during his tenure as a Hollywood director, producer, and actor, did not make the kinds of graphically violent movies that modern critics claim have a negative influence on U.S. values. Nevertheless, he argues that "scrupulous, ethical concern for the sanctity of human life doesn't exist in the same way [it did in the past], and that fact is reflected in the movies." In developing your own essay regarding the cause-effect relationship between movies and modern values, first come up with examples, both from current events in the news and from recent films that you have seen or heard/read about: concrete evidence of violent tendencies, degenerating morals, or a general lack of concern for the value of life, liberty, peace. Then, in the argumentative body of your essay, consider whether, based on these examples, you agree with Pollack that movies only reflect the values of society and do not contribute to their creation.

3. Rent and watch one or more of Pollack's films (titles other than those mentioned in the headnote include *They Shoot Horses, Don't They?*, *Three Days of the Condor,* and *The Electric Horseman*). In an essay, analyze Pollack's work as a reflection of contemporary U.S. life. What themes or messages do you discover beyond his aim to tell a good story? Does he succeed in his stated goal of presenting an "argument"?

Film Criticism in Review

The following piece by Time *magazine movie reviewer Richard Schickel derives from a panel discussion on the current state of film criticism presented in a recent edition of* Cineaste *magazine. The editors of* Cineaste *introduce the panel discussion by describing current film criticism in a state of semi-crisis: they point to the "dumbing down of both movies and moviegoing audiences" as well as marketing pressures that might compel writers to produce less than critical reviews at times. Richard Schickel, while agreeing with certain points in the* Cineaste *editors' assessment, also takes some of their central claims to task in this article. Besides being the main film reviewer for* Time, *Schickel is an author of numerous movie-related books (including* Film on Paper: The Inner Life of Movies, The Men Who Made the Movies, Intimate Strangers: The Culture of Celebrity, Clint Eastwood: A Biography *and* The Disney Version: The Life, Times, Art and Commerce of Walt Disney), *a well-respected journalist (having written for* Life *magazine and the* Los Angeles Times Book Review), *and documentary filmmaker (including Emmy award-nominated works such as* The Men Who Made the Movies, *an eight-part series for PBS, and NBC's* Life Goes to the Movies). *He begins this article by drawing a crucial distinction between film criticism and movie reviewing, noting that he believes that his work fits more appropriately in the latter category because he consciously avoids creating work that smacks of overly academic pomposity. Schickel develops this point by suggesting that he finds an inflated notion of film criticism both pretentious and self-aggrandizing. Instead, to his way of thinking, if one is a movie reviewer whose work appears with regularity in a magazine with a significant national reputation, such as* Time, *then one establishes credibility "not by isolated acts of brilliant writing or thinking," but creating a reliably intelligent and distinctive voice and a clear sense of taste against which potential moviegoers can measure their own filmic likes and dislikes. Schickel concludes this article with a consideration of the future of film reviewing—and of films in general. The revolution in digital technology, he believes, is radically altering both the production and distribution of film, and at this point nobody can accurately predict whether film will survive in its traditional/current form, or whether it will one day be relegated to the status of quaint artifact, a venue to which kids once went on their first dates.*

A definition: critics write for people who have seen or read or heard the object they are writing about; reviewers write for people who are perhaps thinking about—but probably won't—expose themselves to the movie or book or symphony in question.

I, for example, may have written a little movie criticism over the past few decades, but for thirty-five years I've mostly plied the humbler craft of reviewing. Over that time, it has become something of a habit with me. It's not quite as mundane as brushing my teeth every day. It's more like my Tuesday tennis game—something I look forward to, engage in passionately for a finite amount of time, then pretty much forget until the next week. Another way of putting that is that you have to take the task seriously while you're doing it, but it's self-deluding—no, self-aggrandizing—to take it seriously after it's done.

Still, as jobs go, it's not a bad one. You get to shoot your mouth off without causing anyone any lasting harm—least of all yourself. Sometimes you even get to do a little minor good—bringing attention to a neglected film or advancing a worthwhile young career. I also value the work because it keeps me involved, week-in, week-out, in what passes for public life in our times. Without having to get out and see movies I would probably spend a lot more time in bed with the covers pulled over my head. Also I like seeing my name regularly in print in a major American magazine, a privilege not vouchsafed to many. Finally, movies, being the capacious medium they are, provide a nice variety of socio-political-esthetic topics to write about at least glancingly. But that's about it. To make any larger claims for reviewing is to reveal yourself as a pompous ninny. This is a breed not entirely unknown in the trade, and it is one reason reviewing has always been a part-time job for me. It is an occupation that should not become an exclusive preoccupation.

To that end I have, from the beginning, spent more time writing books and writing, producing, and directing television documentaries than I have reviewing. Sometimes in these other jobs I make broader critical gestures than I do when I'm reviewing. I certainly think that making films for television has made me a better reviewer, more alert to the processes—and the often sly tricks—by which movies are put together. These other activities also serve a need I have to make things that are a little larger and more complicated to construct than a movie review, to express myself in ways that reviewing cannot fully accommodate.

Given my rather modest and solipsistic definition of the reviewer's job, the question of what makes a "critique" (a loathsomely pretentious word, by the way) "memorable" strikes me as moot. I can't think of a review I have ever read that I thought ought to outlive, in toto, the shelf-life of the publication in which it appeared. Some old reviews (Agee's, Otis Ferguson's, Manny Farber's) are helpful to the historian and sometimes these writers spin some very nice apercus. But when I go back to them I generally find myself arguing with them.

Politely, of course. Like me, these people were doing their jobs as best they could. That is to say, contingently, in a hurry. They undervalued films we now regard as masterpieces. And vice versa. They had no idea they were writing for the long run. Most of them, indeed, wanted to be doing something else—writing a novel, say, or painting a picture. They were not lifers. They thought there must be an existence beyond the jute mill. Which may, paradoxically, account for the wacky grace of the best prose. They often just grabbed a thought out of thin air and ran with it until the deadline or exhaustion stopped them.

I don't know that any of them particularly confronted the insoluble contradiction that lies at the center of movie reviewing. Which is that words are an awkward and frustrating tool with which to confront an essentially visual medium, a medium that usually creates its best effects through sub- and non-verbal means. All of us who review movies are trapped in narrative—the who, what, why, and whens of the plot—which is often silly and misleading, obliged for reasons of space (and literary logic) to skip the shot or the cut or the series of same where a movie's most profound, if flickering and accidental, logic lies.

Because of this, I am pretty much convinced that it is impossible to write sensible movie reviews—or for that matter art or music reviews—at a very high level. Logically, you would have to paint or compose a response to a painting or a symphony. Perhaps only literary criticism—words applied to words—is possible.

Doubtless, I'm exaggerating this argument for effect. But the thought is, I think, usefully instructive. At the least, it keeps one's own self-regard decently within bounds. All I try to do when I'm reviewing is turn a nice phrase or two, make the pieces as pleasurable to read as I can and offer an honest first word—not a definitive last word—on whatever movie I'm talking about, something that perhaps helps set the terms of any argument that may develop over a given movie—which these days are not many or particularly illuminating.

Eventually, if you are a reviewer who appears regularly in a significant publication, you establish yourself not by isolated acts of brilliant writing or thinking, but by a sort of reliability. People get used to your voice, grow accustomed to your quirks and you become a source against which they measure their own taste: "If that guy likes it, I probably will, too." Or, conversely, "If he likes it, I know I'm going to hate it."

The best short definition of movies I ever heard was offered by Joseph Campbell, the scholar of myth, in a lecture he gave not long before he died: "The genial imaging of enormous ideas." I know, of course, that many great movies are short on "geniality." But even they offer the shimmer and sheen of their imaging, a quality that disarms and seduces us, makes us willing accomplices in their explorations of "enormous"—though often hard to define—"ideas."

I'm thinking now of pictures like *Bonnie and Clyde, Chinatown,* and *Fargo, Double Indemnity, Hail the Conquering Hero,* and *White Heat*—allusive, elusive movies that offer curiously subversive visions of American blandness and terror, permanently nourish our memories and entirely evade firm theoretical and ideological definition. It's the duty of the reviewer to be alert to these rarities, to single them out of the endless rush of film passing before him. That may not be a big deal. But it is not entirely an inconsequential one, either.

For a movie must either live up to its first notices or live them down as it seeks such place as it may have in history. If we are responsible reviewers we must strive not to make too many egregious errors as we confront the new releases. You're bound to make some, of course, but you don't want to be a laughing stock after you're gone; it will embarrass your children.

Beyond that, what? Well, I think it is important to make it difficult for distributors to pull quotes from your pieces to adorn their ads. Who wants to be an unpaid adjunct to their marketing departments? It is also important to be intellectually flexible. Any reviewer who insists on approaching all movies from a fixed ideological perspective—Marxist, structuralist, feminist, auteurist, what-have-you—is by my definition, totally—and joylessly—wet. And bound to miss the delightful point most of the time.

I think reviewing is an instinctive occupation. We respond to a movie viscerally: we like it, we don't like it. Then comes the hard part: analyzing both the movie itself and our response to it. It makes it more interesting if that response is complicated by having seen lots of movies, by having a sense of the careers, the cultural exigencies, that has brought the anxious—not to say quaking—object to its moment of scrutiny. But the main thing is to stay in touch with your instincts. By them—largely—do we find out why a movie works or doesn't work, why it gives us pain or pleasure.

But movie reviewing, even of this modest sort, is in decline—perhaps even approaching that "crisis" the editors speak of in their invitation to contribute. In the Sixties and Seventies, when the literati—as usual well behind the cultural curve—discovered (or permitted themselves to admit) that movies were an 'art form,' more prestige attached to movie reviewing than it now enjoys. Movies, of course, were more stirring then. People were really trying to get a handle on the then-flourishing modern masters of the form—Bergman, Godard, Kurosawa, et al. Also the American movie was in an inspiringly unsettled state and was trying to expand and redefine its generic boundaries. The services of reviewers as mediators and explicators were more centrally interesting to readers then than they are now, when imported films struggle for attention and the American film has settled into largely vulgar display.

Other unpleasant circumstances have also arisen. I don't know if many reviewers have been "co-opted" by the industry, but television has created hundreds of 'critics,' most of whom are what the publicists scornfully call "quote whores"—people who will give you something to run in the ads even before they have written the rest of their imbecilic notices. It is also true that the new pattern of release—2,500 or so prints of a major film going out on the same Friday, a movie's commercial future foretold in that first weekend—diminishes the role of the reviewer, enhances the role of pure hype in drawing crowds. By the time the public gets around to reading the few serious reviewers who are left (who also may have less space than ever for their views), the die has been long since cast. We are, at that point, playing catch-up ball, at best. The studios, we might note, are aware of this and if, as I do, you write for an influential magazine they make it as difficult as possible for you to see the film in time to publish before that first weekend. I suspect our views are irrelevant to the success or failure of the movies on which they have gambled the most money, are therefore most nervous about, but those birds aren't taking any chances.

I don't know if this constitutes an authentic "crisis." But then, I'm not at all certain that movies—let alone movie reviewing—have much of a future. I suppose theatrical distribution of films—almost certainly in some digital format—will continue, if only because adolescents will always require a dating destination. But whether movies for this audience will require attentive reviewers I doubt. Whether movies in general will survive as a genuine art form—with products appealing to every element of a vast audience, some portion of which welcomed serious reviewing as a goad to their own thinking—is also dubious, I think.

The studios and distributors would, naturally, be glad to be rid of us—to turn movie journalism exclusively into a branch of celebrity journalism. And I think a lot of newspapers and magazines would be glad to be done with our gesturings (or are they merely posturings?) as well. It takes up valuable space and annoys some readers. Something punchy in the jejune dot-com manner—consumer guidance rendered in a superficially subjective, purely populist style—would do almost everyone just as well.

Will you miss us when we're gone, you rascals you? Maybe more than you know—the rattle of more or less informed, more or less cogently expressed opinion, appearing in generally accessible venues, has its mysterious, indefinable uses in societies that maintain the democratic pretense. It keeps people buzzing, hopping, stirred up in ways that an in-depth profile of Britney Spears never will. Maybe it's not much. But I'm bound to think, given the time I've devoted to this curious occupation—next to Andrew Sarris and John Simon I guess I'm the longest continuously serving reviewer around—that it is not nothing, either.

SUGGESTIONS FOR WRITING

1. Through a relatively simple Google search, read several examples of film reviews by Richard Schickel. Then write a short analytical essay discussing how Schickel's views on particular movies seem to reflect his understanding of the role of a film critic, as expressed in the above article. Are there ways in which Schickel's published movie reviews or critiques conflict with the ideas he espouses in this *Cineaste* piece, or do his reviews seem to support the central thematic points he expresses here? Cite concrete examples from the text of his reviews as supporting evidence as you develop the body of your analysis.

2. In his article, Schickel offers provocative thoughts on the nature of his profession, its current position in popular culture, and its challenges. Interestingly, the author chooses to adopt a relatively humble stance, downplaying his importance and impact on the tastes and preferences of his readership, the moviegoing public. Prewrite to discover certain of these qualifying statements made by Schickel, and then list them. Next, write an essay in which you analyze Schickel's persuasive purpose in adopting such a stance. How might this apparently genuine humility, in a somewhat ironic way, actually support his credibility as one of the leading practitioners of the reviewer's craft?

3. Using Schickel's prescriptive statements in this essays as guidelines and models, and drawing upon several of his Web-based reviews as illustrations and examples, write your own review of a recent movie you viewed, or of a DVD you've always wanted to check out. In the process of developing your own review, you might focus on the same considerations that Schickel discusses here: The concerns and predilections of your imagined readership (you might pretend you're writing for a certain magazine or blog site), and your own moral/ intellectual stance vis-à-vis the cinematic "text" to which you are responding.

STEPHEN KING

Why We Crave Horror Movies

In this section of the chapter devoted to popular film, we move from a general discussion of the current state of filmmaking and film reviewing/ criticism, to an in-depth examination of certain types of movies, specifically two subgenres: the horror film and the romantic comedy. In the first of the two articles devoted to horror film, Stephen King—perhaps the best-known and most prolific practitioner of the form—provides a thoughtful and provocative backdrop for a discussion of the topic. Consider some of the images that have sprung fully formed from the brain of King: a hotel with blood pouring down its elevator shafts and long-dead people as its guests; a skinny, oppressed teen with superpowers that bring death and devastation to her high school prom; a gigantic and malicious mongrel slobbering hell's own drool; an intelligent and vengeful vintage Plymouth Fury automobile; a small town in Maine in which a nameless, shapeless mist blankets the environs and its inhabitants while concealing ferocious, unearthly beasts. All of these—and many more—are products of the fertile (and some would say twisted) imagination of this article's author. The horror-themed books of Stephen King are so widely read—and the movies made from them (including such classics as Carrie, The Shining, Cujo, Christine, Children of the Corn, Firestarter, Pet Sematary, *and* The Mist) *so popularly viewed—that his creations may well have become part of the U.S. collective consciousness. Along with the above-mentioned creep-show fare, King has also created a large body of novels and novel-based films with serious and sensitive themes, such as* The Shawshank Redemption, *which deals with friendship and honor, and* Stand By Me, *a touching coming-of-age adventure/drama. Nevertheless, King is perhaps best known for his horror*

books and films, and in the following article he takes a break from story-
telling to reflect on the genre that has brought him worldwide recognition.
King begins by stating a bold and not entirely tongue-in-cheek premise:
"I think that we are all mentally ill." Underneath a frequently thin veneer of
civilization, he suggests, we all have "fears, homicidal rages, and sexual
desires"—baser urges which he calls "anticivilization emotions"—and the
function of horror movies is to appeal to those dark elements within our-
selves and therefore reduce their psychic energy. Thus purged of our negative
impulses, we can go on to engage in positive feelings of love, friendship,
loyalty, and kindness. According to King, then, horror movies serve an im-
portant regulating function, defusing people's destructive urges and helping
to maintain a society's psychic equilibrium.

I think that we're all mentally ill; those of us outside the asylums only hide it a little better—and maybe not all that much better, after all. We've all known people who talk to themselves, people who sometimes squinch their faces into horrible grimaces when they believe no one is watching, people who have some hysterical fear—of snakes, the dark, the tight place, the long drop . . . and, of course, those final worms and grubs that are waiting so patiently underground.

When we pay our four or five bucks and seat ourselves at tenth-row center in a theater showing a horror movie, we are daring the nightmare.

Why? Some of the reasons are simple and obvious. To show that we can, that we are not afraid, that we can ride this roller coaster. Which is not to say that a really good horror movie may not surprise a scream out of us at some point, the way we may scream when the roller coaster twists through a complete 360 or plows through a lake at the bottom of the drop. And horror movies, like roller coasters, have always been the special province of the young; by the time one turns 40 or 50, one's appetite for double twists or 360-degree loops may be considerably depleted.

We also go to re-establish our feelings of essential normality; the horror movie is innately conservative, even reactionary. Freda Jackson as the horrible melting woman in *Die, Monster, Die!* confirms for us that no matter how far we may be removed from the beauty of a Robert Redford or a Diana Ross, we are still light-years from true ugliness.

And we go to have fun.

Ah, but this is where the ground starts to slope away, isn't it? Because this is a very peculiar sort of fun indeed. The fun comes from seeing others menaced—sometimes killed. One critic has suggested that if pro football has become the voyeur's version of combat, then the horror film has become the modern version of the public lynching.

It is true that the mythic, "fairytale" horror film intends to take away the shades of gray. It urges us to put away our more civilized and adult penchant for analysis and to become children again, seeing things in pure blacks and whites. It may be that horror movies provide psychic relief on this level because this invitation to lapse into simplicity, irrationality and even outright madness is extended so rarely. We are told we may allow our emotions a free rein or no rein at all.

If we are all insane, then sanity becomes a matter of degree. If your insanity leads you to carve up women like Jack the Ripper or the Cleveland Torso Murderer, we clap you away in the funny farm (but neither of those two amateur-night surgeons was ever caught, heh-heh-heh); if, on the other hand your insanity leads you only to talk to yourself when you're under stress or to pick your nose on the morning bus, then you are left alone to go about your business . . . though it is doubtful that you will ever be invited to the best parties.

The potential lyncher is in almost all of us (excluding saints, past and present; but then, most saints have been crazy in their own ways), and every now and then, he has to be let loose to scream and roll around in the grass. Our emotions and our fears form their own body, and we recognize that it demands its own exercise to maintain proper muscle tone. Certain of these emotional muscles are accepted—even exalted—in civilized society; they are, of course, the emotions that tend to maintain the status quo of civilization itself. Love, friendship, loyalty, kindness—these are all the emotions that we applaud, emotions that have been immortalized in the couplets of Hallmark cards and in the verses (I don't dare call it poetry) of [*Star Trek* actor] Leonard Nimoy.

When we exhibit these emotions, society showers us with positive reinforcement; we learn this even before we get out of diapers. When, as children, we hug our rotten little puke of a sister and give her a kiss, all the aunts and uncles smile and twit and cry, "Isn't he the sweetest little thing?" Such coveted treats as chocolate-covered graham crackers often follow. But if we deliberately slam the rotten little puke of a sister's fingers in the door, sanctions follow—angry remonstrance from parents, aunts and uncles; instead of a chocolate-covered graham cracker, a spanking.

But anticivilization emotions don't go away, and they demand periodic exercise. We have such "sick" jokes as, "What's the difference between a truckload of bowling balls and a truckload of dead babies?

(You can't unload a truckload of bowling balls with a pitchfork . . . a joke, by the way, that I heard originally from a ten-year-old.) Such a joke may surprise a laugh or a grin out of us even as we recoil, a possibility that confirms the thesis: If we share a brotherhood of man, then we also share an insanity of man. None of which is intended as a defense of either the sick joke or insanity but merely as an explanation of why the best horror films, like the best fairy tales, manage to be reactionary, anarchistic, and revolutionary all at the same time.

The mythic horror movie, like the sick joke, has a dirty job to do. It deliberately appeals to all that is worst in us. It is morbidity unchained, our most base instincts let free, our nastiest fantasies realized—and it all happens, fittingly enough, in the dark. For those reasons, good liberals often shy away from horror films. For myself, I like to see the most aggressive of them—*Dawn of the Dead*, for instance—as lifting a trap door in the civilized forebrain and throwing a basket of raw meat to the hungry alligators swimming around in that subterranean river beneath.

Why bother? Because it keeps them from getting out, man. It keeps them down there and me up here. It was Lennon and McCartney who said that all you need is love, and I would agree with that.

As long as you keep the gators fed.

SUGGESTIONS FOR WRITING

1. In a persuasive essay, consider King's premise that we all have "anticivilization emotions." Begin prewriting by listing some activities other than horror movies and "sick" jokes that Americans might use to purge these emotions and "keep the gators fed." Then, as you develop the argumentative body of your essay, consider the extent to which your listed examples might reflect certain unhealthy aspects of contemporary society. Drawing upon those arguments, develop a conclusion and/or thematic premise that explains how our modern psychology might differ from that of people who lived a century or more ago, and why.

2. If you are a fan of horror movies, make a list of several of your favorites. In an analytical essay, examine some movies from your list in light of King's theories about the horror genre's appeal. Do your examples support or disprove King's point about the daredevil, normative, and psychological function of horror movies? If you enjoy horror movies, are you drawn to them for the reasons Stephen King suggests—that is, do you have deep-seated fears, angry urges, or inappropriate sexual drives that need defusing—or are there other factors involved that King has

not considered? On the other hand, if you are repulsed by horror movies, or merely disinterested in them, write an argumentative essay in which you take King's assertions to task, using yourself and others of your acquaintance as examples of people who are not "all mentally ill" at the core of their psyches.

3. Just as Stephen King looks at "Why We Crave Horror Movies," in an essay of your own, explore why we crave another popular genre of movies: futuristic techno-thrillers, movies based on television sitcoms and cartoons, chase movies, menaced-female dramas, psychotic-killer stories, romantic comedies, supernatural comedies, and so forth. Choose a type of movie familiar to you so that you can offer as many specific examples as possible. In approaching this assignment, try to answer some of the same questions King does: What is the fun of seeing this type of film? What sort of psychic relief does it deliver? Are there specific types of people who are likely to enjoy the genre more than others? Does the genre serve any function for society? In what ways do movies in this genre affect us, changing our thoughts or feelings after we have seen them?

KYLE BISHOP

Dead Man Still Walking: Explaining the Zombie Renaissance

In the next article devoted to the horror sub-genre of popular movies, professional "zombie-ologist" Kyle Bishop discusses the recent resurgence of the walking dead in popular movie fare. Actually, Bishop is a well-respected professor of literature who happens to have an abiding interest in filmic monsters—and particularly in zombies, partly because he thinks they're cool, and partly because he sees in their portrayals a reflection of certain mass preoccupations and attitudes. In fact, Bishop's doctoral dissertation addressed the cultural relevance of zombie cinema, and he has written widely on the subject, with article titles such as "Technophobia and the Cyborg Menace: Buffy Summers as Neo-Human Avatar," "The Sub-Subaltern Monster: Imperialist Hegemony and the Cinematic Voodoo Zombie," "Raising the Dead: Unearthing the Non-Literary Origins of Zombie Cinema," and the article presented here, "Dead Man Still Walking: Explaining the Zombie Renaissance." In Bishop's view, since the terrorist attacks of September 11,

2001, zombie movies have become more popular than ever, with multiple remakes, parodies, and sequels. This renaissance of the subgenre, he feels, reveals a connection between zombie cinema and post-9/11 cultural consciousness in America. If horror films can be seen to function as barometers of society's anxieties, then zombie movies represent the inescapable realities of unnatural death while presenting a grim view of the modern apocalypse through scenes of deserted streets, piles of corpses, and gangs of vigilantes. These images have become increasingly common in recent years, according to the following article, and can shock and terrify a population that has become numb to other horror subgenres. As such, zombie films provide a telling touchstone to the prevailing preoccupations, fears, and general worldview of post-9/11 audiences.

Wars and other tragedies affect cultural consciousness like the blast from a high-yield explosive or a massive earthquake. The ensuing shockwaves reach far and wide, and one of the best ways to recognize and understand these undulations is by analyzing the literature and film of the times. For instance, the use of atomic weapons at the end of World War II ushered in nuclear paranoia narratives like the films *Godzilla* (1954) and *Them!* (1954), and fear of the encroaching Communist threat inspired alien invasion stories like Jack Finney's novel *Invasion of the Body Snatchers* (1955) and the movie *Invaders from Mars* (1953). The terrorist attacks of September 11, 2001, caused perhaps the largest wave of paranoia for Americans since the McCarthy era. Since the beginning of the war on terror, American popular culture has been colored by the fear of possible terrorist attacks and the grim realization that people are not as safe and secure as they might have once thought. This shift in cultural consciousness can be most readily seen in narrative fiction, particularly through zombie cinema.

Since 2002, the number of both studio and independent zombie movies has been on a steady rise. Hollywood has re-embraced the genre with revisionist films like *28 Days Later* (2002), video game-inspired action movies like *Resident Evil* (2002), big-budget remakes like *Dawn of the Dead* (2004), and comedies like *Shaun of the Dead* (2004). The zombie craze continued with 2007 seeing the theatrical releases of *Planet Terror*, *28 Weeks Later*, and *Resident Evil: Extinction*—the Sundance Film Festival even featured two zombie films that season[1]—and with a remake of *Day of the Dead*, Romero's own *Diary of the Dead*, and *Zombie Strippers* all coming out in 2008. David Oakes's Zombie Movie Data- Base Web site confirms this increased interest in zombie cinema with data showing a marked rise in all kinds of zombie narratives over the past ten years; more than 575 titles are listed for 2006 alone.[2] Peter Dendle, Pennsylvania State University professor and zombie scholar, observes that the number of amateur zombie movies has "mushroomed considerably" since 2000 (interview). Although the quality of many of these backyard, straight-to-video, and Internet-based productions remains a matter of debate, the striking surge in the genre's popularity and frequency cannot be denied.

The fundamental genre conventions of zombie cinema fit post-9/11 cultural consciousness well. During the latter half of the twentieth century, zombie movies graphically represented the inescapable realities of unnatural death (via infection, infestation, or violence) and presented a grim view of a modern apocalypse in which society's infrastructure breaks down. The twenty-first-century zombie movies are no different from their historical antecedents, but society has changed markedly since the World Trade Center towers were destroyed. Scenes depicting deserted metropolitan streets, abandoned human corpses, and gangs of lawless vigilantes have become more common than ever, appearing on the nightly news as often as on the movie screen. Because the aftereffects of war, terrorism, and natural disasters so closely resemble the scenarios of zombie cinema, such images of death and destruction have all the more power to shock and terrify a population that has become otherwise jaded by more traditional horror films.

The Developmental Cycle of Zombie Cinema: Establishing the Renaissance

The modern zombie movie has been around for almost forty years and, like other genres, it has gone through periods of feast and famine.[3] According to film scholar Darryl Jones, the genre was born in 1968 with the release of George A. Romero's *Night of the Living Dead* (1961), in which a motley group of people, led by an African American antihero named Ben (Duane Jones), must spend the night in a besieged country house, waiting for the authorities to arrive. When the county militia finally does show up, its first response is to shoot and kill Ben, the only survivor of the supernatural abattoir. The violence and graphic images in this low-budget horror film were unprecedented at the time, and the movie functions largely as a metaphor for the atrocities of Vietnam and racism.[4] Called "hippie Gothic" by film theorist Joseph Maddrey (51), *Night* protests the war by graphically confronting audiences with the horrors of death and dismemberment and by openly criticizing those who use violence to solve their problems. The politically sub-versive film gained a cult following and eventually made more than $30 million worldwide ("Business Data for Night").

Recognizing the potential market and profitability of such movies, other filmmakers began to experiment with the story line in little-known films like *Garden of the Dead* (1972), *Return of the Evil Dead* (1973), and *Horror of the Zombies* (1974). In 1978, Romero released *Dawn of the Dead,* a lampoon of capitalism and rampant consumerism. It depicts a group of reporters and SWAT team members forced to barricade themselves for weeks into an abandoned shopping mall surrounded by zombies.[5] *Dawn* was almost immediately followed by Lucio Fulci's un-official sequel *Zombie* (1979), about a global zombie infestation origi-nating on a voodoo-laden Caribbean island. The two films firmly defined the genre, with *Dawn* becoming a huge hit that grossed $55 million worldwide ("Business Data for Dawn"), and they spawned a veritable surge of classical zombie movies, such as *Night of the Zombies* (1981), *Revenge of the Zombies* (1981), *Mansion of the Living Dead* (1982), and *Kung Fu Zombie* (1982).

In spite of the proliferation of these movies and their success on B-reel screens, they seem to have played themselves out by the mid-1980s, especially after the arrival of Michael Jackson's "Thriller" video in 1983. This campy short film tried to be uncanny and frighten-ing, but once the walking dead started to dance and jive with the King of Pop, zombies became nothing more than a joke. Although Romero tried to revitalize zombie films in 1985 with Day of the Dead (the metaphor this time addressing Cold War fears and paranoia[6]), the genre was in its death throes. Day failed at the box office, and Maddrey supposes that "audiences in the carefree, consumer-friendly 1980s apparently did not feel the need for such a serious examination of personal and societal values" (129). Instead consumers wanted comedic movies like Dan O'Bannon's *Return of the Living Dead* (1985), which fla-grantly abuses Romero's genre rules by featuring zombies that can talk and by introducing the now-quintessential eating of brains. With such unmemorable titles as *Zombie Brigade* (1986) and *I Was a Teenage Zom-bie* (1987), things only got worse as budgets plummeted and camp took the place of scripts.

Historically, zombie cinema had always represented a stylized reaction to cultural consciousness and particularly to social and political injustices, and America in the 1990s saw perhaps too much complacency and stability for zombie movies to fit the national mood. The Cold War was over, the Berlin Wall had fallen, Ronald Reagan's Star Wars defense system was proven unnecessary, and George H. W. Bush's Gulf War had apparently been resolved. In fact, aside from some skirmishes in third-world countries, Americans were largely insulated from global warfare. Furthermore, in the Clinton decade, sexual impropriety took headlines away from global genocide and tyrannical massacres. With nothing specific to react to or protest against, cinematic versions of the zombie genre declined steadily throughout the 1990s, although Peter Jackson's *Dead Alive* (1992) provided some fresh ideas by inventing a subgenre commonly called "splatstick" comedy, where blood and guts are the primary comedic medium. Nevertheless, virtually no new or original stories were produced in the decade at all, although Dendle observes that no-budget, direct-to-video productions continued to flourish (*Zombie Movie 10*).

Even though zombies were no longer a source of terror on the silver screen, young people found renewed interest in zombies through violent video games. In 1993, id Software released a revolutionary first-person shooter game called *Doom*, which features zombified marines; however, these basically two-dimensional foes use guns instead of teeth, and the game's plot is more science fiction than horror. While zombies continued to play bit parts in other games, the first true zombie video game—Capcom's *Biohazard* (since renamed *Resident Evil*)—did not appear until 1996. This game takes its central story line directly from Romero's movies, for players must explore an isolated country manor while shooting reanimated corpses and trying to avoid being eaten-although unlike Romero's movies, there is a lot more "fight" than "flight." Nevertheless, the terror and action of zombie movies translated quite logically from the big screen to the video screen, and a nontraditional form of narrative incubated the genre until it was ready to reemerge in theaters in 2002 with the release of two mainstream movies.

By returning to the classical form of Romero's films, British director Danny Boyle began the zombie renaissance with the first truly frightening zombie movie in years. Riding high from his *Trainspotting* (1996) success, Boyle created a new version of the zombie story with *28 Days Later*, in which a man wakes from a coma to find London abandoned and full of decaying corpses. Boyle also introduced faster, more feral zombie creatures, keeping the monsters alive rather than dead, and audiences responded as if the genre were new, instead of just newly re-visioned. The film's $8 million budget eventually resulted in a $45 million gross in the United States alone ("Business Data for 28 Days

Later"). At about the same time, mainstream Hollywood was also trying to kick-start the genre by capitalizing on the popularity of the video game circuit with Paul W. S. Anderson's *Resident Evil*, an action-packed science fiction movie that is more video game than narrative. More big-budget films have followed, like the two *Resident Evil* sequels (2004 and 2007), remakes of *Dawn of the Dead* (2004) and *Night of the Living Dead* (2006), the revisionist comedy *Shaun of the Dead*, and Romero's return with 2005's *Land of the Dead*.

The popularity of the zombie continues to inundate other media as well. The shooting-gallery nature of zombie survival—the more you kill, the more keep popping up—still spawns new video games every year in which players become part of the action. The *Biohazard* series now has over a dozen titles, and Romero's latest zombie movie inspired the game *Land of the Dead: Road to Fiddler's Green* (2005). The zombie also found a logical home in graphic novels, most notably Steve Nile's *George A. Romero's Dawn of the Dead* (2004) and Robert Kirkman's ongoing epic series *The Walking Dead* (2004–present). Zombies can be found outside of narrative fiction in the humorous yet strangely eerie *Zombie Survival Guide* (2003). This parody of popular survival guides is a straightfaced, seemingly nonfiction effort by Max Brooks to prepare the public for an actual zombie infestation. Even a number of hard-rock bands have jumped aboard the zombie bandwagon (e.g., Zombie Ritual and their 2004 album *Night of the Zombie Party*).

However, in spite of this evidence of a resurgence in the popularity of the zombie monster, no one identified the movement as having an official "renaissance" until Romero—the "Shakespeare of zombie cinema" (Dendle, Zombie Movie 121)—re-entered the game with *Land of the Dead*. In early 2006, Steven Wells wrote an article reacting to Showtime's made-for-TV movie *Homecoming* (2004), in which "Americans killed in Iraq rise from their flag-draped coffins and slaughter their way to the polling booths so they can vote out a warmongering president" (2). Wells shows an even broader impact, claiming that "there were zombies everywhere in 2005," from an all-zombie production of *Romeo and Juliet* to online zombie blogs and a zombie appearance on *American Idol* (2). Zombies even showed up in the sixth Harry Potter novel, if only for a brief cameo.

The appearance of zombies in print media other than graphic novels is perhaps the most notable evidence of a renaissance for the more mainstream public. According to Don D'Auria, an editor of horror novels, "Until three years ago [zombies] were really unseen.

Then they just seemed to pop up everywhere" (qtd. in St. John 2). In a 2006 New York Times article, Warren St. John provides a number of examples of the zombie literary invasion: Brian Keene's *The Rising*, a novel about "smart zombies"; David Willington's *Monster Island*, about a zombie infestation in Manhattan; and *World War Z: An Oral History of the Zombie War*, another faux nonfiction creation from Brooks (1, 13). In addition, Stephen King, the unequivocal master of modern literary horror, finally released a full-blown version of the zombie story with his 2006 novel *Cell*, a chilling morality tale in which unnamed terrorists turn the majority of Americans into enraged cannibals by brainwashing them with a mind-scrambling cell phone signal.

While the zombie renaissance is basically a given to zombie scholars and fans, such coverage from mainstream publications like the *New York Times* gives Wells's observations greater credibility as well as publicity. The return of the zombie, most obviously and prolifically in film, has fully come to the public's attention. St. John summarizes the renaissance: "In films, books and video games, the undead are once again on the march, elbowing past werewolves, vampires, swamp things and mummies to become the postmillennial ghoul of the moment" (1). All this evidence points to one unavoidable fact: "zombies are back" (2).

The Primary Characteristics of Zombie Cinema: Understanding the Genre

The twenty-first-century zombie movie renaissance seems fueled in part by the popularity of zombies in other media and by the relatively low cost and ease of making splatterfest films.[7] But to explain this phenomenon and to understand the post-9/11 social relevance of zombie cinema, the essential characteristics of such films must be examined and the genre must be differentiated from other horror genres. Unlike many other tales of terror and the supernatural, the classical zombie story has very specific criteria that govern its plot and development. These genre protocols include not only the zombies and the imminent threat of violent deaths, but also a postapocalyptic backdrop, the collapse of societal infrastructures, the indulgence of survivalist fantasies, and the fear of other surviving humans. All of these plot elements and motifs are present in pre-9/11 zombie films, but they have become more relevant to a modern, contemporary audience.

The most conspicuous feature of zombie movies is naturally the zombies themselves-both what the creatures are and, perhaps more important, what they are not. Audiences fear these ghouls for a number of obvious reasons: they are corpses raised from the dead, and, more significantly, they are the corpses of the known dead, what horror scholar R. H. W. Dillard calls "dead kindred" (15). In addition, the zombies pursue living humans with relentless dedication and kill people mercilessly by eating them alive. Because zombies are technically "dead" rather than the more romantic "undead" (i.e., ghosts and vampires), they possess merely a rotting brain and have no real emotional capacity. Toward that end, zombies cannot be reasoned with, appealed to, or dissuaded by logical discourse. Other supernatural foes devised by authors and Hollywood filmmakers are generally conscious, thinking individuals. In fact, in recent years, traditional supernatural monsters have become sympathetic protagonists and misunderstood heroes, like the ghosts in *The Sixth Sense* (1999) or *The Others* (2001), the vampires in Anne Rice's tales, or characters like Angel and Spike in the television series *Buffy the Vampire Slayer* (1997–2003) and *Angel* (1999–2004). Such qualities for zombies are logical impossibilities.[8]

What's more, in contrast to other supernatural or undead creatures, the zombie directly manifests the visual horrors of death; unlike most ghosts and vampires, zombies are in an active state of decay. Simon Pegg, cowriter and star of *Shaun of the Dead*, observes, "Metaphorically, this classic creature embodies a number of our greatest fears. Most obviously, it is our own death, personified. The physical manifestation of that thing we fear the most" (133). It is no coincidence that the modern cinematic zombie cycle began "on the eve of the Tet offensive in Vietnam" (Maddrey 122), when the general populace was being exposed to graphic images of death and violence on the nightly news. In addition, the inescapable realities of mortality ensure that every viewer could both fear and relate to the zombie; although no one expects to rise from the grave as a cannibalistic ghoul, everyone will die and rot.

As audiences have become more familiar with special effects and more accustomed to images of violence, cinematic depictions of zombies have had to become progressively more naturalistic and horrific. In *Night of the Living Dead*, the ghouls are basically just pasty-faced actors; even the scenes of cannibalistic acts are less shocking because the film is in black and white rather than color. By *Dawn of the Dead*, the zombies have become more realistic (yet strangely blue), and scenes of death and dismemberment are shockingly graphic and naturalistic-thanks for the most part to special effects wizard Tom Savini, who claimed that "much of my work for *Dawn of the Dead* was like a series of portraits of what I had seen for real in Vietnam" (qtd. in Skal 311).

Now, after thirty more years of global warfare and bloodshed, the twenty-first-century audience, largely desensitized by graphically violent video games and other media, almost demands an upping of the ante. In response, *28 Days Later* and *Land of the Dead* feature zombies with missing limbs, decaying flesh, and only partially constituted heads and faces; even the rather light *Shaun of the Dead* (a self-proclaimed "romantic comedy" zombie film) has some particularly gruesome ghouls and nauseating dismemberment scenes.[9]

Yet even though zombies are certainly uncanny and frightening by themselves, such monsters would not prove much of a threat if they appeared in the modern-day world; certainly the police or military would be around to exterminate the monsters. But zombie movies are almost always set during (or shortly after) the apocalypse, when those reassuring infrastructures cease to exist. In *Night of the Living Dead*, the zombie infestation seems limited to just one backwoods county, but by *Dawn of the Dead*, the impression is rather clear that the whole world is overrun. Romero's feckless survivors hide out in a shopping mall for an indeterminate amount of time, waiting in vain for the resumption of media broadcasts and for help that never arrives. *28 Days Later* is based on the premise that all of the United Kingdom has been decimated in just under a month, and *Land of the Dead* is even bleaker: the film is set in a zombie-dominated world, where Pittsburgh has been set up as a city-state unto itself. In all of these scenarios, the virus, plague, or infestation has been so rapid and complete that cities are quickly overrun, buildings abandoned, posts deserted, and airwaves silenced.

One of the greatest—or at least the most detailed—literary imaginings of the apocalypse is King's *The Stand*, a novel with no zombies but with most of the other zombie motifs: the story explores both the utter fall and eventual resurrection of the United States following a devastating and global viral pandemic.[10] King's novel blames the end of modern society on the governmental military complex, tailoring the deterioration of America's infrastructure on William Butler Yeats's description of the end of the world: "Things fall apart; the center cannot hold." This poignant image is central to zombie cinema; Brooks describes the new world order in his *Zombie Survival Guide:* When the living dead triumph, the world degenerates into utter chaos. All social order evaporates. Those in power, along with their families and associates, hole up in bunkers and secure areas around the country. Secure in these shelters, originally built for the Cold War, they survive. Perhaps they continue the façade of a government command structure. Perhaps the technology is available to communicate with other agencies or even other protected world leaders. For all practical purposes, however, they are nothing more than a government-in-exile. (155)

Once people start to die at an uncontrollable rate, panic rages through all levels of the government and the military, and most would be more interested in saving themselves and their families than in doing their jobs.[11]

The breakdown of social order leads to one of the more curious allures of zombie films: their ability to play out survivalist fantasies. Extreme followers of the survivalist credo hoard foodstuffs and ammunition in their isolated mountain cabins and basement bunkers, just hoping for the day when society will collapse and their paranoia will finally be justified. Like Brooks's book parodies, numerous survival manuals and Web sites—such as Jack A. Spigarelli's *Crisis Preparedness Handbook* (2002) and Joshua Piven and David Borgenicht's *The Complete Worst-Case Scenario Survival Handbook* (2007)—encourage and direct such behavior and apocalypse narratives allow their followers some cathartic enjoyment. Furthermore, as realized in movies like *The Omega Man* (1971) and *Night of the Comet* (1984), the end of the world means the end of capitalism, and everything becomes free for the taking. As a matter of survival, looting becomes basically legal-or at the very least, there is no law enforcement presence to prevent wanton theft. Anyone can own a Porsche, wear the latest Paris fashions, or go on an unbridled shopping spree.

The best depictions of this contradictory "fun amidst the terror" are found in the 1978 *Dawn of the Dead* and the 2004 remake by Zach Snyder. Both films take place primarily in shopping malls, locations that afford both security and sustenance. In the '78 version, Romero presents a light-hearted montage showing the four remaining survivors at play among the many shops available to them-playing basketball, eating exotic foods, and putting on makeup and expensive clothes-living out what horror scholar David J. Skal calls "consumerism gone mad" (309). Snyder's film includes a similar montage: finding themselves relatively safe from everything but boredom, the survivors play games, try on expensive clothes and shoes, watch movies on big-screen televisions, and even play golf. In a sick way, the mall is the ultimate vacation resort—they just can't ever go outside. An abbreviated version of the same idea is present in *28 Days Later*: in a parody of game shows like *Supermarket Sweep* (1990–2003), the four survivors race around a grocery store, filling their carts with all the goods they can carry.

Such sequences show that once the survivors take both the law and their protection into their own hands, establishing some kind of defensible stronghold-like a shopping mall, a bunker, an ordinary house, or the neighborhood pubthe zombies cease to be much of a direct threat and become more animals to be avoided. Instead, the real fear comes from the other human survivors—those who can still think, plot, and act.[12] As Dillard points out, "The living people are dangerous to each other, both because they are potentially living dead should they die and because they are human with all of the ordinary human failings" (22). In most zombie films, the human protagonists eventually argue, fight, and even turn against one another; cabin fever can make those inside the strongholds more dangerous than the zombies on the outside (Jones 161-62). In addition, the journey from survivor to vigilante is a short one; with the total collapse of all governmental law-enforcement systems, survival of the fittest becomes a very literal and grim reality. Those with power, weapons, and numbers simply take whatever they want. However, in the new zombie economy, everything is free-except other humans, of course. For lawless renegades, the only real sports left are slavery, torture, rape, and murder, which appease base appetites that cannot be satisfied by simply going to the mall.

In the 1978 *Dawn of the Dead*, the peaceful haven of the shopping mall is destroyed by the violent arrival of a vigilante biker gang. These bandits, whose primary aim is to loot the stores, disrupt the careful balance established between the zombies and the remaining survivors; as a result of the bikers' intrusion, more people die and all security is lost. In *28 Days Later*, this vigilante scenario is all the more frightening because the primary threat comes from the military, soldiers who are supposed to protect citizens, not abuse them. In a misguided attempt to repopulate the world, the soldiers threaten the female protagonists with rape, and Jim (Cillian Murphy) narrowly escapes execution for defending them. The threat of the zombies remains a fundamentally frightening part of the movie, but because the threat of bodily harm and rape are realworld potentialities, they are all the more terrifying.

The Twenty-First-Century Zombie: Explaining the Renaissance

The post-9/11 zombie film remains remarkably true to the genre's original protocols. Although the zombies are not always literally dead, as in Romero's films, the apparent apocalypse and collapse of societal infrastructures remain central features. In addition, the genre tends to emphasize certain causes for the end of the world, including infectious disease, biological warfare, euthanasia, terrorism, and even immigration. Although the genre is forty years old, these concepts resonate more strongly with present-day Americans than ever before, where events like the September 11 attacks, the war in Iraq, and Hurricane Katrina provide comparable forms of shocking ideas and imagery.

The end of the world is the ultimate societal fear, made all the more real by current weapons of mass destruction, and Snyder's remake of *Dawn of the Dead* depicts this apocalypse through a sequence of shocking events most zombie films simply imply. Ana (Sarah Polley), the film's protagonist, wakes one morning to find the world she knew collapsing around her. Her husband is trying to kill her, neighbors are shooting one another with handguns, and explosions of unknown origins rock the skyline. The chaos, disorientation, fear, and destruction she witnesses are disturbingly similar to the initial news footage broadcast on September 11, 2001. Although Jim in *28 Days Later* wakes after the apocalypse is essentially over, the film nevertheless presents a disturbing sequence of images of a metropolitan London void of all human presence. At the time of its conception, this moment in the screenplay was probably intended to simply shock audiences with its foreignness, but after September 11, the eerie street scenes take on new meaning.

Screenwriter Alex Garland joins Boyle on the *28 Days Later* DVD commentary track, where they discuss the historical antecedents of the film's imagery. The screenplay was written and filming had begun before September 11, so Garland and Boyle drew from other international crises and disasters for apocalyptic images. The scene in which Jim picks up stray pound notes off London's empty streets was directly inspired by footage from the "killing fields" of Cambodia during and after the reign of Pol Pot. The street billboard displaying hundred of photos and notes seeking missing loved ones, which has a direct tie to 9/11 now, was based on an actual street scene following a devastating earthquake in China. The abandoned city, overturned buses, and churches full of corpses were all inspired by existing moments of actual civil unrest and social collapse.

Such images of metropolitan desolation and desertion certainly resonate strongly with contemporary audiences. According to Brooks, "People have apocalypse on the brain right now. . . . It's from terrorism, the war, [and] natural disasters like Katrina" (qtd. in St. John 13). During and after the collapse of the World Trade Center towers in New York, numerous journalists and bystanders commented on how the events seemed unreal—like something out of a movie. After Hurricane Katrina, Kevin Lair, who lived with his family near where the 17th Street levee burst, told reporters, "The whole thing looks like something out of a science fiction movie" (quoted in "It's Like"). Additionally, John Graydon, who rode out the aftermath of the storm in the Superdome, called his father in England and said, "It's like a scene from *Mad Max* in there" (qtd. in Beard). Nightly news clips showed the deserted streets of New Orleans as if the city were a film set, with abandoned cars, drifting newspapers, and stray dogs. Of course, these events may not directly affect the production of zombie movies, but they certainly affect an audience's reception of those films.

Romero's movies, like all great fantasy texts, have always offered critical metaphors, and the great twenty-first-century zombie films continue in this vein. According to Andy Coghlan of New Scientist magazine, "Infectious diseases are indeed the new paranoia that's striking Western society" (qtd. in James); fittingly, *28 Days Later* is about the risks of an unstoppable pandemic, in which a blood-borne virus can wipe out the entire United Kingdom in just under a month's time. Furthermore, the film makes the somewhat abstract potential of zombification a much more visceral reality. Boyle's characters refer to the ravenous monsters as "infecteds," not "zombies"-the creatures are not technically dead at all, but hapless people infected with a psychological virus that makes them ultra-aggressive and violent. This kind of zombie is more frightening than the traditional fantasy monster, and instead of just being a horror movie, *28 Days Later* crosses into science fiction: it could happen. In fact, Boyle calls the movie "a warning for us as well as an entertainment" (qtd. in James).

The psychic plague of *28 Days Later* is most likely a reference to AIDS, but it could just as easily reference cholera, smallpox, or anthrax. In fact, in an unsettling irony, England experienced a devastating outbreak of foot-and-mouth disease during the filming of *28 Days Later*, resulting in the slaughter of millions of livestock (Boyle and Garland). Similarly, the *Dawn of the Dead* remake was shot during another scare: the SARS epidemic of 2003. Snyder noticed the alarming parallels between his film and the nightly news; both were fraught with panic and misinformation (Snyder and Newman). The threat of infestation and other biohazards is hardly less significant today; it is hard to view either film-or any zombie movie, for that matter-without thinking of the recent threat of bird flu or avian influenza.

The idea of a terminal, debilitating illness or infection leads to the less obvious issue present in all zombie movies: euthanasia. These films raise the question: is it better to murder loved ones or to allow them to become something monstrous? In Romero's *Land of the Dead*, those bitten by zombies are given the choice of being killed immediately, since the virus takes time to work. Like a terminally ill patient, those infected by the zombie virus have time to say goodbye, put some affairs in order, and determine the method of their own death, enacting a kind of morbidly poignant "living will."[13] In *28 Days Later*, however, anyone infected must be killed at once—and often brutally; the virus takes only twenty seconds to fully manifest its insanity. When Selena's (Naomie Harris) traveling companion is bitten in a zombie attack, Selena immediately hacks off his injured limb and butchers him with a machete. In an even more pathetic scene, young Hannah (Megan Burns) barely gets the chance to say goodbye to her father (Brendan Gleeson) before the British military shoot him. The slaughter of the infected living becomes an essential form of mercy killing; the choices of the zombie landscape are hard ones, but survival is the top priority.

All of these narrative motifs and cinematic images can resonate strongly with modern viewers of the zombie movie, but the primary metaphor in the post-9/11 zombie world is terrorism. According to St. John, it does not take much of a stretch to see the parallel between zombies and anonymous terrorists who seek to convert others within society to their deadly cause. The fear that anyone could be a suicide bomber or a hijacker parallels a common trope of zombie films, in which healthy people are zombified by contact with other zombies and become killers. (13)

The transmission of the zombie infection is a symbolic form of radical brainwashing. Because anyone can become infected (i.e., conditioned) at any time, everyone is a potential threat; thus, paranoia becomes almost as important as survival. Those bitten often hide the injury, so even friends and family members cannot be fully trusted. In fact, the first zombie encountered in the *Dawn of the Dead* remake is a young girl, her apparent innocence making her violence all the more shocking.

Romero's *Land of the Dead* depicts a post-zombied society, a world where the enemy is literally at the gates. Pittsburgh has been converted into an island stronghold, with rivers and electric fencing keeping the zombies out (and the residents safely in). Class division is more critical than in other zombie films: the upper class lives an opulent lifestyle in Fiddler's Green, a luxurious highrise, while ignoring the problem; the commoners, however, must face reality while living in the slums below. In a documentary by Marian Mansi about the making of *Land of the Dead*, Romero comments, "Thematically, what the film is about is a bunch of people trying to live as though nothing has changed. Or at least that's what the administration believes. The protagonists understand that the world has completely changed." To keep the wealthy properly fed and supplied, the poor and industrious must risk their lives by venturing outside the city's fortifications, scavenging the countryside in an ever-increasing radius. They see the grim horrors of death and infection every day, much like soldiers on the front line of combat.

The wealthy elite in Fiddler's Green are literally isolated from the grim facts that make their lifestyle possible. To ensure the status quo, Dennis Hopper's Kaufman, the self-appointed leader of Pittsburgh, constructs the world's most extreme border security-blown up and barricaded bridges make the rivers impassable, and electric fences and armed guards protect the area from any intrusion; in an extreme example of xenophobia, soldiers shoot any intruders on sight. These forms of immigration control have become even more jarringly familiar with recent debates about erecting a fence between the United States and Mexico and the redeployment of National Guard troops to guard the United States' southern border during George W. Bush's presidency. *Land of the Dead* is certainly not subtle in its critique of modern American foreign policy; in fact, in Mansi's documentary, Romero goes so far as to identify the fascist Kaufman as Donald Rumsfeld and the Fiddler's Green tenants board as the Bush administration. Like Americans in the years immediately after the 9/11 terrorist attacks, the residents in *Land of the Dead* are asked both to continue their lives as if no real threat existed and to behave in certain ways because of the threat that does exist.

Conclusion

Although the conventions of the zombie genre remain largely unchanged, the movies' relevance has become all the more clear—a post-9/11 audience cannot help but perceive the characteristics of zombie cinema through the filter of terrorist threats and apocalyptic reality. Dendle emphasizes that the problem is "sorting out whether the movies really are doing something different in the post-9/11 world, or whether it's simply that audiences can't help but see them differently now" (interview). Most twenty-first-century zombies are faster, more deadly, and symbolically more transparent, but otherwise the films follow the mold Romero invented back in the 1960s. Yet they are different now, at least from the perspective of reception. As Dendle says, "we all view the world differently now, and . . . filmmakers and audiences alike are inherently attuned to read themes and motifs through different lenses than they would have before" (interview).

Initially, zombie movies shocked audiences with their unfamiliar images; today, they are all the more shocking because of their familiarity. In fact, fans of horror films, particularly apocalypse narratives like zombie movies, may find that the movies even help prepare them for reality. Dendle was approached in the summer of 2005 by a law student who had survived the horrors of September 11 firsthand. Although the experience was understandably shocking, this student claimed he had been emotionally prepared for the tragedy not by his family, community, or government, but by his long appreciation for zombie movies (interview). Perhaps zombie cinema is not merely a reflection of modern society, but a type of preemptive panacea, and that potential gives the genre both cultural significance and value.

NOTES

1. These were Andrew Currie's Fido and The Signal, written and directed by David Bruckner, Dan Bush, and Jacob Gentry.

2. Oakes uses a rather liberal definition of zombie movies on his Zombie Movie Data-Base, including in his numbers any film that features undead or otherwise reanimated creatures, such as golems, mummies, and creatures possessed by demons.

3. This article is limited in scope to those films that openly embrace the genre conventions established by George A. Romero in his series of zombie movies (i.e., stories that feature hordes of cannibalistic human corpses that relentlessly pursue an isolated group of survivors and can only be killed by a gunshot or blow to the head). While zombies can be found in a variety of films prior to 1968, the majority of zombie movies made since September 11 follow Romero's genre lead, not those films addressing voodoo enslavement or alien invasion.

4. For more detailed readings of Night of the Living Dead, see Maddrey 49–51, 122–24; Jones 160–63; Dillard; and Paul Wells 80–82. For an

in-depth psychoanalytical reading of the film and an investigation of terror in general, see Connolly 422–24.

5. For a discussion of the symbolism and capitalist critique in *Dawn of the Dead,* see Jones 163; Maddrey 126; Paul Wells 82; and Wood 125–27.

6. For more detailed discussions of *Day of the Dead,* see Jones 163–64 and Maddrey 128.

7. For instance, the direct-to-video films *Rise of the Undead* (2005) and *Swamp Zombies* (2005) boast total production budgets of $10,000 and $12,000 respectively, according to the "Business Data" sites for both films.

8. Two notable exceptions must be addressed. First, in the noncanonical "zombedies" of the 1980s and '90s, like *Return of the Living Dead* and *I Was a Teenage Zombie,* the protagonists do become zombies, and the plots of such films often revolve around turning the hapless heroes back to normal. As mentioned earlier, however, such films are not true zombie horror films. Second, Romero has been experimenting with the idea of zombie evolution, a concept progressing toward sentient ghouls. For example, in *Day of the Dead,* a quasidomesticated zombie named "Bub" is taught to use a razor, pick up the phone, and hold and fire a gun; in *Land of the Dead,* a former gas station attendant named "Big Daddy" leads a zombie attack, figuring out how to circumvent the humans' fortifications. Such an evolution seems illogical, but it is hard to argue against Romero, should he choose to adjust his own genre. Nevertheless, in spite of these experiments, the true zombie protagonist has not yet arrived.

9. *Shaun of the Dead* is certainly the most thought provoking and relevant of the zombedies, although the comedy is one of satire rather than just jokes and slapstick. Director Edgar Wright is suggesting that a zombie infestation would probably go unnoticed by the average middle-class worker; as depicted by Simon Pegg's Shaun, modern society has already turned everyone into zombies.

10. In fact, Romero considered filming a screen adaptation of *The Stand,* which Maddrey points out "would have been the one [of King's works] most suited to Romero's vision of America" (127).

11. This unpleasant possibility, that those hired to protect would actually cut and run, was manifested in New Orleans during Hurricane Katrina, when a number of local law-enforcement officers fled with their families ("N.O. Police").

12. This is one of the more interesting aspects of the zombie scenario, but it is one that cannot be fully explored in a two-hour film. Romero's *Land of the Dead* shows the breakdown of social structure most fully, but it would be best demonstrated by serialized narratives, such as Kirkman's graphic novels or a television series.

13. Once again, a zombie movie eerily echoes contemporary headlines: *Land of the Dead* was released the same summer that Americans debated the tragic case of Terri Schiavo, who ultimately was taken off life support at the behest of her husband.

WORKS CITED

Beard, Matthew. "Hurricane Katrina: 'Like a Scene from Mad Max': British Couple." Independent. BNet Business Network, 3 Sept. 2005. Web. 27 Feb. 2009.

Boyle, Danny, dir. 28 Days Later. 2002. Twentieth Century Fox, 2003. DVD.

Boyle, Danny, and Alex Garland. Commentary. 28 Days Later. Dir. Danny Boyle.

Brooks, Max. The Zombie Survival Guide. New York: Three Rivers, 2003. Print.

"Business Data for Dawn of the Dead (1978)." Internet Movie Database. IMDb .com, n.d. Web. 3 May 2006.

"Business Data for Night of the Living Dead." Internet Movie Database. IMDb .com, n.d. Web. 3 May 2006.

"Business Data for Rise of the Undead." Internet Movie Database. IMDb.com, n.d. Web. 3 May 2006.

"Business Data for Swamp Zombies." Internet Movie Database. IMDb.com, n.d. Web. 3 May 2006.

"Business Data for 28 Days Later." Internet Movie Database. IMDb.com, n.d. Web. 3 May 2006.

Connolly, Angela. "Psychoanalytic Theory in Times of Terror." Journal of Analytical Psychology 48 (2003): 407–31. Print.

Dendle, Peter. E-mail interview. 20 Oct. 2005.

——. The Zombie Movie Encyclopedia. Jefferson: McFarland, 2001. Print.

Dillard, R. H. W. "Night of the Living Dead: It's Not Like Just a Wind That's Passing Through." American Horrors. Ed. Gregory A. Waller. Chicago: U of Illinois P, 1987. 14–29. Print.

"It's Like a Sci-Fi Movie." News24.com. 24.com, 10 Jan. 2005. Web. 27 Feb. 2009.

James, Toby, dir. Pure Rage: The Making of 28 Days Later. 28 Days Later. Dir. Danny Boyle. 2002. Twentieth Century Fox, 2003. DVD.

Jones, Darryl. Horror: A Thematic History in Fiction and Film. London: Arnold, 2002. Print.

King, Stephen. The Stand. New York: Doubleday, 1990. Print.

Maddrey, Joseph. Nightmares in Red, White and Blue: The Evolution of the American Horror Film. Jefferson: McFarland, 2004. Print.

Mansi, Marian, dir. Undead Again: The Making of Land of the Dead. Land of the Dead. Dir. George A. Romero. 2005. Unrated Director's Cut. Universal, 2005. DVD.

"N.O. Police Fire 51 for Desertion." Fox News. Fox News Corporation, 30 Oct. 2005. Web. 27 Feb. 2009.

Oakes, David, ed. Zombie Movie Data-Base. Trash Video, n.d. Web. 27 Oct. 2007.

Pegg, Simon. Afterword. Miles Behind Us. By Robert Kirkman. Berkeley: Image Comics, 2004. Print. Vol. 2 of The Walking Dead.

Romero, George A., dir. Dawn of the Dead. 1978. Ultimate Ed. Anchor Bay, 2004. DVD.

——, dir. Day of the Dead. 1985. Anchor Bay, 2003. DVD.

——, dir. Land of the Dead. 2005. Unrated Director's Cut. Universal, 2005. DVD.

——, dir. Night of the Living Dead. 1968. Millennium Ed. Elite, 1994. DVD.

Skal, David J. The Monster Show. New York: Faber, 1993. Print.

Snyder, Zach, dir. Dawn of the Dead. 2004. Unrated Director's Cut. Universal, 2004. DVD.

Snyder, Zach, and Eric Newman. Commentary. Dawn of the Dead. Dir. Zach Snyder.

St. John, Warren. "Market for Zombies? It's Undead (Aaahhh!)." New York Times 26 Mar. 2006, sec. 9: 1+. Print.

Wells, Paul. The Horror Genre: From Beelzebub to Blair Witch. New York: Wildflower, 2002. Print.

Wells, Steven. "G2: Shortcuts: Zombies Come Back from the Dead." Guardian [London] 2 Jan. 2006, Features: 2. Print.

Wood, Robin. "Neglected Nightmares" Horror Film Reader. Ed. Alain Silver and James Ursini. New York: Limelight Editions, 2000. 111–27. Print.

Wright, Edgar, dir. Shaun of the Dead. 2004. Universal, 2004. DVD.

Yeats, William Butler. "The Second Coming." 1919. The Norton Introduction to Literature. Ed. Jerome Beaty et al. 8th ed. New York: Norton: 2002. 1325. Print.

Kyle Bishop is a lecturer of English composition, American literature and culture, film studies, and fantasy literature at Southern Utah University. He has presented and published a variety of papers on popular culture and cinematic adaptations, including *A Hazard of New Fortunes, Metropolis, Night of the Living Dead, Fight Club, White Zombie, Buffy the Vampire Slayer,* and *Dawn of the Dead.* He is currently completing his dissertation on the theoretical and cultural significance of zombie cinema at the University of Arizona.

SUGGESTIONS FOR WRITING

1. In a previous article on zombies, Kyle Bishop, a genre theorist by profession, stated, "The horror of the zombie movie comes from

recognizing the human in the monster; the terror of the zombie movie comes from knowing there is nothing to do about it but destroy what is left; the fun comes from watching the genre continue to develop." Nowadays, Bishop says in the current article, the genre has developed into a type of text that is "perhaps . . . not merely a reflection of modern society, but a type of preemptive panacea, and that potential gives the genre both cultural significance and value." In an analytical essay, first consider the validity of this latter proposition: In your experience or the experience of friends and loved ones, do these types of movies help process feelings of angst and disquietude in post-9/11, terrorist-threatened America? Whether or not you agree with this proposition, list several other reasons why zombie movies may be popular among persons of your generation in particular. Finally, consider Bishop's "panacea theory" as manifest in other films: What other specific films, or discrete genres of film, might confront frightening subjects to reach audiences at the basest primal and archetypal levels, in order to prepare them emotionally tragedy, as Bishop suggests in the conclusion of this article?

2. In the body of this essay, Bishop comments, "Such images of metropolitan desolation and desertion certainly resonate strongly with contemporary audiences. According to Brooks, 'People have apocalypse on the brain right now. . . . It's from terrorism, the war, [and] natural disasters like Katrina.'" In response to this quotation, develop a personal essay in which you discuss your own relationship to the horror film and attempt to propose a psychological theory to explain your particular experience with zombie movies, chainsaw-massacre flicks, monster epics such as *Cloverfield* or *War of the Worlds*, and so forth. If such films do indeed resonate strongly with you in some specific ways, what might this reveal about your character, your upbringing, your hard-wired excitement threshold, your fears and anxieties, and your concerns about death? Further, what might it reveal about the ways in which media coverage of the 9/11 events, the subsequent war on terror, the war in Iraq, natural disasters such as Hurricane Katrina, and so forth, have affected you emotionally, perhaps undermining your sense of security and safety? If, conversely, you find yourself not in the least interested in coming face-to-face with blood, gore and unspeakably brutal practices on the big screen—that is, you are not in the least drawn to zombie or other horror movies and studiously avoid them what might this reveal about you and your complex personality dynamics regarding disturbing world events and/or natural tragedies?

3. The author of this article has asserted elsewhere that immersing oneself in the guts and gore of the cinematic zombie world is a worthwhile scholarly pursuit. For instance, he has commented, "Although zombies are technically dead, their cinematic genre is a living, breathing entity that

continues to grow and evolve." To support this point, Bishop gives evidence of the continuing appeal of zombie-related popular culture artifacts, such as the proliferation of zombie-themed video games. Furthermore, the current popularity of the zombie flick has given rise to a series of successors; such films as *Resident Evil* (2002), and the genre's popularity and longevity have resulted in remakes of both *Dawn of the Dead* and *Day of the Dead (2006)*. In addition to these remakes, with their production values greatly improved over those of the original films, the genre is also constantly reinventing itself with revisionist films such as *Shaun of the Dead* and Romero's own *Land of the Dead* (2005). Bishop concludes these paraphrased points by alluding directly to the rhetorical power of the examples cited: "Such overwhelming contemporary evidence firmly establishes zombie cinema as a valued member of genre studies." In a persuasive essay, critique the validity of these assertions on two fronts: First, in your experience, and perhaps with the aid of a bit of Internet-based research, is the zombie phenomenon as widespread and pervasive as Bishop claims it is in this essay and elsewhere? Second, if the depiction of zombies has indeed proliferated in recent years, does the widespread appearance of a certain pop-culture phenomenon necessarily make it a subject worthy of lengthy academic discussion, as Bishop undertakes here and elsewhere?

On Romantic Comedy in the New Millennium

DAVID DENBY

A Fine Romance

No doubt you've seen several, if not all, of Judd Apatow's films, even if you're not immediately familiar with his name. Apatow is responsible for a remarkable string of recent hits, including: Funny People (2009) (producer); Year One (2009) (producer); Pineapple Express (2008) (producer); Forgetting Sarah Marshall (2008) (producer); Walk Hard: The Dewey Cox Story (2007) (writer/producer); Superbad (2007) (producer); Knocked Up (2007) (director/writer/producer); Talladega Nights: The Ballad of Ricky Bobby (2006) (producer); The 40-Year-Old Virgin (2005) (director/writer/ producer); Anchorman: The Legend of Ron Burgundy (2004) (producer). While this entire body of work is worthy of examination and discussion, given that all Apatow's films reflect attitudes and concerns of contemporary

U.S. culture, the article at hand examines one particular film—Knocked Up—and the messages encoded within it. According to some reviewers, Knocked Up's subtext appears to suggest that, when confronted with choices charged with dire repercussions (e.g., a girlfriend's pregnancy), modern boys and girls should submit to some traditional construction of the nuclear family: Get married, raise 1.5 babies, buy a mini-van, enroll the kids in soccer camp—even when there seem to be few valid relationship dynamics to support such conformity. Other critics contend that, with its seeming advocacy of mild illegal hallucinogen usage, its rapid-fire vulgarity, and its non-missionary coital gymnastics, the film seems almost subversive. In the area of gender studies, still others find a sexist/misogynist position implied in the fact that Alison, the female protagonist, does not have an abortion after discovering that she is pregnant by a mate she chose through the cloudy lenses of beer goggles. Some have gone so far as to accuse the film of being unsubtle propaganda for the pro-life religious right, while others have pointed to the fact that Alison continues to be an admirably career-focused modern gal throughout the narrative, thereby supporting a more positively feminist agenda, if an overly simplistic one. Clearly, then, Judd Apatow's films, and Knocked Up in particular, inspire heated debate on a broad range of cultural and moral concerns. Whatever one's position vis-à-vis such thematic issues, the first article by the highly respected New Yorker film critic David Denby provides an admirable historical backdrop for such dialog, giving the reader succinct and ample historical perspective on the subject by tracing the lineage of romantic comedies from Buster Keaton, through the screwball comedies of the thirties and forties, the highly charged interactions of Hepburn and Tracy, the hilarious, angst-ridden and ultimately doomed loves of Woody Allen, and finishing with a critique of the current crop of romantic comedies, with those of Apatow topping the list.

His beard is haphazard and unintentional, and he dresses in sweats, or in shorts and a T-shirt, or with his shirt hanging out like the tongue of a Labrador retriever. He's about thirty, though he may be younger, and he spends a lot of time with friends who are like him, only more so—sweet-natured young men of foul mouth, odd hair, and wanker-mag reading habits. When he's with them, punched beer cans and bongs of various sizes lie around like spent shells; alone, and walrus-heavy on his couch, he watches football, basketball, or baseball on television, or spends time memorializing his youth—archiving old movies, games, and jokes. Like his ancestors in the sixties, he's anti-corporate, but he's not bohemian (his culture is pop). He's more like a sullen back-of-the-classroom guy, who breaks into brilliant tirades only when he feels like it. He may run a used-record store, or conduct sight-seeing tours with a non-stop line of patter, or feed animals who then high-five him with their flippers, or teach in a school where he can be friends with all the kids, or design an Internet site that no one needs. Whatever he does, he hardly breaks a sweat, and sometimes he does nothing at all.

He may not have a girlfriend, but he certainly likes girls—he's even, in some cases, a hetero blade, scoring with tourists or love-hungry single mothers. But if he does have a girlfriend she works hard. Usually, she's the same age as he is but seems older, as if the disparity between boys and girls in ninth grade had been recapitulated fifteen years later. She dresses in Donna Karan or Ralph Lauren or the like; she's a corporate executive, or a lawyer, or works in TV, public relations, or an art gallery. She's good-tempered, honest, great-looking, and serious. She wants to "get to the next stage of life"—settle down, marry, maybe have children. Apart from getting on with it, however, she doesn't have an idea in her head, and she's not the one who makes the jokes.

When she breaks up with him, he talks his situation over with his hopeless pals, who give him bits of misogynist advice. Suddenly, it's the end of youth for him. It's a crisis for her, too, and they can get back together only if both undertake some drastic alteration: he must act responsibly (get a job, take care of a kid), and she has to do something crazy (run across a baseball field during a game, tell a joke). He has to shape up, and she has to loosen up.

There they are, the young man and young woman of the dominant romantic-comedy trend of the past several years—the slovenly hipster and the female straight arrow. The movies form a genre of sorts: the slacker-striver romance. Stephen Frears's "High Fidelity" (2000), which transferred Nick Hornby's novel from London to Chicago, may not have been the first, but it set the tone and established the self-dramatizing underachiever as hero. Hornby's guy-centered material also inspired "About a Boy" and "Fever Pitch." Others in this group include "Old School," "Big Daddy," "50 First Dates," "Shallow Hal," "School of Rock," "Failure to Launch," "You, Me and Dupree," "Wedding Crashers," "The Break-Up," and—this summer's hit—"Knocked Up." In these movies, the men are played by Vince Vaughn, Owen Wilson, Adam Sandler, John Cusack, Jimmy Fallon, Matthew McConaughey, Jack Black, Hugh Grant, and Seth Rogen; the women by Drew Barrymore, Jennifer

Aniston, Kate Hudson, Sarah Jessica Parker, and Katherine Heigl. For almost a decade, Hollywood has pulled jokes and romance out of the struggle between male infantilism and female ambition.

Knocked Up, written and directed by Judd Apatow, is the culminating version of this story, and it feels like one of the key movies of the era— a raw, discordant equivalent of *The Graduate* forty years ago. I've seen it with audiences in their twenties and thirties, and the excitement in the theatres is palpable—the audience is with the movie all the way, and, afterward, many of the young men (though not always the young women) say that it's not only funny but true. They feel that way, I think, because the picture is unruly and surprising; it's filled with the messes and rages of life in 2007. The woman, Alison (Katherine Heigl), an ambitious TV interviewer in Los Angeles, gets pregnant after a sozzled one-night stand with Ben (Seth Rogen), a nowhere guy she meets at a disco. Cells divide, sickness arrives in the morning—the movie's time scheme is plotted against a series of pulsing sonograms. Yet these two, to put it mildly, find themselves in an awkward situation. They don't much like each other; they don't seem to match up. Heigl has golden skin, blond hair, a great laugh. She's so attractive a person that, at the beginning of the movie, you wince every time Rogen touches her. Chubby, with curling hair and an orotund voice, he has the round face and sottish grin of a Jewish Bacchus, though grape appeals to him less than weed. At first, he makes one crass remark after another; he seems like a professional comic who will do anything to get a laugh. It's not at all clear that these two should stay together.

Authentic as Ben and Alison seem to younger audiences, they are, like all the slacker-striver couples, strangers to anyone with a long memory of romantic comedy. Buster Keaton certainly played idle young swells in some of his silent movies, but, first humiliated and then challenged, he would exert himself to heroic effort to win the girl. In the end, he proved himself a lover. In the nineteen-thirties, the young, lean James Stewart projected a vulnerability that was immensely appealing. So did Jack Lemmon, in his frenetic way, in the fifties. In succeeding decades, Elliott Gould, George Segal, Alan Alda, and other actors played soulful types. Yet all these men wanted something. It's hard to think of earlier heroes who were absolutely free of the desire to make an impression on the world and still got the girl. And the women in the old romantic comedies were daffy or tough or high-spirited or even spiritual in some way, but they were never blank. What's going on in this new genre? "Knocked Up," a raucously funny and explicit movie, has some dark corners, some fear and anxiety festering under the jokes. Apatow takes the slacker-striver romance to a place no one thought it would go. He also makes it clear, if we hadn't noticed before, how drastically the entire genre breaks with the classic patterns of romantic comedy. Those ancient tropes fulfill certain expectations and, at their best, provide incomparable pleasure. But "Knocked Up" is heading off into a brave and uncertain new direction.

Shakespeare knew the Roman farces—by Plautus, Terence, and others—in which a scrambling boy chases after a girl and lands her. He varied the pattern. His comedies were rarely a simple chase, and the best American romantic comedies have drawn on the forms that he devised—not so much, perhaps, in the coarse-grained *Taming of the Shrew* but in *Much Ado About Nothing,* with its pair of battling lovers, Beatrice and Benedick. Why is the contact between those two so barbed? Because they are meant for each other, and are too proud and frightened to admit it. We can see the attraction, even if they can't. They have a closely meshed rhythm of speech, a quickness to rise and retort, that no one else shares. Benedick, announcing the end of the warfare, puts the issue squarely: "Shall quips and sentences and these paper bullets of the brain awe a man from the career of his humor? No, the world must be peopled."

Romantic comedy is entertainment in the service of the biological imperative. The world must be peopled. Even if the lovers are past child-rearing age or, as in recent years, don't want children, the biological imperative survives, as any evolutionary psychologist will tell you, in the flourishes of courtship behavior. Romantic comedy civilizes desire, transforms lust into play and ritual—the celebration of union in marriage. The lovers are fated by temperament and physical attraction to join together, or stay together, and the audience longs for that ending with an urgency that is as much moral as sentimental. For its amusement, however, the audience doesn't want the resolution to come too quickly. The lovers misunderstand each other; they get pixie dust thrown in their faces.

Befuddled, the woman thinks she's in love with a gas-station attendant, who turns out to be a millionaire; an unsuitable suitor becomes a proper suitor; and so on. It's always the right guy in the end. Romantic drama may revel in suffering, even in anguish and death, but romantic comedy merely nods at the destructive energies of passion. The confused lovers torment each other and, for a while, us. Then they stop.

The best directors of romantic comedy in the nineteen-thirties and forties—Frank Capra, Gregory La Cava, Leo McCarey, Howard Hawks, Mitchell Leisen, and Preston Sturges—knew that the story would be not only funnier but much more romantic if the fight was waged between equals. The man and woman may not enjoy parity of social standing or money, but they are equals in spirit, will, and body. As everyone agrees, this kind of romantic comedy—and particularly the variant called "screwball comedy"—lifted off in February, 1934, with Frank Capra's charming *It Happened One Night,* in which a hard-drinking reporter out of a job (Clark Gable) and an heiress who has jumped off her father's yacht (Claudette Colbert) meet on the road somewhere between Florida and New York. Tough and self-sufficient, Gable contemptuously looks after the spoiled rich girl. He's rude and overbearing, and she's miffed, but it helps their acquaintance a little that they are both supremely attractive—Gable quick-moving but large and, in his famous undressing scene, meaty, and Colbert tiny, with a slightly pointed chin, round eyes, and round breasts beneath the fitted striped jacket she buys on the road. When she develops pride, they become equals.

The cinema added something invaluable to the romantic comedy: the camera's ability to place lovers in an enchanted, expanding envelope of setting and atmosphere. It moves with them at will, enlarging their command of streets, fields, sitting rooms, and night clubs; rapid cutting then doubles the speed of their quarrels. Out on the road, in the middle of the Depression, Gable and Colbert join the poor, the hungry, the shysters and the hustlers; they spend a night among haystacks, get fleeced, practice their hitchhiking skills. In screwball comedy, the characters have to dive below their social roles for their true selves to come out: they get drunk and wind up in the slammer; they turn a couch in an upstairs room of a mansion into a trampoline; they run around the woods at a country estate—the American plutocrats' version of Shakespeare's magical forest in "A Midsummer Night's Dream," where young people, first confused and then enlightened, discover whom they should marry.

In many of the screwball classics, including *Twentieth Century, My Man Godfrey, The Awful Truth, Easy Living, Midnight, Bringing Up Baby, Holiday, The Philadelphia Story, The Lady Eve*—all made between 1934 and 1941—the characters dress for dinner and make cocktails, and the atmosphere is gilded and swank. The enormous New York apartments, the country houses with porticoes, the white-on-white night clubs in which swells listen to a warbling singer—all this establishes a facade of propriety and manners, a place to misbehave. Except for the Fred Astaire/Ginger Rogers dance musicals, in which evening clothes are integral to the lyric transformation of life into movement, the lovers are no more than playing at formality. The characters need to be wealthy in order to exercise their will openly and make their choices. The screwball comedies are less about possessions than about a certain style of freedom in love, a way of vaulting above the dullness and petty-mindedness of the sticks. (In these films, no matter how rich you may be, you are out of the question if you hail from Oklahoma or Albany—you are Ralph Bellamy.)

Many of the heroines were heiresses, who, in those days, were prized for their burbling eccentricities—Carole Lombard's howl, Irene Dunne's giggle, Katharine Hepburn's Bryn Mawr drawl. Pampered and dizzy, they favored spontaneity over security when it came to choosing a man. As for the men, they came in two varieties. Some owned a factory or a mine, or were in finance—worldly fellows who knew how to float a debenture or hand a woman into a taxi—and others were gently cartooned intellectuals. Innocents preoccupied with some intricate corner of knowledge, they gathered old bones (Cary Grant, in *Bringing Up Baby*), or new words (Gary Cooper, in *Ball of Fire*), or went up the Amazon and discovered unspeakable snakes (Henry Fonda, in *The Lady Eve*). The man is the love object here—passive, dreamy, and gentle, a kind of Sleeping Beauty in spectacles—and the woman is the relentless pursuer. Katharine Hepburn in "Baby" nearly drives Cary Grant crazy with her intrusions into his work, her way of scattering his life about like pieces of lawn furniture. She's attracted by his good looks but also by what's unaroused in him, and she will do anything to awaken him. Equality in these comedies takes a new shape. The man is serious about his work (and no one says he shouldn't be), but he's confused about women, and his confusion has neutered him. He thinks he wants a conventional marriage with a compliant wife, but what he really wants is to be overwhelmed by the female life force. In the screwball comedies, the woman doesn't ask her man to "grow up." She wants to pull him into some sort of ridiculous adventure. She has to grow up, and he has to get loose—the opposite of the current pattern.

The screwball comedies were not devoted to sex, exactly—you could hardly describe any of the characters as sensualists. The Production Code limited openness on such matters, and the filmmakers turned sex into a courtship game that was so deliriously convoluted precisely because couples could go to bed only when they were married. The screwball movies, at their peak, defined certain ideal qualities of insouciance, a fineness of romantic temper in which men and women could be aggressive but not coarse, angry but not rancorous, silly but not shamed, melancholy but not ravaged. It was the temper of American happiness.

Sometimes the couple in a romantic comedy are already married, or were formerly married, but husband and wife go at each other anyway, because they enjoy wrangling too much to stop. Who else is there to talk to? In a case like that, romance becomes less a dazed encounter in an enchanted garden than a duel with slingshots at close quarters—exciting but a little risky. The most volatile of these comedies was "His Girl Friday," Howard Hawks's 1940 version of the 1928 Ben Hecht/Charles MacArthur play *The Front Page*. In the original, the star reporter Hildy Johnson is a man. In Hawks's version, Hildy (Rosalind Russell) is a woman who has fled the barbarous city desk and plans to marry a timid businessman (Ralph Bellamy). Her former husband and editor, Walter Burns (Cary Grant), will do anything to get her back to the paper. He doesn't seem drawn to her as a woman, yet he woos her in his way, with scams, lies, and one important truth—that she's the only person good enough to cover the hottest story in town. She knows him as an indifferent and absent husband, yet she's attracted, once again, by the outrageous way this man fans his tail. And, despite her misgivings, she's caught, too, by the great time they have together toiling in the yellow journalism that they both love. Vince Vaughn, in some of his recent roles, has displayed a dazzling motormouth velocity, but he has never worked with an actress who can keep up with him. Rosalind Russell keeps up with Grant. These two seize each other's words and throw them back so quickly that their dialogue seems almost syncopated. Balance between the sexes here becomes a kind of matched virtuosity more intense than sex.

If Russell and Grant were exactly alike in that movie, Spencer Tracy, slow-talking, even adamantine, with a thick trunk and massive head, and Katharine Hepburn, slender, angular, and unnervingly speedy and direct, were opposites that attracted with mysterious force. In the classic comedy *Adam's Rib* (1949), their sixth movie together (they made nine), they were an established onscreen married couple, rising, drinking coffee, and getting dressed for work. How can you have romantic comedy in a setting of such domestic complacency? *Adam's Rib*, which was written by a married couple, Garson Kanin and Ruth Gordon, and directed by George Cukor, takes these two through combat so fierce that it can be ended only with a new and very desperate courtship. They become opposing lawyers in a murder case. He prosecutes, and she defends, a woman (Judy Holliday) who put a couple of slugs in her husband when she caught him in the arms of his mistress. As the two lawyers compete in court, and Tracy gets upstaged by Hepburn, the traditional sparring at the center of romantic comedy intensifies, turns a little ugly, and then comes to an abrupt stop with a loud slap—Tracy smacking Hepburn's bottom in a proprietary way during a late-night rubdown session. The slap is nothing, yet it's everything. The husband has violated the prime rule of mating behavior by asserting a right over his wife physically. The drive for equality in movies can lead to bruising competitions, and in *Adam's Rib* the partnership of equals nearly dissolves. Suddenly anguished, the movie uneasily rights itself as husband and wife make concessions and find their way back to marriage again.

Achieving balance between a man and a woman in a romantic comedy can be elusive. Marilyn Monroe, her tactile flesh spilling everywhere, was either lusted after or mocked, but only Tony Curtis, appearing in Cary Grant drag in *Some Like It Hot*, knew how to talk to her. Rock Hudson and Doris Day, in their films together, were exclusively preoccupied with, respectively, assaulting and defending Day's virtue, and they both seemed a little demented. Tom Hanks matched up nicely with Daryl Hannah and with Meg Ryan, as did Richard Gere and Hugh Grant with Julia Roberts, whose eyes and smile and restless, long-waisted body charged up several romantic comedies in the nineties.

In recent decades, however, Woody Allen and Diane Keaton have come closest to restoring the miraculous ease of the older movies. Short and narrow-jawed, with black-framed specs that give him the aspect of a quizzical Eastern European police inspector, Allen turned his worried but demanding gaze on Keaton, the tall, willowy Californian. In their early films together, they seemed the most eccentric and singular of all movie couples; it was the presence of New York City, in *Annie Hall* (1977) and *Manhattan* (1979), that sealed their immortality as a team. Allen, narrating, presented himself as the embodied spirit of the place, sharp and appreciative, but also didactic, overexplicit, cranky, and frightened of lobsters off the leash and everything else in the natural world. The idea was that beauty and brains would match up, although, early in *Annie Hall*, the balance isn't quite there—Keaton has to rise to his level. Initially, she's nervously apologetic—all floppy hats, tail-out shirts, and tremulous opinions—and she agrees to be tutored by Allen, who gives her books to read and takes her repeatedly to *The Sorrow and the Pity*. For a while, they click as teacher and student. If Tracy and Hepburn were like a rock and a current mysteriously joined together, these two neurotics were like agitated hummingbirds meeting in midair.

Working with the cinematographer Gordon Willis, Woody Allen created the atmosphere of a marriage plot in conversations set in his beloved leafy East Side streets—his version of Shakespeare's magical forest. But *Annie Hall,* surprisingly, shifts away from marriage. The quintessential New Yorker turns out to be a driven pain in the neck, so insistent and adolescent in his demands that no woman can put up with him for long. And the specific New York elements that Allen added to romantic comedy—the cult of psychoanalysis and the endless opinions about writers, musicians, and artists—also threaten the stability of the couple. Psychoanalysis yields "relationships" and "living together," not marriage, as the central ritual, and living together, especially in the time of the Pill and the easy real-estate market of the seventies, is always provisional. Opinions about art—the way the soul defines itself in time—are provisional, too. In "Annie Hall," Keaton outgrows Allen's curriculum for her and moves on, and in *Manhattan,* perhaps the best American comedy about selfishness ever made, she returns to the married man she was having an affair with. Allen loses her both times; the biological imperative goes nowhere. *Annie Hall* and *Manhattan* now seem like fragile and melancholy love lyrics; they took romantic comedy to a level of rueful sophistication never seen before or since.

The louts in the slacker-striver comedies should probably lose the girl, too, but most of them don't. Yet what, exactly, are they getting, and why should the women want them? That is not a question that romantic comedy has posed before.

The slacker has certain charms. He doesn't want to compete in business, he refuses to cultivate macho attitudes, and, for some women, he may be attractive. He's still a boy—he's gentler than other men. Having a child with such a guy, however, is another matter, and plenty of women have complained about the way *Knocked Up* handles the issue of pregnancy. Alison has a good job, some growing public fame, and she hardly knows the unappealing father—there's even some muttering about "bad genes." Why have a baby with him? Well, a filmmaker's answer would have to be that if there's an abortion, or if Alison has the child on her own, there's no movie—or, at least, nothing like this movie. And this movie, just as it is, has considerable interest and complication as fiction.

What's striking about *Knocked Up* is the way the romance is placed within the relations between the sexes. The picture is a drastic revision of classic romantic-comedy patterns. Ben doesn't chase Alison, and she doesn't chase him. The movie is not about the civilizing of desire, and it offers a marriage plot that couldn't be more wary of marriage. *Knocked Up*, like Apatow's earlier *40-Year-Old Virgin*, is devoted to the dissolution of a male pack, the ending of the juvenile male bond. Ben and his friends sit around in their San Fernando Valley tract house whamming each other on the head with rubber bats and watching naked actresses in movies. The way Ben lives with his friends is tremendous fun; it's also as close to paralysis as you can get and continue breathing. Apatow, of course, has it both ways. He squeezes the pink-eyed doofuses for every laugh he can get out of them, but at the same time he suggests that the very thing he's celebrating is sick, crazy, and dysfunctional. The situation has to end. Boys have to grow up or life ceases.

Ben and Alison's one-night stand forces the issue. Willy-nilly, the world gets peopled. Yet the slowly developing love between Ben and the pregnant Alison comes off as halfhearted and unconvincing—it's the weakest element in the movie. There are some terrifically noisy arguments, a scene of Rogen's making love to the enormous Heigl ("I'm not making love to you like a dog. It's doggy style. It's a style"), but we never really see the moment in which they warm up and begin to like each other. That part of the movie is unpersuasive, I would guess, because it's not terribly important to Apatow. What's important is the male bond—the way it flourishes, in all its unhealthiness, and then its wrenching end. Alison lives with her sister, Debbie (Leslie Mann), and brother-in-law, Pete (Paul Rudd), and Ben begins to hang out with Alison at the house of the married couple, who are classically mismatched in temperament. Pete is restless, disappointed, and remorselessly funny, and Ben links up with him. Whooping with joy, they go off to Las Vegas, but they don't gamble or get laid. Instead, they hang out and eat "shrooms." They merely want to be together: it's as if Romeo and Mercutio had left the women and all that mess in Verona behind and gone off to practice their swordsmanship. When Ben and Pete get high, crash, and then return, chastened, to the women, the male bond is severed at last, the baby can be born, and life continues. In generic terms, *Knocked Up* puts the cart before the horse—the accidental baby, rather than desire, pulls the young man, who has to leave his male friends behind, into civilization.

As fascinating and as funny as *Knocked Up* is, it represents what can only be called the disenchantment of romantic comedy, the end point of a progression from Fifth Avenue to the Valley, from tuxedos to tube socks, from a popped champagne cork to a baby crowning. There's nothing in it that is comparable to the style of the classics—no magic in its settings, no reverberant sense of place, no shared or competitive work for the couple to do. Ben does come through in the end, yet, if his promise and Alison's beauty make them equal as a pair, one still wants more out of Alison than the filmmakers are willing to provide. She has a fine fit of hormonal rage, but, like the other heroines in the slacker-striver romances, she isn't given an idea or a snappy remark or even a sharp perception. All the movies in this genre have been written and directed by men, and it's as if the filmmakers were saying, "Yes, young men are children now, and women bring home the bacon, but men bring home the soul."

The perilous new direction of the slacker-striver genre reduces the role of women to vehicles. Their only real function is to make the men grow up. That's why they're all so earnest and bland—so nice, so good. Leslie Mann (who's married to Apatow) has some great bitchy lines as the angry Debbie, but she's not a lover; she represents disillusion. As Anthony Lane pointed out in these pages, Apatow's subject is not so much sex as age, and age in his movies is a malediction. If you're young, you have to grow up. If you grow up, you turn into Debbie—you fear that the years are overtaking you fast. Either way, you're in trouble.

Apatow has a genius for candor that goes way beyond dirty talk—that's why *Knocked Up* is a cultural event. But I wonder if Apatow, like his fumy youths, shouldn't move on. It seems strange to complain of repetition when a director does something particularly well, and Apatow does the infantilism of the male bond better than anyone, but I'd be quite happy if I never saw another bong-gurgling slacker or male pack again. The society that produced the Katharine Hepburn and Carole Lombard movies has vanished; manners, in the sense of elegance, have disappeared. But manners as spiritual style are more important than ever, and Apatow has demonstrated that he knows this as well as anyone. So how can he not know that the key to making a great romantic comedy is to create heroines equal in wit to men? They don't have to dress for dinner, but they should challenge the men intellectually and spiritually, rather than simply offering their bodies as a way of dragging the clods out of their adolescent stupor. "Paper bullets of the brain," as Benedick called the taunting exchanges with Beatrice, slay the audience every time if they are aimed at the right place.

SUGGESTIONS FOR WRITING

1. Denby compares the comedies of Judd Apatow to the earlier romantic comedies in this way: ". . . it represents what can only be called the disenchantment of romantic comedy, the end point of a progression from Fifth Avenue to the Valley, from tuxedos to tube socks, from a popped champagne cork to a baby crowning." In Denby's opinion, how does *Knocked Up,* and films like it, represent a de-evolution of the romantic genre? In an argumentative essay, discuss the accuracy of the author's critique: Do you agree with Denby that in the new romances "There's nothing in it that is comparable to the style of the classics—no magic in its settings, no reverberant sense of place, no shared or competitive work for the couple to do"? Or on the contrary, do you find in these movies a shared magic that reverberates for individuals of your generation—some set of qualities that Denby, who is older, might be missing? If the latter, what specific qualities might make Apatovian comedy qualify as enchanting? Cite specific examples from the "text" of the movie as you develop your supporting points in the body of your essay.

2. At the beginning of this article, Denby documents a certain kind of character that appears in Judd Apatow's romantic comedies: the contemporary young male. Here is part of Denby's description of this character: "His beard is haphazard and unintentional, and he dresses in sweats, or in shorts and a T-shirt . . . he spends a lot of time with friends who are like him, only more so—sweet-natured young men of foul mouth, odd hair, and wanker-mag reading habits. When he's with them, punched beer cans and bongs of various sizes lie around like spent shells; alone, and walrus-heavy on his couch, he watches football, basketball, or baseball on television, or spends time memorializing his youth—archiving old movies, games, and jokes . . . he's anti-corporate, but he's not bohemian (his culture is pop). He's more like a sullen back-of-the-classroom guy, who breaks into brilliant tirades only when he feels like it. . . . He may not have a girlfriend, but he certainly likes girls . . ." Using the rhetorical form of comparison/contrast, write an essay in which you discuss your opinion of the real-life accuracy of this depiction: If you're a guy, how does this character resemble you and/or your buds, and in what ways does it completely miss the mark? If you're

not a guy, in what ways does this characterization resemble guys you know (and love) and in what ways do the males of your acquaintance differ from the Apatovian stereotype?

3. After the general introduction in this essay, Denby goes on to provide a brief survey of romantic comedy through history. As the first stop in this comedic time-travel, he discusses the comedies of William Shakespeare. Shakespeare, says Denby, was well grounded in classical drama. He "knew the Roman farces—by Plautus, Terence, and others—in which a scrambling boy chases after a girl and lands her." However, part of Shakespeare's genius and innovation was in varying the pattern of classical comedy. Shakespeare's comedies "were rarely a simple chase." In *Much Ado About Nothing*, "its pair of battling lovers, Beatrice and Benedick," have much sexually charged conflict because "they are meant for each other, and are too proud and frightened to admit it. We can see the attraction, even if they can't." From this narrative tension and ultimately satisfying resolution arises a second point: that, as Denby says, "Romantic comedy is entertainment in the service of the biological imperative. The world must be peopled [as Benedick says toward the end of the play]." Historically, romantic comedy has served a crucial social function: It "civilizes desire, transforms lust into play and ritual—the celebration of union in marriage." As a writing project, conduct research into one of Shakespeare's comedies, such as *Twelfth Night, The Winter's Tale,* or *Much Ado About Nothing,* and compose an essay in which you compare themes and concerns in that play with those in *Knocked Up,* pointing out both areas of similarity and areas of striking difference.

KIRA COCHRANE

Where Have All the Good Women Gone?

A recent issue of Genders *magazine contains a lengthy analysis of the current state of romantic comedy, specifically as concerns the portrayals of women in general, and of hip-hop and film star Queen Latifah in particular. According to that article's author, "The traditional romantic comedy ends in the coupling of an often unlikely couple, but the pleasure of the narrative is the lively, quarrelsome give-and-take of the courtship, fired by the struggle for egalitarianism between the unruly woman and the man who is her match." This suggests that in romantic comedies before, say, the year 2000, women and men were portrayed as relative equals in terms of their intelligence* and social roles, and that the narrative tension in such films derived from the role-reversal of women and men: Comedy derived from fact "unruly" feminine heroines challenged traditional expectations of women in the prevailing culture of the time, and comedy derived from the interplay between those women and their staid male counterparts. The Genders article goes on to find fault with more recent romantic comedies on a variety of fronts, and it focuses on one in particular—Bringing Down the House—for its ultimate failure to consider Queen Latifah as a viable romantic comedy heroine because of her body type and ethnicity. The current article, by Kira Cochrane—a journalist and novelist who studied American literature at the Universities of Sussex and California before moving to London to work as a journalist, currently as deputy weekly editor for The Guardian—finds serious deficiencies in contemporary romantic comedies for some similar reasons, although she uses a different methodology to arrive at her conclusions. Interviewing a group of teenagers and exposing them to some current rom-com fare, she concludes from her conversations with these young "experts" that the current string of recent comedies portrays women as merely ditzy and needy—a far cry from female traits that once made such films great. As such, she bemoans the fact that the new female protagonists perpetuate certain negative stereotypes in romantic comedy, which through film history "has been a genuinely positive genre for women."

When Rosalind Russell strides across the screen in the first scenes of *His Girl Friday*—arguably the greatest romantic comedy of all time—she is intent on a safe, boring life as the wife of an insurance salesman. The trouble is, the script just won't let her do it. Russell plays Hildy Johnson, a brilliant newspaper reporter, and when she tells her ex-husband and editor, Walter Burns, played by Cary Grant, that she intends to leave work and settle down in the suburbs, he springs into action to stop her. This is, of course, because he loves her, but also because he needs her, for Johnson is clearly brilliant: the best reporter on the newsroom floor, a woman who can outmatch any man in repartee, who is clever and glamorous and angry and vital and alive. "I'm no suburban bridge player, I'm a newspaper man!" cries Johnson, hammering at her typewriter, forgetting her boring fiance and nailing the story.

Compare this with the lead character of the recently released romantic comedy, *Confessions of a Shopaholic*. Becky Bloomwood, played by Isla Fisher, is also a journalist, but she is so far from the template laid down by Johnson in 1940 as to be unrecognizable. As the film's title suggests, Bloomwood is obsessed with shopping. The mannequins in boutique windows literally beckon to her and her twelve credit cards are almost all maxed out. She is also incomparably stupid. In a job interview for *Successful Savings* magazine she is unable to open her bag to retrieve her CV, mixes up the words "fish" and "fiscal," and walks into a glass wall. When she finally becomes a well-known writer, she can only blink in befuddlement.

I watch *Confessions of a Shopaholic* with a group of teenage girls whom I've brought along to find out how the target audience for romantic comedies responds to them. And I am particularly interested because of the turn the genre has taken. Romantic comedies have, of course, long been formulaic, and often palpably dumb, but recently they actually seem to have become contemptuous of women.

Take another recent release, *He's Just Not That Into You*, which offers up some of the most depressing female characters ever committed to celluloid. This was directed by Ken Kwapis, from a script by Abby Kohn and Marc Silverstein—the fact that there were women involved in its production seems incredible. It includes a character played by Ginnifer Goodwin who is so needy that she stages "drive-bys" of places where she knows potential dates hang out, and is complimented by her eventual love interest with the immortal line: "I like you like I like bassett hounds – there's something kind of desperate about you." There's Scarlett Johansson's character, who takes up with a married man, and is then forced to sit in a closet and listen while he has a sexual encounter with his wife. And there's Drew Barrymore, who draws murmurs of approval from her workmates when she receives a phone message from a new boyfriend—only to redden sharply and sadly as he accidentally leaves a message for another woman immediately afterwards. If you had to sum up this film in one word, it would be humiliation. That word would be capitalized.

It's not only women who have noticed the shift in the romantic comedy genre. Peter Travers, a film critic for *Rolling Stone* magazine described *He's Just Not That Into You* as "a women-bashing tract disguised as a chick flick" and Kevin Maher has written in the *Times* that the "so-called chick flick has become home to the worst kind of regressive pre-feminist stereotype". Dr Diane Purkiss, an Oxford fellow and feminist historian, feels that we have reached a nadir in the way that women are portrayed on screen, and says that there's been "a depressing dumbing down of the whole genre. That's not to say that I want all movies to be earnest and morally improving. But I think that you can actually have entertainment with sassy, smart heroines, rather than dimwitted ones."

You can, but at the moment, we don't. In fact, the women who people today's romantic comedies seem to have three main obsessions. There's shopping, of course, as seen in *Confessions of a Shopaholic* and *Sex and the City*. There's babies, as witnessed in *Baby Mama*, *Juno* and *Knocked Up*. And there's marriage, which was front and center of the noxious recent release *Bride Wars*, featuring Kate Hudson and Anne Hathaway fighting over their dream wedding—described by Purkiss as "what some drunken bozo who never got a date in high school thinks women are like."

Marriage is also at the centre of *Made of Honor*, *License to Wed*, *The Wedding Date*, *The Wedding Planner* and *27 Dresses*. It's something that the teenagers find bemusing. I ask whether they're obsessed with marriage themselves, and they laugh—not surprising, since recent figures show that fewer and fewer of us are actually tying the knot. "I see marriage as a bit of a negative thing," says Bronté Norman Terrell, 17. "You're signing your life away. Very few of our parents are still together, so why would we want to go through all that?"

What's sad is that over the years the romantic comedy has been a genuinely positive genre for women. It sailed off to a fine start in 1934, with *It Happened One Night*, featuring Claudette Colbert as a famous heiress on the run from her father, and Clark Gable as a luckless journalist, who encounters her on a bus and sniffs out a story. The relationship between the two is initially sarcastic—as with the relationships between countless rom-com couples—but most of all it is equal.

This sets the tone for most of the great classics of the genre, the male and female characters are finely balanced. So, of course, in *His Girl Friday*, Russell and Grant trade witticisms at terrifying speed, as do Katharine Hepburn and Grant in *The Philadelphia Story*. This trend continued through classics such as *Pillow Talk* (1959), in which Doris Day's clever, capable interior designer could never be bested by Rock Hudson's rakish composer; *Annie Hall* (1977), in which Diane Keaton's eponymous character is clearly much less scared than Woody Allen's character is by a room of marauding lobsters; and on through *When Harry Met Sally*, in which the two titular protagonists are equally intelligent, witty, and proud, and, in the famous fake orgasm scene, Meg Ryan's character teaches Billy Crystal's that perhaps his lovers haven't been having quite such a riot in bed as he thinks.

The girls are initially unenthusiastic when I give them these classic romantic comedies to watch at home, but when we discuss them later, their voices light up. Naile Ahmet, 17, describes a scene in *His Girl Friday* where the male and female protagonists "are arguing for five minutes, non-stop, really fast—he wants to get his point across, she wants to get her point across—and they both have just as much to say." She sounds genuinely surprised by this turn of events. Shanice Calica, 16, says that she thought *Pillow Talk* "was going to be really old-fashioned and lovey-dovey, but it was quite modern and funny. The female character wasn't throwing herself at the man, whereas in the newer films they're willing to do anything for the guys." Bronté was surprised by *Annie Hall*, in which the female character was "almost portrayed in a better light than the man—she was the one who let him down, whereas quite often now you just see a poor woman on screen who everyone feels sorry for, who's let down by her lover." And Rhiannan Brown, 17, is impressed by Meg Ryan's character in *When Harry Met Sally*. "She's more subtle, more real life than the women in rom-coms today. She's working, she has her own house, she knows what she wants, and what she wants is very similar to what the average woman of today wants—even though," she adds, as only a teenager can, "it was made back in the eighties."

Rhiannan's comments reflect the fact that in the classics of the genre, women are regularly portrayed as high-powered, competent, capable career women. Following *His Girl Friday*, Russell assured her fame by playing strong, determined women in the workplace, while Doris Day took roles including a college professor in *Teacher's Pet* (1958), and an advertising executive in *Lover Come Back* (1961).

Now, at a time when 70% of women are in the workforce, career women in romantic comedies are generally either portrayed as incompetent, cruel, or both. Dr. Tamar Jeffers McDonald, an expert on romantic comedies, says that she finds it "quite insulting that a career woman now is something that is so frowned upon. You see depictions of women who are supposedly at the top of their game, yet they can't walk down a corridor in a white suit without pouring coffee on themselves or walking into a bush. The films are not very subtly saying 'yes, they may be at the top in their jobs, but actually what they really need is a man. In fact, a husband.'"

A big part of the problem with romantic comedies, says Purkiss, is that "there aren't enough women involved with the film industry", which is borne out by the fact that, for instance, women made up only

15% of the directors, writers, producers and editors of the top 250 films of 2007. The result is that those making romantic comedies often have no idea of their audience, and simply resort to outlandish female stereotypes. Purkiss points to the fights in *Bride Wars*: "People sort of sneaking in and poisoning each other's perms, which wasn't only improbable, but was on an index of probability that could only be set by someone who isn't a woman, but looks at them doing their strange, funny female stuff with an outsider's eye." Compare that with *Mamma Mia!*, released last year, which had a female writer, director and producer, and was warm and respectful towards women, showing no judgment, for instance, about the fact that Meryl Streep's character had clearly slept with three men in quick succession. The film was an enormous hit with its female audiences.

The people making these films don't just seem to misunderstand their audiences, though, but genuinely dislike them – there is a huge whiff of feminist backlash about the genre. As women make the slow crawl towards equality in the workplace, freedom in our relationships, and parity with men, romantic comedies seem determined to remind us of "our place," to suggest that we're incapable of further progress, and should really give up. As Brontë says of Bloomwood in *Confessions of a Shopaholic*, "She was very dopey, wasn't she—a woman who can't grasp love or a job or manage her bills." She adds that she "can't think of a film where the main female character has been someone successful, someone normal." "And if they are successful," says Shanice, "it's like they have to get married so that they're not so concentrated on their work."

The group writes off many of today's rom-coms as predictable, clichéd and exaggerated, but they're not too bothered. They prefer horror films. I ask whether there are any female characters that have particularly captured their imagination, and while rom-coms come up short, Brontë finally plumps for Angelina Jolie's character in the thriller *Mr. and Mrs. Smith*—an assassin on a mission to kill her own husband. When I relay this to Purkiss, she sounds distinctly relieved. "I'll sleep better tonight," she says. "That just shows that no matter how powerful the cultural forces raining down on you are, you can always find a role model somewhere."

SUGGESTIONS FOR WRITING

1. Using your vast experience as a viewer of movies, consider this article's central premise that the romantic comedies of today demonstrate a

disappointing trend toward portraying women in a negatively stereotypical light: air-headed, materialistic, and subservient to men. Based on the movies with which you are familiar, do you agree with this assessment, or has author Cochrane only focused on certain movies that support her thesis, ignoring contemporary romantic comedies that portray women in a more positive light . . . more along the lines of "traditional" comedies of bygone eras of cinema? If, by your prior knowledge and possibly through some additional research, you conclude that Cochrane is correct in her assessment of this negative trend, then write a persuasive essay in which you amplify her discussion by providing additional examples of films that support her gender-based conclusions. If, on the other hand, you discover a body of modern comedies whose heroines are portrayed more favorably— and which therefore contradict the conclusions made by Cochrane— then write a comparison/contrast essay in which you develop a thesis that all women in modern rom-coms are in fact *not* portrayed negatively, as Cochrane contends, but instead are portrayed by contemporary comedic filmmakers in a variety of ways, some positive and some less so.

2. The *Genders* magazine article mentioned in the introduction uses academic scholarship to make its points about negative portrayals of women in romantic comedies. Its author brings in a wide range of source material, incorporating literary and feminist theory. [If you're curious to read it, the article can be found at http://findarticles.com/ p/articles/mi_7085/is_46/ai_n28529866/ on the Web.] By contrast, since Kira Cochrane is a journalist, the tone of this article is more conversational and its appeals to academic sources less extensive. Nevertheless, Cochrane does bring in a wealth of evidence from previous movies and film commentators, and additionally she conducts a kind of mini-ethnographic study of a group of teenage girls, in order to determine their responses to several film comedy "texts." While this study might not be considered serious scholarly research, since the study group is so small, it does make for compelling journalism, yielding results interesting enough for the resulting article to be included in a major newspaper and in this popular culture anthology. For the purposes of composing a short primary-source research essay, conduct a similarly limited ethnographic essay on film opinion. Pick a small group of people with certain common traits—age, gender, ethnicity, eating habits, and so on—and expose them to a film from a genre which you are familiar and interested; it could be romantic comedy, as in the above article, but it could just as easily be science fiction, horror, or slasher films. For each member of your sample group, ask specific questions about his or her responses to certain implied

themes or attitudes you believe to be present in the film. Then, from the data generated by these questionnaires and the resulting responses, draw some conclusions about the way members of this particular category of people perceive certain aspects of film. From these conclusions will evolve a thesis for your essay, which you can support with quotes from your subjects' responses, along with other research-based supporting material, as Cochrane did in her article.

3. Write a comparison/contrast essay in which you first list and summarize the central points made in David Denby's article on the comedies of Judd Apatow, and then perform the same action (i.e., list and summarize) the main points made in Kira Cochran's article about portrayals of women in contemporary romantic comedies. Having completed this first prewriting stage, arrive at some conclusions about whether you agree or disagree with the opinions expressed in the two articles. Try to be as specific as possible here, teasing out discrete intellectual threads expressed in both articles and responding directly to each of these. From your prewriting at the first two stages, you should arrive at a clear sense of how you feel about the portrayals of men and women in the cinematic subgenre of romantic comedy—at least those comedies with which you are familiar, either by firsthand experience or by reading these two articles and others. Finally, in developing the body of your essay, hold your own conclusions up against the assertions made in each of these essays. In developing a comparison/contrast of this type, you can structure your essay point-by-point, going back and forth between each of the above-mentioned intellectual threads, or you can use the whole-to-whole method, examining all of your points about males in romantic comedy, and then comparing them to all your points about women in this film genre.

CHAPTER 7

Popular Reading

THE BOOK IS DEAD. OR IS IT? MUCH HAS BEEN WRITTEN LATELY about the impending demise of the book, widely lamented as a quaint, antiquated artifact to be replaced by a variety of digital and other electronic media. Likewise, cultural pundits have commented upon a general decline in reading interest and activity in contemporary U.S. culture, especially among the younger generation(s). To take one example, Jeff Jarvis, television critic, creator of *Entertainment Weekly*, associate publisher of the *New York Daily News*, and a columnist for the *San Francisco Examiner,* calls the book in its traditional form "an out-moded means of communicating information. And efforts to update it are hampered because, culturally, we give undue reverence to the form for the form's sake." Jarvis goes on to list a number of fatal flaws in spine-bound, paper-based volumes: "They are frozen in time without the means of being updated and corrected. They have no link to re-lated knowledge, debates, and sources. They create, at best, a one-way relationship with a reader. They try to teach readers but don't teach authors. They tend to be too damned long because they have to be long enough to be books. . . . They limit how knowledge can be found because they have to sit on a shelf under one address; there's only way to get to it. . . . They aren't searchable. They aren't linkable. They have no metadata. They carry no conversation. They are thrown out when there's no space for them anymore." Jarvis sums up the current state of books thus: "Print is where words go to die."

However, other researchers believe that, while the format of books is no doubt in a state of rapid change, reading as a fundamental human activity is alive and well. For instance, Tom Peters, writing in a recent issue of *Library Journal*, notes that while new digital formats are challenging traditional forms of reading matter, "Never before has so much reading material been so easily and quickly available to so many people." This, Peters believes, is a positive development; so long as writers, librarians, and publishers keep up with the technologies and the changing reading habits of individuals, reading will continue to be as popular an activity as it has always been.

The first reading in the Popular Reading chapter of this book weighs in on the gloom and doom side of the discussion. Using a variety of factual sources, critic Caleb Crain demonstrates that both general adult and children's books have shown dramatic declines in new offerings; furthermore, he points to an increasing public feeling that written language is an artificial, painful, and ineffective way of conveying meaning, evidenced by slumping book sales and literacy rates. These factors, Crain believes, will have profoundly deleterious ramifications in Western civilization in the future.

Having set that somewhat bleak stage, this chapter then undercuts the negative predictions somewhat by presenting two literary subgenres vital within contemporary popular culture: young adult novels and the range of forms that blend word and image, including cartoons, comic strips, comic books, and graphic novels. For the first reading in the young adult section, "J. K. Rowling's Ministry of Magic" the famous (and infamously horrific) author Stephen King uses the Harry Potter book series to launch an attack on those "bighead" (his somewhat unflattering term) intellectuals who would suggest that books are dying and that young people aren't reading. Following this broad introduction to young adult literature, the chapter next focuses on two other popular series in the same genre. In "Talk to the Animals," social commentator Laura Miller sets her sights on the *Chronicles of Narnia* series, responding to the religious subtexts found in those novels and finding much to admire in the writing of C. S. Lewis, despite some of the allegorical underpinnings that she finds troublesome. The young adult section of this chapter ends with the extremely popular *Twilight* series of vampire novels. In "What Girls Want," commentator Caitlin Flanagan explains why these books are particularly appealing to preadolescent girls and concludes that their near-obsession with the novels is, on balance, a healthy thing—again supporting King's thesis that reading yet thrives in contemporary Western culture.

Along with young adult fiction series, illustrated texts—and the reading of these artifacts—are also quite popular in contemporary culture, although cultural commentators are likely to disagree on whether this is cause for pride or despair. We're not talking about thirteenth-century illuminated religious manuscripts here, but rather the Sunday funnies in your local newspaper, the cartoons in magazines and on the Web, and the comic books and graphic novels in specialty stores and increasingly in their own sections of mainstream bookstores. As our culture becomes generally more visual, it's natural that the texts we read incorporate more visual elements, and we as readers are called upon to interpret the meaning and assess the appeal of texts that combine word and image. Offering a model of this kind of response, Stephen J. Lind takes *Peanuts* as his object of analysis, explaining the secular and sacred interpretations of this immensely popular comic strip by Charles M. Schulz. John Catalini offers a different perspective on word/image combinations by showing their potential educational value; he describes his practice of asking students to create pictographs or academic graffiti as a strategy for improving their critical thinking skills.

CALEB CRAIN

Twilight of the Books

In an article included later in this chapter, prolific writer (and reader) Stephen King sums up the current state of reading in America. Commenting specifically on the reading habits of the younger generation—and echoing a famous pop song lyric by sixties super-group The Who—King makes the statement, "The kids are all right." By so asserting, he makes the point that, despite encroachments by the World Wide Web, text messaging, and OMG-style slang contractions, books are alive and well in modern civilization, and that young people are reading as much as ever, with every bit as much enthusiasm. King counters a currently popular sentiment that literature generally, and the reading of books in particular, is on the decline in our contemporary culture. The first article in this chapter exemplifies the kind of scholarship that King disagrees with and takes to task in his own opinion piece. In the following article, New York Times book reviewer and prolific author in his own right, Caleb Crain, assimilates factual evidence from a variety of reputable sources, including surveys, historical data, biological hypotheses and experiments, field ethnographies, and psychological studies, to argue that reading is in fact on a precipitous decline, despite Stephen King's assurances to the contrary. With persuasive documentation, Crain makes a convincing argument, adding that the erosion of our reading behaviors will yield a number of near-catastrophic effects on our society, both immediately and in the long term.

In 1937, twenty-nine per cent of American adults told the pollster George Gallup that they were reading a book. In 1955, only seventeen per cent said they were. Pollsters began asking the question with more latitude. In 1978, a survey found that fifty-five per cent of respondents had read a book in the previous six months. The question was even looser in 1998 and 2002, when the General Social Survey found that roughly seventy per cent of Americans had read a novel, a short story, a poem, or a play in the preceding twelve months. And, this August, seventy-three per cent of respondents to another poll said that they had read a book of some kind, not excluding those read for work or school, in the past year. If you didn't read the fine print, you might think that reading was on the rise.

You wouldn't think so, however, if you consulted the Census Bureau and the National Endowment for the Arts, who, since 1982, have asked thousands of Americans questions about reading that are not only detailed but consistent. The results, first reported by the N.E.A. in 2004, are dispiriting. In 1982, 56.9 per cent of Americans had read a work of creative literature in the previous twelve months. The proportion fell to fifty-four per cent in 1992, and to 46.7 per cent in 2002. Last month, the N.E.A. released a follow-up report, "To Read or Not to Read," which showed correlations between the decline of reading and social phenomena as diverse as income disparity, exercise, and voting. In his introduction, the N.E.A. chairman, Dana Gioia, wrote, "Poor reading skills correlate heavily with lack of employment, lower wages, and fewer opportunities for advancement."

This decline is not news to those who depend on print for a living. In 1970, according to Editor & Publisher International Year Book, there were 62.1 million weekday newspapers in circulation—about 0.3 papers per person. Since 1990, circulation has declined steadily, and in 2006 there were just 52.3 million weekday papers—about 0.17 per person. In January 1994, forty-nine per cent of respondents told the Pew Research Center for the People and the Press that they had read a newspaper the day before. In 2006, only forty-three per cent said so, including those who read online. Book sales, meanwhile, have stagnated. The Book Industry Study Group estimates that sales fell from 8.27 books per person in 2001 to 7.93 in 2006. According to the Department of Labor, American households spent an average of a hundred and sixty-three dollars on reading in 1995 and a hundred and twenty-six dollars in 2005. In "To Read or Not to Read," the N.E.A. reports that American households' spending on books, adjusted for inflation, is "near its twenty-year low," even as the average price of a new book has increased.

More alarming are indications that Americans are losing not just the will to read but even the ability. According to the Department of Education, between 1992 and 2003 the average adult's skill in reading prose slipped one point on a five-hundred-point scale, and the proportion who were proficient—capable of such tasks as "comparing viewpoints in two editorials"—declined from fifteen per cent to thirteen. The Department of Education found that reading skills have improved moderately among fourth and eighth graders in the past decade and a half, with the largest jump occurring just before the No Child Left Behind Act took effect, but twelfth graders seem to be taking after their elders. Their reading scores fell an average of six points between 1992 and 2005, and the share of proficient twelfth-grade readers dropped from forty per cent to thirty-five per cent. The steepest declines were in "reading for literary experience"—the kind that involves "exploring themes, events, characters, settings, and the language of literary works," in the words of the department's test-makers. In 1992, fifty-four per cent of twelfth graders told the Department of Education that they talked about their reading with friends at least once a week. By 2005, only thirty-seven per cent said they did.

The erosion isn't unique to America. Some of the best data come from the Netherlands, where in 1955 researchers began to ask people to keep diaries of how they spent every fifteen minutes of their leisure time. Time-budget diaries yield richer data than surveys, and people are thought to be less likely to lie about their accomplishments if they have to do it four times an hour. Between 1955 and 1975, the decades when television was being introduced into the Netherlands, reading on weekday evenings and weekends fell from five hours a week to 3.6, while television watching rose from about ten minutes a week to more than ten hours. During the next two decades, reading continued to fall and television watching to rise, though more slowly. By 1995, reading, which had occupied twenty-one per cent of people's spare time in 1955, accounted for just nine per cent.

The most striking results were generational. In general, older Dutch people read more. It would be natural to infer from this that each generation reads more as it ages, and, indeed, the researchers found something like this to be the case for earlier generations. But, with later ones, the age-related growth in reading dwindled. The turning point seems to have come with the generation born in the nineteen-forties. By 1995, a Dutch college graduate born after 1969 was likely to spend fewer hours reading each week than a little-educated person born before 1950. As far as reading habits were concerned, academic credentials mattered less than whether a person had been raised in the era of television. The N.E.A., in its twenty years of data, has found a similar pattern. Between 1982 and 2002, the percentage of Americans who read literature declined not only in every age group but in every generation—even in those moving from youth into middle age, which is often considered the most fertile time of life for reading. We are reading less as we age, and we are reading less than people who were our age ten or twenty years ago.

There's no reason to think that reading and writing are about to become extinct, but some sociologists speculate that reading books for pleasure will one day be the province of a special "reading class," much as it was before the arrival of mass literacy, in the second half of the nineteenth century. They warn that it probably won't regain the prestige of exclusivity; it may just become "an increasingly arcane hobby." Such a shift would change the texture of society. If one person decides to watch "The Sopranos" rather than to read Leonardo Sciascia's novella "To Each His Own," the culture goes on largely as before—both viewer and reader are entertaining themselves while learning something about the Mafia in the bargain. But if, over time, many people choose television over books, then a nation's conversation with itself is likely to change. A reader learns about the world and imagines it differently from the way a viewer does; according to some experimental psychologists, a reader and a viewer even think differently. If the eclipse of reading continues, the alteration is likely to matter in ways that aren't foreseeable.

Taking the long view, it's not the neglect of reading that has to be explained but the fact that we read at all. "The act of reading is not natural," Maryanne Wolf writes in "Proust and the Squid" (Harper; $25.95), an account of the history and biology of reading. Humans started reading far too recently for any of our genes to code for it specifically. We can do it only because the brain's plasticity enables the repurposing of circuitry that originally evolved for other tasks—distinguishing at a glance a garter snake from a haricot vert, say.

The squid of Wolf's title represents the neurobiological approach to the study of reading. Bigger cells are easier for scientists to experiment on, and some species of squid have optic-nerve cells a hundred times as thick as mammal neurons, and up to four inches long, making them a favorite with biologists. (Two decades ago, I had a summer job washing glassware in Cape Cod's Marine Biological Laboratory. Whenever researchers extracted an optic nerve, they threw the rest of the squid into a freezer, and about once a month we took a cooler-full to the beach for grilling.) To symbolize the humanistic approach to reading, Wolf has chosen Proust, who described reading as "that fruitful miracle of a communication in the midst of solitude." Perhaps inspired by Proust's example, Wolf, a dyslexia researcher at Tufts, reminisces about the nuns who taught her to read in a two-room brick schoolhouse in Illinois. But she's more of a squid person than a Proust person, and seems most at home when dissecting Proust's fruitful miracle into such brain parts as the occipital "visual association area" and "area 37's fusiform gyrus." Given the panic that takes hold of humanists when the decline of reading is discussed, her cold-blooded perspective is opportune.

Wolf recounts the early history of reading, speculating about developments in brain wiring as she goes. For example, from the eighth to the fifth millennia B.C.E., clay tokens were used in Mesopotamia for tallying livestock and other goods. Wolf suggests that, once the simple markings on the tokens were understood not merely as squiggles but as representations of, say, ten sheep, they would have put more of the brain to work. She draws on recent research with functional magnetic resonance imaging (fMRI), a technique that maps blood flow in the brain during a given task, to show that meaningful squiggles activate not only the occipital regions responsible for vision but also temporal and parietal regions associated with language and computation. If a particular squiggle was repeated on a number of tokens, a group of nerves might start to specialize in recognizing it, and other nerves to specialize in connecting to language centers that handled its meaning.

In the fourth millennium B.C.E., the Sumerians developed cuneiform, and the Egyptians hieroglyphs. Both scripts began with pictures of things, such as a beetle or a hand, and then some of these symbols developed more abstract meanings, representing ideas in some cases and sounds in others. Readers had to recognize hundreds of symbols, some of which could stand for either a word or a sound, an ambiguity that probably slowed down decoding. Under this heavy cognitive burden, Wolf imagines, the Sumerian reader's brain would have behaved the way modern brains do when reading Chinese, which also mixes phonetic and ideographic elements and seems to stimulate brain activity in a pattern distinct from that of people reading the Roman alphabet. Frontal regions associated with muscle memory would probably also have gone to work, because the Sumerians learned their characters by writing them over and over, as the Chinese do today.

Complex scripts like Sumerian and Egyptian were written only by scribal élites. A major breakthrough occurred around 750 B.C.E., when the Greeks, borrowing characters from a Semitic language, perhaps Phoenician, developed a writing system that had just twenty-four letters. There had been scripts with a limited number of characters before, as there had been consonants and even occasionally vowels, but the Greek alphabet was the first whose letters recorded every significant sound element in a spoken language in a one-to-one correspondence, give or take a few diphthongs. In ancient Greek, if you knew how to pronounce a word, you knew how to spell it, and you could sound out almost any word you saw, even if you'd never heard it before. Children learned to read and write Greek in about three years, somewhat faster than modern children learn English, whose alphabet is more ambiguous. The ease democratized literacy; the ability to read and write spread to citizens who didn't specialize in it. The classicist Eric A. Havelock believed that the alphabet changed "the character of the Greek consciousness."

Wolf doesn't quite second that claim. She points out that it is possible to read efficiently a script that combines ideograms and phonetic elements, something that many Chinese do daily. The alphabet, she suggests, entailed not a qualitative difference but an accumulation of small quantitative ones, by helping more readers reach efficiency sooner. "The efficient reading brain," she writes, "quite literally has more time to think." Whether that development sparked Greece's flowering she leaves to classicists to debate, but she agrees with Havelock that writing was probably a contributive factor, because it freed the Greeks from the necessity of keeping their whole culture, including the Iliad and the Odyssey, memorized.

The scholar Walter J. Ong once speculated that television and similar media are taking us into an era of "secondary orality," akin to the primary orality that existed before the emergence of text. If so, it is worth trying to understand how different primary orality must have been from our own mind-set. Havelock theorized that, in ancient Greece, the effort required to preserve knowledge colored everything. In Plato's day, the word mimesis referred to an actor's performance of his role, an audience's identification with a performance, a pupil's recitation of his lesson, and an apprentice's emulation of his master. Plato, who was literate, worried about the kind of trance or emotional enthrallment that came over people in all these situations, and Havelock inferred from this that the idea of distinguishing the knower from the known was then still a novelty. In a society that had only recently learned to take notes, learning something still meant abandoning yourself to it. "Enormous powers of poetic memorization could be purchased only at the cost of total loss of objectivity," he wrote.

It's difficult to prove that oral and literate people think differently; orality, Havelock observed, doesn't "fossilize" except through its nemesis, writing. But some supporting evidence came to hand in 1974, when Aleksandr R. Luria, a Soviet psychologist, published a study based on interviews conducted in the nineteen-thirties with illiterate and newly literate peasants in Uzbekistan and Kyrgyzstan. Luria found that illiterates had a "graphic-functional" way of thinking that seemed to vanish as they were schooled. In naming colors, for example, literate people said "dark blue" or "light yellow," but illiterates used metaphorical names like "liver," "peach," "decayed teeth," and "cotton in bloom." Literates saw optical illusions; illiterates sometimes didn't. Experimenters showed peasants drawings of a hammer, a saw, an axe, and a log and then asked them to choose the three items that were similar. Illiterates resisted, saying that all the items were useful. If pressed, they considered throwing out the hammer; the situation of chopping wood seemed more cogent to them than any conceptual category. One peasant, informed that someone had grouped the three tools together, discarding the log, replied, "Whoever told you that must have been crazy," and another suggested, "Probably he's got a lot of firewood." One frustrated experimenter showed a picture of three adults and a child and declared, "Now, clearly the child doesn't belong in this group," only to have a peasant answer:

Oh, but the boy must stay with the others! All three of them are working, you see, and if they have to keep running out to fetch things, they'll never get the job done, but the boy can do the running for them.

Illiterates also resisted giving definitions of words and refused to make logical inferences about hypothetical situations. Asked by Luria's staff about polar bears, a peasant grew testy: "What the cock knows how to do, he does. What I know, I say, and nothing beyond that!" The illiterates did not talk about themselves except in terms of their tangible possessions. "What can I say about my own heart?" one asked.

In the nineteen-seventies, the psychologists Sylvia Scribner and Michael Cole tried to replicate Luria's findings among the Vai, a rural people in Liberia. Since some Vai were illiterate, some were schooled in English, and others were literate in the Vai's own script, the researchers hoped to be able to distinguish cognitive changes caused by schooling from those caused specifically by literacy. They found that English schooling and English literacy improved the ability to talk about language and solve logic puzzles, as literacy had done with Luria's peasants. But literacy in Vai script improved performance on only a few language-related tasks. Scribner and Cole's modest conclusion—"Literacy makes some difference to some skills in some contexts"—convinced some people that the literate mind was not so different from the oral one after all. But others have objected that it was misguided to separate literacy from schooling, suggesting that cognitive changes came with the culture of literacy rather than with the mere fact of it. Also, the Vai script, a syllabary with more than two hundred characters, offered nothing like the cognitive efficiency that Havelock ascribed to Greek. Reading Vai, Scribner and Cole admitted, was "a complex problem-solving process," usually performed slowly.

Soon after this study, Ong synthesized existing research into a vivid picture of the oral mind-set. Whereas literates can rotate concepts in their minds abstractly, orals embed their thoughts in stories. According to Ong, the best way to preserve ideas in the absence of writing is to "think memorable thoughts," whose zing insures their transmission. In an oral culture, cliché and stereotype are valued, as accumulations of wisdom, and analysis is frowned upon, for putting those accumulations at risk. There's no such concept as plagiarism, and redundancy is an asset that helps an audience follow a complex argument. Opponents in struggle are more memorable than calm and abstract investigations, so bards revel in name-calling and in "enthusiastic description of physical violence." Since there's no way to erase a mistake invisibly, as one may in writing, speakers tend not to correct themselves at all. Words have their present meanings but no older ones, and if the past seems to tell a story with values different from current ones, it is either forgotten or silently adjusted. As the scholars Jack Goody and Ian Watt observed, it is only in a literate culture that the past's inconsistencies have to be accounted for, a process that encourages skepticism and forces history to diverge from myth.

Upon reaching classical Greece, Wolf abandons history, because the Greeks' alphabet-reading brains probably resembled ours, which can be readily put into scanners. Drawing on recent imaging studies, she explains in detail how a modern child's brain wires itself for literacy. The ground is laid in preschool, when parents read to a child, talk with her, and encourage awareness of sound elements like rhyme and alliteration, perhaps with "Mother Goose" poems. Scans show that when a child first starts to read she has to use more of her brain than adults do. Broad regions light up in both hemispheres. As a child's neurons specialize in recognizing letters and become more efficient, the regions activated become smaller.

At some point, as a child progresses from decoding to fluent reading, the route of signals through her brain shifts. Instead of passing along a "dorsal route" through occipital, temporal, and parietal regions in both hemispheres, reading starts to move along a faster and more efficient "ventral route," which is confined to the left hemisphere. With the gain in time and the freed-up brainpower, Wolf suggests, a fluent reader is able to integrate more of her own thoughts and feelings into her experience. "The secret at the heart of reading," Wolf writes, is "the time it frees for the brain to have thoughts deeper than those that came before." Imaging studies suggest that in many cases of dyslexia the right hemisphere never disengages, and reading remains effortful.

In a recent book claiming that television and video games were "making our minds sharper," the journalist Steven Johnson argued that since we value reading for "exercising the mind," we should value electronic media for offering a superior "cognitive workout." But, if Wolf's evidence is right, Johnson's metaphor of exercise is misguided. When reading goes well, Wolf suggests, it feels effortless, like drifting down a river rather than rowing up it. It makes you smarter because it leaves more of your brain alone. Ruskin once compared reading to a conversation with the wise and noble, and Proust corrected him. It's much better than that, Proust wrote. To read is "to receive a communication with another way of thinking, all the while remaining alone, that is, while continuing to enjoy the intellectual power that one has in solitude and that conversation dissipates immediately."

Wolf has little to say about the general decline of reading, and she doesn't much speculate about the function of the brain under the influence of television and newer media. But there is research suggesting

(margin text, right side)

that secondary orality and literacy don't mix. In a study published this year, experimenters varied the way that people took in a PowerPoint presentation about the country of Mali. Those who were allowed to read silently were more likely to agree with the statement "The presentation was interesting," and those who read along with an audiovisual commentary were more likely to agree with the statement "I did not learn anything from this presentation." The silent readers remembered more, too, a finding in line with a series of British studies in which people who read transcripts of television newscasts, political programs, advertisements, and science shows recalled more information than those who had watched the shows themselves.

The antagonism between words and moving images seems to start early. In August, scientists at the University of Washington revealed that babies aged between eight and sixteen months know on average six to eight fewer words for every hour of baby DVDs and videos they watch daily. A 2005 study in Northern California found that a television in the bedroom lowered the standardized-test scores of third graders. And the conflict continues throughout a child's development. In 2001, after analyzing data on more than a million students around the world, the researcher Micha Razel found "little room for doubt" that television worsened performance in reading, science, and math. The relationship wasn't a straight line but "an inverted check mark": a small amount of television seemed to benefit children; more hurt. For nine-year-olds, the optimum was two hours a day; for seventeen-year-olds, half an hour. Razel guessed that the younger children were watching educational shows, and, indeed, researchers have shown that a five-year-old boy who watches "Sesame Street" is likely to have higher grades even in high school. Razel noted, however, that fifty-five per cent of students were exceeding their optimal viewing time by three hours a day, thereby lowering their academic achievement by roughly one grade level.

The Internet, happily, does not so far seem to be antagonistic to literacy. Researchers recently gave Michigan children and teen-agers home computers in exchange for permission to monitor their Internet use. The study found that grades and reading scores rose with the amount of time spent online. Even visits to pornography Web sites improved academic performance. Of course, such synergies may disappear if the Internet continues its YouTube-fuelled evolution away from print and toward television.

No effort of will is likely to make reading popular again. Children may be browbeaten, but adults resist interference with their pleasures.

It may simply be the case that many Americans prefer to learn about the world and to entertain themselves with television and other streaming media, rather than with the printed word, and that it is taking a few generations for them to shed old habits like newspapers and novels. The alternative is that we are nearing the end of a pendulum swing, and that reading will return, driven back by forces as complicated as those now driving it away.

But if the change is permanent, and especially if the slide continues, the world will feel different, even to those who still read. Because the change has been happening slowly for decades, everyone has a sense of what is at stake, though it is rarely put into words. There is something to gain, of course, or no one would ever put down a book and pick up a remote. Streaming media give actual pictures and sounds instead of mere descriptions of them. "Television completes the cycle of the human sensorium," Marshall McLuhan proclaimed in 1967. Moving and talking images are much richer in information about a performer's appearance, manner, and tone of voice, and they give us the impression that we know more about her health and mood, too. The viewer may not catch all the details of a candidate's health-care plan, but he has a much more definite sense of her as a personality, and his response to her is therefore likely to be more full of emotion. There is nothing like this connection in print. A feeling for a writer never touches the fact of the writer herself, unless reader and writer happen to meet. In fact, from Shakespeare to Pynchon, the personalities of many writers have been mysterious.

Emotional responsiveness to streaming media harks back to the world of primary orality, and, as in Plato's day, the solidarity amounts almost to a mutual possession. "Electronic technology fosters and encourages unification and involvement," in McLuhan's words. The viewer feels at home with his show, or else he changes the channel. The closeness makes it hard to negotiate differences of opinion. It can be amusing to read a magazine whose principles you despise, but it is almost unbearable to watch such a television show. And so, in a culture of secondary orality, we may be less likely to spend time with ideas we disagree with.

Self-doubt, therefore, becomes less likely. In fact, doubt of any kind is rarer. It is easy to notice inconsistencies in two written accounts placed side by side. With text, it is even easy to keep track of differing levels of authority behind different pieces of information. The trust that a reader grants to the New York Times, for example, may vary sentence by sentence. A comparison of two video reports, on the other hand, is cumbersome. Forced to choose between conflicting stories on television, the viewer falls back on hunches, or on what he believed before he started watching. Like the peasants studied by Luria, he thinks in terms of situations and story lines rather than abstractions.

And he may have even more trouble than Luria's peasants in seeing himself as others do. After all, there is no one looking back at the television viewer. He is alone, though he, and his brain, may be too distracted to notice it. The reader is also alone, but the N.E.A. reports that readers are more likely than non-readers to play sports, exercise, visit art museums, attend theatre, paint, go to music events, take photographs, and volunteer. Proficient readers are also more likely to vote. Perhaps readers venture so readily outside because what they experience in solitude gives them confidence. Perhaps reading is a prototype of independence. No matter how much one worships an author, Proust wrote, "all he can do is give us desires." Reading somehow gives us the boldness to act on them. Such a habit might be quite dangerous for a democracy to lose.

SUGGESTIONS FOR WRITING

1. Crain draws on evidence from a range of academic disciplines in his discussion of reading: sociological surveys, historical records, theories and experiments in evolutionary biology, anthropological interviews, psychological experiments. In order to explore what types of evidence you find most persuasive, create a table with three columns. In the first column, list the specific pieces of evidence that Crain discusses; in the second column, describe what you see as the strengths of this type of evidence; and in the third column describe its weaknesses. For instance, with the five surveys of reading practices that Crain mentions in the first paragraph, one strength might be that they yielded statistical evidence, whereas a weakness might be that the statistics vary widely depending on how the questions were phrased. After you've examined each type of evidence, write a paragraph in which you discuss whether you think this diversity of evidence makes Crain's case stronger or more fragmented.

2. At the end of the article, Crain draws some fairly broad conclusions about the potential effects that the decline in reading will have on our culture. Make a list of Crain's proposed consequences. For each, write your own comments on whether you think it is likely to happen. What other consequences do you envision if reading continues to decline and if video watching and Internet use continues to increase?

3. Take a few minutes to think about your own childhood TV watching habits and about your current reading habits so as to compare your own experience to the general statistics proposed by Crain. After reflecting, write down some notes, perhaps in the form of a timeline that records your TV and reading habits for each year you've been alive. As a child and teenager, how much TV did you watch? Did you have a television in your bedroom? How did TV function for your family? What sort of books did you read as a child and teenager? How many hours per day do you typically read? From these notes, develop an autobiographical essay about your lifetime of experience watching TV and reading. Note in particular any connections you can discern between your TV watching and your reading practices, as well as any connections you can make to Crain's observations in his article.

STEPHEN KING

J. K. Rowling's Ministry of Magic

Now that the dust has settled on the final J.K. Rowling literary release,
Harry Potter and the Deathly Hallows, prolific author Stephen King offers
a historical reflection on the Potter phenomenon, focusing on two specific
areas of inquiry. First, he discusses the literary merit of the Harry Potter
novels, both on their own terms and in comparison to other, less well-known
literature for children and young adults. In doing so, he brings to light some
specific elements that make author Rowling's ministry—that is, her creation
of the universe of Hogwart's School—so magical. Having covered this first
topic, author King moves from an analysis of the Potter texts themselves to
the issue of their popularity among young people. This leads him to question
suppositions made by certain academics that the mythical "young people of
today" are, considered as a whole, less literate than children of previous
generations. King takes these education theorists to task, calling them
"bigheads" and proposing his own theory: that contemporary young people,
despite their cell phones, iPods, and Wiis, are reading every bit as much, and
with as much enthusiasm, as young people of previous generations.

And so now the hurly-burly's done, the battle's lost and won—the Battle of Hogwarts, that is—and all the secrets are out of the Sorting Hat. Those who bet Harry Potter would die lost their money; the boy who lived turned out to be exactly that. And if you think that's a spoiler at this late date, you were never much of a Potter fan to begin with.

The outrage over the early reviews (Mary Carole McCauley of *The Baltimore Sun*, Michiko Kakutani of *The New York Times*) has faded . . . although the sour taste lingers for many fans.

It lingers for me, too, although it doesn't have anything to do with the ultimately silly concept of "spoilers," or the ethics of jumping the book's pub date. The prepublication vow of *omertà* was, after all, always a thing concocted by publishers Bloomsbury and Scholastic, and not—so far as I know—a part of either the British Magna Carta or the U.S. Constitution. Nor does Jo Rowling's impassioned protest ("I am staggered that some American newspapers have decided to publish . . . reviews in complete disregard of the wishes of literally millions of readers, particularly children . . .") cut much ice with me. These books ceased to be specifically for children halfway through the series; by *Goblet of Fire*, Rowling was writing for *everyone*, and knew it.

The clearest sign of how adult the books had become by the conclusion arrives—and splendidly—in *Deathly Hallows*, when Mrs. Weasley sees the odious Bellatrix Lestrange trying to finish off Ginny with a Killing Curse. "NOT MY DAUGHTER, YOU BITCH!" she cries. It's the most shocking *bitch* in recent fiction; since there's virtually no cursing (of the linguistic kind, anyway) in the Potter books, this one hits home with almost fatal force. It is totally correct in its context—perfect, really—but it is also a quintessentially adult response to a child's peril.

The problem with the advance reviews—and those that followed in the first post-publication days—is one that has dogged Rowling's magnum opus ever since book 4 (*Goblet of Fire*), after the series had become a worldwide phenomenon. Due to the Kremlin-like secrecy surrounding the books, all reviews since 2000 or so have been strictly shoot-from-the-lip. The reviewers themselves were often great—Ms. Kakutani ain't exactly chopped liver—but the very popularity of the books has often undone even the best intentions of the best critical writers. In their hurry to churn out column inches, and thus remain members of good standing in the Church of What's Happening Now, very few of the Potter reviewers have said anything worth remembering. Most of this microwaved critical mush sees Harry—not to mention his friends and his adventures—in only two ways: sociologically ("Harry Potter: Boon or Childhood Disease?") or economically ("Harry Potter and the Chamber of Discount Pricing"). They take a perfunctory wave at things like plot and language, but do little more . . . and really, how can they? When you have only four days to read a 750-page book, then write a 1,100-word review on it, how much time do you have to really *enjoy* the book? To *think* about the book? Jo Rowling set out a sumptuous seven-course meal, carefully prepared, beautifully cooked, and lovingly served out. The kids and adults who fell in love with the series (I among them) savored every mouthful, from the appetizer (*Sorcerer's Stone*) to the dessert (the gorgeous epilogue of *Deathly Hallows*). Most reviewers, on the other hand, bolted everything down, then obligingly puked it back up half-digested on the book pages of their respective newspapers.

And because of that, very few mainstream writers, from *Salon* to *The New York Times*, have really stopped to consider what Ms. Rowling has wrought, where it came from, or what it may mean for the future. The blogs, by and large, haven't been much better. They seem to care about who lives, who dies, and who's tattling. Beyond that, it's all pretty much *duh.*

So what did happen? Where did this Ministry of Magic come from?

Well, there were straws in the wind. While the academics and bighead education critics were moaning that reading was dead and kids cared about nothing but their Xboxes, iPods, Avril Lavigne, and *High School Musical*, the kids they were worried about were quietly turning on to the novels of one Robert Lawrence Stine. Known in college as "Jovial Bob" Stine, this fellow gained another nickname later in life, as—ahem—"the Stephen King of children's literature." He wrote his first teen horror novel (*Blind Date*) in 1986, years before the advent of Pottermania . . . but soon you couldn't glance at a *USA Today* best-seller list without seeing three or four of his paperbacks bobbing around in the top 50.

These books drew almost no critical attention—to the best of my knowledge, Michiko Kakutani never reviewed *Who Killed the Homecoming Queen?*—but the kids gave them plenty of attention, and R. L. Stine rode a wave of kid popularity, partly fueled by the fledgling Internet, to become perhaps the best-selling children's author of the 20th century. Like Rowling, he was a Scholastic author, and I have no doubt that Stine's success was one of the reasons Scholastic took a chance on a young and unknown British writer in the first place. He's largely unknown and uncredited . . . but of course John the Baptist never got the same press as Jesus either.

Rowling has been far more successful, critically as well as financially, because the Potter books grew as they went along. That, I think, is their great secret (and not so secret at that; to understand the point visually, buy a ticket to *Order of the Phoenix* and check out former cutie

Ron Weasley towering over Harry and Hermione). R.L. Stine's kids are kids forever, and the kids who enjoyed their adventures grew out of them, as inevitably as they outgrew their childhood Nikes. Jo Rowling's kids *grew up* . . . and the audience grew up with them.

This wouldn't have mattered so much if she'd been a lousy writer, but she wasn't—she was and is an incredibly gifted novelist. While some of the blogs and the mainstream media have mentioned that Rowling's *ambition* kept pace with the skyrocketing popularity of her books, they have largely overlooked the fact that her *talent* also grew. Talent is never static, it's always growing or dying, and the short form on Rowling is this: She was far better than R. L. Stine (an adequate but flavorless writer) when she started, but by the time she penned the final line of *Deathly Hallows* ("All was well."), she had become one of the finer stylists in her native country—not as good as Ian McEwan or Ruth Rendell (at least not yet), but easily the peer of Beryl Bainbridge or Martin Amis.

And, of course, there was the magic. It's what kids want more than anything; it's what they crave. That goes back to the Brothers Grimm, Hans Christian Andersen, and good old Alice, chasing after that wascally wabbit. Kids are always looking for the Ministry of Magic, and they usually find it.

One day in my hometown of Bangor, I was walking up the street and observed a dirty-faced boy of about 3 with scabbed knees and a look of extreme concentration on his face. He was sitting on the dirt strip between the sidewalk and the asphalt. He had a stick in his hand and kept jabbing it into the dirt. "Get down there!" he cried. "Get down there, dammit! You can't come out until I say the Special Word! You can't come out until I say so!"

Several people passed by the kid without paying much attention (if any). I slowed, however, and watched as long as I could—probably because I have spent so much time telling the things inhabiting my own imagination to get back down and not come out until I say so. I was charmed by the kid's effortless make-believe (always assuming it *was* make-believe, heh-heh-heh). And a couple of things occurred to me. One was that if he had been an adult, the cops would have taken him away either to the drunk tank or to our local Dreamboat Manor for a psychiatric exam. Another was that kids exhibiting paranoid-schizophrenic tendencies are simply accepted in most societies. We all understand that kids are crazy until they hit 8 or so, and we cut their groovy, anything-goes minds some slack.

This happened around 1982, while I was getting ready to write a long story about children and monsters (*It*), and it influenced my thinking on that novel a great deal. Even now, years later, I think of that kid—a little Minister of Magic using a dead twig for a wand—with affection, and hope he didn't consider himself too old for Harry Potter when those books started appearing. He might have; sad to think so, but one thing J.R.R. Tolkien acknowledges that Rowling doesn't is that sometimes—often, really—the magic goes away.

It was children whom Ms. Rowling—like her Fear Street precursor, but with considerably more skill—captivated first, demonstrating with the irrefutable logic of something like 10 bazillion books sold that kids are still perfectly willing to put aside their iPods and Game Boys and pick up a book . . . if the magic is there. That reading itself is magical is a thing I never doubted. I'd give a lot to know how many teenagers (and preteens) texted this message in the days following the last book's release: DON'T CALL ME TODAY I'M READING.

The same thing probably happened with R.L. Stine's Goosebumps books, but unlike Stine, Rowling brought adults into the reading circle, making it much larger. This is hardly a unique phenomenon, although it seems to be one associated mainly with British authors (there was *Huckleberry Finn*, of course, a sequel to its YA little brother *Tom Sawyer*). *Alice in Wonderland* began as a story told to 10-year-old Alice Liddell by Charles Dodgson (a.k.a. Lewis Carroll); it is now taught in college lit courses. And *Watership Down*, Richard Adams' version of *The Odyssey* (featuring rabbits instead of humans), began as a story told to amuse the author's preteen daughters, Juliet and Rosamond, on a long car drive. As a book, though, it was marketed as an "adult fantasy" and became an international best-seller.

Maybe it's the British prose. It's hard to resist the hypnotism of those calm and sensible voices, especially when they turn to make-believe. Rowling was always part of that straightforward storytelling tradition (*Peter Pan*, originally a play by the Scot J.M. Barrie, is another case in point). She never loses sight of her main theme—the power of love to turn bewildered, often frightened, children into decent and responsible adults—but her writing is all about story. She's lucid rather than luminous, but that's okay; when she does express strong feelings, she remains their mistress without denying their truth or power. The sweetest example in *Deathly Hallows* comes early, with Harry remembering his childhood years in the Dursley house. "It gave him an odd, empty feeling to remember those times," Rowling writes. "[I]t was like remembering a younger brother whom he had lost." Honest; nostalgic; *not* sloppy. It's a small example of the style that enabled Jo Rowling to bridge the generation gap without breaking a sweat or losing the cheerful dignity that is one of the series' great charms.

Her characters are lively and well-drawn, her pace is impeccable, and although there are occasional continuity drops, the story as a whole hangs together almost perfectly over its 4,000-plus page length.

And she's in full possession of that famously dry British wit, as when Ron, trying to tune in an outlaw news broadcast on his wizard radio, catches a snatch of a pop song called "A Cauldron Full of Hot Strong Love." Must have been some witchy version of Donna Summer doing that one. There's also her wry send-up of the British tabloids— about which I'm sure she knows plenty—in the person of Rita Skeeter, perhaps the best name to be hung on a fictional character since those of Jonathan Swift. When Elphias Doge, the perfect magical English gentleman, calls Rita "an interfering trout," I felt like standing up and giving a cheer. Take *that*, Page Six! There's a lot of meat on the bones of these books—good writing, honest feeling, a sweet but uncompromising view of human nature . . . and hard reality: NOT MY DAUGHTER, YOU BITCH! The fact that Harry attracted adults as well as children has never surprised me.

Are the books perfect? Indeed not. Some sections are too long. In *Deathly Hallows*, for instance, there's an awful lot of wandering around and camping in that tent; it starts to feel like Ms. Rowling running out the clock on the school year to fit the format of the previous six books.

And sometimes she falls prey to the *Robinson Crusoe* syndrome. In *Crusoe*, whenever the marooned hero requires something, he ventures out to his ship—which has conveniently run aground on the reef surrounding his desert island—and takes what he needs from stores (in one of the most amusing continuity flubs in the history of English literature, Robinson once swims out naked . . . then fills his pockets). In much the same manner, whenever Harry and his friends get into a tight corner, they produce some new spell—fire, water to douse the fire, stairs that conveniently turn into a slide—and squiggle free. I accepted most of these, partly because there's enough child in me to react gleefully rather than doubtfully (in a way, the Potter books are *The Joy of Magic* rather than *The Joy of Cooking*) but also because I understand that magic is its own thing, and probably boundless. Still, by the time the Battle of Hogwarts was reaching its climax of clumping giants, cheering portraits, and flying wizards, I almost longed for someone to pull out a good old MAC-10 and start blasting away like Rambo.

If all those creative spells—produced at the right moment like the stuff from Crusoe's ship—were a sign of creative exhaustion, it's the only one I saw, and that's pretty amazing. Mostly Rowling is just having fun, knocking herself out, and when a good writer is having fun, the audience is almost always having fun too. You can take that one to the bank (and, Reader, she did).

One last thing: The bighead academics seem to think that Harry's magic will not be strong enough to make a generation of nonreaders (especially the male half) into bookworms . . . but they wouldn't be the first to underestimate Harry's magic; just look at what happened to Lord Voldemort. And, of course, the bigheads would never have credited Harry's influence in the first place, if the evidence hadn't come in the form of best-seller lists. A literary hero as big as the Beatles? "Never happen!" the bigheads would have cried. "The traditional novel is as dead as Jacob Marley! Ask anyone who knows! Ask us, in other words!"

But reading was *never* dead with the kids. *Au contraire*, right now it's probably healthier than the adult version, which has to cope with what seems like at least 400 boring and pretentious "literary novels" each year. While the bigheads have been predicting (and bemoaning) the postliterate society, the kids have been supplementing their Potter with the narratives of Lemony Snicket, the adventures of teenage mastermind Artemis Fowl, Philip Pullman's challenging *His Dark Materials* trilogy, the Alex Rider adventures, Peter Abrahams' superb Ingrid Levin-Hill mysteries, the stories of those amazing traveling blue jeans. And of course we must not forget the unsinkable (if sometimes smelly) Captain Underpants. Also, how about a tip of the old tiara to R.L. Stine, Jo Rowling's jovial John the Baptist?

I began by quoting Shakespeare; I'll close with the Who: The kids are alright. Just how long they stay that way sort of depends on writers like J.K. Rowling, who know how to tell a good story (important) and do it without talking down (more important) or resorting to a lot of high-flown gibberish (vital). Because if the field is left to a bunch of intellectual Muggles who believe the traditional novel is dead, they'll kill the damn thing.

It's good make-believe I'm talking about. Known in more formal circles as the Ministry of Magic. J.K. Rowling has set the standard: It's a high one, and God bless her for it.

1. With the most recent novel, *Harry Potter and the Deathly Hallows,* J. K. Rowling brings the seven-book Harry Potter series to a conclusion. The first book in the series was written almost a decade and a half ago, when you were still quite young, and new Harry Potter books continued to arrive regularly, thanks to the prolific Rowling, through much of your childhood, adolescence, and young adulthood. In a first-person autobiographical narrative essay, comment upon the effect that the Harry Potter phenomenon had upon you. If you were an avid reader of the series, recall as accurately as you can the impression that certain books, or passages within books, made upon your impressionable younger mind. Feel free also to describe settings such as long lines in bookstores, characters such as Potter-fanatic friends, and narrative incidents relating to your experiences with any of the books. Contrarily, if you were an avid avoider of the whole Harry Potter craze throughout your childhood, describe the phenomenon from your point of view, most likely using a jaded or even sarcastic tone, and reflect upon why you reacted negatively, both to the publicity hype surrounding each book's release, and the cultish following that seemed to grow with each successive volume.

2. In the above article, Stephen King examines the popularity of the Harry Potter series of novels while commenting on the state of reading preparedness and interest in young people. Of the latter, he comments, "While the academics and bighead education critics were moaning that reading was dead and kids cared about nothing but their Xboxes, iPods, Avril Lavigne, and *High School Musical*, the kids they were worried about were quietly turning on to the novels of one Robert Lawrence Stine." Who is this Stine fellow, and why have we heard much less about him than we have about J. K. Rowling, in the opinion of Stephen King? If you have read any of Stine's novels, write an essay comparing them to any of the Harry Potter books with which you became familiar in younger days. If you have not read any of Stine's works, do a bit of research, find several pages of his writing online or in your school library, and write an explication/analysis of the text, commenting on the quality of the writing in comparison to that of the Harry Potter books, and speculating on its potential appeal, both for children and young adults of your own age.

3. Harkening back to Stephen King's comment about the bighead education critics in the previous question, why do you think King has such a negative view of professional academics who bemoan the state

of literacy in today's youth? Might education critics have some valid points in suggesting that today's children are less likely to read than are children of previous generations; if so, what specific reasons can you cite by way of supporting the bighead critics in their opinions? Conversely, what arguments can you make in support of King's secondary thesis, namely that children and young adults of today "are alright" as readers—that they engage with popular and even literary texts as actively and energetically as kids in the past did? In an argumentative essay, balance the two sides of this controversy, elaborating on each and ultimately arriving at a thesis that articulates your own opinion on the subject.

LAURA MILLER

Talk to the Animals

During his lifetime, British author C. S. Lewis was frequently praised for his entire literary oeuvre, but especially for his Chronicles of Narnia: *seven volumes of young adult fantasy fiction that portray Christian ideals through allegory while recreating some biblical stories in the process. Praise for Lewis's writing has continued to the present day, and both children and adults continue to find the world of Narnia captivating: some because of the aforementioned spiritual resonance, and others simply because the universe he creates, and the stories he tells, are so irresistibly magical. Laura Miller, the author of the following essay, falls into the latter camp of readers. The Catholic faith in which she was raised bred in Miller a distrust for organized religion generally, and for Christianity specifically, especially the dogmatic variety. Nevertheless, she was drawn from an early age into the Narnia series, and Miller describes, in this essay from her recent* The Magician's Book: A Skeptic's Adventures in Narnia, *how she loved the Lewis stories when she was a child while she was blissfully unaware of their Christian subtext. Later, in her teen years, when she learned of the hidden religious messages, she turned against the books, associating them with the Catholicism she had come to distrust, and even going to far as to malign Lewis for instances of racial stereotyping and social class elitism in the books. Later in life, however, she reversed this position to some degree, rediscovering the joys in his fictive world, and it is this newfound understanding and appreciation that she articulates in the following text.*

One of the first stories I found both true and terribly sad is a chapter that comes in the middle of P. L. Travers' "Mary Poppins," an interlude devoted to the infant twins, John and Barbara Banks, in their nursery. (Jane and Michael, the older and better-known Banks siblings, have gone off to a party.) The twins can understand the language of the sunlight, the wind and a cheeky starling who perches on the window sill, but they are horrified when the bird informs them that they will soon forget all of this. "There never was a human being that remembered after the age of one—at the very latest—except, of course, Her." (This "Great Exception," as the starling calls her, is Mary Poppins, of course.) "You'll hear all right," Mary Poppins tells John and Barbara, "but you won't understand."

This news makes the babies cry, which brings their mother bustling into the nursery; she blames the fuss on teething. When she tries to soothe John and Barbara by saying that everything will be all right after their teeth come in, they only cry harder. "It won't be all right, it will be all wrong," Barbara protests. "I don't want teeth!" screams John. But, of course, their mother can't understand them any better than she can understand the wind or the starling.

It's at age one that we acquire our first words. This story, which made me so melancholy as a girl, is, among other things, about the price we pay for language, for the ability to tell our mothers that it's not our teeth that are upsetting us but something else. It alludes to what we have given up to be understood by her and all the other adults, our lost brotherhood with the rest of creation. Words are what separate us from the animals, or as Travers would have it, from the elements themselves, from everything that can simply be without the scrim of consciousness intervening.

In C.S. Lewis' Chronicles of Narnia, this mournful rift is healed; there, people can talk to animals, to trees and sometimes even to rivers (as happens in "Prince Caspian"). People have longed to communicate with the universe since time immemorial—a profound, mystical longing. Lewis' friend, J.R.R. Tolkien, described this as one of the two "primordial desires" behind fairy tales (after the desire to "survey the depths of space and time"): We want to "hold communion with other living things." But since children are literalists and materialists, not mystics, their love for animals, and for stories about people who can talk to animals, is seldom understood as a manifestation of this desire.

To say that, as a child, I—and my brothers and sisters and most of our friends—loved animals would be an understatement; much of the time we wanted to *be* animals. Take us to a park or some place with a rambling yard, and we'd immediately begin mapping out the territory for one of our elaborate games of make-believe. At first, we pretended to be various woodland fauna, inspired by the "Old Mother West Wind" books by Thornton Burgess, a series our mother read to us. At home, one of us would clamber up onto the roof of our ranch house (via the top bar of the swing set) to play the eagle who came swooping down to pounce on the squirrels and chipmunks below.

This preoccupation with animals starts early. Two friends of mine, twins named Corinne and Desmond, began pointing at themselves and saying "This is a puppy" almost as soon as they learned to talk. As time goes by and the impossibility of such imaginings becomes obvious, the ache for contact grows more desperate. By age seven, when I first read "The Lion, the Witch and the Wardrobe," I longed for some better rapport with the family cats and the neighborhood dogs, with any kind of beast, really. Animals seemed like relatives left behind in the Old Country, except that the growing expanse that separated us wasn't a physical ocean but a cognitive one. They stood on the dock, getting ever smaller, while we children watched from the deck, on the way to a new, supposedly better way of being in the world, haunted by the image of what we were losing.

Animals, like infants, belong to the vast nation of those who communicate without words, through gesture, expression, scent, sound and touch. Children are immigrants from that nation, and like most recent immigrants still have a mental foothold on the abandoned shore. I believed, probably correctly, that I understood animals better and cared about them more than the adults around me. I could still faintly remember what it was to be like a beast, before language complicated things. But I didn't appreciate the inverse relationship between the individual self I was building out of the new words I acquired every day and the inarticulate world that moved away from me as my identity gained definition.

Watching Corinne and Desmond grow up, I have noticed another drawback to learning to talk: Speaking also ushers in the stage at which grown-ups stop doing anything you want just to make you stop crying. It's only when you can ask for something with words that people expect you to understand the word "no." So age one also marks the beginning of our entry into human society proper, where compromise is the price of admission. Many adults—and especially the authors of great children's books—view growing up as a kind of tragedy whose casualties include innocence and the capacity for whole-hearted make-believe. But kissing Puff the Magic Dragon good-bye happens later, on the brink of pre-pubescence. Travers, in her chapter on poor John and Barbara Banks, seems to be saying that even the smallest children have *already* suffered a heart-breaking separation, before they leave their cribs.

Words also introduce us to our most implacable enemy: time. Developmental psychologists believe that memory begins with the learning of language; to speak (or more accurately, to understand speech, since most children can comprehend before they can articulate) is to remember. With memory comes the capacity to dwell on the past and to anticipate the future; without memory, how could we know our lives and our selves? And without knowing these things, how could we own them? But as Travers' mournful little parable would have it, to speak is also to forget—to forget what it is not to remember, to forget what it feels like to live the way animals do, in a perpetual now, unaware of death and outside of time.

Animals inhabit the world of raw experience we've left behind; animals are the people of our lost homeland. To a child, an animal seems like a compatriot. The attachments that I had to the animals I knew were every bit as powerful as my feelings toward, say, my siblings (and less ambivalent, too, since I wasn't competing with the family cats for my parents's attention or a bigger share of the french fries). It's true that some adults still feel this way about their pets, and if you ask them why, the explanation often has to do with the transparency of animals' affection, their sincerity, which also turns out to be connected to their lack of language. Animals can't speak, ergo, they can't lie.

Yet the most cherished creatures in children's fantasy are *talking* animals. If we have mixed feelings about the gifts of language and consciousness, we have no intention of surrendering them. Instead, we want to bring animals along with us, into the solitude of self- knowledge, perhaps hoping that they'll make it a less lonely place for us. Children are more likely than adults to fantasize about talking beasts because kids don't have the logical faculties to see that giving animals the power of speech would surely spoil everything we like about them.

Talking animals were one of the things I loved most about the Chronicles as a child, but over the years that aspect of the books has lost its old allure. Once I would have given anything to join the Pevensie siblings at the round dinner table in Mr. and Mrs. Beaver's snug little house, trading stories about Aslan and eating potatoes and freshly caught trout. What I now like about animals—their lack of self-consciousness—I know to be intimately bound up in their speechlessness. As a little girl, I suspected them of having inner lives much like my own, if only they could (or would) tell me about it; now, I recognize that their charm lies in their lack of such secret thoughts. If my neighbor's cat, my friend's dog, the squirrel who sometimes treks along my fire escape, peering in on me while I'm reading on my sofa, could speak, would they really have anything to say that they can't already communicate well enough in their usual way: by purring, snuffling, wagging, chittering?

Stories about talking animals are not, of course, solely the province of children's literature. Folklore—which is made by and for adults—has its share of them, too, but it always uses talking beasts didactically, to personify a particular principle or trait: the wily fox, the fearsome wolf, the methodical tortoise. The animals of fable and fairytale are used to signify an identity that is simple and unchanging. Take the scorpion who breaks his promise by stinging the frog who has agreed to carry him across a river; when asked how he could betray his rescuer, he replies, "It's my nature." People repeat this parable as a way of asserting that a thief is always a thief, and a liar is always a liar, so it's best not to trust either one.

Adults rarely tell each other real stories (as opposed to fables and parables) about animal characters because the adult notion of a good story—especially now, a few hundred years into the history of the novel—demands psychological change, enlightenment, growth. When a contemporary novel with animal characters appears—Richard Adams' "Watership Down," for example—even if in most ways it meets the criteria of adult fiction, its moorings there are never secure. Chances are it will drift, sooner or later, to the children's bookshelves.

Children freely and delightedly identify with the characters in animal stories, often more easily than they identify with child characters. Children's authors know that what insults an adult reader—being likened to an animal—delights a young one. Robert McCloskey's celebrated picture book, "Blueberries for Sal," for example, is simply an extended conceit on the similarities between the toddler Sal and Little Bear—to the degree that at one point the two youngsters accidentally swap mothers. Curious George is ostensibly a mischievous monkey, but his most devoted readers recognize that he is also a wayward three-year-old.

And in Narnia, even God is an animal. Although as a girl I adored Aslan, the lion god Lewis invented to reign over the imaginary country of Narnia, he is another part of the Chronicles that no longer moves me as it once did. This is only partly because I now see, all too clearly, the proselytizing Christian symbolism, the theological strings and levers behind Lewis' stagecraft; the great lion seems less a character than a creaking device. I also stopped loving Aslan because I have since grown into the autonomy I was only tentatively experimenting with at seven. The kind of story in which a distant, parental presence hovers behind the scenes, ready to step in and save the day at the moment when hope seems lost—a narrative safety net of sorts—annoys rather than comforts me. I no longer need this in same way that I no longer need to hold someone's hand while crossing the street.

Still, being able to navigate traffic on your own doesn't keep you from wanting to hold somebody's hand every once in a while, if for different reasons. Holding hands feels nice, and this is one aspect of Aslan that has retained its charm for me. Unlike the God I was raised to worship, he is a god you can touch, and a god who asks to be touched physically in his darkest hour. In the darkest hour in "The Lion, the Witch and the Wardrobe," he says to Lewis' two little girl characters, Lucy and Susan, "Lay your hands on my mane so that I can feel you there and let us walk like that." Later, the girls climb onto his "warm, golden back," bury their hands in his mane and go for a breathless cross-country ride through a Narnia you can almost taste, thanks to one of Lewis' most exhilarating descriptions:

"Have you ever had a gallop on a horse? Think of that; and then take away the heavy noise of the hoofs and the jingle of the bits and imagine instead the almost noiseless padding of the great paws. Then imagine instead of the black or gray or chestnut back of the horse the soft roughness of golden fur, and the mane flying back in the wind. And then imagine you are going about twice as fast as the fastest race-horse. But this is a mount that doesn't need to be guided and never grows tired. He rushes on and on, never missing his footing, never hesitating, threading his way with perfect skill between tree trunks, jumping over bush and briar and the smaller streams, wading the larger, swimming the largest of all. And you are riding not on a road nor in the park nor even on the downs, but right across Narnia, in spring, down solemn avenues of beech and across sunny glades of oak, through wild orchards of snow-white cherry trees, past roaring water-falls and mossy rocks and echoing caverns, up windy slopes alight with gorse bushes, and across the shoulders of heathery mountains and along giddy ridges and down, down, down again into wild valleys and out into acres of blue flowers."

It is almost impossible to find the plain, untrammeled joy in being alive that Lewis captures in Lucy and Susan's "romp" with Aslan in the traditional Judeo-Christian canon. The scene is blissfully sensual. It ends with all three "rolled over together in a happy laughing heap of fur and arms and legs." It would be hard to imagine the two girls sharing the same intimacy with a god in the form of a man—or, rather, it's imaginable, but only with uncomfortable undertones.

"Animal" is a word sometimes used as a synonym for "carnal," and not in a good way, but Lucy and Susan's desire to touch Aslan, and Aslan's desire to be touched by them is carnal without ambivalence because he is an *actual* animal. Like most adults of his time and place (or adults of most times and places, for that matter), Lewis had mixed feelings about sex, but in this scene, at least, he escapes into a pure delight in physicality that's almost, but not quite, erotic. And although I myself am ambivalent about having to use the word "pure" to characterize that delight or—worse yet, the word "innocent," which I've so far managed to avoid—there is no other adjective for it. Even if I would prefer not to think that sexuality *contaminates* experiences, I have to admit that ambivalence about sexuality does just that. Lucy and Susan's romp with Aslan is as much pleasure as you can have in a body without sex—that is, without sex and the ambivalence that comes with it.

It's also transcendent. "Whether it was more like playing with a thunderstorm or playing with a kitten, Lucy could never make up her mind," Lewis writes. What Susan and Lucy are tumbling around with on Narnia's springy turf is something titanic and formidable, not just their own carnality with all its dormant, unpredictable potential, but a divinity who has just unleashed snowbound Narnia into the rampant vitality of spring. Yet if you're going to romp with a thunderstorm, what better form could it take than a gigantic kitten? Play and youth, too, are forces of nature.

When I read picture books to my toddler friends, Corinne and Desmond, they like to sidle up close to me. Their little fingers creep under my watchband and twine around my thumbs like the ivy that, under Aslan's direction in "Prince Caspian," pulls down all the man-made structures in Narnia. The twins can't sit still; they have to fiddle with locks of my hair, climb onto my shoulders and into my lap. I usually wind up with a foot in my solar plexus and a head blocking my view of the book I'm supposed to be reading. They make me feel like a patient old dog, beset by puppies, my ears chewed on and paws squashed. I suppose they'll only be able to get away with behaving like this for a few more years, when, inevitably, self-consciousness will set in. Except, of course, with animals, who have only ever had this way of showing their love.

SUGGESTIONS FOR WRITING

1. Laura Miller's recent *The Magician's Book: A Skeptic's Adventures in Narnia*—from which the above piece was excerpted—received many positive notices from reviewers, who appreciate its heart and insight. It also received some criticism from other reviewers, who take Miller's writing to task for its perceived bias against Christianity. One key element of *The Magician's Book* is an examination of the ways in which people develop and change as readers over the course of a lifetime. As we get older and develop intellectually and emotionally, we find new ways of engaging with authors and with the texts they produce. In a personal essay, discuss your own development as a reader, from your earliest exposure to printed books, right up to this moment. You might begin the essay exercise by simply constructing a list of all the books you can recall as having been particularly important to you, for whatever reason: kid-lit from the Curious George series, the Little Engine that Could, Hardy Boys mysteries; then, as you moved into adolescence, Harry Potter, or books from the Narnia series; then, most recently, the texts that speak to you now. Working from this list, discuss the ways in which each of the books reflects your developmental stage at the time you were reading it, along with ways in which that book might have helped shape your personality today.

2. Question 1 suggests that you make a list of books that have been important to you throughout your life thus far. If you have not already done that activity because you skipped Question 1, please do that now. Even if you have not become a fan of C.S. Lewis' writing, you will no doubt have read some of the books to which Laura Miller alludes in her writing: the *Little House on the Prairie* series, the novels featuring the magically whimsical Mary Poppins, the enchanting *Island of the Blue Dolphins,* George Orwell's allegorical and politically charged *Animal Farm*. If you haven't read any of those books on Laura Miller's list of favorites, extend your list to include others, such as the middle-school staple *Lord of the Flies,* any or all of the books from the Harry Potter series, or, more recently, the *Twilight* series of vampire books. Next, from your list, select a single book or series that has endured for you as meaningful and engaging. For Laura Miller, one such text was the

Narnia series, and she has written an entire book of her own in which she discusses the reasons why the Narnia series resonated for her as a youth, and why it continues to resonate to this day. While this assignment does not require that you write an entire book, as Miller did, it does ask you to write an essay in which you examine the reasons why your chosen text was meaningful to you at a relatively early age, and why your interest in that book has grown, or waned—or fluctuated, as Miller's interest in the Narnia series did—over the years.

3. A portion of Miller's book consists of a critique of organized religion from the point of view of a popular culture artifact—in this case, the series of Narnia novels. In an analytical essay, consider your own personal history with, and current attitudes about, organized religion. Were you raised in a particular faith? Did your parents, elders, clergy, and/or peers expect you to adhere strictly to that faith, or were you granted a certain amount of latitude in discovering your own spiritual predilections? If you were raised in a strictly religious household, has your connection to that faith continued to that day, or has it fallen by the wayside in recent years? Conversely, if you were not raised in a religious way, have you recently embarked upon a particular spiritual path, or has your lack of childhood religious direction solidified into a comfortable agnosticism? Finally, whatever your history and current position, draw some connections between your religious development/upbringing and popular culture, as Laura Miller does in the reading. Begin with the literary, as Miller does, discussing any books or other writings that reflect or helped inform your religious (or irreligious) development. However, unlike Miller, feel free to extend your examination into other areas of popular culture covered in this textbook: What role might certain television programs, movies, or song lyrics have played in defining and/or reflecting your spiritual self?

CAITLIN FLANAGAN

What Girls Want

One would be hard pressed to find a reader of the English language under the age of 25 who has not heard of the Twilight series of novels by Stephenie Meyer. With a target audience of adolescent and preadolescent girls, the books feature a young protagonist, Bella, who moves to a small and very rainy town in Washington state, develops a relationship with her high school biology lab partner, Edward—a vampire, as it turns out—and engages in a series of dangerous adventures as her romantic connection with Edward deepens and is at the same time continually challenged. The novels have been well received by most reviewers, including the venerable New York Times, which praised the novels for successfully capturing "the teenage feeling of sexual tension and alienation." The vast majority of teens, especially girls, have likewise responded positively—if not downright obsessively—to the books, although some are not quite as enchanted as those in the mainstream; in the words of one young Amazon.com reviewer, "Unlike the doting fangirls who seem to make up about 80% of the reviewers, I found it to be a bit like pudding: simple and easy to swallow, but with absolutely no nutritional value." However, while this detractor comments that "Twilight may be unoriginal, poorly written, and flimsy," she adds that "it has a strange addictiveness to it that makes you want to keep reading." In the following essay, U.S. writer and social critic Caitlin Flanagan dissects that addictiveness, discussing the ways in which Stephenie Meyer understands and skillfully appeals to the deepest desires and drives of young girls, creating texts that are virtually irresistible to girls in ways that Flanagan finds mainly positive and healthy.

Children's books about divorce—which are unanimously dedicated to bucking up those unfortunate little nippers whose families have gone belly-up—ask a lot of their authors. Their very premise, however laudable, so defies the nature of modern children's literature (which, since the Victorian age, has centered on a sentimental portrayal of the happy, intact family) that the enterprise seems doomed from the title. Since the 1950s, children have delighted in the Little Bear books (Mother Bear: "I never did forget your birthday, and I never will")—but who wants to find a copy of Cornelia Maude Spelman's *Mama and Daddy Bear's Divorce* wedged onto the shelf? Still, the volumes fill a need: helping children understand that life on the other side of the custody hearing can still be happy and hopeful, that a broken family is not a ruined one.

But pick up a novel written for adolescents in which the main character is a child of divorce, and you're in very different waters. Divorce in a young-adult novel means what being orphaned meant in a fairy tale: vulnerability, danger, unwanted independence. It also means that the protagonists must confront the sexuality of their parents at the moment they least want to think about such realities. It introduces into a household the adult passions and jealousies that have long gone to ground in most middle-aged parents, a state of affairs that is particularly difficult for girls, who have a more complicated attitude toward their own emerging sexuality than do boys, and who are far more rooted in the domestic routines and traditions of their families, which constitute the vital link between the sweet cocooning of childhood and their impending departure from it.

The only thing as difficult for a girl as a divorce—if we are to judge from stories aimed at the teen market—is a move. Relocating is what led to the drug addiction, prostitution, and death that freaked out a generation of readers in *Go Ask Alice*, and to the teenybopper dipsomania of *Sarah T.: Portrait of a Teenage Alcoholic*. In the most perfectly constructed young-adult novel of the past few decades, *Are You There God? It's Me, Margaret*, Judy Blume heightened the anxiety in her tale of a girl awaiting her first period by beginning the story with Margaret's move to the suburbs. The drama and anguish with which girls confront such disruptions to their domestic lives are typical both of the narcissism that can make living with a teenage girl one of the most unpleasant experiences God metes out to the unsuspecting, and of the ways that, for women, puberty is the most psychologically complex and emotionally alive experience of their lives. Why wouldn't a girl buck against leaving her hometown? Never again will she have such intense friendships, such a burning need to be in constant contact with the circle of girls (the best friend, the second-best friend, the whole court as carefully considered and clearly delineated as a bridal party) who sustain her through their shared experience of the epic event of female adolescence.

Twilight is the first in a series of four books that are contenders for the most popular teen-girl novels of all time. (The movie based on the first book was released in November.) From the opening passage of the first volume, the harbingers of trouble loom: 17-year-old Bella Swan is en route to the Phoenix airport, where she will be whisked away from her beloved, sunny hometown and relocated to the much-hated Forks, Washington, a nearly aquatic hamlet of deep fogs and constant rains. The reason for the move is that Mom (a self-absorbed, childlike character) has taken up with a minor-league baseball player, and traveling with him has become more appealing than staying home with her only child. Bella will now be raised by her father, an agreeable-enough cipher, who seems mildly pleased to have his daughter come to live with him, but who evinces no especial interest in getting to know her; they begin a cohabitation as politely distant and mutually beneficial as a particularly successful roommate matchup off Craigslist. Bella's first day at her new school is a misery: the weather is worse than she could ever have imagined, and the one silvery lining to the disaster is the mystery and intrigue presented by a small group of students—adopted and foster children of the same household—who eat lunch together, speak to no one else, are mesmerizingly attractive, and (as we come rather quickly to discover) are vampires. Bella falls in love with one of them, and the novel—as well as the three that follow it—concerns the dangers and dramatic consequences of that forbidden love.

I hate Y.A. novels; they bore me. That's a disappointing fact of my reading life, because never have I had such an intense relationship with books as when I was a young girl. I raged inside them and lived a double emotional life (half real girl, half inhabitant of a distant world). *To Sir, With Love* and *A Tree Grows in Brooklyn*, *Forever* and *Rebecca*, *Mr. and Mrs. Bo Jo Jones* and *Mrs. Mike*, *Gone With the Wind* and *Rich Man, Poor Man*, and even *Valley of the Dolls* (an astonishing number of whose 8 million readers turned out to be teenagers) and *Peyton Place*, as well as any movie-star biography I could get my hands on (Judy Garland, Greta Garbo—in those days, you had to have been long dead or seriously faded to be worthy of such a biography) and a slew of far less famous books written exclusively for the teen-girl market and published in paperback, never to be heard of again—all of these books consumed me in a way that no other works of art or mass culture ever have. I chose books neither because of, nor in spite of, their artistic merit, only for their ability to pull me through the looking glass.

When I read in "The Dead" that Lily was "literally run off her feet," I did not care about, or even notice, the misuse of the word *literally*, nor did it occur to me to observe that this subtle deployment of a Dublin colloquialism hinted at the story's point of view. What I cared about, intensely, was what it would feel like to be sent running up and down the stairs of a house as a teenage maid, with holiday gaieties in full force, and everyone being mean to me, instead of pampering and babying me the way my parents did on Christmas Eve. I can remember lying on my bed in a Dublin row house at 15, so immersed in Margaret Mitchell that I faked three days of illness to keep reading, and I remember lying in my own bed in Berkeley—the cat dozing at my feet, the bay wind brushing the tree branches against my dormer windows—and roaring through *A Tree Grows in Brooklyn* completely at home in turn-of-the-century Williamsburg, a place I had never even heard of before picking up the book but which I could navigate, in the landscape of my imagination, as easily as I could the shady streets and secret hillside staircases that connected my house to the record shop and ice-cream parlor down on Euclid Avenue.

The salient fact of an adolescent girl's existence is her need for a secret emotional life—one that she slips into during her sulks and silences, during her endless hours alone in her room, or even just when she's gazing out the classroom window while all of Modern European History, or the niceties of the *passé composé*, sluice past her. This means that she is a creature designed for reading in a way no boy or man, or even grown woman, could ever be so exactly designed, because she is a creature whose most elemental psychological needs—to be undisturbed while she works out the big questions of her life, to be hidden from view while still in plain sight, to enter profoundly into the emotional lives of others—are met precisely by the act of reading.

Twilight is fantastic. It's a page-turner that pops out a lurching, frightening ending I never saw coming. It's also the first book that seemed at long last to rekindle something of the girl-reader in me. In fact, there were times when the novel—no work of literature, to be sure, no school for style; hugged mainly to the slender chests of very young teenage girls, whose regard for it is on a par with the regard with which just yesterday they held *Hannah Montana*—stirred something in me so long forgotten that I felt embarrassed by it. Reading the book, I sometimes experienced what I imagine long-married men must feel when they get an unexpected glimpse at pornography: slingshot back to a world of sensation that, through sheer force of will and dutiful acceptance of life's fortunes, I thought I had subdued. The Twilight series is not based on a true story, of course, but within it is *the* true story, the original one. *Twilight* centers on a boy who loves a girl so much that he refuses to defile her, and on a girl who loves him so dearly that she is desperate for him to do just that, even if the wages of the act are expulsion from her family and from everything she has ever known. We haven't seen that tale in a girls' book in a very long time. And it's selling through the roof.

Bella and Edward meet on that unpleasant first day of school, in biology class. The only free spot in the room is next to Edward, a vacancy she initially falls into with a glimmer of excitement—like Dracula's Lucy and Mina, and like every other young woman who has ever come to the attention of a vampire, Bella is enthralled. But Edward demonstrates none of the pickup-artist smoothness of his kind. As she glances shyly at him before sitting down, he meets her eyes "with the strangest expression on his face—it was hostile, furious." As she takes the seat beside him, he leans away from her, "sitting on the extreme edge of his chair and averting his face like he smelled something bad."

In short, Edward treats Bella not as Count Dracula treated the objects of his desire, but as Mr. Rochester treated Jane Eyre. He evinces the most profound disdain and distaste for this girl. Even after they have confessed their love for each other, he will still occasionally glare at and speak sharply to her. At the end of that long first day at Forks High, Bella goes to the school office to drop off some paperwork, and who is there but Edward—trying to get himself transferred out of the class they share.

And yet they are such kindred spirits! They are both crackerjack biology students (Bella because she took an AP course back in Phoenix, and Edward because he has taken the class God knows how many times, given that he is actually 104 years old); they both love the arts; they share a dim view of the many young men who would be Bella's suitors if only she would take an interest in them. All of these facts, combined with Edward's languid, androgynous beauty—slim and feline, possessed of tousled hair and golden eyes—predictably anger and confuse Bella, although they do nothing to cool her awakening physical passion for her smoldering, obdurate antagonist. (This poignant aspect of the female heart proves once again a theory advanced by a high-school chum of mine, an improbable lothario who replied when I demanded that he explain his freakish success with the ladies: "Chicks thrive on rejection.") Edward puts the young girl into a state of emotional confusion and vulnerability that has been at the heart of female romantic awakening since the beginning of time.

Bella is an old-fashioned heroine: bookish, smart, brave, considerate of others' emotions, and naturally competent in the domestic arts (she immediately takes over the grocery shopping and cooking in her father's household, and there are countless, weirdly compelling accounts of her putting dinner together—wrapping two potatoes in foil and popping them into a hot oven, marinating a steak, making a green salad—that are reminiscent of the equally alluring domestic scenes in Rosemary's Baby). Indeed, the book, which is set in contemporary America and centers on teenage life and culture, carries a strange—and I imagine deeply comforting to its teenage-girl readers—aura of an earlier time in American life and girlhood. The effect is subtle, and probably unintentional on the part of its author, a first-time novelist, who was home with three small boys when she blasted out this marvelous book. Like the Harry Potter series, the

Twilight books are ostensibly set in the present, but—in terms of the mores, attitudes, and even the central elements of daily life portrayed within them—clearly evoke the culture of the author's adolescence. The Harry Potter series, feats of wizardry aside, is grounded in a desperate curiosity about the life of the English public school, which was a constant in the imaginative lives of middle- and working-class children in the Britain of J. K. Rowling's youth, and was also a central subject of the comics and novels produced for British children. Stephenie Meyer has re-created the sort of middle-class American youth in which it was unheard-of for a nice girl to be a sexual aggressor, and when the only coin of the realm for a boy who wanted to get lucky was romance and a carefully waged campaign intended to convince the girl that he was consumed by love for her.

Twilight is a 498-page novel about teenagers in which a cell phone appears only toward the very end, and as a minor plot contrivance. The kids don't have iPods; they don't text-message each other; they don't have MySpace pages or Facebook accounts. Bella does have a computer on which she dutifully e-mails her mother now and then, but the thing is so slow and dial-up that she almost never uses it, other than on the morning that she decides to punch the word *vampire* into her wood-burning search engine to learn a thing or two about her squeeze. But the world of the past is alive in other, more significant ways: Bella's friends, all in search of "boyfriends," spend weeks thinking about whom they will invite to a Sadie Hawkins dance. After a friend (toward whom Bella has gently been directing one of her own admirers) finally goes on a big "date" (a lost world right there, in a simple word), she phones Bella, breathless: "Mike kissed me! Can you believe it?" It was a scene that could have existed in any of the books I read when I was an adolescent; but in today's world of Y.A. fiction, it constitutes an almost bizarre moment. (Few things are as bewildering to contemporary parents as the sexual mores and practices of today's adolescents. We were prepared to give our children a "sex is a beautiful thing" lecture; they were prepared to have oral sex in the eighth grade.)

Think, for a moment, of the huge teen-girl books of the past decade. *The Sisterhood of the Traveling Pants* is about female empowerment as it's currently defined by the kind of jaded, 40-something divorcées who wash ashore at day spas with their grizzled girlfriends and pollute the Quiet Room with their ceaseless cackling about the uselessness of men. They are women who have learned certain of life's lessons the hard way and think it kind to let young girls understand that the sooner they grasp the key to a happy life (which essentially boils down to a distaff version of "Bros before hos"), the better. In *Sisterhood*, four close friends might scatter for the summer—encountering everything from ill-advised sex with a soccer coach to the unpleasant discovery that Dad's getting remarried—but the most important thing, the only really important thing, is that the four reunite and that the friendships endure the vicissitudes of boys and romance. Someday, after all, they will be in their 50s, and who will be there for them—really there for them—then? The boy who long ago kissed their bare shoulders, or the raspy-voiced best friend, bleating out hilarious comments about her puckered fanny from the next dressing room over at Eileen Fisher? *Gossip Girl*, another marketing sensation, replaces girls' old-fashioned need for male love and tenderness—these chippies could make a crack whore look like Clara Barton—with that for shopping and brand names.

Notoriously set in an Upper East Side girls school that seems to combine elements of Nightingale-Bamford with those of a women's correctional facility after lights-out, the book gives us a cast of young girls whose desire for luxury goods (from Kate Spade purses to Ivy League–college admissions) is so nakedly hollow that the displacement of their true needs is pathetic. *Prep*—a real novel, not the result of a sales-team brainstorm—derives much of its pathos from the fact that the main character is never sure whether the boy she loves so much, and has had so many sexual encounters with, might actually constitute that magical, bygone character: her "boyfriend." The effect of *Prep* on teenagers is reminiscent of that of *The Catcher in the Rye*: both books describe that most rarefied of social worlds, the East Coast boarding school, and yet young readers of every socioeconomic level have hailed them for revealing the true nature of their inner life. In *Prep*, the heroine wants something so fundamental to the emotional needs of girls that I find it almost heartbreaking: she wants to know that the boy she loves, and with whom she has shared her body, loves her and will put no other girl in her place.

Bella, despite all of her courage and competence, manages to end up in scrape after scrape: finding herself in the path of a runaway car, fainting at school, going shopping in a nearby city and getting cornered by a group of malevolent, taunting men. And over and over, out of nowhere, shoving the speeding car out of her way, or lifting her up in his arms, or scaring the bejesus out of the men who would harm her, is Edward. And at last, while she is recuperating from the near-rape, with a plate of ravioli in a café near the alley, he reveals all. Not since

Maxim de Winter's shocking revelation—"You thought I loved Rebecca? . . . I hated her"—has a sweet young heroine received such startling and enrapturing news. As he gradually explains, Edward has been avoiding and scorning Bella not because he loathes her but because he is so carnally attracted to her that he cannot trust himself to be around her for even a moment. The mere scent of her hair is powerful enough that he is in a constant struggle to avoid taking—and thereby destroying—her. This is a vampire novel, so it is a novel about sex, but no writer, from Bram Stoker on, has captured so precisely what sex and longing really mean to a young girl.

The erotic relationship between Bella and Edward is what makes this book—and the series—so riveting to its female readers. There is no question about the exact nature of the physical act that looms over them. Either they will do it or they won't, and afterward everything will change for Bella, although not for Edward. Nor is the act one that might result in an equal giving and receiving of pleasure. If Edward fails—even once—in his great exercise in restraint, he will do what the boys in the old pregnancy-scare books did to their girlfriends: he will ruin her. More exactly, he will destroy her, ripping her away from the world of the living and bringing her into the realm of the undead. If a novel of today were to sound these chords so explicitly but in a nonsupernatural context, it would be seen (rightly) as a book about "abstinence," and it would be handed out with the tracts and bumper stickers at the kind of evangelical churches that advocate the practice as a reasonable solution to the age-old problem of horny young people. (Because it takes three and a half very long books before Edward and Bella get it on—during a vampiric frenzy in which she gets beaten to a pulp, and discovers her Total Woman—and because Edward has had so many decades to work on his moves, the books constitute a thousand-page treatise on the art of foreplay.) That the author is a practicing Mormon is a fact every reviewer has mentioned, although none knows what to do with it, and certainly none can relate it to the novel; even the supercreepy "compound" where the boring half of *Big Love* takes place doesn't have any vampires. But the attitude toward female sexuality—and toward the role of marriage and childbearing—expressed in these novels is entirely consistent with the teachings of that church. In the course of the four books, Bella will be repeatedly tempted—to have sex outside of marriage, to have an abortion as a young married woman, to abandon the responsibilities of a good and faithful mother—and each time, she makes the "right" decision. The series does not deploy these themes didactically or even moralistically. Clearly Meyer was more concerned with questions of romance and supernatural beings than with instructing young readers how to lead their lives. What is interesting is how deeply fascinated young girls, some of them extremely bright and ambitious, are by the questions the book poses, and by the solutions their heroine chooses.

Bella's fervent hope—one that will not be realized until the final novel—is that Edward will ravage her, and that they will be joined forever; the harrowing pain that is said to be the victim's lot at the time of consummation means nothing to her. She loves him and wants to make a gift to him of her physical body—an act fraught with ambiguous dangers (the Twilight series so resonates with girls because it perfectly encapsulates the giddiness and the rapture—and the menace—that inherently accompany romance and sex for them). The ways in which his refusal and her insistence are accommodated are at the heart not only of this novel but of the entire series, and that inspires the rapture young girls feel for the books. This is not your seventh-grade human-development teacher passing around a dental dam and thereby making you want to send a plume of fifth-period taco salad and Gatorade into her outstretched palm. This is sex and romance fully—ecstatically, dangerously—engaged with each other. At last, at last.

As I write this, I am sitting on the guest-room bed of a close friend, and down the hall from me is the bedroom of the daughter of the house, a 12-year-old reader extraordinaire, a deep-sea diver of books. She was the fourth person through the doors of the Westwood Barnes & Noble the midnight that the series' final volume, *Breaking Dawn*, went on sale, and she read it—a doorstop, a behemoth—in six hours, and then turned back to page one as though it were the natural successor to the last page.

Posted on this girl's door—above the fading sticker of a cheery panda hopping over a pink jump rope, and one of a strawberry and a lollipop (their low placement suggesting the highest reach of a very small child), and to the right of an oval-shaped decal bearing the single, angry imperative STOP GLOBAL WARMING—is a small, black, square-shaped sticker that reads MY HEART BELONGS TO EDWARD. In the middle is a photograph of a pair of shapely female hands proffering a red Valentine heart. Also taped to this girl's closed door is a single piece of lined paper, on which she has written, in a carefully considered amalgam of block letters and swirly penmanship and eight different colors of crayon:

EDWARD'S FAN CLUB
YOU MAY ONLY ENTER IF YOU KNOW THE PASSWORD

That she had made her declaration for Edward on such a pretty, handmade sign was all-girl—as was her decision to leave up the old stickers from her childhood. One of the signal differences between adolescent girls and boys is that while a boy quickly puts away childish things in his race to initiate a sexual life for himself, a girl will continue to cherish, almost to fetishize, the tokens of her little-girlhood. She wants to be both places at once—in the safety of girl land, with the pandas and jump ropes, and in the arms of a lover, whose sole desire is to take her completely. And most of all, as girls work all of this out with considerable anguish, they want to be in their rooms, with the doors closed and the declarations posted. The biggest problem for parents of teenage girls is that they never know who is going to come barreling out of that sacred space: the adorable little girl who wants to cuddle, or the hard-eyed young woman who has left it all behind.

Years and years ago, when I was a young girl pressing myself into novels and baking my mother pretty birthday cakes, and writing down the 10 reasons I should be allowed to purchase and wear to the eighth-grade dance a pair of L'eggs panty hose, I knew that password. But one night a few years after that dance, I walked into a bedroom at a party and saw something I shouldn't have, and a couple of months after that I unwisely accepted a ride to the beach from a boy I hardly knew, and then I was a college girl carrying a copy of Hartt's *History of Renaissance Art* across campus and wondering whether I should take out a loan and go to graduate school, and somewhere along the way—not precisely on the day I got my first prescription for birth control, and not exactly on the afternoon I realized I had fallen out of love with one boy and had every right to take up with another—somewhere along the way, I lost the code. One day I was an intelligent girl who could pick up almost any bit of mass-market fiction that shed light on the mysteries of love and sex, and the practicalities by which one could merge the two, and read it with a matchless absorption. *Valley of the Dolls* had been so crucial in my life not because of its word to the wise about the inadvisability of mixing Seconal and Scotch, but for the three sentences that explained how to go about getting undressed before the first time you have sex: go into the bathroom, take your clothes off, and reemerge with a towel wrapped around yourself. One day I was that girl, and one day I was not, and from then on, if you wanted to tempt me to read a bit of trash fiction, I was going to need more compelling information than that.

Midway through *Twilight*, after Edward and Bella have declared their feelings for one another, she emerges from a classroom with a pal, uncertain whether she will eat lunch with Edward, or whether he will once again have vanished into the air, as he has a tendency to do. "But outside the door to our Spanish class, leaning against the wall—looking more like a Greek god than anyone had a right to—Edward was waiting for me."

It's a small moment in the book, but it lit aglow some tiny room of memory, if only for a maddening moment. I thought about how romantically charged high schools are for their young inmates. In 12th grade, I had a class next to the student parking lot. As I sat there one grayish day, I saw my boyfriend emerge from a side door of the massive school, along with half a dozen of his friends. They were clearly in the grip of some new plan, and they stood around their parked cars for a few minutes, talking. Where were they going, and why couldn't I go along?

The boy I was dating leaned against his car and listened to them, and he laughed, but then something happened—I could see he had changed his mind, and as the others drove away, he stood there for a while, looking after them, and then he pushed away from the car and disappeared back into school. Maybe, at long last, he was taking seriously his father's warnings that he might not graduate if he kept ditching school.

The bell rang, the room emptied—and there he was, in the hallway outside my class. "Let's ditch," he said.

I was in worse academic shape than he was; my graduation and college admission depended on passing—as a senior!—my eighth-period geometry class (many trusted souls had assured me that I'd have a bright future, provided that I passed that damn course). And standing in front of me was a boy who had just abandoned his friends to spend the afternoon with me.

I can't remember a thing about geometry except the useless phrase *side-angle-side*, but for the rest of my life I'll remember the bottle of red wine we bought at a package store a mile from school, and the certainty (since proved) that in the scheme of things, I had made exactly the right decision.

SUGGESTIONS FOR WRITING

1. Critique the passage in the above text that reads:

   > The salient fact of an adolescent girl's existence is her need for a secret emotional life—one that she slips into during her sulks and silences, during her endless hours alone in her room, or even just when she's gazing out the classroom window . . . This means that she is a creature designed for reading in a way no boy or man, or even grown woman, could ever be so exactly designed, because she is a creature whose most elemental psychological needs—to be undisturbed while she works out the big questions of her life, to be hidden from view while still in plain sight, to enter profoundly into the emotional lives of others—are met precisely by the act of reading.

   If you are a twentysomething female who has passed successfully (or not) through adolescence, hold each of Flanagan's assertions in this passage up to the lens of your own experience and evaluate the validity of each, using the form of an analytical expository essay to develop your thoughts and reactions. If you are a twentysomething male, construct a similarly analytical essay in which you explain whether or not you agree with Flanagan's points about the differences in the male and female adolescent's psyche with regard to reading behavior—both the choices of reading material and the very act of reading itself.

2. Flanagan makes an interesting pronouncement halfway through this article, observing that "few things are as bewildering to contemporary parents as the sexual mores and practices of today's adolescents. We were prepared to give our children a 'sex is a beautiful thing' lecture; they were prepared to have oral sex in the eighth grade." Write a brief research essay in which you explore your library's online database to find articles that discuss this phenomenon from a legitimate, scholarly point of view. Based upon your findings there, discuss whether or not sex practices and mores have in fact changed from your parents' generation to that of you and your younger siblings. If so, what evidence do researchers produce to substantiate the opinion Flanagan expresses here? On the other hand, if your research turns out to contradict Flanagan's statement, then why do parents make such assumptions? Finally, try to draw some general conclusions about the role popular culture artifacts such as movies, television shows, song lyrics and books such as those of the *Twilight* series have played in this shift?

3. Toward the end of this piece, the author purposely changes rhetorical modes, moving from opinion/analysis to memoir. This change is signaled by the passage, "It's a small moment in the book, but it lit aglow some tiny room of memory, if only for a maddening moment. I thought about how romantically charged high schools are for their young inmates. In 12th grade, I had a class next to the student parking lot. As I sat there one grayish day, I saw my boyfriend emerge . . . " and from there the author goes on to recount a personal anecdote that relates her own life to the *Twilight*-related themes she is discussing in this article. Using the creative non-fictional first-person "I" voice, construct a similar story in which you describe a moment of romantic awakening in your own life. In selecting such an incident, you might go as far back as a crush you had in the second grade, or you might select something that happened as recently as this week, or any time in between. As you write this memoir, keep in mind that such writing is not thesis driven, and that, unlike in academic discourse, you don't necessarily need to prove an assertion or hypothesis so much as relate a story that might have timeless and universal resonance for your readers, and that will keep them engaged through vivid descriptions and inventive use of language.

On Cartoons, Comics, and Pictographs

STEPHEN J. LIND

Reading Peanuts: The Secular and the Sacred

Charlie Brown and Snoopy. These two comic creations of Charles M. Schulz have achieved a stature in popular U.S. culture that few others can claim, right up there with Barbie and Elvis. It is quite remarkable that a six-year-old, bald-headed boy prone to grief and rejection and his imaginative, über-cool beagle should have become such a quintessential part of U.S. culture. It is even more remarkable that a mere comic strip has come to have such a profound and lasting influence on our culture.

In the article that follows, Stephen J. Lind explains some of the reasons for the popularity and appeal of Peanuts *as he discusses the two predominant ways that this comic strip has been interpreted. On the one hand,* secular readings of Peanuts *take a fairly straightforward view, focusing on how the comic strip fits into popular culture and attending to the 12 devices that Schulz used repeatedly to give meaning and consistency to his work. Sacred readings, on the other hand, see* Peanuts *as embodying a certain theology and conveying a religious, Christian message; they see Schulz as intentionally using the comic strip to spread his own Christian beliefs. As Lind puts it imidway through the article, "When the secular reader looks at* Peanuts, *he or she sees the characters in various plots; when the sacred reader looks at* Peanuts, *he or she sees deeper meaning being unearthed and proclaimed." Originally published in the online journal* Interdisciplinary Comics Studies, Lind's *article serves as an excellent example of how scholarly attention to a seemingly mundane and common element of our culture can reveal rich possibilities and new understandings.*

Introduction

Charles Monroe "Sparky" Schulz's *Peanuts* comic strip was like none before it. The children-filled frames took the world by storm, fulfilling Sparky Schulz's childhood dreams. Though he was "a barber's son brimming with insecurity, depression, loss, and resentment" (Lorberer), Schulz was able to take a kid, a dog, and some ragamuffin friends and turn them into an historic franchise—one literally for the record books. For Schulz, the success was no surprise: "Well, frankly, I guess I did expect *Peanuts* would be successful, because after all, it was something I had planned for since I was six years old" (Larkin and Schulz 6).

Schulz's interest in comics began in childhood. As he would walk home with his father, who was the local barber, the two would discuss current strips, agonizing over possible futures that lay in store for the various characters. After seeing Schulz draw a picture of a man shoveling snow, Schulz's kindergarten teacher told him, "Someday, Charles, you're going to be an artist" (6). In order to further his dream, Schulz enrolled in a correspondence course. He submitted countless cartoons to major magazines, but merely received rejection—something he was used to. It was at *Timeless Topix*, though, that Schulz got his real start. Through *Topix*, Schulz was able to produce strips for several Catholic-based magazines. Eventually, Schulz created *Li'l Folks* and sold it as a weekly feature to the St. Paul Pioneer Press (7–9). Schulz continued to work on his skills and sent his work out to major syndicates. Eventually, he mailed off some of his best cartoons to United Feature Syndicate in New York City and was given his big break (9). Once signed, Schulz's strip began to evolve, the characters changing closer to those we know now. Unfortunately for Schulz, however, the strip could not maintain the name *Li'l Folks* because of its similarity to a former strip entitled *Little Folks*. An editor who had never seen Schulz's work was asked to produce some possible names for a comic strip. One of these names, *Peanuts*, was chosen as the new banner for Schulz's strip. Schulz later said that he was "horrified" when he found out the name. The first *Peanuts* strip was then printed on October 2, 1950 (14, 25–26).

Though the first strip ended with Shermy saying, "Good Ol' Charlie Brown . . . How I hate him!" the world disagreed. Schulz went on to create a total of 18,170 strips total (Schulz *Complete Peanuts* 301). It was not a strip, though, that cemented Schulz's place in history. In 1965, Schulz's story, *A Charlie Brown Christmas*, was brought to life for television viewers. Early speculation by everyone involved was that the show would be a failure. The use of child voice actors, no canned laugh-tracks, poor animation, slow action, and an explicit religious message seemed surefire marks of the project's doom. The public thought otherwise, and the show was a sensation. When it was replayed in 1969, fifty-five million viewers tuned in to see "what Christmas was really all about." According to Garrison Keiller, "on that one night in 1969, he [Schulz] reached a larger, more diverse audience than any other single popular artist in American history. What was more, *Peanuts* was single-handedly expanding an industry that would revolutionize worldwide entertainment into the next century" (Schulz *Complete Peanuts* 300).

The engines of the franchise certainly were rolling and brought in the kind of success that the night in '69 foretold. *A Charlie Brown Christmas* and other *Peanuts* classics became holiday regulars. Many *Peanuts* classics have received nods from the movie industry. *A Charlie Brown Christmas* won an Emmy and a Peabody, despite the show's early criticism. Emmys were also won for *A Charlie Brown Thanksgiving*; *You're A Good Sport, Charlie Brown*; *Happy Anniversary, Charlie Brown*; *Life Is a Circus, Charlie Brown*; and *What Have We Learned, Charlie Brown?*. Outside of the monstrous movie industry, the *Peanuts* characters have worked in marketing campaigns for *MetLife* and the Ford Falcon (Wikipedia). In 1960, *Hallmark* began producing *Peanuts* greeting cards, a connection that has created a lasting market for the franchise. Camp Snoopy began in Knotts Berry Farm and has become a staple of several theme parks. Snoopy has made his way into Holiday on Ice and national museums. He was also featured in *The Guinness Book of World Records* after the strip sold to its 2,000th newspaper in 1984. *Peanuts* has also graced the covers of *Time*, *Saturday Review*, *Newsweek*, and other major publications. Schulz himself has received numerous and diverse honors for his greatly cherished work, including honorary degrees and international accolades (Larkin and Schulz 253).

Schulz and his body of work have made history. According to Keiller, "at the peak of Schulz's popularity, *Peanuts* captured three hundred and fifty-five million readers, and the merchandising of the brand created a franchise unlike any of the funny papers had ever known, with the cartoonist himself earning from $30 million to $40 million a year" (Schulz *Complete Peanuts* 301). Keiller continues:

At all levels of society *Peanuts* had a profound and lasting influence on the way people saw themselves and the world in the second half of the 20th century. Schulz's achievement was singular and planetary. An artist, a storyteller, he was now a worldwide industry, too. This had never happened to a newspaper cartoonist before. The new markets that *Peanuts* was dominating in stage, television, film, book, record and subsidiary forms, simply hadn't been open to newspaper comic strip artists in 1950, when United Media had given Schulz the chance to dream his dream. (Schulz *Complete Peanuts* 300).

With such wide success and circulation, *Peanuts* has elicited a variety of responses. There are two categories of such readings that I will discuss here—the *secular*, and the *sacred*. The secular reading takes *Peanuts* at its face value as a loveable pop culture comic strip with little baggage. It is simply good ol' Charlie Brown, Snoopy as Joe Cool, and endless missed football kicks. While the strip may make occasional philosophical inquiries into the human condition, no spiritual meaning is attributed to the franchise by the secular reader. This reading is the dominant reading, as Charlie Brown is not explicitly labeled as a "Christian comic" in the same way that other franchises like *VeggieTales* are. The sacred reader, however, sees *Peanuts* as existing in a moral universe and articulating a distinct religious message. Linus's philosophizing, recitation of Scripture, and belief in The Great Pumpkin are all indicators of and critical elements to the construction of an ideology Schulz is articulating through his work. While there are differing interpretations of what these acts say about Schulz's particular ideology, the acts are nonetheless seen as symbolic pieces of a Schulzian religion.

These are two distinct polar readings of *Peanuts*: the secular and the sacred. Each has its own set of reading practices that produce the resulting interpretations. In this paper I do not seek to argue for one reading's superiority, but rather I endeavor to uncover the characteristics of each reading practice, showing that it is not just the interpretations that differ, but also the process by which the reader gets to the interpretation. *How* the reader reads *Peanuts* will determine how he or she sees the franchise, as either secular or sacred. This paper will thus proceed to take up the elements of the ardent secular and sacred readings, examining their characteristics and problematizing their polarity.

The Secular and the Sacred

The secular reading is the dominant reading. As noted above, this is evidenced by the fact that *Peanuts* is not culturally labeled as a "Christian franchise" in the way that *VeggieTales*, *StoryKeepers*, and others are. Snoopy is not the marketing product of Christian bookstores, but instead fills the shelves of *Hallmark* and dances for *MetLife*. I do not intend, though, to argue that there is a singular secular reading that exists in relation to the ubiquitous Snoopy apparel, Charlie Brown mascots at theme parks or by the original comic strip itself. Instead, a secular reading has as its unifying feature the absence of religious, theological, or overtly spiritual interpretation. The results of this style of reading obviously depends on many variables, but the readings are all still in a singular category of secular, given their absence of sacred interpretation.

I do not seek to create a monolithic secular reading, but rather wish to explicate elements of secular interpretation. Because of this, I will not utilize a particular singular text as emblematic of this reading style. Instead, a multitude of texts will be utilized. Mass media reports, editorial comments, *Peanuts* anthologies, and even museum exhibits will be employed as representative of a secular style of reading. Because the secular reading is the dominant reading, and because it is represented in many ways, my objective is to examine a cross-section of these various texts in order to isolate similar characteristics of their reading practices. What is it that they are attending to in their secular interaction with Schulz's works? Three such characteristics will be examined. The secular interpretation reads *Peanuts* through the success of the franchise, through a distinct view of the characters, and through Schulz's 12 devices.

The sacred reading is set in distinct contrast to the secular reading, as it seeks to unearth a system of religious belief within *Peanuts*. From scriptural references to metaphorical Christ-figures, the *Peanuts* texts are built on and proclaim, at varying degrees of subtlety, a particular theological framework. As with the secular reading, I do not seek to create a singular notion of the sacred reading. Individuals have viewed the sacred meaning in radically different ways, and thus to claim that there is a unified sacred discourse would be unsound. Additionally, because there are a variety of particular sacred readings, it would be unwise for me to make my case for sacred reading practices reading practices based on any one sacred reading. To establish trends in sacred reading practices, I will thus utilize a variety of sacred readings, from journal articles, to sermons, to news clippings, to blog postings. There are three distinct characteristics of this reading style, which sit in convenient contrast to the secular reading style. These characteristics are a focus on intentionality, meaning, and what I call lightning rods.

Success and Intentionality

One element that secular references to *Peanuts* rest upon is the success of the franchise. As described above, *Peanuts* has enjoyed immense success in many different venues. When coming into contact with a *Peanuts* text, secular readers often read it through this success. That is to say, *Peanuts* is not seen as a religious text. Instead, *Peanuts* is read as a popular, mainstream mega-product. It is "the most successful comic strip in newspaper history," has "appeared in some 2,600 newspapers in 75 countries and was translated into 21 languages," and "has sold more than 300 million copies worldwide" (Lambiek). *People* tells the reader that "as creator of the most widely syndicated comic strip in history, Schulz added 'security blanket' to the popular lexicon; his quote 'Happiness is a warm puppy' is in Bartlett's; and Snoopy, perhaps his most enduring icon, was stenciled on the helmet's of American soldiers in Vietnam" (Chin). The secular reader does not see *Peanuts* without simultaneously seeing its cultural vitality.

The term "icon" is used frequently across the secular readings. It is seen in *People* magazine, quoted above, and a publication by *Time* asked the question, "How did a comic strip about a depressed kid become a cultural icon?" (Grossman). "Classic" is another term often used in this same way (Strauss). Elements of *Peanuts* such as Charlie Brown and Snoopy are seen as representative of American culture. They are not seen as abstract preachers atop a pulpit, but rather they are read as *part of* and *representative of* mainstream culture: "Schulz has transformed a comic strip into part of the very essence of American life. [. . .] His characters have become legends in their own comic strip lifetimes" (Berger 193). By linking *Peanuts* with the dominant culture, the reader secularizes the text. *Peanuts* is not an enclaved religious text, but is instead part of the dominant culture. That dominant culture is by its nature secular. Charles Taylor has argued that the long march of society's progress has brought us into a current "social imaginary" whereby our understanding of our society is an understanding not connected to "God or the beyond" (Taylor 187). Our culture is one that is "disenchanted," reading prominent texts through a lens of the individual instead of the divine. It is a "modern secular society" and *Peanuts* is a part of it. Taylor does not argue that God is "altogether absent" from mainstream culture, but that the sacred is now contained in personal devotion and particular political identities (193). Successful pop culture is now conceived of as independent from the sacred.

Further evidencing this phenomenon, The Charles Schulz Museum and Research Center in Santa Rosa, California, opened in Schulz's honor in 2002, "with the mission of preserving, displaying, and interpreting the art of this legendary cartoonist." Very little, if any, however, of the material in the museum reflects anything but secularity. The biography of Schulz mentions nothing of his religious affiliations. Sacred texts articulate a biography full of religious connections, from Schulz's family to his position as a Sunday School teacher. The museum's version has none of this in the biography. Nowhere on the museum's website can any potentially sacred references be found—not even a mention of Short's highly successful interpretative The Gospel According to *Peanuts*. Likewise, the successful *Charles M. Schulz: 40 Years Life and Art* by Giovanni Trimboli, triumphed for its inclusion of a preface by Umberto Eco, never explicitly addresses the question of the sacred, and only has a few strips, among the many reprints, that make scriptural references.

Hallmark is another popular source for *Peanuts* texts to come into contact with its readers outside of the traditional comic strip. A quick glance through the stores or the online Hallmark.com reveals secular dominance. There are no explicit markings of sacred meaning in any of the pieces for sale. The closest to non-secular material is the *A Charlie Brown Christmas* merchandise that one can find amidst the mounds of Snoopy products. Even this Christmas material, however, is secularized, with most depictions simply showing the children and the Christmas tree. The secular reader thus reads *Peanuts* through its success. When a reader sees Snoopy, he or she sees a part of this classic, iconic franchise that has reached millions in the dominant secular society. Discussion of the franchise is then placed in light of the success, not in light of any potential sacred meaning. This reading is further established by the secular display and merchandising that have become an integral part of the franchise's success.

While much of the secular reading sees *Peanuts* through the lens of its enormous mainstream success, the sacred reading attends more closely to an alleged intended meaning inscribed into *Peanuts* by creator Schulz. Sacred readings note "cartoonist Schulz's world," "an inhospitable world that Charles. M. Schulz has sketched," "lucid depictions of the struggle between existentialism and religious determinism," and "brilliant self-reflexive moves from Schulz" (Koresky). Other sacred readings note, "Schulz's genius lies in his simplicity, which points to some greater reality" (Cunningham). "The thing is, the heart of the special isn't Charlie Brown, or Charles Schultz's [sic] humor, but instead it's his parable of belief surrounding Linus. [. . .] he found a humorous way to express how important believing in something was to him" (Seger). "It's a rare comic strip that can include explicit theological references. [. . .] More significant theologically, however, was the world Schulz created" ("Charles M. Schulz Retires" 53); "[Schulz defined a] moral universe" (DeLuca 302). "[He] is the best at bringing religion into comics" (Foss and Howard); and "[he] considered his work far more than a job—it was a vocation. [. . .] His medium [for preaching] was the cartoon" (Gilbert).

To establish this element of intentionality, sacred readings attend to Schulz's biography. Throughout his life, Charles Schulz had a variety of interactions with Christianity. Based on that information, the reader views *Peanuts* as an outgrowth of those experiences. Because Schulz had consistent interactions with the church, it is assumed that *Peanuts* can justifiably be read as an outgrowth of that sacred involvement. The emphasis on Schulz's biography is made clear by the explicit references to it in sacred interpretations. Deluca notes that "When he [Schulz] returned from the war, he began attending church services and studying the Bible" (301). Likewise, "Schulz was a devout Christian, and he was never afraid to include that into his comic" (Seger). "Schulz, who was raised Lutheran, is active with the Church of God," (Foss and Howard). Additionally, "a conservative Protestant and member of the Church of God, [. . .] Schulz created characters that broke from strict parameters or denominations, yet reflected the beliefs ingrained from his upbringing. [. . .] He [also] taught Sunday School, and, through his Peanut gallery, searched for some sort of meaning" (Koresky).

Regardless of the success of the comic strip, the sacred reader reads *Peanuts* through a set of data that seems to reflect Schulz's intentions. Schulz was from a Christian family, studied the Bible, was active in the church, and even taught Sunday School. Therefore, if there are elements in *Peanuts* that appear to create a moral universe and express a religious truth, then the sacred reader believes that meaning was intended. This intended meaning is of great importance as it connects to 'God and beyond', and therefore forms the backbone for the sacred reader's interpretation of *Peanuts*, as opposed to circulation figures or profit margins.

The secular reader is not wholly unaware of this biographical information, however, and it seems pertinent for me to address a sort of "data debate" concerning Schulz. Blogger Mark2000 points clearly at this issue, stating, "[Schulz] was a Methodist Sunday School teacher for a time, after all. Entire books have been written about the Christian undertones in *Peanuts*; however, Schultz [sic] himself claimed later in life to be a secular humanist and is quoted as saying 'the only theology is no theology' (Farinas). The secular reader may thus refute the sacred interpretation by denying the intentions of Schulz. This denial is backed by quotes from Schulz. To answer Mark2000's subsequent question, "Just what did this guy believe in?" is rather difficult. Joanne Greenberg, author of *I Never Promised You a Rose Garden*, gave Schulz the label "secular humanist". Schulz himself once admitted in an interview, "I don't even know what secular humanism is" (Schulz *Complete Peanuts* 330). In the same interview, Schulz's belief system is articulated as clearly as anywhere else, as Schulz himself often skirted the issue, but a distinct answer is hard to identify. Perhaps he dodged the question because he wanted his strip to maintain its mainstream appeal, or perhaps he was shy in answering the question because of his lifetime of pain and rejection, suffering shyness, weak stature, failure in physics and English, rejection from publishers, his mother's death, and the marriage proposal rejection by Donna Johnson (Chin). That may explain why *Peanuts* could serve as a great outlet for his beliefs. It is also possible that his theology was difficult for him to articulate, as he said, "the more I talk about it the more difficult it gets for me to express it and it just simply gets away from me!" (Conversations 41).

The finality of the intentionality debate is impossible, as Schulz himself makes it so. He once said, "Maybe if we looked through [the strips] I could point out a few where I might be trying to say something against hypocrisy, I really don't know" (Schulz *Complete Peanuts* 329). Ultimately, though, the debate does not need to be settled to point to the characteristic of the sacred readings. A key element in how the reader interprets *Peanuts* as sacred is often the use of intention to frame the perception of the text. For the sacred reader, *Peanuts* is not a cute or classic franchise that dominates the market place with unparalleled success. Instead, it is the intentionally crafted work by a studier of Scripture and Bible teacher and has sacred meaning written in it.

Ultimately, though, it would be foolish to deny the success of *Peanuts* and the impact it has had on viewers. Certainly, the success of the franchise, along with its merchandising and consumption, has propagated a simpler secular view of *Peanuts* sitting on the store shelves. That is not to say, though, that this success forecloses the possibility of something more than commercialism being the heart of Schulz's work. While Schulz was certainly trying to sell strips that would sell papers, he has also indicated that there is occasionally something more lurking behind the beagle. While Schulz's comments about his faith, or the function of that faith, in his strips are anything but unambiguous, they do point to instances of sacred meaning within the text. In fact, the ambiguity of his statements speaks towards a desire for Schulz to have his cake and eat it too . . . desiring to maintain the pop culture success of his strip while holding onto the ability to occasionally interject a thought of sacred value. Having *Peanuts* proclaim the gospel message in a Christmas classic or having the strip contain comments about it "raining on the just and the unjust" certainly draws one's attention to Schulz's desire to have a particular ideology manifested through his work. That does not mean, though, that he intended his strip to be a sacred text in its totality, for Schulz was still trying to create a successful strip that he had been dreaming about since he was six years old. The sacred attention to intentionality segments Schulz's intentions into the sole category of the sacred, shutting off perception of other successful and intentional elements of the strip. Schulz's work is a combination of strips that investigate the human condition, strips that speak toward a sacred meaning, and strips that are simply there because they are humorous. Despite the often secular/sacred polarity, the success of the strip and Schulz's intentionality are not mutually exclusive: they are part of the complexity that is Schulz.

The Characters and Meaning

According to Berger, "We enjoy *Peanuts* because it is extremely funny. [. . .] he [Schulz] is a master of representing expressions in his characters" (183). It is these characters that drive the franchise. One way that the secular reader reads the *Peanuts* texts is through an attention to the characters in a manner that is distinct from the sacred reader. The characters of comics are "reassuring," and give the reader "something steady in their lives" (Kennedy qtd. in Astor). The secular reading focuses on the characters, not a sacred meaning behind them.

Secular readers tend to focus their attention on two key characters of *Peanuts*, namely Charlie Brown and Snoopy. I do not say this to state the obvious fact that a franchise is driven by its main characters, but rather to highlight a commonality in the secular readings that is unlike most sacred readings. A *USA Today* report on the Schulz museum notes that "it will contain permanent and rotating displays of *Peanuts* cartoons featuring Charlie Brown, Snoopy and the gang" (Sloan). Charlie Brown and Snoopy are the central and representative characters of *Peanuts*. The rest, while certainly loved and important to the history of the franchise, are ultimately 'part of the gang'. The *BBC News* postings reflect the Charlie Brown/Snoopy centrality: "I've had so much familiar attachment to his [Schulz's] characters, especially Snoopy, since I was a kid."—Maki Darwin; "No one can write a good character like Snoopy, Charlie Brown, etc."—Eli Geisinger; "Everybody have [sic] a little Charlie Brown (or 'Carlitos' in Spanish) in our heart."—Jesus Quintero; "I will always identify with Charlie Brown . . . you [Schulz] are sadly missed, but you, Charlie Brown and his friends will always be remembered fondly."—Steven Dunn; and "Snoopy is my favourite."—Ching ("Your Tributes").

As mentioned before, *Hallmark*'s merchandising is focused on key characters like Snoopy and Charlie Brown. This may begin to explain why the secular reader is attracted predominantly to Charlie Brown and Snoopy as representative of *Peanuts*. Naming is another way in which the reader is inundated with the overwhelming Charlie Brown/Snoopy centrality. It is *Camp Snoopy*, not *Peanuts* Park, and it is "*A Charlie Brown Christmas*" not "*A Peanuts Christmas*." This is certainly due in part to Schulz's unaffectionate response to the title "*Peanuts*," but also serves as a source and reflection of the dominant social association of *Peanuts* with Charlie Brown and Snoopy, not a deep ideological framework or the particularities of the gang.

As David Michaelis says in "The Life and Times of Charles M. Schulz" in *The Complete Peanuts*, Charlie Brown is a national symbol. Charlie Brown is not alone, though:

Conceived as the protagonist of Peanuts, Charlie Brown remains the eccentric hub around which all the action wobbles. He is the only player to ever get billing: *Peanuts, featuring Good Ol' Charlie Brown*. But face it, Charlie Brown, Snoopy has stolen the show. He is the figure most readily identified with the strip—or without the strip—and Schulz concedes that *Peanuts* reached the height of its popularity on Snoopy's bi-wings (Johnson 78).

While sacred meaning can be found in these two characters, as Short argues in detail, most of the explicit sacred references such as scriptural recitation come from a character simply lumped in "the gang"—Linus. For sacred readers, Linus becomes a lightning rod, attracting sacred interpretations. By reading *Peanuts* through Charlie Brown and Snoopy, the secular reader is able to avoid ideational contest with potential sacred meaning.

This is not to say, though, that reading *Peanuts* through these characters makes the secular reading necessarily flat and "meaningless," for as Condit notes, texts are rarely read as pure pleasure without further meaning (Avery and Eason 383). Instead, the reading of the strip is focused on the characters instead of a sacred message. *Peanuts* is about "Charlie Brown, Snoopy, and the gang," not about Christianity or religious conviction. Deeper meaning in the strip is then read through its relationship to the characters, not to a sacred ideology. The characters themselves are seen as "ever-so-loveable," "precocious," and "angst-ridden" (Sloan). Charlie Brown is loved because "we recognize ourselves in Charlie Brown—in his dignity despite doomed ballgames, his endurance despite a deep awareness of death, his stoicism in the face of life's disasters—because he is willing to admit that just to keep on being Charlie Brown is an exhausting and painful process" (Michaelis in Schulz *Complete Peanuts* 295). The rather existential issues discussed are not part of an overall Schulzian ideology preached through *Peanuts*, but rather are seen as elements of a particular character, namely Charlie Brown. When grief or failure or philosophical inquiry are entered into the scene, they are a part of these characters, not part of a Schulzian sermon. Linus, the one who recites the biblical Christmas story in *A Charlie Brown Christmas*, is certainly not ignored by the secular reader. Rather, he is seen as simply 'the philosophical one' in the gang. *Peanuts* is read with Charlie Brown and Snoopy as the central figures. Linus is thus part of the gang, his own character not a reflection of a totalizing *Peanuts* system of belief. Instead, he simply "has a scripture-quoting philosophical bent" (Trimboli 39).

Umberto Eco is often quoted, saying that Schulz's characters are "monstrous infantile reductions of all the neuroses of a modern citizen of the industrial civilization" (qtd. in Koerner). This philosophical discussion in *Peanuts*, however, paired with the use of children and the focus on key consumable characters like Charlie Brown and Snoopy, serves to inoculate the reader against any possible sacred reading. If the reader moves beyond consumption of the widespread *Peanuts* franchise and sees deeper meaning, then the focus on "concerns all people have" causes the reader to read the texts through a lens of universal grief, not a distinctly sacred ideological system. The occasional deep read by the secular reader sees humanity's foibles personified in the characters. There is a distinction between seeing *Peanuts* as about grief and rejection and seeing *Peanuts* as about Charlie Brown who constantly suffers grief and rejection. Even if that distinction is weak, though, the focus on characters still tends to limit philosophical inquiry and discussion of "modern neuroses" to a secular discussion, as sacred investigation is tied to Linus who is just part of the gang.

Conversely, while the secular reading views the characters, primarily Charlie Brown and Snoopy, as lovable, endearing characters with congenial insights into a universal human existence, the sacred reader sees *Peanuts* as a system driven primarily by meaning, not characters. The characters are merely vehicles for that meaning to be articulated. When the secular reader looks at *Peanuts*, he or she sees the characters in various plots; when the sacred reader looks at *Peanuts*, he or she sees deeper meaning being unearthed and proclaimed.

The focus on meaning is the central element that truly makes the sacred reading a sacred reading (though that's not to say that the other two characteristics I explain are irrelevant). The sacred meaning found within *Peanuts* may vary, but *Peanuts* is seen as being a world unto itself, a moral universe, and thus meaning can be sought out. As Marshall says, "the comic world can usefully be conceived of as a whole, as a complete universe with its own rules and regulations" (Marshall 421). As Thomas Inge further explains, "a key element in all of Schulz's work is his sense of man's place in the scheme of things in a theological sense" (qtd. in Nichols). The sacred reader attempts to understand that moral universe and identify what Schulz argues is that place. For example, it was said of *It's the Great Pumpkin, Charlie Brown*, that "the moral of the story is no matter what happens, no matter who ridicules or who falls away: Never stop believing. [. . .] [T]his special captures the core of Charles Schulz: Belief" (Seger). As Short argues (and I shall return to him later), "*Peanuts* [. . .] often assumes the form of a modern-day, Christian parable" (Short *Gospel* 21). Often, the sacred reading attends to *Peanuts* through this lens, seeing the storylines as Schulz's metaphors or parables containing a sacred meaning. For instance, "Think of Linus, the prophet without a people, who unwavers [sic] in his belief in the Great Pumpkin. [. . .] Schulz's genius lies in his simplicity, which points to some greater reality. [. . .] Jesus lived 30 years in unrecorded simplicity" (Cunningham).

Further examples illustrate this attention to deeper meaning beyond the characters themselves: "Schulz establishes that the Great Pumpkin represents something far greater than childish want; the Pumpkin is the messiah of Linus's Halloween, the holiday itself defined by longstanding religious objection and centuries-old attempts to Christianize it, becoming conflated with Christmas" (Koresky). Or more cynically:

To get a full picture of the theological beliefs of Charles M. Schultz [sic] I think *A Charlie Brown Christmas* needs to be matched up with its lesser known younger brother: *It's the Great Pumpkin, Charlie Brown*, which is a not so subtle criticism of blind faith. [. . .] Linus tries to recruit followers, passes up pleasures of the flesh, and attempts to chastise and shame nonbelievers. Linus is convinced that his suffering will result in rewards the heathens don't deserve, and they will live to regret their folly. It's pretty classic zealot behavior. In the end Linus succumbs to the same fatal attitude that got Lot's wife turned into sodium chloride (Farinas).

Further, in a sermon, Reverend McPike of the Trinity Lutheran Church says, "Lucy's little brother Linus goes to the pumpkin patch each year waiting for The Great Pumpkin to rise up and go through with lots of toys for the children. [. . .] Jesus warned of false expectations concerning the coming of the Kingdom of God" (McPike).

In a different sermon, another reverend asks, "How could anybody not see the deep theological aspects of this animated cartoon? You just have to peel away the surface in order to dig into the spirituality that lies within" [italics mine] (Reverend Steve). A Leonard E. Greenberg Center article seems to answer the question partly, saying, "In one sense, the media's relative lack of interest in the religion angle should not be surprising: Schulz had a way of injecting his distinctive Christian perspective into the main arteries of American mass culture without raising secularist eyebrows" (Hoover). The reason the meaning may be missed is the same argument that sacred readers point to for their interpretation—it's in parable or metaphor form. For sacred readers, the meaning is not laid out in *Peanuts* in four-point sermon form, but is rather hidden within and behind the characters for the sacred reader to discover, for the sacred reader to find after 'peeling away the surface'. It is in effect a system of code by which the sacred reader must look beyond the characters themselves to unlock the ultimate meaning. This thus gives rise to varying interpretations of the message, as has already been seen above with The Great Pumpkin being a symbol of both faith and heresy. While Mark2000 argues that the Schulzian system is one critiquing faith, the Greenberg article claims that "there was a substructure of decidedly non-sugarcoated Christian theology—God is sovereign, no matter how difficult things get; humanity is fallen, sustained only by the grace of God" (Hoover).

This dichotomy of the characters and deeper meaning, however, stands in over-simplified opposition. While the secular reader tends to view *Peanuts* as the Charlie Brown and Snoopy show, and the sacred reader looks for meaning behind that, both views miss the complex interweaving as they stand at wrongful extremes. *Peanuts* certainly is about Charlie Brown, Snoopy, and the gang. Schulz makes it so throughout his work. However, Schulz also has much of his work investigate themes of the human condition—grief, loss, hope, etc. For the sacred reading to stand in opposition to this is naive. Much complexity can be seen in Schulz's packaging of grand philosophers in six-year-old bodies. Charlie Brown is the prime example of a character with afflictions and deeper meaning. He constantly suffers loss and rejection, only to continue on the next day, ever hoping to kick that football. Schulz speaks to his adult readers through these common themes, but in no way speaks a message of simplicity. Schulz's interrogation of humanity through Charlie Brown's constant rejection also betrays the notion that only the sacred reader holds claim to Schulz's intentionality. Schulz's biography may read to the ardent sacredist as ripe for the pulpit, but it also reads to the objective reader as being full of rejection and loss that is later mirrored in *Peanuts*. For instance, the Little Red Haired Girl is a representation of Donna Johnson, the woman that rejected Schulz's marriage proposal. She does not share the spotlight with Charlie Brown and Snoopy, and is actually only a fringe member of "the gang," but she symbolizes for Schulz and the interested reader a truth of rejection that is deeper than a quick read of Joe Cool. Schulz's characters are not simple. They are also not averse to deeper theological meaning as the Gospel message is read every Christmas, and Scripture is occasionally invoked, but the meaning found in Luke is certainly not the only meaning Schulz investigates.

Schulz's 12 Devices and Lightning Rods

The final way that the secular viewer reads *Peanuts* is through Schulz's 12 devices. These devices serve to reinforce a sense of steadiness, simplicity, and universal appeal in *Peanuts*. These "devices" are the recurring elements throughout *Peanuts*: "Schulz identifies [these devices] that have worked so well he is willing to attribute to them his strip's historic popularity. He is particularly proud of the ideas, for they are products of his unique intellect, things no one else would have thought of. Or at least no one did. To Schulz, [these are] the twelve things that helped make *Peanuts*" (Johnson 74). (These twelve devices are: the kite-eating tree; Schroeder's music; Linus's blanket; Lucy's psychiatry booth; Snoopy's doghouse; Snoopy himself; The Red Baron; Woodstock; the baseball games; the football episodes; The Great Pumpkin; and The Little Redhaired Girl (72–83)).

The secular reader often reads *Peanuts* through these recurring themes. *Peanuts* is 'about' these twelve devices—they 'are' *Peanuts*. For instance, one journalist wrote, "No more Charlie Brown? Think what that means. No more Charlie trying and trying and trying to kick a football [. . .]. This is terrible. Because if you love sports for what sports can be, you had to love good ol' Charlie Brown" (Kindred 70). The covers of the 40th and 50th year anthologies feature Snoopy and Snoopy's doghouse, respectively. An article that referred to Charlie Brown as a "cultural icon" explained that "Charlie Brown tried to kick a football for the first time in November 1951" (Grossman). Another report says, "For millions, it's a sad day for the funny pages. [. . .] [Charlie Brown] has spent nearly half a century trying to kick a field goal, avoid kite-eating trees, and work up enough courage to say 'hello' to his secret crush" (Koerner). The *BBC News* postings reflect the same sentiments: "I will always remember my most favourite stuffed animal growing up-my Snoopy dog."—E. Price; "My favourite strip was one about 25 years ago where Lucy asks Charlie Brown what are the 3 certainties in life while he starts to run up to kick the football. He replies 'death and taxes' but cannot remember the third until Lucy inevitably takes the ball away at the last minute and he lands flat on his back. Then he remembers!"—Richard

Barnett; and "[Linus and Snoopy's] eternal struggle over Linus's blanket fills many warm memories from my childhood."—Matt Tedone ("Your Tribute"). It was also in the sixties that Snoopy's doghouse burned in the strip, prompting a flood of sympathy letters from fans.

Schulz said, "A cartoonist is someone who has to draw the same thing day after day after day without repeating himself" (Schulz *You Don't Look* 35). That is what Schulz did through these twelve devices. He created the world of *Peanuts* such that these twelve repeating elements become *Peanuts* for the reader. The creative repetition tells readers that this is what *Peanuts* is really all about. If scripture is quoted from the pitcher's mound, the theological reference is not what *Peanuts* is about, but rather *Peanuts* is about the baseball game that we are seeing once more, and all the zaniness that comes with nonchalant shortstops and Beethoven-loving catchers. The scripture references are simply a new twist on the device; the device is not a new twist on scripture. Umberto Eco says, "[comics] continue to repeat the same story ad nauseam, but they do, however, give viewers or readers the impression that they are reading a new story. Readers believe they're reading a new story, and yet they're gratified to find they're reading exactly the same story all the time" (in Trimboli 8–9). The twists on the device make the comic enjoyable, but at its core, the device itself is the constant that the secular reader can read *Peanuts* through. *Peanuts* is not about 'God or the beyond'; *Peanuts* is about these little kids dealing with pumpkins, kites, footballs, and crushes.

The discussion brings us now to the final characteristic of the sacred reading style, an element that for many sacred readers is really the starting point. This characteristic is the attention to what I call lightning rods as opposed to the twelve devices. By lightning rods, I mean elements found throughout the discourse that attract a distinct interpretation or style of reading. For *Peanuts*, there are three key lightning rods: *A Charlie Brown Christmas*, scriptural references, and Robert Short's works. These elements attract sacred analysis and for the sacred reader justify a sacred interpretation. The sacred reader sees *Peanuts* in light of these elements, as opposed to seeing *Peanuts* as a composition of the repeated twelve devices. A given strip is not another football episode, but is rather a place where deeper meaning, biblical truth, or parable may be found.

A Charlie Brown Christmas is the first lightning rod. Set as a Christmas tale, this Charlie Brown escapade is inherently positioned within a potentially theological realm. Other Christmas classics, however, like

Rudolph and The Grinch, are not seen as theologically centered. It is Linus's recitation of the Gospel of Luke that declares *A Charlie Brown Christmas* as a Christian proclamation. As Linus says, "That's what Christmas is all about." For the sacred reader, Schulz's distinctly Christian classic is a proclamation that 'That's what *Peanuts* is all about.' The story of the "Christmas classic that almost wasn't," the Christmas special being too genre-breaking to be a success, reinforces the notion that this is an important benchmark in the *Peanuts* franchise. As Bill Melendez said, "[Schulz] wanted to be very straightforward and honest, and he said what he wanted to say because he was a very religious guy. When I first looked at that part of the story I told Sparky, 'We can't do this, it's too religious.' And he said to me, 'Bill, if we don't do it, who else can? We're the only ones who can do it'" (Mendelson 39–40). Subsequently, *Peanuts* is read as extensions of this message that only Schulz and company could give. In Condit's terms, *A Charlie Brown Christmas* serves as an "historical agent" to ground further reflection on related texts (Avery and Eason 377–378). For instance, *It's the Great Pumpkin, Charlie Brown*, aired the year after the Christmas Special, is seen in relation to the real meaning of Christmas. Koresky argues that because of his place as prophet in *A Charlie Brown Christmas*, "even before the start of *It's the Great Pumpkin*, Linus has already been waiting for a sign, something that will literally drop from the sky and make itself known as a messenger of good tidings." For Koresky, the connection between Halloween and Christmas in the discussions of The Great Pumpkin further reinforces a connection between the two stories. Additionally, Mark2000's blog post, quoted earlier, which argues that the Halloween special must be read in addition to the Christmas special in order to "truly" understand Schulz's theology, speaks to the tendency for sacred readers to view the implications of Schulz's work in light of *A Charlie Brown Christmas*.

Unlike the secular reading, focusing on Charlie Brown, Snoopy, and "the gang," the sacred reading gives Linus a higher place of prominence, in that he is the one with that prophetic-bent. Linus is not the only character, though, to articulate concepts of theological merit. This brings us to our second lightning rod, scriptural references. These scriptural references are located within the strips themselves, though, as noted before, it is often easy to forget that the franchise is driven by "a strip that runs in the local funnies." Charlie Brown once read to his sister, ". . . But David won the fight when he hit Goliath in the head with a stone . . ." to which Sally replied, "What did Goliath's mom say about that?" (Larkin and Schulz 141). Snoopy quoted The Song of Solomon when writing a letter to his sweetheart Truffles (Short *Short Meditations* 73). Charlie Brown once quoted from the book of Isaiah to Snoopy at dinner, saying "The dogs have a mighty appetite . . . they never have enough;" Sally once made Christmas cards where "each one has a little bunny on it dressed like a shepherd," prompting her to warn "Don't say I'm not religious!!" and Lucy once noted, "I was praying for greater patience and understanding but I quit . . . I was afraid I might get it" (Schulz *You Don't Look* 35). According to Short, approximately ten percent of Schulz's strips contain explicit theological references. While this means that 90 percent of the strip is of a more on-face secular nature, the sacred reader sees it as a large amount of a comic strip that has a consistent reflection on a system of sacred meaning. To the sacred reader, it 'makes sense' to read *Peanuts* as an extension of biblical truth because it is biblical truth that the characters are quoting. The scriptural references within the strip thus attract broader sacred readings of the franchise.

We are now brought to a work of broader sacred reading and our final lightning rod, the works of Robert L. Short. Short first wrote *The Gospel according to Peanuts* in 1964, and it has subsequently become the most prominent sacred reading of *Peanuts*, even included in some chronologies of the franchise (Larkin and Schulz 253). Because of its prominence, selling over ten million copies, Short's work, along with his two subsequent books, *The Parables of Peanuts* and *Short Meditations on the Bible and Peanuts*, has attracted an increasing amount of sacred interpretations. Short's work strays from the typical sacred reading practices that I have outlined above, though, in that he believes that "*Peanuts* lends itself easily to this kind of Christian interpretation, whether these thoughts were always in the artist's mind or not" (Short *Gospel* 124). His reading is one built on a purpose—to share the Gospel—and he sees *Peanuts* as a vehicle to do so. *Peanuts* strips serve as parables, conveying truth in a similar manner to the stories that Christ told in the gospels. Short reads *Peanuts* for his own teleological purposes, not for Schulz's theological intentions. In contrast to most sacred readings, Short claims to read *out of*, not *into Peanuts* (26). Nonetheless, his project has been simplified to a work that establishes a connection between Christian Truth and *Peanuts* and thus attracts further sacred reading. These readings are attracted by these lightning rods, and in light of Schulz's theological ties, focus on the deeper meaning behind the characters.

While the secular reader has a tendency to read *Peanuts* through the twelve devices, and the sacred reader is attracted to theological themes through the various lightning rods, neither view speaks of the whole truth. Schulz himself declared that he was proud of making *Peanuts* revolve around his twelve devices, and the readings of the strip show that he was successful. As with the discussion of characters, that does not mean that these twelve devices foreclose the possibility of deeper meaning being found (though that deeper meaning is not necessarily always of sacred kind). The ardent secular reader sees *Peanuts* solely through the lens of the twelve devices, missing the signal that explicit sacred references give. To the ardent secular reader, The Great Pumpkin is simply a cute part of the Halloween tradition, but this interpretation misses the cues that Schulz gives that something more is potentially being said. It is no accident that The Great Pumpkin is conflated with Christmas, set in opposition to materialism, and couched in explicit terms of religion and denomination. Something is being missed by the strict secular reader. The sacred reader, however, is not without fault. Schulz may be saying something at particular times through The Great Pumpkin, but that is not to say that the twelve devices that Schulz loved so dearly are merely there for the rare occasion to shine forth the light of the Gospel. To view the twelve devices solely as vehicles for sacred meaning reduces the strip down to a simplicity while the sacred reader simultaneously accuses the secularist of utter simplicity. While *A Charlie Brown Christmas* may be telling of Schulz's beliefs, this does not mean that a strictly sacred reading of all of *Peanuts* is justified. Instead, these lightning rods should be viewed as indicators of potential messages within *Peanuts*. They should open the eyes of the reader, allowing for the possibility that one may see sacred references in the strip, but they should not instruct the reader to search out sacred meaning in every instance of the franchise. These lightning rods are cues, not instructions. Generally speaking, the extreme secular reading tends to be too shallow, while the ardent sacred reading is too narrow. Both extremes miss the mark.

Conclusion

There are two polarized ways of reading Peanuts. It has been read by some as a part of our secular mainstream society. Others view it as a sacred text—a sermon-in-a-strip. The processes of reading differ as much as the ultimate interpretation. I said in the Introduction that I was not going to argue for the superiority of either the sacred or secular readings. I believe I have kept that promise, for both the sacred and secular readings are one-sided. It is not even enough to say that they are two sides to the same coin, but rather they are more like two lenses to the same pair of 3-D glasses. A seemingly complete figure may be seen by looking through only one lens, but it closes off the truth that the other eye could see, and further, it hides the simple intricacies visible only through both lenses. Both the secular and sacred interpretations contain valid arguments for their positions. The error in either way is seeing interpretation as an activity of strictly dichotomous results—as *either* secular or sacred. Perhaps it is a little bit of both. *Peanuts* is a complex topography of simplicity crafted by an artist with a personal ideology that inevitably shaped the final three-dimensional product. At times this shaping takes the form of explicit message or parable; at other times, this ideology has no explicit ties to a final proclamation. Is *Peanuts* secular? Is it sacred? Yes. Both views have merit, but both are too polar. *Peanuts* is not simply a secular or a sacred text, it's the artistic working of a man who suffered loss, had an interest in the sacred, wanted people to laugh, had a dog, knew a girl, had some kids, and ultimately drew it all on paper for the world to see.

The exploration of reading practices does allow for further investigation. In particular, other texts are read through the secular/sacred dichotomy, such as C. S. Lewis's *Chronicles of Narnia* and J.R.R. Tolkien's tales of Middle Earth. An examination of the rhetorics of the readings in conjunction with the texts offers insight in many avenues, such as audience interpretation, intentionality, and encoded meaning. This study of *Peanuts* is merely a minor representation of the work that could take up questions comparing *Narnia's* great box office results to Bruner and Ware's *Finding God in the Land of Narnia*, and the like. The characteristics of reading practices described here, while specifically tied to *Peanuts*, will likely serve as a rough map for the ways readers take up these other texts. Additionally, by attention to potential lightning rods, the critic may be able to draw even more works into this particular field of inquiry.

This examination of *Peanuts* also cues us in on more fundamental elements of reading practices. The elements of the polarities highlight critical elements of texts that must be attended to . . . intentionality, repeated devices, etc. More importantly, these elements do not always receive equal attention. This serves the critic by expanding his/her field of vision when exploring the interaction between the text and the audience. Just because a text enjoys great cultural success, for instance, does not mean that all of its audience will view it through that lens. Nor do an author's vocalized intentions guarantee that the text will be viewed in that light. The critic must be careful not to wrongfully assume that an audience has or will interpret a text through any given mode. Likewise, when a critic endeavors to posit his/her own interpretation of a text, the intricate possibilities must each be considered with an ever-present guard against oversimplification and false dichotomies. As seen here, these practices are of particular importance when dealing with the secular and the sacred. Ultimately, this particular paper joins the ranks of the countless responses to the late Charles M. Schulz's work. The strip drove a franchise into success and circulation that has afforded such extreme and diverse readings. What drove the strip was a boy, his dog, and some friends. What drove them was a master artist, Sparky Schulz.

REFERENCES

Astor, David. "The Cartoon Dilemma." *Brandweek* 08 May 2000: 40–45.

Avery, Robert and David Eason. *Critical Perspectives on Media and Society*. New York: The Guilford Press, 1991.

Berger, Arthur Asa. *The Comic-Stripped American; What Dick Tracy, Blondie, Daddy Warbucks and Charlie Brown Tell Us About Ourselves*. New York: Walker, 1973.

Bruner, Kurt and Jim Ware. *Finding God in the Land of Narnia*. Wheaton: Tyndale House Publishers, 2005.

"Charles M. Schulz." *Conversations*. Ed. M. Thomas Inge. Jackson: University Press of Mississippi, 2000.

"Charles M. Schulz Biography." Charles M. Schulz Museum and Research Center. 11 Apr 2006 http://www.schulzmuseum.org.

"Charles M. Schulz Retires." *Christian Century* 19 Jan 2000: 53.

Chin, Paula. "Gentle Genius." *People* 28 Feb 2000: 52–60.

Cunningham, Andy. "The Beauty of Simplicity." Online Posting. 01 Nov 2005. Blogspot. 11 Apr 2006 http://southern...rsion.blogspot.com.

DeLuca, Geraldine. "I Felt a Funeral in My Brain": The Fragile Comedy of Charles Schulz." *The Lion and the Unicorn 25* 25 (2001): 300–09.

Farinas, Mark. "Exactly What Kind of Christian Was Charles Schultz?" Online Posting. 23 Dec 2005. 11 Apr 2006 http://mark2000.com/?p=41.

Foss, Sarah and Scripps Howard. "Subtle Blend of Humor and Religion in the Comics." *Plain Dealer* 12 Feb 2000: 1F.

Gilbert, Richard. "The Gospel According to *Peanuts*: A Tribute to Charles Schulz." First Unitarian Church of Rochester, 2000. 12 Apr 2006 http://www.roch...2000/20000514.html.

Grossman, Lev. "Suffer the Little Children." *Time* 03 May 2004: 72–73.

Hoover, Dennis R. "*Peanuts* for Christ." *Religion in the News* Summer 2000.

Johnson, Rheta Grimsley. *Good Grief: The Story of Charles M. Schulz*. 2nd rev. ed. Kansas City: Andrews and McMeel, 1995.

Kindred, Dave. "A good man, that Charlie Brown." *The Sporting News* 10 Jan 2000.

Koerner, Brendan I. "Good Grief! Charlie Brown Says So Long." *U.S. News & World Report* 27 Dec 1999: 28.

Koresky, Michael. "The Book of Linus." *Reverse Shot* 2004.

Lambiek. "Comic Creator Charles Schulz." 2006. 12 Apr 2006 http://www.lambiek.net.

Larkin, David and Charles M. Schulz. *Peanuts: A Golden Celebration: The Art and the Story of the World's Best-Loved Comic Strip*. New York: HarperCollins, 1999.

Lorberer, Eric. "Charles M. Schulz." *CityPages* 927. 9 Sept 1998.

Marshall, Geoffrey. "Comic Worlds within Worlds." *College English* 32.4. (1971): 418–427.

McPike, Jeffrey D. "Thy Kingdom Come." Trinity Lutheran Church. 2001. 10 Apr 2006 http://lcmsserm...m/index.php?sn=333.

Mendelson, Lee. *A Charlie Brown Christmas: The Making of a Tradition*. Carbondale: HarperCollins, 2000.

Nichols, Bill. "The Christmas Classic That Almost Wasn't." *USA Today* 06 Dec 2005.

Reverend Steve. "Lessons 16 and 17 of Wood." *The Holy Lessons of Wood*, 1999. 17 Apr 2006 http://lessons....od.org/L16-17.html.

Schulz, Charles M. *The Complete Peanuts*. Seattle: Fantagraphics Books, 2004.

——. *You Don't Look 35, Charlie Brown!* 1st ed. New York: Holt, Rinehart, and Winston, 1985.

Seger, Sean. "Jaded Geek Reviews It's the Great Pumpkin Charlie Brown." *JadedGeek*, 2005. 10 Apr 2006 http://www.jade.../great_pumpkin.htm.

Short, Robert L. *The Gospel According to Peanuts*. Louisville: Westminster/John Knox Press, 1965.

——. The Parables of *Peanuts*. San Francisco: HarperCollins, 2002.

——. *Short Meditations on the Bible and Peanuts*. Louiseville: Westminster/John Knox Press, 1990.

Sloan, Gene. "You're a Good Topic for a Museum, Charles Schulz!" *USA Today* 09 Aug 2002: 01d.

"'Sparky' Schulz, Newspaperman." *Editor & Publisher* 133.8 (2000): 16.

Strauss, Gary. "Compilation Grows from Early '*Peanuts*'." *USA Today* 15 Mar 2004.

Taylor, Charles. *Modern Social Imaginaries*. Durham: Duke University Press, 2004.

Trimboli, Giovanni. *Charles M. Schulz: 40 Years Life and Art*. New York: Pharos Books, 1990.

Wikipedia, The Free Encyclopedia. *"Peanuts."* 2006.

"Your Tributes to the Creator of *Peanuts*." *BBCNews*, 2000. 11 Apr 2006 http://news.bbc...g_point/641394.stm.

SUGGESTIONS FOR WRITING

1. Lind discusses three key points that support each of the two ways of interpreting *Peanuts*. In this exercise, create a diagram or other visual representation of these six points discussed by Lind. Do this by first summarizing each point and condensing it to perhaps 30–40 words; handwrite or print these summaries and then cut them out. On a larger sheet of paper, decide where to place the summary of each point and how to show the connections between points. Include labels or additional text if this helps clarify your diagram. Finally compare your visual overview of Lind's article to overviews created by other students in your class; how do they represent Lind's article similarly and differently?

2. Although Lind claims that both the secular and the sacred interpretations of *Peanuts* have validity, this exercise asks you to choose one of the interpretations and argue for its superiority. Working with the evidence that Lind provides as well as with any additional evidence you find through research, write an essay that argues that either the secular or the sacred way of reading *Peanuts* is correct. Consider showing both the strengths of the interpretation you're arguing for as well as the weaknesses of the interpretation you're arguing against.

3. In his conclusion, Lind states that the secular and sacred readings of *Peanuts* are one-sided: "It is not even enough to say that they are two sides to the same coin, but rather they are more like two lenses to the same pair of 3-D glasses." With both perspectives, in other words, we get a fuller and more accurate interpretation of *Peanuts*. Lind also suggests that this is the case for all practices of reading and interpretation, and that critics need to see texts through multiple lenses. Follow up on this concept by developing multiple interpretations of a single cultural item. Choose a famous person or character (for example, Barbie, Elvis, Tiger Woods); a popular event (for example, Halloween, the Olympics, election day); or a well-known symbol (for example, the Nike swoosh, the red carpet at the Oscars, a skateboard). Then make a list of different possible meanings that this item might have for different audiences (young and old, male and female, rich and poor, secular and sacred). Choose three or four possible interpretations and develop each

of them in a brief descriptive paragraph. Finally, comment on whether these multiple interpretations do indeed give you the metaphorical 3-D glasses of interpretation that Lind discusses.

JOHN CATALINI

Pictographs Go Pop: How Classroom Posters Can Transform Words and Images Into Learning Strategies

Like most popular writing, cartoons, comic strips, and comic books are intended primarily for our entertainment. They differ from other forms of fiction and nonfiction in that they use images as well as words to captivate their readers, but still, the ultimate goal is to amuse and interest us. As you can see in the next article, though, word/image combinations can be more than entertaining; they can be—yikes!—downright educational. John Catalini, a wonderfully inventive writing instructor at UC Santa Barbara, uses what he calls "pictographs" in his classes to help his students read carefully and think critically. He asks his students to literally picture their thinking by responding to texts not only with writing but also with drawing. As students visualize and write about the books they're reading—and about other "texts" they encounter daily, such as music, TV shows, or current events— they can draw connections and come to new kinds of insights, accessing both their verbal and visual brainpower. In the article that follows, Catalini shows us three examples of his own pictographs and he discusses, in a unique and engaging style, the general method and rationale behind his approach.

A Primer for Your Perusal

One thing to remember about reading anything is that some person created it, at some time, in some place, and for some reason. That person wrote it, sketched it, painted it, photographed, sculpted, or cooked it. And she or he had you in mind. Really. So your job is to be actively engaged. Swing along. Think critically, but also feel, relate. See, hear, taste, smell or touch with pizzazz. Enjoy the work of it.

Thoughts Are Images, Images Thoughts

In her 1994 book, *Bird by Bird: Some Instructions on Writing and Life*, Anne Lamott suggests to beginning writers that they write down what they see "through a one-inch picture frame" (17). She goes on to tell an anecdote about her ten-year-old brother's being overwhelmed by trying to write a three month research report on birds, in just one night. Comforting them, their father advised, " 'Bird by bird, buddy. Just take it bird by bird' " (19).

So we all learn to write and read, word by word—or line by line, color by color, image by image, by states or by meals. "You come, too," the speaker says in Robert Frost's poem *The Pasture*. Let's clear away the winter debris from the meadow spring. It's an open invitation, like learning to read gestures and seasons. We all want to make sense of things.

But it takes practice, and patience. Twigs, leaves, ideas and words can seem hopelessly intertwined. Where to begin?

You already know one strategy: take notes. And most of us mix our notebook jottings with underlining, highlighting, circles, stars, doodles or sketches. We draw stuff to emphasize, prioritize, illustrate, or just plain "picture" our thinking, or someone else's. It helps us to "figure" it out. Study medieval manuscripts, Leonardo de Vinci's notebooks, or storyboard concepts for films; they bristle with words and pictures.

Are you keeping up? Good—no, great! Words are just images with attitudes. Can you visualize a concept? Is a wave water?

Don Quixote, Linguistic Athlete

Some words have back stories the way iconic images have cultural ancestries. Edvard Munch's painting *The Scream* begat Andy Warhol's prints, begat the mock horror film series, begat the Halloween mask for children. Yikes! Dante's *Inferno*, Mary Shelley's *Frankenstein*, and the North American Iroquois' false face masks probably belong in there, too. We read the pictures, name the contexts, and write them down: expressionism, pop art, scary movies, and rituals. Pictures and words, words and pictures.

The notes and images in Figure 1 form a pictograph study aid. Stolen from prehistoric cave dwelling artists, it is a technique to make meaning and memory stick with us. It's part of the broad spectrum of our shared design alphabet, of how we "keep track" of stuff.

Let's take a simple word like *tilt*, for instance. In the lexicon of the modern sports writer, that's a somewhat old-fashioned word that can

Figure 1

come off the bench for *match, game, contest, encounter, meeting,* and the like. (The use of *battle* and its technowarfare metaphors is cliché, baby.) *Tilt* also lit up old school pinball machines when the operator's game got too violent, as in tipping the whole contraption. It can be a verb as well, when the field or pitch or court *tilts* against a team and the players have to fight uphill.

Speaking of the Middle Ages (manuscripts, remember?), way back in the day, *tilt* was about thrusting a lance in a joust. Two knights rode their horses at each other—everybody in armor—and tried to knock each other down to win a tournament championship and some cash. Today, we still say people are moving *at full tilt* when they smash into each other; think demolition derby or teenage romance.

The superstars in this sinister field (that's a heraldric pun) are King Arthur, Lancelot (an unwitting pun?), Ivanhoe, Heath Ledger (*A Knight's Tale*, the film), and the baddest of them all in real battle, Joan of Arc—and many wannabes. (Some undergraduate students would say a *plethora*. Ugh.) The real "people's choice" should be the Weary Dreamer himself.

The Ingenious Gentleman Don Quixote of La Mancha is the creation of Spanish writer Miguel de Cervantes Saavedra (1547–1616). The Don is a knight errant who suffers from his own errors. With his famous sidekick Sancho Panza, the madman sets out to perform heroic deeds for Dulcinea, a "lady" of questionable repute. *Don Quixote* is a satire dressed up as a romance.

One episode features the self-proclaimed redoubtable warrior in full gear on his nag Rosinante, charging a giant; only it is a foe made of wood and gears—a windmill. People who today take on perceived enemies, real or not, without much chance of success, may be accused of *tilting at windmills*.

Don Quixote is idealistic, a romantic who is unaware of practicalities; he is capricious and impulsive. That's what the dictionary gives as the meanings for *quixotic*. What it fails to add is that everyone who reads about the old geezer's exploits loves him. It's why the 1972 film musical *Man of La Mancha* was a smash hit, about all our impossible dreams.

So what's the deal with the poster in Figure 1? It's a "teacherly" device to capture the spirit of linear and global thinking, to juxtapose words and pictures for study and discussion. Someone once called the process "Rorschach-ing around," after the psychologists' ink stain test named after Hermann Rorschach (1884–1922). Think of the classroom handout as pumped-up note taking, with quotable quotes from Nabokov and Kundera. The "Idol" scenario was copied from cartoonist Mike Peters.

One more note on Don Quixote: he's Cervantes' version of a *picar* or *picaro*, a rogue or clever adventurer who survives by wit and cunning, interacting with people from different social levels. The book affords Cervantes the opportunity to deconstruct the popular tradition of the *picaresque* novel, commenting on its literary shortcomings and on the culture that produced it. Mark Twain's *Huckleberry Finn* is a picaresque work, and a *Bildungsroman* (coming of age, rite of passage) as well.

Whew! That may be too much information for a pictograph cartoon. But, as Scott McCloud points out in his 1993 classic *Understanding Comics: The Invisible Art*, Egyptian hieroglyphics, the *Bayeux Tapestry* about the Norman conquest in 1066 C. E., and pre-Columbian codices are all complex and serious entertainments. They're just "the funnies" to some, like newspaper comic strips, but they can set us to thinking, nonetheless.

Pictographs and Critical Thinking

Defining terms such as those generated by the *Don Quixote* pictograph is one of our most basic critical thinking skills. It's like the forensic work done by laboratory nerds in police procedural television shows. They ask simple questions: *What have we got here? What's it called?* There follows a close, critical reading of the crime by the investigating detectives, an explication.

Franz Kafka's 1915 novella *The Metamorphosis* (Figure 2) features a character who wakes up one morning and discovers that he has changed into a big bug. As we walk around the house, everything else seems normal. There are human rooms, walls, tables, chairs, a door, a window, and a staircase. Yet nothing is a set piece. The author animates the scenes with descriptions that bear the marks of the emotions of the other family occupants. It's a home freighted with portents. The psychological whole is greater than the sum of its glass and plaster parts. The pictograph attempts to capture that inner world with architectural trappings slightly skewed.

So critical thinking moves from definition through explication and analysis. How do the parts relate to each other? How do they work together to form a cohesive, articulated shape? What are the weft and the warp of the fabric as the shuttle flies back and forth on the loom? Hey, let's mix our metaphors, just for fun, eh?

No type of critical thinking is pure. No critical response to a work is just a linear sequence, from simple to complex. Oxygen mixes with blood, which engorges the organs, who send messages via the nerves to the brain, that commands us to breathe more deeply, and doing so, the open mouth declares, "What a day! How fresh the air." All this while we are walking through a field and looking for four-leaf clovers.

The art making of these pictographic study aids is an amateur's avocational interest, for an educator who loves his work perhaps too much. But there's no law against your joining in the fun. It's just

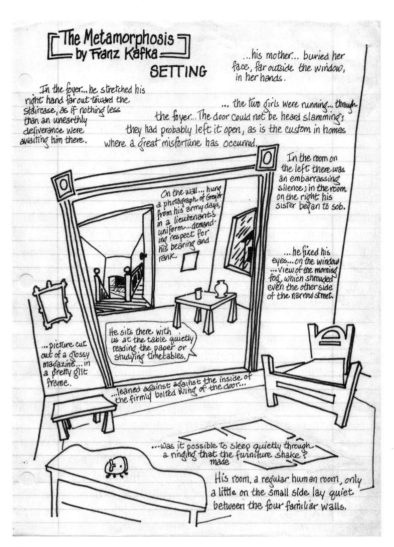

Figure 2

academic graffiti, after all. Designing your own pictograph can be a first step in exploring a text, creating a new perspective, and developing an alternative style of note taking.

We're complex beings, so it should come as no surprise that our thinking is fancy, too. Once upon a Saturday afternoon, a little girl was climbing inflatable stairs toward the high perch of an inflatable slide—in a children's fun house, on her birthday. She looked behind her to see if her grandfather was negotiating the ascent and conquering his fears. "Don't worry," she reassured him. "It's tricky, but it's fun."

And so it was.

The upper levels of critical thinking are also tricky, but fun. When definition, explication, and analysis have established a reasonably empirical trail of evidence, we can start climbing. Interpretation, comparison, and evaluation are signposts for the journey through the subjective realm of critical thinking: criteria from outside a given work are allowed. A thing is not just itself, but many things to many people. There's a whole lot of co-opting going on. We've dipped into the world of biases already in the two pictographs shown. First, we integrated quotes from literary critics with the *Don Quixote* sketches and definitions. Then, we celebrated the transmogrifying of Kafka's protagonist into an anthropomorphic being, making invidious comparisons that entomologists might question. People who study insects, in other words, could get upset because a beetle transforms a human's world view into something oblique, er, slanted, dude.

And another thing: using big words doesn't make a critical thinker right, or more insightful than, say, we might be! It's Kafkaesque, a little bit.

While we are talking about change and shape-shifting, you could add to your library on words and pictures by finding a copy of Anne Sexton's 1971 book *Transformations*. Her deliciously visceral stories are accompanied by Barbara Swan's drawings. It's the kind of work that will inspire you to be more daring in your pictographs.

One transformation that seems to fascinate all of us is how introspection affects artistic expression. Cartoonist Lynda Barry has taken a page from the "alternative comix" of the 1960s and 1970s and combined that counterculture tradition with the informal personal essay. She mixes printed words and cursive handwriting in the same sentences. Her cross-hatching and shading seem to add heightened psychic realism to figures and titles alike. The landscape is filled with animals, globule people, and alter ego commentators, all of whom can be grotesque and lyrical at the same instant. It's prickly critical thinking, with a thorny skin like a cactus; but when cut, it reveals a succulent core. Google "Two Questions" to see one of her best efforts.

Questions To Answer in Figure 3 is this author's attempt to copy Lynda Barry's technique, to express his own struggles with using cartoons and pictographs as learning and teaching tools. It was fun to do, a challenge that stretched personal boundaries. Try it yourself. Don't be shy. It may appear that spending time on producing your own

Figure 3

pictographs is choosing to do a lot of extra work. It's just a different kind of fun—unplugged but interactive, raucous but contemplative.

A Final Question

Well, that's a start. Thanks for riding along. This article has briefly examined one permutation of using popular culture as a learning and teaching strategy—with cartoon pictographs. The reading of these pictures and texts is an acquired skill and taste. Our focus has been on literary works, but it could have been on music, painting, fashion, automobiles, or anything. Andy Warhol started off painting pictures of women's shoes for magazines.

Will thinking about popular culture help you succeed in your career as a doctor, lawyer, accountant, banker, business owner, mechanic, scientist, realtor, professional surfer, or any other money-making venture? Who's to say? It can't hurt, can it? Okay, maybe if you obsessed over it. But then you could become a film director, advertising executive, talk show host, wedding crasher, or country music composer.

Seriously, with all that you've read in this textbook, I shouldn't need to convince you that popular culture matters. Should I?

Now It's Your Turn

Choose something important from one of your courses. Maybe it's a little complex and you need to study it for an exam. What's the central idea or image? Make a quick sketch of it in the middle of your notebook page. Find a phrase or sentence from the text or critical commentary and write it under your sketch. What would the sketch think about it? Write that as a piece of dialogue in a speaker's balloon. Keep going. Don't stop to judge your work. You have four corners of your page to add secondary ideas/images. Then connect everything with doodles. Have fun. Give it all a title you will remember. Close your notebook. Wait two days. Look at it again and try to recall other details from the original source/work. Fiddle with it. Shade or color it. Make the study subject or object your own. As a final touch, draw a stick figure of yourself, moving and saying something funky or profound. Nice job. Next page.

REFERENCES

Lamott, A. (1995). *Bird by bird*. New York: Anchor Books/Doubleday.
McCloud, S. (1993). *Understanding comics: The invisible art*. New York: HarperCollins.

SUGGESTIONS FOR WRITING

1. Write a brief description of Catalini's writing style in this article, using specific quotations of his words, phrases, and sentences to illustrate the claims you make about his style. Then write a brief reflection on your experience of reading Catalini's article. How did his distinctive

style of writing influence you? Do you think the style made you more or less inclined to trust Catalini and embrace the points he made?

2. Take a careful look at Figure 1 and reread Catalini's discussion of this pictograph on pages 373–376. Then give it a try yourself. Imitate Catalini's method of illustrating a word that has an interesting etymology or rich cultural references. Here are a few possibilities: *addict, chocolate, demon, glamour, idol, pagan, robot, weird*. You might also research and illustrate one of the many Latin phrases that we commonly use, such as *et cetera*, *ad nauseam*, *status quo*, or *carpe diem*. After looking up the word's etymology and making a list of all of its different meanings and cultural references, sketch out several possibilities for illustrating some of the more interesting aspects of the word. You can do the final drawing yourself, or you can create a collage by cutting and pasting images that you find in magazines and elsewhere. After you've created your pictograph, write a paragraph or two in which you discuss whether and how the process of visualizing the word added to your understanding of it.

3. Choose a short story, poem, song, or other text with which you are very familiar, and imitate Catalini's method in Figure 2 by representing some of the words from the text along with an illustration that also represents part or all of the text. Catalini describes this as an exercise in critical thinking, and in his pictograph he chooses quotations that describe the setting of Kafka's "The Metamorphosis" and places them in a slightly skewed drawing of a room. You can choose quotations that have to do with setting, or with a certain theme or character or plot element in the text you're working with. You can draw the illustration yourself, as Catalini did, or you can create a collage of images on which to place the quotations. After you've created your pictograph, write a paragraph or two in which you discuss whether and how the process of illustrating a text added to your understanding of it.

credits

index

385

Additional Titles of Interest

Note to Instructors: Any of these Penguin-Putnam, Inc., titles can be packaged with this book at a special discount. Contact your local Allyn & Bacon/Longman sales representative for details on how to create a Penguin-Putnam, Inc., Value Package.

Allison, *Bastard Out of Carolina*

Alvarez, *How the Garcia Girls Lost Their Accents*

Augustine, *The Confessions of St. Augustine*

Austen, *Persuasion*

Austen, *Pride and Prejudice*

Austen, *Sense and Sensibility*

Bloom, *Shakespeare: The Invention of the Human*

C. Brontë, *Jane Eyre*

E. Brontë, *Wuthering Heights*

Burke, *Reflections on the Revolution in France*

Cather, *My Ántonia*

Cather, *O Pioneers!*

Cellini, *The Autobiography of Benvenuto Cellini*

Chapman, *Black Voices*

Chesnutt, *The Marrow of Tradition*

Chopin, *The Awakening and Selected Stories*

Conrad, *Heart of Darkness*

Conrad, *Nostromo*

Coraghessan-Boyle, *The Tortilla Curtain*

Defoe, *Robinson Crusoe*

Descartes, *Discourse on Method and The Meditations*

Descartes, *Meditations and Other Metaphysical Writings*

de Tocqueville, *Democracy in America*

Dickens, *Hard Times*

Douglass, *Narrative of the Life of Frederick Douglass*

Dubois, *The Souls of Black Folk*

Equiano, *The Interesting Narrative and Other Writings*

Gore, *Earth in the Balance*

Grossman, *Electronic Republic*

Hawthorne, *The Scarlet Letter*

Hutner, *Immigrant Voices*

Jacobs, *Incidents in the Life of a Slave Girl*

Jen, *Typical American*

M. L. King Jr., *Why We Can't Wait*

Lewis, *Babbitt*

Machiavelli, *The Prince*

Marx, *The Communist Manifesto*

Mill, *On Liberty*

THE
THIRD
ACT